Bob Woodward

WIRED
The Short Life and Fast Times of
John Belushi

faber and faber
LONDON · BOSTON

First published in the USA in 1984
by Simon and Schuster, Inc., New York
First published in Great Britain in 1985
by Faber and Faber Limited
3 Queen Square London WC1N 3AU

Printed in Great Britain by
Butler & Tanner Ltd, Frome and London

British Library Cataloguing in Publication Data

Woodward, Bob
Wired: the short life and fast times of John Belushi.
1. Belushi, John   2. Comedians——United States——Biography
I. Title
791.43′028′0924   PN2287.B423

ISBN 0–571–13577–3
ISBN 0–571–13596–X Pbk

Acknowledgments

Washington Post editor Benjamin C. Bradlee and Simon and Schuster president Richard Snyder were, as they had been on three previous occasions, the sponsors of this work. I cannot thank them enough for their many indulgences and kindnesses. Without them this project would not have been undertaken. Others who provided invaluable assistance include: Jane Amsterdam, for support, editing and toughness that aided at every step; Milton Benjamin for sound guidance; David Maraniss for advice, support and mature judgment; Carol Melamed for a lawyer's careful read; Andrea Kingsley and Barbara Feinman for countless assists; Olwen Price for expert typing; Jennifer and Laughlin Phillips for housing on Martha's Vineyard; Broadway Video for tapes, photos and research assistance; Marcia Resnick for photos; various newspapers and magazines as noted in the text, especially *Rolling Stone,* for its chronicle of Belushi, the show business and youth culture.

Special thanks to *Washington Post* managing editor Howard Simons for prodding me along the way.

Others at Simon and Schuster who deserve many thanks are Ann Godoff, Michael Gast, Joni Evans, Dan Green, Judy Lee, Maria Iano and Alex Gigante.

Alice Mayhew, my editor at Simon and Schuster, worked hard and provided more attention and time than any author should expect. Her wisdom and honesty could not have been found elsewhere.

And to Elsa Walsh, my esteem and affection for direction, advice, an editor's sharp pencil and a friend's gentle encouragement.

John Ward Anderson, a 1981 Harvard graduate, assisted me in all aspects of producing this book—its conception, the reporting, research, writing and organization. His role could not have been greater. He is a dedicated journalist and tireless worker. This book is as much his as it is mine.

Note on Sources and Methods

In the summer of 1982 I received a call at *The Washington Post,* where I work, from Pamela Jacklin, a sister-in-law of John Belushi, who had died of a drug overdose three months earlier. She said there were still many unanswered questions surrounding John's death, and she suggested I look into it. John Belushi was not a natural subject for my reporting; I had concentrated on Washington stories and knew very little about his show business world—television, rock and roll, and Hollywood. But I was curious.

On Thursday, July 15, I took the shuttle to New York City to meet his widow, Judy Jacklin Belushi. My notes taken that day say: "The house is subdued, a very dark place, and Judy is a peppy, small woman . . . she has a very precise memory and exact sense of what she knows, what she has heard, and where others she has spoken with get their information." Three weeks later I visited her again, this time for three days on Martha's Vineyard. She spent hours explaining John, his career and his life, perhaps to retrieve a memory and also an understanding. She did not romanticize; she seemed to stick to the facts as she knew them, and it became apparent that she, many of her friends, and many more of John's former associates were willing to provide me with a detailed, relatively uncensored recollection of him, his career, and the events leading up to his death.

These were the first of twenty-one interviews and a dozen or more other discussions I had with Judy Belushi over the next year. She and her sister, Pam Jacklin, who is the attorney for John Belushi's estate, provided me with access to his financial records and many of his personal papers. They encouraged others to help me but neither requested nor received any assurances about what I would write. (They did not see the manuscript before publication.)

The project was conceived as a series of articles for the *Post,* but Bernie Brillstein, John's former manager, warned me, "John's a book, not a series of articles." It was soon apparent that he was right.

All the information in this book comes firsthand from witnesses or records. Of those interviewed, 217 spoke on the record and the information they gave me makes up the core of the book. The source of each section of the book is listed by name in the chapter notes. Another group of about fifty people spoke on background, meaning the information they provided could be used but not directly attributed to them. This information was generally supplementary, and these background sources were used mainly to confirm details provided on the record by others. In several cases, as noted, information given to police or prosecutors was used. On the few occasions that people mentioned in the book declined to be interviewed or could not be located, this fact is noted in the chapter notes.

In addition, written records provided important information as well as a chronology and a guide to interviewing the key people in Belushi's life. These records included appointment calendars, diaries, telephone records, credit card receipts, medical records, handwritten notes, letters, photographs, newspaper and magazine articles, stacks of accountants' records covering the last several years of Belushi's life, daily movie production reports, contracts, hotel records, travel records, taxi receipts, limousine bills and Belushi's monthly cash disbursement records.

A number of drug suppliers and users are named. In several cases, there is some disagreement over the extent to which certain individuals were suppliers, dealers or users. That disagreement is reflected in the text.

This book, like any other project of comparable length, has primary sources—people who were relied on more than others, who were close to the subject and were found to be reliable. They are also the major figures in the story of John Belushi's life. If they are present in a scene in the book, the information came from them or it was generally confirmed by them. This applies particularly to matters regarding personal thoughts, conclusions, feelings and states of mind.

The use of quoted dialogue comes directly from the participants as they said they recalled it.

John Belushi and I both grew up in Wheaton, Illinois, and went to the same high school. He graduated in 1967, six years after I graduated. But we never met. The streets, stores, teachers, coaches, families, and the character of that small Midwestern town are familiar to me, but Wheaton is just a small part of this story.

His story, however, emerges from and reflects three American cities —Chicago, where his comedy and acting career were rooted; New York, where it grew and flourished; and Los Angeles, the entertainment capital, the city of the greatest temptations, the place where he died.

To follow Belushi's path I traveled from coast to coast many times, visiting everyone possible and everywhere possible. The trail led me from the lavish suites at the Beverly Hills Hotel, the bungalows and the Polo Lounge, to the seedy little apartments of the drug dealers off Sunset Boulevard, and to New York City and the accountants' files, the Central Park West apartments of friends, and the downtown underground clubs that he loved.

In one interview I found myself led down to a cramped, windowless office in the basement of an uptown bar where the owner recalled his experiences with Belushi. For another I had to go to bed early and set my alarm for 3:30 A.M. to visit one after-hours club—one of John's favorites—that didn't open until 4 A.M.

I visited the Warner Brothers lot to see director Steven Spielberg and actor Chevy Chase. At the Universal lot I interviewed director Louis Malle and Belushi's former partner, Dan Aykroyd. At Paramount there were the executives who run the studio and actress Penny Marshall. When Belushi's former agent, Mike Ovitz, declined my interview request, Marshall took me uninvited to a party at Ovitz's home. He later agreed to several long phone interviews.

I visited the offices of Belushi's doctors, the Playboy Mansion, and Jack Nicholson's house for poolside discussion. Half the interview with Carrie Fisher was conducted in a limousine that was taking her to the airport. After she was dropped off, the limousine driver described an extraordinary 24-hour period driving Belushi around Hollywood six months before his death.

In Washington I spent most of the afternoon of December 3, 1982, with Columbia Pictures president Frank Price who was in town for that evening's world premier of *Gandhi*. Much of the last week of Belushi's life was spent with two people who a year after his death were waiting table in D.C., one at a posh Pennsylvania Avenue restaurant several blocks from the White House, and the other at the Georgetown Hamburger Hamlet. I found these two quite by accident when a close friend brought one of them to a party at my house.

I spent two weekends in Toronto, Canada, talking with Cathy Smith, the woman who gave Belushi heroin and cocaine injections the final week of his life.

Since I never met Belushi, his perspective is reflected only through others, their recollections of what he did and said. Over the years Belushi gave many interviews to journalists, but he seemed to dislike doing so and often evaded the questions or central issues, perhaps just to be funny. On several occasions he seemed to open up slightly, and those are quoted in part during the narrative as they occurred. And finally I made use of the video tapes of his television performances, his musical recording, and the seven movies in which he acted.

A character of Belushi's extreme was an embodiment of the energy and will of the 1970s. And American show business can be so glamorous, full of fun, even inspiring. Belushi could have been, should have been, one of those comedians whose work was measured in decades, across generations. But it wasn't. Why? What happened? Who was responsible, if anyone? Could it have been different or better? Those were the questions raised by his family, friends and associates. Could success have been something other than a failure? The questions persist.

Nonetheless, his best and most definitive legacy is his work. He made us laugh, and now he can make us think.

BOB WOODWARD
February 1984

Part One

1

Chicago. Friday, July 6, 1979. Judy Jacklin Belushi, wife of comedian John Belushi, woke up with a hangover, an ugly thumping headache. A July 4 celebration had extended into a July 5 celebration—a Chicago Cubs game, fireworks from a rooftop, a nighttime tour of the city with John, a visit to Second City, the famous improvisational comedy troupe where he once worked, the old bars, pinball at one, and the cocaine, which she had turned down but which John had taken. And this time the cocaine had come from John's movie producer, Robert K. Weiss, a bearded giant of a man.

John was in Chicago to begin work on *The Blues Brothers* movie, a musical comedy about two hipsters and their blues band. Keeping drugs away from him would be difficult enough without the authority figures on the set contributing theirs. Judy called Weiss and pounced hard.

"Don't give him fucking coke!" she shouted. John couldn't handle it. They were trying to get it out of their lives. She herself had abstained for six weeks and was going to beat it. John could too, but he needed help. He'll wreck the movie with cocaine, Judy said. Weiss's ass was on the line. "It's your career," she pleaded, "but it's my life."

Weiss said he hadn't known that John's drug problem was that great.

Judy reminded Weiss that John considered Chicago home. Being back with a Hollywood movie crew was like a drug picnic. John, now thirty, was being treated like a counterculture mayor, and all his old social and drug networks had been reactivated.

Weiss said he understood. He promised to talk to the members of the Blues Brothers band, some of whom were cocaine users, and enlist their support.

That night Judy sat down to make an entry in her diary, which she had begun six months earlier, just after John's fame had really hit. He'd been on the cover of *Newsweek* magazine the previous fall as the fraternity slob Bluto from *Animal House,* which was now on its way to becoming the biggest moneymaking comedy in Hollywood history. Six months ago, John and his partner, Dan Aykroyd, had had the number-one-selling record album in the country, the first album by the Blues Brothers. It had sold 2.8 million copies. John was still the popular star of NBC's "Saturday Night Live," the top-rated late-night television show that had an audience of more than 20 million.

Instant fame had meant the end of their struggling low-rent existence. It meant more money and more drugs. Giving or selling drugs to John was a kind of game, like feeding popcorn to the seals at the zoo; give him a little and he would perform, be crazy and outrageous; a little more and he'd stay up all night, outdancing, outdoing, outlasting everyone around him.

Judy, twenty-eight, a small woman who had been mistaken on movie sets for a messenger several times because of her informal clothes and quick talk, had been with John since high school in Wheaton, Illinois, a small town 25 miles west of Chicago. They had been married three years, and she was still very much in love with him. Nearly everything about him and his show-business life appealed to her. John could be awful, could be gruff and demanding, but there was a real sense of decency and strength in him.

As she wrote in her diary that night, Judy felt she might have been a little unfair to Weiss. He seemed to have been genuinely unaware. But she couldn't stand it any longer. There had to be a change, and she had at least taken some action by calling him. "I feel better now," she scribbled. "Things should work out."

Several days later, Dr. Bennett Braun, a thirty-nine-year-old Chicago physician and psychiatrist who was coordinating the medical support for the movie, came down to the set. John said he wanted his regular B_{12} vitamin shot.

"There is no documentation that this makes a difference," Braun said.

"It keeps me going," John replied.

Braun figured there was no reason to argue. He gave John the injection and performed a cursory physical examination. It was clear John was taking far too many drugs. Braun could see it and feel it—excessive weight, unclear eyes, clogged nasal passages, pale, almost colorless skin, the sigh and rasp of his breathing. Braun asked a few questions. Yes,

John answered, he was using cocaine to take him up. Then he needed something to bring him down. Braun could see that John was battering his body and mind.

"You're burning out," Braun said. "The cocaine will shorten your life."

John just listened.

Braun left it at that. If John were a regular patient, he'd jump on him. Maybe his regular doctors were too much in awe of their famous patient to take any action. John might fire a meddling doctor, and then the doctor would have achieved nothing but the loss of an influential patient.

Braun went to see Weiss. John needed psychiatric help, and Braun offered to see him professionally. "You've got to get him off drugs," he said deliberately. "If you don't, get as many movies out of him as possible, because he has only two to three years to live."

Weiss was shocked by Braun's prognosis, especially after Judy's call. But the doctor's assessment was almost too much, it was too stark to repeat. His only course was to focus on John's health and do whatever he could to lighten the pressure. It would be hard, almost impossible. There was no putting any kind of leash on John, and it was precisely that absence of control, that daredevil quality, that had made him such a box-office hit.

The following month, August, the filming began, and the schedule was tough, the drug use constant. Judy saw no way out. And she realized there were many lapses on her own part—some pot, and occasionally some speed or LSD, a strong hallucinogen. On September 27 and 28, Judy, actress Carrie Fisher (Princess Leia in the hit movie *Star Wars*) and Penny Marshall (one of the stars of the television series "Laverne and Shirley") took some LSD. Judy called it a "sixties weekend"; they had made Polaroid pictures and tape recordings of their conversations as they hallucinated.

Fisher, twenty-three, the daughter of singer Eddie Fisher and actress Debbie Reynolds, was cast as John's angry ex-girlfriend in *The Blues Brothers* movie. In real life, she was romantically involved with Dan Aykroyd, the other Blues Brother. Fisher and Aykroyd planned to get married. They spent a great deal of time with John and Judy and the two couples had become a kind of package. It seemed to Fisher that she and Aykroyd would be with John and Judy the rest of their lives.

Fisher and John had a close relationship. She was attracted by his inability to handle his own intensity. He would say *"I've got an idea!"* with such belief and conviction that he enrolled everybody around. John seemed always to be starting a club. Intuitively he could gather up all the loose energy in a room, amplify it and change everything. Fisher trusted in him; she couldn't find it in herself to judge him.

John too sensed a kinship. "Hey," he once told her, "you're just like me. They're different," he said of Judy and Danny. "We're alike." John seemed always somewhat dissatisfied, as if he were protesting, "This can't be it. This can't be all of it. This isn't enough. There has to be more, something else!" Fisher felt it, too.

He had once shouted at her, *"I'm an addict!"* And he hadn't meant drugs. He was referring to his life, the excitement, the possibility of more.

John could get Carrie to try almost anything. She didn't like liquor, but John got her to drink Wild Turkey, a Kentucky bourbon. And once they smoked some opium together.

She figured John was taking about four grams of cocaine a day, but it was difficult to tell. He had so much that she would kid him, "Hey, give us some." And he usually did. Fisher knew both the appeal and dreadful toll of drugs. Her father had been addicted to shooting speed for more than a dozen years.

As Judy and others were trying to reduce John's drug intake, Judy laid down a law at the Blues Bar, an old bar John and Aykroyd had reopened as a private retreat in Chicago: "No coke at the bar," Judy would tell people with cocaine. "I know you don't want to hurt John."

One night at the bar Fisher was asked to keep an eye on John. He pulled out a big stash of coke and passed it to her. "You want some blow?" he asked.

"Should you be doing that?" Fisher replied, trying to be a good enforcer.

"You want some or not!" John screamed.

She decided to let others play cop. It wasn't for her. She didn't want a new-model John.

Morris Lyda, a twenty-nine-year-old Texan who had been hired as the road manager for the Blues Brothers band, became John's personal overseer during the movie. Lyda was responsible for getting John up in the morning, driving him to the set and seeing him through the night.

Free time was the killer—those hours, an afternoon, a half-day or even a couple of days when John wasn't needed on the set. Lyda, who rarely went more than two days without some cocaine, was trying to control John's cash flow. Drug purchases were made in cash, and without it, he couldn't buy. John called at all hours of the day or night wanting money, once at 5 A.M. for $600. Lyda didn't want to give it to him, and he called John's assistant manager, Joel Briskin, who was also in Chicago to help John.

"Yeah, go ahead and give it to him," Briskin said. "John will be what he's going to be."

Some members of the crew were supplying John, often palming off cocaine that had been cut several extra times (increasing the amount but decreasing the potency with nonactive ingredients like lactose). Lyda called it "crap blow," and John had it more often than not.

Lyda kept a supply of Valium on hand to help John come down. John called him any time of the night—at times twice the same night—and Lyda would take the tranquilizer to John's hotel.

It was a depressing time for Lyda. He had become a kind of drug valet, and he hated himself for it. He was sacrificing too much of his energy and dignity to John's habits. But he couldn't take a stand because of his own drug use. It would have been laughable. He was both facilitator and regulator of John's drugs: it was an impossible contradiction.

Late in the afternoon Thursday, October 25, John Landis, the director of *The Blues Brothers,* was in a rage as he got up and moved across the movie set, which that day was on the outskirts of the city. The film crew was waiting to begin the next scene. It was day 64 on location, nearly the last day of filming in Chicago, and Belushi was refusing to come out of his private trailer.

Like many in the movie business, Landis kept in close touch with the Hollywood grapevine and the gossip about his project was painful and true. The film was weeks behind schedule and millions over budget. Drugs were readily available on the set. *The Blues Brothers* script, initially 324 pages—nearly three times the normal length of a movie script —had been cut but had never been properly finished. Its author was listed as "Scriptatron GL-9000"—Aykroyd, who liked to think of himself as an automated writer.

The executives at Universal Studios were having fits, pressuring Landis to get control of his movie. They had rushed the project into production without much thought following *Animal House* and the Blues Brothers hit record.

Landis, twenty-nine, a short, strong-willed man with glasses and a full beard, felt like a helpless onlooker in his own movie. His mood alternated between giddiness and despair. He was anxious to solve the problem of John's irresponsibility once and for all.

Landis reached the trailer and opened the door. There sat Belushi, a five-foot-nine ghastly, bloated, semi-adult parody of Bluto. His curly black hair was dishevelled; his gaze was fixed at a point several feet in front of his eyes. Courvoisier cognac had been spilled all over. There was urine on the floor. On a table was a mound of cocaine, piled high and white.

"John, you're killing yourself!" Landis shouted. "This is economically unfeasible. Do not do this to my movie!"

John's head bobbed up and down.

"Don't do this to me. Don't do this to Judy. Don't do it to yourself!"

Belushi just stared up.

"I'm going to get the stills man and get pictures of this and show it to you," Landis threatened.

John gave no sign, not even a shrug, that he was comprehending.

Was there no way out of this madness? Landis wondered. He scooped up the white powder, carried it over to the toilet and flushed it.

John stood unsteadily, muttering, and began advancing on Landis—220 pounds to Landis's 165. Landis made a tight fist, reeled back and hit John square in the face. John went down. Landis didn't know who was the more surprised, but he thought, My God, I just slugged the star of my movie—a friend and collaborator—and he's big enough to kill me.

John didn't get up, and at first he didn't move. Then he lowered his head and burst into tears. "I'm so ashamed, so, so ashamed." He rose, trembling, and threw his arms around Landis. "Please understand."

Landis didn't. What was John finding in drugs? So much was being placed in jeopardy—career, family, life itself. Why? he asked John.

"I need it. I need it," John replied weakly. "You couldn't possibly understand."

Judy arrived at John's Winnebago about two hours later, just as the sun was setting. John was asleep. That morning Judy had discovered about a dozen Quaaludes in his jacket and had taken away four so he wouldn't have so many. John liked downers like Quaaludes which, when taken two or three at a time, produce muscle relaxation, a sense of contentment, passivity resembling a mild state of drunkenness on the edge of sleep, a disconnection between mind and body. Quaaludes, he had said, were perfect for taking the edge off the restlessness of the cocaine high. The previous day she had taken a packet of coke from him. There had been several grams.

Yesterday cocaine, today Quaaludes. Obviously her hope from July, her optimism about reducing his drug use, was a pathetic one.

John woke up a few minutes later and poured out his story. He'd been downtown in Chicago when a call had come at 4 P.M. ordering him out to the set at once for a dusk shot; he didn't get on the road until four-thirty and got caught in the rush-hour traffic and was late.

Judy tried to downplay the incident.

"You don't understand," John said on the verge of tears. "You don't understand what they've done. . . . They've humiliated me." He did not say that Landis had hit him but simply that Landis was placing all the blame and guilt for the delay on him. John felt betrayed, particularly after all the other times he'd spent waiting to do a scene or being called for no reason. The movie was a disorganized mess.

"They can't treat me like this," John said. "I've been working too hard. They can't blame me for fucking the whole day, costing them money." John said he wanted some cocaine.

No, Judy said.

"I've got to have it. I can't possibly do this scene without it." But the cocaine had been thrown out. John took out some more cognac and beer and began drinking fast. Judy decided to join him. You either joined John or you were quickly left behind. When Landis came back to the trailer, again to say John had to come for the scene, John screamed: "Fuck you! I'm not ready. Get out of here or I'll kill you!"

Landis hesitated and then left. Judy had not seen John in such bad shape for an entire year. Perhaps her efforts were in vain; perhaps she was no good for him; maybe drugs were the only way to get through the filming of a movie like this.

John got up and went to the bathroom, and she saw him take some Quaaludes.

Aykroyd came in and tried to coax John to the set, arguing that no matter what had happened they had to get it rolling. It was a simple scene: John was to sit on the edge of a car in a gas station, smash a bottle of booze and announce they had to get to a concert. John finally agreed, but after ten minutes on the set, he passed out and was carried back semiconscious to the trailer.

Judy rummaged through his pockets and found only three Quaaludes. Those three plus the four she had taken from him earlier accounted for seven. That left about five he could have taken—a huge dose. On top of the liquor, it was dangerous: a mixture of Quaaludes and alcohol could induce a coma and even cause death. Judy called the staff nurse on the set, who came and made John vomit. The nurse told Judy to watch John's eyes carefully for possible signs that he was slipping into a coma.

John and Judy were then driven back to their rented two-bedroom apartment in Chicago at the Astor Towers. Aykroyd came by to sit up with Judy. He was John's best friend and business partner—a tall, lanky twenty-seven-year-old who, in his own way, was as crazy and hyper as John. Yet Aykroyd kept both his feelings and most of his drug use private. He was indulgent of John but sympathized with Judy. He reminded her that they had been through this before with John, and that things would get better.

Judy felt lost, caught in a spiderweb of drugs. John continued to vomit through the night, but later he seemed to feel better. After Aykroyd left, Judy wrote in her diary: "What could be going on inside this person to make him so unhappy?"

On Saturday, October 27, Landis filmed the final scene in Chicago, the blowing up of a gas station; and on Sunday the entire cast and crew headed for Los Angeles for three more months of filming and technical work to complete the movie.

After spending several nights at the Beverly Hills Hotel, John and Judy moved into actress Candice Bergen's house, which they rented for $2,000 a month. It was a small, elegant cottage-cabin, hidden in several dozen acres of woods in Coldwater Canyon, fifteen minutes from Universal Studio, where they were filming.

On Friday night, November 9, John and Judy went over to the house of Ron Wood of the Rolling Stones and freebased cocaine for the first time. Wood wrote out the instructions of how to heat and purify street cocaine and then inhale the fumes. They left early, about 1:30 A.M. Judy wrote in her diary: "Good time. We need to blow out every once in a while."

Despite the freebasing, Judy was beginning to feel a little better. Just two weeks out of Chicago and their life seemed back on track. She was given an office at Universal Studio so she could work on a book she was doing on the movie—a humorous series of files and pictures giving the background on her husband and Aykroyd as Jake and Elwood Blues, their Blues Brothers names.

John and Danny were preparing and doing scenes with Aretha Franklin and Ray Charles, and the work seemed to be going very well. John was getting up early, swimming, working out a little, taking vitamins. Judy had brought a blender and juicer with her and made a special drink each morning for the two of them with freshly squeezed juice from a dozen oranges, a little wheat germ, yeast, one raw egg and one banana. On November 15 she wrote in her diary about John: "He looks very happy, healthy, wealthy and wise. I am proud of him for the way he is working. I am very happy and in love."

The next week John hurt his knee and had to go to the hospital emergency room to have blood drawn out to relieve the pressure. He was in great pain, and so on the Sunday after Thanksgiving when two Blues Brothers band members provided some cocaine for John, Judy was not too worried. She had convinced herself that conservative use was acceptable. The filming proceeded at a reasonable pace through Christmas. On New Year's, their third wedding anniversary, they gave a big party at their house with three cases of champagne. Unexpected guests included Cher (of Sonny and Cher) and California Governor Jerry Brown. John turned thirty-one on January 24.

The filming took another week, and on February 1, 1980, Landis was finished, figuring he had enough to put together the movie.

Soon after, John disappeared. No one had any idea where he had gone, not Judy, nor Landis, nor Aykroyd. Landis expected to hear it on the news at any moment: "John Belushi, the famous comedian, was found dead. . . ."

But a few days later, John popped up, acting as if nothing had happened and seemingly unaware of the anguish he had caused. Landis felt obligated to make a serious effort to do something and called Judy.

John needs to be helped, Landis said. We've got to get him treated, hospitalized, detoxed—formally committed if necessary.

Judy agreed; she'd do anything to stop him. Moderation hadn't worked. There had been more ups and downs—too many drugs, and it was killing their marriage, killing her. Both Judy and Landis agreed that the key was Bernie Brillstein, who had been John's manager for nearly five years now, since the first "Saturday Night" shows in 1975. Brillstein, a forty-nine-year-old Burl Ives look-alike, loved John like a son. John might listen to him.

Since Landis and Brillstein didn't get along, Landis asked Weiss and other Universal executives to call Brillstein separately and urge forcefully that John be put away to dry out, put away until he got off cocaine.

Finally Landis made his own pitch to Brillstein.

"Get him committed," Landis said. "Save him, Bernie. He'll only listen to you. He's going to die. You've got to put him away. He's out of control. Only you, only you, Bernie, only you can do it. He'll only listen to you."

Brillstein said that they had seen this before. It was a phase, a stage, a binge. He is going to wake up and realize what's happening.

"No," Landis pleaded. "Bernie, this can't go on. It can't be permitted any longer. There's no coming back really, not from this."

Brillstein knew John inside out. Landis was overreacting.

"You fuck!" Landis screamed. "You can't make money off a corpse!"

Brillstein loathed people to make pronouncements about John, or his own relationship with John. Everyone knew about the cocaine. That was show business. People could have it in their ears, and John practically did. As long as it didn't interfere with making the movie, no one would raise a peep. Brillstein pondered his responsibility. Judy and Aykroyd knew that John couldn't be controlled. When there was idle time, John would go get drugs, or go get three pizzas, a blow job, or a nap.

Why hadn't Landis taken control during the filming? Why didn't the studio stop production if it was so bad? So now they were dumping it in his lap. Now that the movie was over, it was so serious that something had to be done.

Brillstein wanted to stay out of John's private life. He understood obsessive behavior. Like John, he ate obsessively. Fifteen years earlier Brillstein had had a serious gambling problem, always trying to make the extra thousand bucks. Eventually he got about $20,000 in debt and was scared that he would never dig himself out. It took three years to pay off, but Brillstein had learned a lesson. He was convinced that John was smart enough to learn his. John, like Brillstein himself, had a strange sixth sense. He would know when to pull back.

One morning in L.A., John went to Brillstein's fourth-floor corner office on Sunset Boulevard. He had clearly been up all night, and he looked disgusting. John gave Brillstein a big bear hug in show-business tradition. He reeked of a foul odor. He was overweight and a mess. It was an embarrassment. There could be no more pretending, no more half-measures.

"John," Brillstein said, "you've got to stop. You've got to get some help. You've got to get healthy."

"I can handle it," John said. "I have the heart of a high school senior."

"You're going to kill yourself," Brillstein said. "You can't do this, you can't abuse yourself. You're going to put yourself out of show business. You can't hang out with this scum that you're hanging out with.''

John's eyes flashed. He got up and shut Brillstein's office door.

"Look," John screamed, "I'm not paying you to be my best friend!"

It was the first time that John had ever called Brillstein an employee. Brillstein tried to interrupt, but John was boiling. "I don't ask what you do after six o'clock, don't ask me!" This was where the line was drawn, he said. No one, no one whatsoever, was going to tell him what to do. "Don't ask me where I go! Don't tell me where to go!"

"You can't tell me not to love you!" Brillstein shouted. "I'm not talking about goddamn business! I'm talking about *your life!*"

"I know what you're saying," John said. "I know it's for my good . . . but I got to run my own life."

They hugged.

"You worry about your business," John said. "I'll worry about me."

Brillstein saw there was no resolving it. He had taken his best shot, and John had turned into a madman. At least he knew enough to stay out of this from now on.

Universal had bought *The Blues Brothers* script over the phone. That had been eighteen months ago when John had become unbelievably successful. Brillstein could have sold the studio air if it had been for sale. But John was now idle again, and Brillstein figured he had better get another movie or project fast, if only to keep John's mind on something besides drugs. Brillstein knew that Landis had not overstated the problem, but his solution wouldn't work.

Judy called Dr. Michael A. Rosenbluth, a prominent Fifth Avenue internist in New York, where John and Judy had their home. Rosenbluth had seen John three years earlier when the drug problem had also been out of hand.

John went to see Rosenbluth on March 27, 1980. After the appointment the doctor wrote in his file: "Patient very hostile, alternately agitated and drowsy. *Paranoid!* He's been using cocaine heavily, according to wife. Patient states he doesn't want to stop using it now! Case discussed with wife. Advised that patient should be hospitalized for detoxification."

But Judy and Brillstein finally concluded that commitment was out of the question. John had to go of his own free will, and he would not even begin to listen. His will was too overpowering on the smallest matters. He insisted that he was in control and that he could stop when, and if, he wanted.

Some compromise would have to be found.

One week later, the first weekend in April, John flew to Chicago to see his younger brother, Jimmy, twenty-five, act in a play.

Jimmy was concerned about their eighty-four-year-old grandmother, Vasilo Belushi, who lay dying in California. Nena, as they called her, had had three heart attacks.

She had been a beloved, maternal figure around their house in Wheaton when they were growing up, a second mother, a court of appeal. She granted things denied by their mother, if only a laugh of approval, a snack, some comforting. She spoke little English and called John "Johnny Nena's," which meant he belonged to her, was her favorite. She was small, fragile, sweet and doting. Nena always wore a black hairnet and almost never left the house.

As they talked, Jimmy cried over the prospect of Nena's death.

"Hold it together," John said, lecturing him about the need to be strong. He had expressed the absurd notion that if Nena was waiting to say goodbye to them, she would continue to live until they arrived; by staying away, John reasoned, they were postponing her death.

"You know," Jimmy said, "she's waiting for you."

"That's why I'm not going," John replied.

"You got to go."

John waved his brother off.

Later that week, Brillstein called Jimmy, who was also one of his clients. "We're worried about John," he said. "Judy is worried. Maybe you can do something. I think it's time for the younger brother to be the older brother. You've got to talk to him."

Jimmy got into his jeep and began searching for John. With a mandate from Judy and Brillstein to take control, he could try to do something. He tracked down John at the apartment of Del Close, forty-five, the director of Second City. Close, a fierce intellectual in the Lenny Bruce tradition and a former heroin junkie, had directed both John and Jimmy at Second City and had had a tremendous influence on their lives.

Jimmy knocked on the door of Close's first-floor apartment and walked in. John and Close obviously had been doing drugs.

"You've got to come with me," Jimmy said, grabbing John's arm and dragging him toward the door.

"Okay, okay, okay, *okay!*" John said, and walked out with him.

Jimmy reached into his brother's pocket and confiscated a packet of cocaine. They took a cab over to Clark Street, where Jimmy had parked his jeep.

John suggested they hit the town together.

No, Jimmy said stiffly, we're going home.

John said he wanted to go out, not home.

Home, Jimmy said, indicating he was here to straighten out his big brother.

"So you want to fight?" John asked.

"Yes," Jimmy replied. He wanted to fight; the anger and the rivalry surfaced in a flash. His heart pumped and his mouth was dry, right out there by Clark Street in the middle of the evening: big brother, little brother, careers, parents, private, old history.

"If I win, we go out," John said, taunting. "If you win, we go home."

They squared off. From certain angles the brothers were perfect likenesses. It was like boxing in front of a mirror. But Jimmy was quicker and in better shape. He swung hard and landed a fist to John's mouth. They both swung, ducked and charged at each other. When they stopped for a moment, Jimmy felt he had clearly won, having landed the only punch. John's lip was already swelling and discolored.

"This is like *East of Eden*," John said, referring to the brothers' fight scene in the James Dean movie. John was panting and winded.

Jimmy thought they could go home now, and he walked to the jeep. John jumped into the driver's seat. "Come on, let's go," he said, taking the wheel and racing off across town, driving right over Jimmy's victory. They went to a blues club, then to Lincoln Park, and later on a tour of underground Chicago nightlife. John had a Polaroid camera, and he snapped pictures along the way. Soon Jimmy was smiling. They stayed out for four hours. John was fun when he took charge. They were kids again.

The next day Jimmy felt guilty about lecturing, fighting. John was too hard to stop, and maybe even a brother had no right to try. How could he tell how much cocaine was too much? He apologized to John several times.

"Hey, it's over," John said. "Don't worry. I've forgotten about it. I don't even remember it. Forget it."

"John, I'm sorry," Jimmy said. "I didn't mean it."

"Hey, forget it, don't worry about it."

Jimmy went to California alone to see Nena. John stayed in Chicago. Several days later Judy flew to Chicago from New York to tell John that she was going to California to see Nena, and John decided to go with her. They arrived and he went to the hospital, where he talked to Nena for a while and fell asleep on her bed. Judy, Jimmy and the doctors thought that John looked so sick himself that he should be checked by a doctor.

"Look," Judy told John, "I just think you should tell him straight off what you've been doing this last week so he can understand what's wrong with you."

"I'm going to tell him," John said belligerently. "I'm going to tell him."

John was examined. His problem: too many drugs.

Nena died the next day, and John paid $4,066 to fly fourteen relatives to Chicago for the funeral. He broke down and wept at the service, the tears dripping from his face as he went around hugging dozens of friends and relatives.

The next week John agreed to hire a personal bodyguard to help control his drug use. Both John and Morris Lyda had heard about a former Secret Service agent who had successfully helped the Eagles' ("Hotel California") lead guitarist, Joe Walsh.

Richard G. Wendell, called "Smokey" because of the bear tattoos on his arms, was just tall and heavy enough to be physically impressive, but not overbearing. With seven years in the Secret Service and the Executive Protection Agency, Smokey, thirty-four, was a professional watcher, a proven drug enforcer. He had a soft voice, soft manner and enough natural authority and tact to be effective. Walsh recommended him highly and then, half joking, warned Smokey: "I may have done the worst thing in your life for you and your family. I've set you up with John Belushi."

"I don't really know him," Smokey replied, though he had met John briefly with Walsh months earlier in Chicago.

"John doesn't know John," Walsh said.

Brillstein agreed to pay Smokey $1,000 a week plus expenses. "It's going to be very hard," Brillstein warned. "He's a difficult man. I'm sure you're well aware of John's problem."

On Wednesday, April 16, 1980, Smokey flew from his home in the Washington, D.C., suburbs to New York. He was scheduled to meet John that afternoon at the Record Plant, a recording studio on West Forty-fourth Street. From what everyone had said, Smokey realized it was a question not just of moderating John's cocaine use but of stopping it entirely. John apparently knew no moderation; if he took a little, he took a lot; once he got started he would take what he could find. Smokey would have to be unsparing.

Smokey went to the Record Plant about two o'clock that afternoon with Walsh, who had agreed to help John record a version of "Gimme Some Lovin' " for *The Blues Brothers* movie sound-track album. Morris Lyda came along.

Bob Tischler, the producer of the album, told Smokey, "I want to wish you a lot of luck. John's hard."

Then they all waited for John, who came in three hours late, apparently unconcerned that he had kept Walsh, one of the highest-paid rock-and-roll stars, waiting. John was bouncing, flying on cocaine, Smokey concluded.

"Hey, oh," John said. "What's going on?"

He was wearing blue corduroy trousers, sneakers and a double-breasted sports jacket that couldn't be buttoned because he was too overweight. His pockets were stuffed with eight small Dixie cups of Haagen-Dazs ice cream. He offered them around and began eating some himself.

"Hey, Smokey," John said, coming over and shaking hands tentatively, giving a sharp glance, the Belushi stare, his eyes riveting and holding Smokey. Smokey looked back as if to say, I *know* that you *know* that I *know* my job is to stop the drugs. It was a simple but clear communication on the matter.

"Hey, processed hair," John said to Smokey.

"Yeah, mine used to look like yours before I fixed it," Smokey replied.

"One for you," John said, walking away, strutting around the room rapidly with nervous, jerky movements. He put on some headphones to start the recording session.

A few minutes later a well-dressed stranger entered the recording studio. He was toting a fancy walking cane, escorting two women and carrying three bottles of champagne.

John obviously knew the man and appeared very pleased to see him. A bucket was brought out for the champagne.

"This is Smokey," John said, introducing everyone. "He's going to be traveling with me, helping me, taking care of me. Today's the first day."

Smokey looked over the newcomers. He and Walsh eyed each other uncomfortably. The strangers were obviously drug people, Smokey concluded. He wondered how this was going to work. Would he be able to tell if some buy or drug transfer was taking place?

"I've got to go to the bathroom," John said, a little too smoothly. "But I'll listen to this first." He put the headphones back on and turned away.

The stranger immediately went to the bathroom and came out shortly afterward.

Smokey darted in without John noticing. In the small room, his hands and eyes began to search. In the chrome paper-towel dispenser, he found a small packet of cocaine. Smokey slipped it into his pocket and walked back into the studio.

John finished listening and headed for the washroom. After several minutes, he pushed open the door, rushed out frowning and walked over to the stranger. Smokey strained to overhear the mumbled conversation.

"That's impossible," the stranger said, and went to the washroom. He came out looking bewildered.

Smokey watched as John poked around the room. There was the usual clutter from a recording session—food, drinks, coffee, fresh cigarettes—all lying on a table. A Vantage Blue hanging from his mouth, John walked over and with studied nonchalance picked up a pack of Dunhill cigarettes.

"Let me see the cigarettes," Smokey said, walking up to the table.

"What cigarettes?" John snapped. "What are you talking about?"

Smokey said he thought John smoked Vantage.

"I don't smoke these, but I want to try them," John said.

Smokey grabbed the Dunhill box and tightened his grip. John swung around. Smokey did not let go. Neither would give up, and soon they had tumbled to the floor and were yanking at the box, wrestling each other for it. Smokey finally pulled it out of John's hand, stood up and flipped open the top. Inside was another packet of cocaine.

John got up and ran around the room shouting, threatening. Tischler was astonished.

Smokey addressed Tischler: "Bob, is it your custom to have all these people in the studio when recording?"

No, Tischler said.

"These are my friends," John shouted. "If I want them here, they can stay."

"Here's what we are going to do," Smokey said softly, addressing the stranger. "You can stay, but the more 'blow' you leave around, the more expensive it's going to be. I have in my possession two grams. I know John can afford it. It's painful when you lose blow, but it's worse when it's wasted. Now if this were Sweet 'n Low . . ." In one motion Smokey quickly ripped open the packets, and before anyone could stop him, he had dumped the white powder into a cup of coffee on the table.

John was like a pinball machine on tilt, out of control, and he raced into the soundproof recording room. Through the window the others could see that he was throwing things around, shouting so loudly they could hear his muffled voice.

"I can't believe this," Tischler said.

John finally came back and motioned Smokey over to the side.

"Don't you ever! Ever! Ever again embarrass me like that again in front of my friends."

Smokey explained that there would have been no incident if John had let him see the cigarette box. Those were the rules, Smokey indicated. He had to be able to do his job without interference.

John glared.

Smokey figured he had better try to get and hold the psychological edge as soon as possible, even if it meant being fired the first day on the job.

John went back to work. Walsh told him how to mix honey and tea to help his voice. As they were all leaving, Walsh wished John luck with Smokey.

"You're right," John said. "I'm not going to like him." John gave Smokey a pat on the back and shook his hand.

John, Smokey and Lyda went to a nearby Italian restaurant. Smokey had worked with rock stars before but had never seen so many autograph seekers as those who came in a steady stream to their table. It was also Smokey's first chance to see John eat: first an antipasto, then spaghetti, ravioli, a main meat course and dessert. After dinner John and Smokey went to John's house at 60 Morton Street, a row house on a pretty tree-lined street in Greenwich Village. On the first floor, which was really the basement level, John and Judy had their bedroom. Next to it John had a room he called the vault, a large music room with sophisticated stereo equipment and soundproofing on the walls and door.

John took Smokey into the vault, shut the door, put on a recording and turned the volume way up. John looked at Smokey to see how he liked the sound. "Is this too loud?" John asked.

Without saying anything, Smokey walked over to the amplifier and turned the volume up.

Bored, John turned off the music and went upstairs to the main parlor floor, where there was a large living room and dining room.

John said he wanted to go to the Blues Bar, another private bar (with the same name as the one in Chicago) that he and Aykroyd rented several blocks away. Smokey should call a limousine, John said, adding that he didn't like Cadillacs or stretch limousines. He wanted a Lincoln Town Car.

Smokey called for a Lincoln, and while they waited, John made a few phone calls, then outlined Smokey's responsibilities.

"Do whatever you did for Joe Walsh," John said, adding, "I don't go anywhere without Judy. Never leave her behind. Take care of her. She is very important to me. Remember that."

Smokey explained that he would get up with John in the morning and put him to bed at night; and he would try to handle everything—cars, food, phones, security, travel arrangements, whatever John wanted.

John seemed to relax. "Now, as far as myself and my problem," he said, ". . . I'm going to give you lots of ifs, ands and buts, and you're going to have to deal with it. Don't you want to write any of this down?"

Smokey said he would remember.

"I suppose you know in this business drugs are one of the biggest problems along with alcohol. Well, I'm no drinker. . . . When I was thirty, I was told that I'm a millionaire. I used to scrimp with Judy in one-room apartments."

John returned to his problem. "It's hard to go back and be constantly funny." He explained that there was incredible pressure from everyone, expectations from everyone and from himself. "I'm sure it comes as no surprise that people in this business need something to keep themselves up and their minds going. You *need* drugs. You've got to be on top, got to store everything to use it." He said he always had to be alert to the comic possibilities in everything that happened around him and to him.

They sat in silence for a moment. Smokey was beginning to like John.

One of his favorite places, John said, one of the few places he could go to relax, was the Tenth Street Baths, an old Russian and Turkish bathhouse—the *schvitz,* or "sweat," as it was called. An old guy named Al ran the place, which also had a small restaurant. You've got to meet him, John said, and called Al on the phone. Soon John was ordering a second dinner—steaks, fries and salads. "I have this good friend of mine who'll come over and pick it up," John said. "Smokey."

John autographed some pictures of himself for the people at the baths and sent Smokey out when the limousine arrived.

Smokey walked to the car, told the driver the address of the baths and sent him off to pick up the food. Smokey then climbed the outside steps to the second floor and waited. As soon as the limousine rounded the corner, John stepped out of the ground-floor door. He commenced a fast, happy walk up Morton Street. Smokey came down the steps and followed along, increasing his own pace until he was in step right beside John.

John noticed Smokey, stopped abruptly and yelled, "What the hell are you doing here?"

"Where are you going?" Smokey asked.

"I told you to go get dinner."

"How heavy can two dinners be in the back of a Town Car? And besides, the driver looks strong enough to me."

"Goddamn," John shouted, and swung his arm up and slapped a street sign hard with the palm of his hand. He turned and went back to the house. Smokey followed.

Smokey checked the house to make sure there were no back exit escape routes and sat down to watch television. About 10 P.M. the food came and John devoured his second dinner. They then took the limousine to the Blues Bar. After a few minutes John started to inch his way to the door, and he finally tried to run out alone. But Smokey managed to get out first through another door. When John finally reached the car and opened the door, Smokey was waiting in the back of the limousine.

"Son of a bitch!" John yelled, slamming the door. He went back into the bar.

A little bit later John raced out and got into the car alone. This time Smokey was too late and had to chase the car down the street. He finally caught up and pounded on the back. John ordered the driver to stop, then start again, then stop quickly. Smokey chased the lurching car down Hudson Street for a block until it finally halted. Smokey opened the door and got in.

John was laughing hysterically. "I finally got you!"

"That depends on how you look at it," Smokey said. "Aren't we in the same car together?"

"Yeah," John said. "I told the guy to stop."

"Why did you?"

"I don't know," John replied.

2

Wheaton, Illinois. March 1967.
Dan Payne, a thirty-four-year-old drama and speech teacher at Wheaton
Central High School, hurried out in the cold rain one Saturday to his
Ford station wagon. He was uncomfortable about his day's plan. He was
going to drive his star senior, John Belushi, 25 miles to Chicago to audi-
tion for a seven-week acting job in a summer-stock theater. He wanted
John to get the job but was worried that, as an unofficial father, he might
be pushing John too hard.

Belushi was eighteen, and he was the kid everyone wanted a piece
of: "Killer Belushi," cocaptain of the varsity football team, 170 pounds,
five feet nine, all-conference middle linebacker. John was popular; he had
been elected homecoming king by the student body; he played drums in
a rock-and-roll band, the Ravins, and the band had cut a record. He was
also a brilliant actor, everything from ballerinas to Marlon Brando in the
student variety show.

In the six years he had been at Wheaton, Payne had never seen such
talent or charm in a young adult. Belushi's skits and jokes and his imitations were the way he communicated. His irreverence was pie-throwing
funny, not bomb-throwing angry, and he turned it to everything in his
experience—family, religion, teachers, coaches.

Thrusting his belly over his belt, Belushi could play Howard Barnes,
the football coach, to perfection, as the coach explains how to grade a
physical education class:

"One fifth for wrestling, one fifth for basketball, one fifth on calis-
thenics, one fifth on volleyball and one fifth on football."

Pause. "And one half on attitude."

John also played both the head coach and his alcoholic assistant
giving the football team a pep talk before the big game.

The head coach delivers the usual exhortations: stomp fingers, break arms, legs, necks, kick, bite; send the opponents to the hospital, cover the field with blood. Then the coach glances out of the corner of his eye, hesitates, wonders whether he ought to call on his assistant. He might be too drunk to stand. Finally the coach does, and the assistant, waving his arms, staring vacantly into space, says:

"All right! How many of you guys beat off last night? How many times do I have to tell you? Don't masturbate. It saps your strength. Did any of you touch yourself before the game? I'll bet you did."

Payne had probably laughed too much at that.

He turned right on Elm Street and stopped at 904, a small, one-story, three-bedroom house that John shared with his parents, grandmother, an older sister and two younger brothers. It was in a working-class section of Wheaton, which was mainly an affluent Republican suburb.

Payne honked, and Belushi dashed out, wearing a suit and necktie, looking the perfect clean-cut straight-arrow with his close-cropped black hair. Payne had never seen John so dressed up. John was treating the audition seriously. It had taken much time and many phone calls to arrange the tryout with Adrian Rehner, who ran the Shawnee Summer Stock Theater. Normally, auditions were given only to college and graduate students who were studying theater.

"I'm not sure I really want to do this," John said softly, looking away from Payne.

Surprised and irritated, Payne inquired why.

"I can't be in shows if I play football."

Payne thought football had won out, but John's explanation was more complicated. John needed a scholarship to go to college. His father's two restaurants in Chicago were not doing well, and there wasn't much money. "And I don't want to go into the Army." If he didn't have a draft deferment, he would probably be sent to Vietnam. He wasn't particularly antiwar, but he didn't want the Army to interfere with his life. Payne suggested that they drive over to the high school and talk.

They pulled into the parking lot by Grange Field, the vast stadium where 10,000 fans came on fall Friday nights to watch football. Grange Field was named for halfback Red Grange, the 1922 Wheaton High graduate who had gone on to become the legendary "galloping ghost" of the University of Illinois and later of the Chicago Bears. Playing on the team was the biggest thing at the Wheaton high school.

John explained that football looked like not only a path to college and out of the Army but a career. He had to choose—football or acting.

Payne urged him to slow down. They were not talking about a career, just a summer job. John kept fretting about the future. Okay, Payne said, what about football as a career? He didn't know much about the National Football League except that 170-pound linebackers were a rarity. After twenty minutes John agreed to go to the audition.

They got several miles closer to Chicago when John said he wanted to get a soda and think things over again. They went into the White Hen Pantry in Glen Ellyn. It was still raining, a blustery, chilly rain, almost snow.

John told Payne he was angry with his father. Adam Belushi had come to America in 1934 at sixteen and had worked his way up in the restaurant business, from dishwasher and busboy to managing and then owning restaurants. He was never home. The restaurants had not merely dominated his father's life, they had obliterated it. He spent his week-nights at an apartment above the restaurant, returning to Wheaton only on the weekends to issue decrees and orders for the coming week. Holidays were often the biggest business days in the restaurant business so they were ignored or postponed.

John said his older sister was getting married, and though there was very little money, they were going to do it up big, buying furniture on time, putting on an expensive party for the family. "If they can pay for the wedding, why can't they pay for my college?"

About the only good thing John could say about his father was that he had bought him a motorcycle, a BMW 250, two years ago. That's it, John said. Now his parents wanted him to get a summer job and bring in some money. He had to make $50 a week: that was their minimum.

Look, Payne said, you have nothing else to do this afternoon and no other plans for summer work. Let's see what happens.

Even with the delays, they arrived at Rehner's house only about ten minutes late. Payne waited in the car while John went for the tryout; it was to be a cold reading from material John had never seen before. When John emerged, he said, "I wasn't very good. I didn't do very well."

Payne doubted it. Both he and the football coaches knew that John could be lazy in practice or rehearsal, but when the lights went up, when the band was playing, and when the audience or fans were there, he went all out. About 50 to 60 people were auditioning for the twelve places in the summer company. After the formal auditions were over, Payne and John went inside together. Rehner had a number of the auditioners do some informal readings and some scenes. John did several and broke everyone up, including the others who were there trying out.

Rehner motioned Payne to the kitchen.

"Does he have problems memorizing lines?" Rehner asked.

"No, no," Payne lied, "he can learn lines very well." In fact, John was always improvising, trying to improve on the lines. And he didn't like to stay in his assigned place on stage. Also, his acting tended to excess. Payne recalled John's Marlon Brando impersonation with the Brando ripped T-shirt. At each performance John had ripped the shirt a little more so that by the final show, it was barely hanging on his back. But there was no doubt that when John took the stage, all eyes were on him. He always stole the show. But Payne kept quiet about John's shortcomings.

Rehner promised to call Payne that night with his decision.

Back in the station wagon, John was beaming.

"That's what I want to do," he said. The others were so much older. But he knew he had been the focus, and he had got the laughs. He was full of questions. Would he get the $50 a week he needed? Who is Rehner? Where does he teach? How long have you known him? There were many "what if" questions about his future. He had forgotten football. Did Payne think he'd be hired? Soon John's confidence flagged, and he was full of doubts. It was dark when Payne dropped him back at Elm Street. A half-hour later Rehner called Payne.

"He's the most talented son of a bitch I've ever seen," Rehner said. Of course they would take him. "It's $45 a week," Rehner said. "That's all we can afford."

Payne said he would supplement John's pay by $5 out of his own pocket, but it would have to be done through the theater so John wouldn't know. He'd send a check for $35 to cover the seven weeks. Rehner agreed.

Payne called John with the good news.

"Great! Wow!" John said. "Now, how about the money?"

Shawnee would pay him $50 a week, Payne said, and after congratulating him he hung up. It had been an exhausting day. He hoped he had done the right thing.

John had a steady girlfriend, a skinny sixteen-year-old All-American–looking sophomore named Judy Jacklin. She was five feet five with long, straight bleached hair.

Judy had first noticed John the previous year when he had played a Nazi camp counselor in the variety show. They had met during the summer at Herricks Lake, a small lagoon near her house. A group of her friends and a group of his had rented boats, and a water fight had erupted. John had grabbed an oar and banged the water ferociously at the girls' boat. His oar took a wild bounce and hit Judy's arm. He apologized and called her the next day to check on the arm. It was fine. He called again. On the third call he asked her to go to the Homecoming dance that fall. She said yes. At the dance John was crowned homecoming king and received a small tin crown. He was sheepish and seemed embarrassed.

They went out for several months until Judy broke it off. After two days she felt a longing for John and sent him a note. Soon they were back together, seeing a great deal of each other, and Judy realized she'd fallen in love with him.

John also spent many of his free hours playing the drums for the rock-and-roll band the Ravins. Wearing red shirts, black pants and black turtleneck collars called dickies, John and some friends, including Dick Blasucci and Tony Pavilonis, performed at school dances and the Wheaton Youth Center. The Ravins played popular records over and over until they could imitate them as closely as possible.

When the Rolling Stones had released "(I Can't Get No) Satisfaction" with Mick Jagger singing, John was the first to get the record and learn the words. The Stones toured America that year, and John convinced some of his fellow Ravins to take the train to Chicago for the concert. John thought the Stones were the greatest and was obsessed with their music.

The Ravins also made a recording, funded by Blasucci's father, called "Listen to Me Now." They all thought it was destined for the top of the charts. A hundred copies were made, and it was sent to the local radio stations, but none of them would play it. Later, the Ravins used the records as prizes for dance contests and, in mockery of their dreams, painted a few copies gold and tossed them around like Frisbees.

John finally turned down a football scholarship at Western Illinois in favor of Illinois Wesleyan; both the football coach and the drama department wanted him, and it seemed like a good compromise. But his grades, mostly Cs, were not good enough, and he wasn't accepted. So at the last minute, he chose the University of Wisconsin at Whitewater, which had no football team but an acceptable drama department. He told Judy he was going to study to become a professional actor and that she might have to support him during the first years after he got a drama degree. At least until he was thirty. If he didn't make it by then, he would find something else to do.

He graduated with the class of 1967 (voted "Most Humorous") and was off on his motorcycle to his summer job at Shawnee.

The summer company did seven shows in as many weeks, including *Anne of the Thousand Days,* in which John played Cardinal Wolsey. The local newspaper reviewer said: "Cardinal Wolsey is played with fine sensitivity by John Belushi. Brooding, towering and a pillar of strength and power, he brings some strong moments to Shawnee." And for Agatha Christie's *Ten Little Indians,* another reviewer pointed out that Belushi was "especially good as a comic detective, much in the Peter Sellers line, but not so bumbling."

In addition to working on his acting that summer, John used marijuana for the first time.

Late in August, Tom Long, an older actor who had been at Shawnee that summer, mentioned to Payne what a wonderful job the Albanian had done.

Payne looked perplexed. "The Albanian?"

John.

"No," Payne said, "he's not Albanian." John had told Payne that his father was Greek and his mother Italian. It was unlikely that he'd make up something like that. Sometime later he asked John about it.

"Hey, Tom told me you're Albanian. You got bombed one night and told him you don't tell anyone?"

"Yeah," John said quietly, "you know I am. The people in Wheaton . . . ." John added, hesitating, "There was enough trouble around here without telling anyone . . . we didn't want it known, didn't want to get in trouble around town. It's been with me so long, that's the story we've been telling. But I really am Albanian."

Payne was dismayed. It was all too believable—a family from Albania, a small, impoverished Communist country, coming in the 1950s to an upper-middle-class Republican suburb during the McCarthy era, and concluding that it would be prudent to cover up their ethnic origin.

All this made Payne more determined to help John. Shawnee had worked out better than anyone's wildest dream. Payne and his wife, Juanita, wondered about the next step for John, and they decided to take Judy and him to see Chicago's famous Second City comedy troupe, whose better-known alumni included Mike Nichols, Elaine May, Shelley Berman, Alan Arkin, Joan Rivers and Alan Alda.

On the way Payne told them how it had started. In 1955 a group had set itself up in Chicago's Hyde Park area as a backroom improvisational theater. Originally called The Compass, it became, in 1959, the Second City, the title of a famous *New Yorker* article that poked fun at Chicago. Disposing of tradition—sets, scripts and strict routine—the company created a special interaction with the audience by using the news of that week or that day for their subject matter, which included politics, education, sex, family, psychiatry and childhood, used-car salesmen, blind dates. Each show started with rehearsed sketches, but those were followed by an improvisational performance based on suggestions and questions from the audience.

John sat through the show. Barely. It seemed to the Paynes and to Judy that he was dying to go on stage and join in. "Hey, I could do that," he announced in the car afterward, offering his criticisms, reenacting some of the sketches, shaking his head, throwing his arms about. John had admired David Steinberg, who'd done a stand-up monologue on the Bible and God. He established an almost physical contact with the audience. Steinberg looked out into the room, searching, locking eyes, playing combative, unfriendly characters and then switching back to his own natural charm. John couldn't stop talking about it. Later he told Judy that Second City was what he wanted to do.

Early the next month John was off to Whitewater, Wisconsin, to enroll as a college freshman. He let his hair grow longer, and he hitch-hiked home many weekends to see Judy, who was now the president of her junior class at Wheaton High. Her parents expressed their disappointment that she was still going out with John. He looked like a hippie, and high school girls weren't supposed to go out with college boys. But she told them that she loved John.

His first semester John flunked the college speech class and was angry. He told Judy that he was the best in the class. He was not a failure, he could control the room better than anyone, but instead of doing the assignments, he liked to improvise. Assignments and professors were too rigid.

Adam Belushi was having trouble paying the expenses for John's college. There simply was no money. He would be able to finish the year at Whitewater, but he would have to move back to Wheaton and find a college nearby for next fall.

Adam had always wanted John to take over his restaurants, and that pressure was mounting. John said no, that was not his life, that was not what he wanted; he was going to become an actor; just couldn't do it; please understand.

"I'll give you my business," Adam Belushi said. The old way was for the son to help his father, to carry on. "I'll sign it over to you right now."

"No," John said again.

In the summer of sixty-eight, after his freshman year, John rented a barn on the outskirts of Wheaton which he shared with two other boys for $40 a month and did odd jobs.

He became an enthusiastic supporter of Senator Robert F. Kennedy, who had launched his presidential campaign. Judy wasn't so sure; her parents thought Kennedy was a radical. John explained to Judy that he considered himself a patriot but the war in Vietnam was wrong, "immoral," "Fascist." If drafted, he would run away to Canada.

Tom Long took John to Chicago during the 1968 Democratic Convention. The night of Hubert Humphrey's nomination, August 28, they joined the protest march to the International Amphitheater, more as observers than demonstrators. The National Guard, helmets fastened and billy clubs drawn, had set up a barricade of jeeps covered with barbed wire along the route. As the marchers advanced, the National Guard opened fire with liquid tear gas from pressurized hoses. John was one of the first to get hit, and the power of the blast knocked him off his feet.

Later that night he appeared at the door of Rob Jacklin, Judy's older brother, who was living in Chicago. Reeking of tear gas, John was barely conscious as he stumbled through the door. Rob took off John's clothes and led him to the shower. Later John called Judy in Wheaton. The violent confrontation was all over the news.

"I can't believe how much tear gas hurts," John said to Judy. "I was following Dick Gregory and he said"—John lowered his voice to imitate the black activist comedian—" 'We are not an illegal assembly. We are going to my house for some coffee.' " And the police, who John said were trained to give demonstrators or a crowd an avenue of escape, had blocked all the alleys and trapped everyone. "I couldn't believe it! . . . I saw one cop beating this kid, and I went over, and the cop jabbed me in the ribs. I was scared and promised to go home. . . . I walked away and the cop just went back beating on the kid!"

In the fall of 1968, John transferred to the College of DuPage, a new two-year junior college in Glen Ellyn. Money was an increasing problem. The Paynes gave him some household jobs—$2 an hour to clean the windows. He was slow, not a great cleaner, but they could see he needed the work. The son of the restaurateur seemed always to have a big appetite, so he often ate at the Paynes'. Their baby had colic and was often up much of the night. Sometimes John came by about 2 A.M. and, if there was a light on, scratched on the back window. He wanted just to talk.

There was not much campus life at the College of DuPage, but John formed close relationships with Steve Beshekas and Tino Insana, two tall, husky graduates of a nearby high school. They got together at a friend's house in Wheaton, and Beshekas saw immediately that there was an incredibly funny chemistry between John and Insana as they sat around for hours telling stories and cracking jokes. One day, John proposed that they form a comedy group—Belushi, Beshekas and Insana—and call themselves the West Compass Players, after the forerunner to Second City.

By the end of the year the West Compass Players were performing regularly—short skits in the student union and at local coffee houses. John was the driving force. Most of the skits were slapstick and sight gags, and John taught Insana and Beshekas the techniques he had learned at Shawnee. The three also did night janitorial work to earn money. Whenever possible, John went to see the Second City show in Chicago. He borrowed their ideas and bent their material to his own style.

He also learned how to use material from his own experience. Evangelist Billy Graham had graduated from Wheaton College in 1943, and Graham's fundamentalism was widely subscribed to in the town. John invented a skit to show how religion had kept him from getting laid in high school:

"I'd go over to her house, up to her bedroom and we'd get close, so close to making it, and then she'd scream, 'God is in the closet watching us!' and she'd run out."

Soon Adam Belushi lost both his restaurants and found a job as a bartender. Agnes Belushi, John's mother, worked as a cashier at the local pharmacy.

One night in late 1968, John went by the Elm Street house. Jimmy, fourteen, had just started high school. He was uncertain about school and had just had a fight with their mother. Jimmy lay in his pajamas on the bed in the little alcove by the chimney, between the kitchen and garage—the spot where John and Jimmy had shared bunk beds for years. There was a religious icon hanging in the corner, and the only light came from a 60-watt bulb in a wall lamp John had built in wood shop half a dozen years earlier.

"Just use this place to sleep," John told his brother, indicating that's what he had done. "Go to school all day, go to football, come back here and eat and go out all night and come here and sleep. Go out for football, wrestling. Go out for the speech team. Go out for dramatics. Do whatever you want to do, but just do it. And stay out of here."

John tried to explain to Jimmy how he felt about their parents. They lived their own lives, and the kids had to live theirs; that was the only way. Their parents didn't understand the pressure, how their ethnic heritage and the restaurants didn't fit into Wheaton. Their parents made decisions and didn't understand how those decisions affected their children. It was better not to get too involved with the family. Their parents, as they both knew, were unhappy with each other and had been for years. Shield yourself with sports and school and absence. Most of all, keep busy, John said.

Jimmy didn't exactly understand, but he took down all the newspaper clippings about John from the bulletin board. Now there would be room for what he was going to do in high school.

Jimmy thought John knew how to work things out at home. One day, years before, their mother had swatted them. She had been the disciplinarian since their father was generally away, and John had told Jimmy, "Just laugh when she hits us." They did, and pretty soon she was laughing with them.

When their father took a rare day off, he often declared it yard day and would direct everyone to a task. One day while their father was at the restaurant, John did an imitation.

"Number one," John mimicked, getting halfway out of his seat like his father. "You take out the garbage.

"Number two, you do the lawn.

"Number three, I want you to help your mother with the dishes.

"Number four, turn over the garden for Nena."

John's mother and the rest of the family were in hysterics. John had captured his father perfectly, and he could make his mother laugh so hard that no sound came out. Jimmy could see how John worked his magic around the house to break the rules to get his way.

John was smoking marijuana more frequently. He did not particularly try to hide it, but John and Judy burned incense in her parents' car, which they often used, to cover the smell. Her father raised the issue.

"Why are you so stupid to smoke that stuff?" Leslie Jacklin asked. "It will only lead to something worse. It will lead to heroin."

In the fall of 1969, Judy started college at the Urbana-Champaign campus of the University of Illinois. Carol Morgan, a classmate from Wheaton, was her roommate in the campus dormitory, and almost every weekend John hitchhiked down 120 miles to visit. Occasionally he brought Insana and Beshekas, and they would perform comedy skits at the school coffee shop. They were developing more of an edge: their new theatrics were not merely good-natured takeoffs on coaches, but bricks aimed at politicians, moms, dads.

Morgan noticed that John had changed from his high school days. He had donned the mantle of the angry young radical—antiwar, anti-Nixon, anti-clean-clothes. He joined in demonstrations on their campus, especially that spring, after the Kent State shootings.

John also announced that he hated alcohol and that anybody who drank was "straight." And he introduced Judy to marijuana. Morgan, John and Judy would put masking tape and wet towels around the door of the girls' dormitory room and smoke pot for hours, listening to hard-rock groups like Led Zeppelin. There were other drugs available around the college, and John began to experiment with downers and hallucinogens. Morgan was afraid to use LSD, and John kidded her about it. It's fun, he said, you'll enjoy it, it's a great high, it will make you laugh. Morgan knew that everyone was experimenting with acid and that John would try anything and everything for a new experience, but that stuff wasn't for her.

During her freshman year, Judy told John she was pregnant. They loved each other, but marriage and a child? They were not ready. They didn't tell their parents but went together to a clinic in Chicago for an abortion. John was proud that he had gone with her.

On June 5, 1970, John graduated from the College of DuPage with an associate of arts degree in general studies. Now out of school, he was vulnerable to the draft, and his lottery number was distressingly low—59 out of 365. He had a good chance of being called. He found a doctor who was helpful in getting people medical exclusions. John had slightly high blood pressure, so he took lots of salt and exercised strenuously before going to see the doctor. The regimen had caused his blood pressure to go up, and John concluded that he could do it again to get himself rejected if he was called. But to play it safe, John, Insana and Beshekas enrolled in the University of Illinois, Circle Campus, in Chicago.

John found an apartment on Taylor Street, in an Italian neighborhood, and shared it with Tom Long and an Iranian student. He also discovered a small coffee shop in the basement of the Universal Life

Church, about a block from the campus, that was in financial straits. Beshekas, Insana and John rented the space for $100 a month and opened the Universal Life Coffee House, home of the West Compass Players. The room held about four dozen people and they charged $1 admission. They served Kool-Aid and developed 60 to 70 very short comedy skits, called "blackouts," which evolved over the weeks.

John sat for hours each morning, reading the newspaper, looking for things to make fun of. He loved impersonating Chicago Mayor Richard Daley, and the audience loved it too.

During their sophomore year, Judy and Carol Morgan moved off campus to a $150-a-month apartment about twelve blocks from the college. John still hitchhiked down regularly to spend the night.

Once he convinced the girls to go exploring with him. They got in Morgan's 1962 Buick, and John gave directions. About three miles from the apartment, he told Morgan to pull over. Growing wild in the flat, wide-open farm fields of central Illinois, there was a huge patch of marijuana. It was called Rantoul Rag, named for the nearby town and for the harsh effect it had on the throat.

Carol and Judy refused to leave the car. John hopped out, loaded two pillowcases and jumped back into the car, and they raced back to the apartment. Morgan, paranoid about the police, locked the door. They dumped the contents of the pillowcases onto the living room floor and started smoking it. It tasted horrible, and no matter how much they smoked, they didn't really get high, only dizzy. The three of them stayed in the apartment for the rest of the day and night, playing music on Morgan's portable stereo and smoking. John taught Morgan and Judy how to clean the pot and then showed them how to dry it in the gas oven. At the end of the weekend, John filled up 30 Baggies with an ounce of pot each and took them back to Chicago to smoke and sell.

The West Compass Players continued to travel down to the Urbana-Champaign campus to perform, and the Rantoul Rag was one of the reasons. Beshekas regularly loaded up for the trips back north.

One day, he heard a knock at the door of his Glen Ellyn home. There were policemen with a search warrant. He was busted for possession of twelve pounds, but he was a good soldier and took the rap alone. He got two years probation. John was relieved and grateful. Part of the pot had been his.

3

Chicago. February 1971. Bernard Sahlins, forty-seven years old, balding, five feet eight—Hollywood agents claimed he looked like a TV repairman—left his apartment and rushed by foot the five blocks to the home of the Second City comedy troupe in the Old Town section. Sahlins was the sole remaining founder of the twelve-year-old farm team for American comedy and was now its producer, owner, president, and godfather. His six-member cast was on its way to New York for a revue, and Sahlins was auditioning new talent. He was looking a little harder this week since he was going to direct the next show himself. Second City was thriving on weekends when Chicago's professionals and students—the hip, generally antiwar elite, eighteen- to thirty-five-year-olds—flocked to the show and paid $4 a seat. On weeknights ($3 a seat) the gate was down, and Sahlins had recently taken out a $10,000 bank loan to keep going.

He walked into the empty cabaret-theater, 80 by 50 feet, filled with small round tables and chairs for an audience of 325. He stepped halfway to the back of the playhouse, up a 30-inch riser, and took a seat on the right side. Unwrapping one of his skinny Brazilian Danneman cigars, he lit up, set an elbow on the table and waited. Sahlins had seen thousands of auditions. He had spotted and hired David Steinberg, Joan Rivers and Robert Klein.

His assistant, Joyce Sloane, the nuts and bolts producer, came in along with several members of the current cast. The three-member comedy team that had been performing at the Universal Life Coffee House was being given a private audition. Sahlins had heard their show was satirical and topical—their version of Second City. He was making an exception by letting the trio perform some prepared material. He wanted to see his budding competition at its best.

The theater was quiet as Belushi walked onto the bare stage. It was just the way Sahlins liked it. Empty stages don't forgive an actor anything.

Glasses askew, trenchcoat a size too large and wrinkled, Belushi carried a large stack of books and a look of rejection—the high school wimp, the class brain. He was waiting at a bus stop, shy, frightened (like Jonathan Winters, whom John had imitated before a mirror when he had been a high-schooler), half-genius, half-reject, apparently alone in the world, terrified by it.

Tino Insana came on stage, a tough hood, shouting, "Hey, you!"

Belushi turned slowly, doubtful, and opened his mouth. No words came out. Insana began calling Belushi names, mocking his appearance, playing the bully, jeering at a cowering, frozen Belushi. He knocked the books from under Belushi's arm.

Belushi stepped back, suddenly firm, confident, authoritative, and threw his coat open. His head snapped up. He altered his posture, his eyes, his walk, the reach of his arms, his forehead. His cheek muscles tensed. The axis and shape of his physical form changed in a half-dozen ways.

"Is this a greaser that I see before me?" Belushi demanded. Under his coat he had two swords, and he threw one to Insana. Now transformed into Errol Flynn's Captain Blood, John cast off his meek exterior and fought menacingly, dominating Insana and quoting lines from *Hamlet* and *Macbeth* (what he termed his gobbledygook Shakespeare). He was a swashbuckling adventurer; he gained supremacy, he selected his moment.

"And thee I thrust." He lunged gracefully and stabbed Insana in the groin. "Thrust home."

Sahlins had rarely seen such a strong audition—such self-conviction, intensity and control. John's ability to accelerate through two such diverse roles was spectacular; he had made all the right choices. He had not trembled or walked feebly as the wimp but had conveyed his timidity by staying still. He had used his costume well. He had executed both parts with economy, had not tried to overpower the stage, had not used his hands too much like most amateurs. It was a mature performance.

Belushi, Insana and Beshekas did a few more skits and a reading. Sahlins didn't want to break up the trio, but the performers were very uneven. Insana showed promise, Beshekas was relatively hopeless, Belushi was one in a hundred, one in a thousand.

48

"I want you to come to work. I should put you in the touring company," he told Belushi, referring to the minor-league company that played college campuses, "or one of the workshops, but I'm not. I hope you vindicate my judgment."

Sahlins explained that John would be in the replacement cast, and when the others came back they would make a place for him in the regular six-member cast or else add him as a seventh member. In twelve years that had not been done; everyone else had gone on tour or to workshops. The pay was $150 a week.

Belushi accepted deadpan. He said he wanted Insana and Beshekas hired also. Sahlins said no. Insana would be put in the touring company; Beshekas was not ready.

Sahlins also admonished Belushi that the company functioned as a group; he would be expected to be a team player, to support the others and hold back some of his own impulses.

John assured him that he understood and went off to call Judy, his parents and the Paynes to tell them he had his first job, Second City, the big time.*

Sahlins suspected he was hiring not only a great deal of talent but also some trouble. At twenty-two, Belushi would be by far the youngest member of the troupe ever. And he would be their first true creature of the 1960s. On first look, Belushi seemed to suggest some of those new, stronger forces. He would be likely to push the comedy in more extreme directions and extend the boundaries beyond the 1950s University of Chicago version of the Beat Generation. John reflected the political outrage of the times. Sahlins believed that pure acting was transmitted and received unconsciously. Pure talent was largely a mystery. But here it was. Sahlins explained to John that his motto was "Play bright" or "Play

* On a nine-page public relations form Belushi filled out several months after he started, he gave his nationality and then scratched it out so it was unreadable. "I tried to stay unemployed as long as possible," he wrote. To the question about his second choice of career: "Commander of a star ship." Under his home phone he wrote "disconnected."

"Has your life ever been in danger?" the questionnaire asked. "Only when I thought of suicide." On the subject of his musical interests, he said, "Someday I'd like to buy a big stereo outfit and learn to play records at full volume." How extensive is your wardrobe? "I don't need many clothes, but I wish I could find some clean socks."

He closed with this handwritten comment: "Right now I love my work and the people I work with. I don't have much time for outside activities."

Later somebody graded the form and wrote at the top: "C—sloppy and incomplete."

the scene at the top of your intelligence." That meant several things: be cutting but not gross; straightforward but not simpleminded; zany, wicked, but not slapstick.

Joe Flaherty, thirty, was an easygoing two-year veteran cast member in the Sahlins–Mike Nichols image of the cerebral, verbal, satiric comic performer. He looked on Belushi's arrival with mixed feelings. John had a good eye, and his ear was wonderful: he was accomplished at accents. The trouble was his real voice; he sounded like a Chicago teenager, all nasal twang, not exactly Gregory Peck. Belushi was a child of his times —longer, wilder, frizzy hair, a bit too knee-jerk in his antiestablishment politics, more extreme and impatient.

Flaherty soon discovered that it was all too easy for Belushi to steal a scene. In one, Flaherty was talking to someone on stage during a cocktail-party skit when suddenly he heard a huge roar from the audience and turned to see John pretending to shoot up drugs, then fall dead. The audience loved it. "Don't go for the focus all the time," Flaherty told John after the show. "You have to be more of a group player, and when the audience is supposed to be concentrating on someone else, let the scene play out." John was racing to the laugh lines.

"Okay," John said, "I'm sorry. I won't do that."

Yet Flaherty realized that he could work well with Belushi. The show was a series of set skits or scenes, revamped every two or three months, that ran about 90 minutes with an intermission. After a second break the cast came back for the free-for-all improvisational hour.

Sahlins was convinced that the audience's involvement was central. He cast Flaherty as the facile conservative columnist William F. Buckley, Jr., and Belushi as the writer Truman Capote, and had them debate topics suggested by the audience.

As Capote, John, his black hair combed and plastered straight back, wore a white jacket, rose-colored sunglasses and a shoulder bag carried high under his arm. The incongruity of the husky, dark East European sashaying around got a laugh. John was sweet and innocent. He put his hand out in the air gently; he moved his head from side to side. "Well," he said with a delicate, fluttery, drawn-out lisp.

Flaherty, as the verbal Buckley, had to read Buckley's *National Review* magazine to keep up on the latest Lord So-and-So quotes or the current favored Hungarian freedom fighter intellectual. Belushi did it all with attitude, and he stole the laughs with his eyes or eyebrows or simply by saying, "Well," or "Oh, my!" Whenever Flaherty's Buckley picked a fight with John's Capote, the audience sided with Capote. Belushi had a few set gags. Several were long animal stories, and one was about a tiger catching a duck—Capote's new book, "In Cold Duck."

When the audience asked about homosexuality, Flaherty said, "If the good Lord wanted us to be homosexuals, he would have made Adam and *Steve*"—a good line that got a nice laugh each time. Belushi simply replied, "Oh, don't be silly, Bill." It got a bigger laugh.

The Capote-Buckley debate was so successful that Sahlins wanted them to repeat it in the next revue.

"We can't do that," Belushi said. "They'll kill us, the fucking critics and the audience, for doing something twice." But Sahlins insisted, and it was an even bigger hit the second time.

Belushi's repertoire was growing. He did his Mayor Richard J. Daley ("If a man can't give his own son a job . . ."). In the improvisational hour the audiences called for it, shouting from their seats, "Daley, Daley!" John also played a belligerent coach at a PTA meeting; a kid who'd been caught smoking pot being visited by his father and his priest in jail; a stoned citizen stumbling nonsensically with paranoid pauses through a pro-drug editorial reply entitled "No Hope Without Dope." Then there was his bumbling tax adviser, H. R. Rock, who asked clients, "About how many children do you have?" He played a college student bluffing his way through Professor Flaherty's final oral exam in Russian history. In another, Belushi played Hamlet and sang:

> To be, to be
> Sure beats the shit
> Out of not to be.

John played a hippie who had written a threatening letter to President Nixon ("Don't come into town if you know what's good for you"). Two FBI agents, one played by Flaherty, come to question him and beat him up. Each time, Belushi would say "God bless Jack Anderson," for no other reason than to plug Anderson's muckraking column, which he read each day. It got a laugh.

In the fall of 1971, six months after he'd started, John was getting a good deal of attention in the Chicago press. Sydney J. Harris of the *Chicago Daily News* reviewed the latest show, *Cum Grano Salis* (*With a Grain of Salt*), and singled him out. "We all have our personal favorites, however, and mine was John Belushi, who has only to step out on the stage to start me tittering like a schoolboy." Harris said he hadn't laughed so hard or so continuously since the great, long-lost days of Alan Arkin and Barbara Harris.

John cut out a copy of the review and put it in his wallet. Flaherty and other cast members noticed it one day and ganged up, taunting him about having a clipping service, asking whether he always had the article with him.

"Yes," John said, "I carry that article around."

"John," Flaherty replied, "you really want to make it big in this business, don't you?"

"Damn right I do!"

Actor Cliff Robertson came backstage one night after the show, praised Belushi and hinted that he would like to work with him someday.

"Jesus, Cliff Robertson," John repeated for several days, and started talking Hollywood dreams. Flaherty left a phony message at the box office for Belushi: "John, call me at once. Have a movie I want you to be in. Cliff Robertson."

An hour later John was backstage telling everyone, "Cliff Robertson called!"

"Yeah, yeah, John," Flaherty said, smiling, "you're going to be a big star."

Harold Ramis, a tall, curly-haired member of the cast, had thought of himself as Second City's radical, crazed-out zany until John arrived. He was annoyed by Belushi's calculated and exaggerated stunts. If a skit called for John to choke someone on stage, John left his colleague sputtering for breath. Ramis viewed Belushi as a hippie who was bringing rock and roll into Second City. John did a parody of Elton John and James Taylor called Elton Taylor, and he introduced a flawless imitation of singer Joe Cocker. He had the voice and the anguished, jerky body movements that suggested the words started at his toes.

Ramis noticed too, especially during the improvisational hour, that if someone passed the ball to John, often it didn't come back. John had developed a habit of performing solo for several minutes—a time almost unheard of—and beating his subjects into submission. He went on as long as it took. It was clear to Ramis that John knew his strengths and that he didn't think he needed the other players. He would get behind everyone on stage—the power spot—and communicate with the audience privately. He was noticed when he walked onstage, even when he had nothing to do.

Some time after the Robertson visit, Belushi approached Flaherty backstage: "I'm having trouble getting people to work with me in the improv hour. . . . What's wrong? . . . No one in the cast will really talk to me."

"It's a group, you've got to remember that, John," Flaherty said, figuring it was time to slap Belushi down a little. "Unless you're just doing a solo scene, there are other people in the scene, and you've got to remember about the give-and-take. . . . And a scene usually isn't any good if the focus is on just one person. The other people tend to get discouraged. You have to share the focus, even though you may be the dominant figure in the scene."

"Do I do that?" Belushi asked.

"Yeah, you have a tendency to get into yourself up there . . . especially after that article."

Belushi seemed full of self-reproach. "Yeah, I guess maybe you're right. I haven't been thinking too much in terms of the other people."

Flaherty thought that perhaps he'd been too hard. "You know, whatever it is, you always have to sacrifice something for the good of the scene, let someone in even if they're not that good."

Judy had come to live with John that first summer, a fact they kept from her parents. He had a place near Second City, a large three-bedroom apartment they shared with Tino Insana and Flaherty's brother Paul. Later, Judy transferred to the University of Illinois Circle Campus in Chicago and moved in with John permanently. A few days after Judy's twenty-first birthday in January 1972, they went to visit her parents, the Jacklins, figuring they'd better describe the new living arrangements.

Judy sat down in a chair in her parents' bedroom and began crying. John asked the Jacklins to turn off the television, and then he said, "Judy and I want to live together. We love each other. I now have a good paying job, and we've decided to live together."

"Why don't you get married?" asked Mrs. Jacklin.

"It's not the right time," John explained, "and we don't need a piece of paper to prove we love each other."

The Jacklins did not understand and protested. Mrs. Jacklin started to cry. John said there was no give in their position. Judy was astonished at John's strength, his confidence and self-assurance.

John's work was now consuming his life, taking him on the average day no farther than several blocks from Second City. The show ran six nights a week; Monday was his only day off. On work days he slept until about noon and then went to Lum's, an inexpensive restaurant and a central meeting place right across the street from the theater. There he'd meet Flaherty, Ramis and some other members of the cast, read the papers, eat fried mushrooms and drink coffee or beer.

During these sessions they planned new skits and talked shop. Sahlins, and the choices he was making, were a favorite topic. He doesn't pay enough, Belushi said. No one was making more than $200 a week. "We should be on TV," John said another afternoon, complaining that Sahlins wasn't making the most of Second City by keeping it locked in the 1950s and in Chicago. They should agitate for Sahlins to get them a film deal. The cast was that good, Belushi said. The others laughed.

After the performance, too, the cast tended to stick together and go out to bars—folk music at the Earl of Old Town, drinks at the Saddle Club or at John's favorite, the Sneak Joint, a small bar right across from the theater that had last call at 4 A.M. Often the sun was coming up as they left.

At Lum's or the bars after the show, there was much talk about the cast's experimentation with new drugs. John was using marijuana frequently, sometimes before the show or before the improv hour. He had also tried amphetamines and liked the energy drive they provided. He was trying it all—LSD, mushrooms, peyote, sunshine acid. "Yeah, I tried this, man. It was great." "Man, you really get off on this." There was a blond man with a strange voice around the neighborhood. He was nicknamed Dr. Psychedelic; he supplied drugs.

Flaherty didn't think there was anything wrong with taking drugs, but they scrambled his brain and he didn't use many. His wife, Judith, liked to experiment, and on one occasion John and Judith took some mescaline, a hallucinogen that is a little less intense than LSD. It turned out to be a nice mild high.

Judith, who had done some acting with Second City, loved John and called him "My Oak Tree" because he was so strong. Underneath the macho walk and flying hair she had found a gentle, sweet friend. They had a platonic relationship that she found better than sex.

John even exchanged information with Sahlins on the best kinds of pot and other experimental substances. As long as drugs did not interfere with the cast's work, Sahlins didn't worry much. Belushi didn't seem to be doing more than anyone else in his generation. It was true that drugs fired some creative powers in some cast members at times. It seemed that the people who had those powers were going to use drugs no matter.

For Judy it was becoming important and liberating to get stoned. New drugs and more drugs were a kind of test: a comparatively easy way to cross frontiers—personal ones, and group barriers—and to break out of society's bonds. Drugs were the only way to get *away*. There wasn't the time or the money for real vacations. Drugs were a necessary recreation; $5 or $10 was well spent for some pot or several "tabs" of the latest mind-bender.

Flaherty was amazed that John could take so many drugs and still perform. Once, before the show, John had told him that he had taken some wild new hallucinogen. Flaherty asked if he was all right, and John insisted he was. That night, the company did their regular Biblical soap-opera spoof on the birth of Christ. Flaherty was playing Joseph, and his wife Mary said that she was expecting.

"Who?" he asked.

"An angel of the Lord came upon me," she said.

Joseph looked skeptical. Suddenly, John appeared as Gabriel, the Angel of the Lord, at the other side of the stage with orange international distress gloves and cardboard wings attached to his back. John's entrance was always a hit because, if he walked just right, he could get the wings to flap with each step. As usual, the audience laughed. The noise died down. Flaherty looked at John. He was still walking across the stage, in slow motion. By the time he made it to Flaherty, the laughs had subsided. The drug had destroyed John's timing.

Eventually, Flaherty called John on his drug use, on stage. During a segment called "Make a Speech," members of the cast would give speeches on subjects suggested by the audience. Flaherty had just finished one, and he had turned to introduce Belushi. "Look at him, ladies and gentlemen, he's stoned!"

John fired him a dirty look.

"Yeah, look at his eyes, ladies and gentlemen," Flaherty continued.

John broke into a heavy sweat during his speech, which wasn't very funny. Off stage Flaherty said, "Boy, John, you were real bad out there. How come?"

"What the fuck!" John screamed. "What are you doing? You don't do that. You don't say that in front of all those people."

"Relax," Flaherty said, "the audience doesn't know if you're stoned or not."

"Never tell anybody on stage that they're stoned. Do you realize how paranoid you get when you're high? Don't do it again."

Sahlins thought that John was charting a more subversive ground, turning against the satiric tradition of the institution that had found him and was supporting him. "Play bright" was going up in smoke; it was yielding to a scathing, wise-guy, dirty-mouth assault.

One night during the improvisational hour, John, playing the obnoxious person, said, "Eat a bowl of fuck." It got a giant laugh. He said it again. After the show, Sahlins said it might be permissible if it fitted into what was happening on stage. But it wasn't necessary. It was simply a foul line that John had tossed off for its shock value, to cross the taste barrier.

Sahlins wasn't sure what to do. He wanted to encourage taking chances, and the cast had to have the freedom to try new things. Also he had a rule: Never just say no flatly. He approached John again.

John stood by his right to exercise his creative instincts. It worked, he said; the audience laughs.

"I don't give a damn if it's a success with the audience," Sahlins replied.

"Come on, come on," John said, combat-ready.

"Listen, John," Sahlins said, breaking his own rule. "No. You may be right, but 'No!' this time."

So John said "Eat a bowl of fuck" only when Sahlins wasn't around.

Flaherty thought Belushi played the obnoxious guy too well. In one show John ran on stage, looked first at the other actors and then the audience and stated, "Wait, I got to take a shit," and ran off. A short while later he strolled back: "Boy, you should have seen the size of that one!" It was funny, but then John was almost always funny. Flaherty tried to push him to refine his humor: bathroom humor was childish.

In any case it was becoming clear to Sahlins that his young find had become the star of the show, the favorite. The anguish of the other cast members was legitimate. Belushi's mere presence on stage could over-shadow them and mow them down. If he'd been, at first, a natural, but a little bland, now he had an edge. He was surer, and he wore an "I don't take any shit" look. And Belushi was ambitious. Perhaps he had had one foot out the door the day he arrived.

Del Close, a thirty-six-year-old former Second City actor who had directed some of the revues in recent years, came back in 1972 to put together the forty-third revue, the *43rd Parallel*. Close didn't care too much for Sahlins's highbrow instincts, and he was attracted to John im-mediately. John was in italics and the other cast members were in regular print. They were comedians, John was the one human being; they were playing parts and characters, Belushi played real people. Belushi's pres-ence revived Close's feeling of the old days—the Beat Generation, drugs and the vital Lenny Bruce era—nastiness, fuck-you, sick-comic daring.

"How is it that you look so totally relaxed on stage and so in com-mand?" Close asked him.

"Because that's the only place I know what I'm doing," John replied. The communication was so truthful. John worked his eyebrows and gave Close a lecherous look, not sinister, but boyish and honest, as if he'd confessed. Close, a thin, fierce, former stand-up comic, had a small mattress-on-the-floor apartment across the street from Second City. He had been a heroin addict and had had dependencies on speed and Valium at various times. His current problem was alcohol, but he relished his narcotic past, and he wore his track marks from the needles like a badge of honor. The marks confirmed his status as an outsider, the precise quality that he wanted to impress on the show. Actors comprised an alien subculture; they were supposed to be spokesmen for outrage. Second City was supposed to be picking at society's scabs.

Close saw an instrument in Belushi—a trainable, ticking, bad-boy time bomb.

Close had known Lenny Bruce, who had died of a heroin overdose in 1966. Close had once gone with Second City's founding director, Paul Sills, to see Bruce perform, and afterward Sills had told him, "If you can ever find out what Lenny is taking, by all means do it." Drugs were central to the outlandish performances Close wanted. Belushi didn't need to be convinced.

"Lenny Bruce," Close told John one night, "took his work seriously. You have no idea how seriously he took it, pinned his entire life on it. And he had courage, not just through the drugs, but in his art." How long do you think Lenny could go without a laugh? Once he went nearly twenty minutes and then pulled nine trains of thought together. The audience laughed at the same moment like a snap of a sheet, not only a laugh for the jokes but for the brilliance and for the release of tension.

Close found John a most unusual student; he didn't need to be taught to relax or to be spontaneous. His timing was exact. John approached his skills as if they were simply a personality quirk, so Close undertook to teach John structure. That meant more complex material.

Close believed that the most complex subject for a comedian to handle on stage was death. First he guided John in parts calling for him to deal with the death of someone else. In one skit, John plays a taxidermist who brings his fiancée home to meet his parents. The parents are stuffed. John is meant to appear quite natural, to wear an expression of "What did you expect?" The fiancée is, of course, horrified. When she realizes she is next, she calls the police. John leaves the stage and returns with a stuffed policeman.

Close instructed him that the object was to end the sketch with a scream rather than a laugh. And he wanted the scream to be so loud it was a laugh. John carried it off.

For the *43rd Parallel,* subtitled "Macabre and Mrs. Miller," John developed an angry, hip comic character of the early sixties modeled on Close. On stage, he predicts his death. ("And by then the needle will be in my arm and I'll be six feet underground, and there'll be nothing you can do to stop it.") Often he died on stage. Close taught John that the dying had to come unexpectedly; it had to be a surprise.

Marlon Brando, whom John had mimicked when he was still a schoolboy, became increasingly a role model. He'd seen *On the Waterfront* (1954) a dozen times, and he loved everything Brando played. Flaherty could see that John was thinking of himself heading in that direction, the next Marlon Brando. Judith Flaherty felt that John was right to see in Brando a style that fit him—encompassing both courage and range, the young, unjaded Terry Malloy to the burnt-out, wise Don Corleone of *The Godfather.*

John explained to a reporter for *Tempo* at Chicago State College how one imitation led to another: "Well, what I did, I happened to see Brando in a picture called *Reflections in a Golden Eye* in which he played a homosexual. Not long afterwards, I saw Capote being interviewed on TV and I suddenly realized, 'Hey, Brando was doing Capote!' Now if Brando can do Capote and I can do Brando—well then, I can do Capote."

In the spring of 1972, after John had been at Second City for fourteen months, *Chicago Daily News* writer Marshall Rosenthal interviewed him. "Obsessed with Marlon Brando, John Belushi polishes off a slice of pizza, stuffs the greasy napkin into his cheeks and becomes The Godfather," Rosenthal wrote.

"The Brando character, in fact, runs through much of Belushi's hilarious impersonations at Second City, but it never overtakes him because beneath the macho-Mafioso pose always beats the vulnerable heart of a hippy-dippy chump. . . . Belushi has only to step on stage to get laughs."

Rosenthal quoted John: "But a funny thing happens at Second City. A year after you're there, you start to get this fear that you'll die there, and you start wondering when you'll leave."

Rosenthal concluded:

"The pizza has turned into specks of sausage and cheese scattered in the deep-dish baking pan. We step across Wells Street at 3 A.M. to have the last beer at the Earl of Old Town. Folksinger Ed Holstein is on stage, and he calls to John, 'Hey, Valachi, c'mon up and do your Brando!' Not too reluctantly Belushi ambles on stage, takes a long swig of draft beer, and says, 'I could'a been a contendah. . . .' "

4

New York. October 1972. Tony Hendra, a Cambridge-educated Englishman who was working as an editor for *National Lampoon* magazine, boarded a plane to Chicago. He had heard about Belushi's Joe Cocker imitation, had listened to a tape, and he now wanted to see the boy wonder in person.

Hendra was in charge of developing an off-Broadway production that would showcase the bitter insult humor and raunchy, borderline taste of the magazine, which had become an overnight success by mocking sickness, religion, sex and death. Hendra and Sean Kelly, a thirty-three-year-old schoolteacher from Montreal who wrote satire for the *Lampoon* on the side, had an idea of doing a job on their own generation, a parody of one of its most sacred cows, the rock concert. They had found a 1969 *New York Times* editorial blasting Woodstock, the granddaddy of all such gatherings: "The dreams of marijuana and rock music that drew 300,000 fans and hippies to the Catskills had little more sanity than the impulses that drive the lemmings to march to their deaths in the sea."

Hendra thought it was a wonderful analogy—the fans at Woodstock as furry little rodents who make mass suicidal leaps into the ocean. *Lemmings* would be the name of the show.

There were certain rock deities they *had* to parody—Crosby, Stills, Nash and Young, Bob Dylan, James Taylor, Joe Cocker. Kelly began working on the lyrics while Hendra started recruiting a seven-member cast. He needed people who could sing, play instruments and do impersonations. At least on tape, Belushi's Cocker sounded impeccable.

At Second City what Hendra saw, mostly, was the John Belushi Hour, a special performance dedicated shamelessly to the *National Lampoon* talent scout sitting in the audience. Belushi muscled his way into every improv sketch, appearing on stage and capturing attention, throwing in irrelevant impersonations of Brando and Capote and appearing oblivious to his colleagues' visible anger.

It was the sort of blatant self-promotion that Hendra detested in an actor. At the same time, he was fascinated by Belushi, who talked with his eyes and his body. Hendra felt that the bearded comic might jump over the floodlights and go after the audience. His talent was overwhelming, unpredictable but undeniable. The guy was cute and scary, good-natured and dangerous. Exactly the person to play the emcee of *Lemmings*—a menacing teddy bear.

When Hendra went backstage after the show, John almost jumped on him. "Hey, come on back to my place," he said. "We'll do some drugs, have some drinks and talk."

But most of the cast went to John's apartment after the show, and it was difficult for Hendra to talk to John, because all the Second City people were interested in *Lemmings* and there was no privacy. Hendra told John there were parts of the Second City performance he hadn't liked. In fact, he didn't particularly care for improvisational humor. With a straight face, John said he agreed entirely. Hendra said he'd be in touch. Back in New York, he called Sean Kelly. "Don't worry about Cocker. We found him."

John told Judy that he was upset that Hendra hadn't liked the show. When two weeks passed with no word, he announced that it looked as though he wasn't going to get an offer. Then Hendra called and offered Belushi a job, and John accepted at once. New York was the place to go, he explained to Judy; it was the heart and center of real show business.

She asked him whether his plans included her.

Yes, of course, he said. He had read that companies sometimes found jobs for their employees' wives, and he would see if she could get something with the *Lampoon*.

Sahlins was not surprised to hear that Belushi would be leaving. He had watched dozens of his talented people move on. "Make sure it's not a dead end," he warned. "You don't want to ever turn into the most boring thing there is—an out-of-work actor, even a talented one."

As with many people who come from the Midwest to the East, Judy realized that they brought feelings of awe and resentment, fears about being the unsophisticated hayseeds, wearing the wrong clothes, saying the wrong things. But, particularly on John's part, there was a defiance and a will to succeed and conquer.

The first month the *Lampoon* put John and Judy up at the Roosevelt

Hotel, but they soon found a walk-up sublet for about $250 a month on Third Avenue, between Thirteenth and Fourteenth streets near the Village and SoHo. It was more than they were used to paying, but the place looked comfortable at first. Gradually, though, they became disenchanted. At night the building and streets were noisy, hookers hung around the hallways, and the place was full of cockroaches. About all they had was a bed and a television. It was too depressing.

So John went to see Matty Simmons, who had financed the start-up of *National Lampoon* magazine three years earlier; as the publisher, he was also providing the financial backing to *Lemmings*. Simmons, an outspoken man of forty-six, had amassed a fortune as cofounder of the Diners Club and as chairman of the company that published *Weight Watcher's Magazine*.

"I have to go back to Chicago," John said. "Judy, my girlfriend, is not happy here. She has no job, no friends."

"You can't go back," Simmons said. "What can Judy do?"

John said she had studied art, and Simmons quickly gave her a job in the *Lampoon* art department at $175 a week.

In the meantime, Hendra had hired the rest of the cast, including a tall, sophisticated twenty-nine-year-old named Chevy Chase. He was a member of "Channel One," an underground video revue that was eventually packaged into a feature film, *The Groove Tube*. It was immediately clear to Hendra that there was going to be tension between Belushi and Chase. Chase was as much a product of upper-middle-class New York as Belushi was of Chicago. Chase shared Belushi's interest in music and satire, but he was more political. A boyishly handsome amateur with little experience, Chase was constantly pushing Hendra for a higher profile. John, long-haired, bearded and slightly overweight, had more theatrical experience than anyone else in the cast, and he expected to be billed as the star of the show. Hendra refused. He wanted everyone to start even. If there was to be a star, he or she would emerge in the performance.

While the rest of the cast carried their own weight musically, John wasn't much good at the guitar. Hendra put him on bass and turned the volume down. But in other ways John was expanding and creating an extraordinary role for himself. There were a lot of transitions to make between the songs, and John helped Kelly develop the character of the emcee stage announcer, the demonic instigator of the mass suicide. John ad-libbed and improvised as Kelly took notes that he later typed into the script.

But from time to time Belushi threatened to go "home" to Chicago.

Having transplanted himself from England right after college, Hendra was sympathetic. John was young, nervous and frightened, sometimes to the point of tears.

The day the show was to open at the Village Gate theater, January 25, 1973, Simmons received a call from the manager. The state tax collector had just closed the place because of $26,000 in back taxes. When Simmons arrived, the doors were padlocked. The only way to get the padlocks off was to pay the bill in full. Convinced that *Lemmings* was going to be a hit, Simmons put up the money.

Lemmings opened that night with a skit about high school sex. It was followed by a hospital operating-room scene in which doctors, including John, are high on drugs and kill the patient, Chase. There was a reading from "Mrs. Agnew's Diary"—the wife of Vice President Spiro Agnew. And Chase played a Hell's Angel who was upset that a flower child had touched his beloved motorcycle. In a spoof of *Jesus Christ Superstar* called "Jackie Christ Superstar," John played Pontius Pilate at the Last Supper Club—in the style of Brando's Godfather.

In the second half, John as the stage announcer and master of ceremonies for the "Woodshuck Festival of Love, Peace and Death," prepared the mass suicide.

"Can I have your attention please," he began in a high, whiny, authoritarian voice. *"Can I have your attention!*

"Okay, we all know why we came here. A million of us. We came here to off ourselves. . . . As you know, there isn't enough food to go around. There just isn't enough food. So remember," he continued, mocking the Woodstock notion that the person on either side was a brother or sister, "the man next to you is your dinner."

After a few songs, John said, "All right, I don't want to bring anyone down. . . . [But] if you're not a black homosexual working-class woman, you're an oppressor pig. You deserve to die." He complained that businessmen controlled the "means of self-extermination," including razor blades, and suggested that everyone find some creative way to kill himself.

"Now it gives me great pleasure to introduce the All-Star Dead Band," Belushi said.

"Lead vocals, Janis Joplin and Jim Morrison." Laughter. Both Joplin and Morrison had died of drug overdoses.

"Rhythm guitar, Brian Jones." More laughter: Jones had been another overdose death.

"Slide guitar, Duane Allman." Allman had died in a motorcycle accident.

"Lead guitar, Jiiiiimi Hendrix." Laughter. Hendrix, too, had died of a drug overdose.

"And on the keyboard, Harry Truman." Laughter too. The former president was, of course, also dead.

"I want to hear lots of 'Right ons' out there."

John's Cocker imitation with the deep, gravelly voice brought down the house as he sang "Lonely at the Bottom of the Barrel," which had been written for John. The show ended with an extraordinary dance and light show to a group song called "Megadeath."

There is one review, even for a semi-underground revue, that really counts, and that is in the *New York Times*. John and Judy went to get the early edition. Under a headline "LEMMINGS" FAILS EARLY, RECOVERS LATER, they read: "The discovery of 'Lemmings' is John Belushi, a bushy-bearded clown with a deceptively off-handed manner." John's Pontius Pilate was praised as "perfect."

"For example," Mel Gussow's review said, "one need not know that Belushi is doing (and doing in) Joe Cocker to relish his extraordinary limb-twitching performance. He looks as if he were plugged into an electric socket. Tripping over his legs, he falls down with a thud and never stops playing while vainly attempting to lift himself from the floor feet first."

John was elated. He was the star of the show for sure, indelibly certified in the newspaper of record, the *New York*-fucking-*Times*. Something forever in the archives, no matter what.

On February 3, *The New Yorker* magazine hailed *Lemmings* as "very, very good and very, very funny," and "funniest of all is Mr. Belushi as Joe Cocker. . . . Mr. Belushi is a witty and inspired mimic . . . a real discovery."

The next day, Walter Kerr, in the *New York Times,* put the show down with complaints that the young crew in *Lemmings* didn't draw vital distinctions between parody and imitation; too much *Harvard Lampoon* (forerunner of the *National Lampoon*), *Mad* magazine and comic-book stuff on the stage, he wrote. Tony Hendra got some copies of the review, wrapped a dead fish inside them and sent the package over to the *Times*.

Time magazine added its seal of approval on February 19, calling the show "high-voltage humor" and "uproariously funny." The second act, *Time* said, "is a well-etched commentary, held together by an endearingly bumbling announcer, John Belushi."

Three months later the *New York Times* ran a favorable, prominently displayed story on the front page of the Sunday entertainment section: WHY DO YOUNG PEOPLE LOVE "LEMMINGS?" The long story, by Eric Lax, began: "The real message of the '60s wasn't love and peace, it was death—from needles or bullets, take your pick. Death is what 'Lemmings' is about. It is also implicitly about laughter as a vital life sign."

After that article the show was even more of a hit.

In 1973, John's brother Jimmy, now eighteen and in his first year at the College of DuPage, hitchhiked 27 hours to New York to visit John during his spring break. Jimmy went to see the show and was in awe.

After the show John took Jimmy down to the White Horse, a famous pub on Eleventh and Hudson streets. They sat at a table just inside the door.

"Right over there," John said, pointing fifteen feet over to the second stool from the left at the bar, "is where Dylan Thomas died, in that very seat, after he'd had eighteen straight whiskeys."

Jimmy was impressed but vague about who Thomas was.

A great poet who toyed with death, John told him, a tormented man who died young—at thirty-nine. Too much whiskey; Old Grand Dad was his favorite. This was his favorite tavern. "An acute insult to the brain," John said, quoting from the death report of November 1953. Thomas passed out here and was taken to a nearby hospital.

The death, his youth, the energy of Thomas's poetry, seemed to have stuck to John. At twenty-five, John seemed on top of the world, but he was drawn to Thomas. He seemed intense and restless and weary and was romanticizing death. John recited:

> "The force that through the green fuse drives
>   the flower
> Drives my green age; that blasts the roots of
>   trees
> Is my destroyer. . . ."

John kept returning to the Dylan Thomas legend, saying, "*He* died right there; he died right fucking there." *

* Dylan Thomas did consider the White Horse his favorite American tavern and did probably die from too much liquor; it is questionable whether he had eighteen straight whiskeys, although he was in the White Horse drinking heavily a day or two before he went into a coma.

Things were looking up for John and Judy. They had found another apartment to rent but broke the lease when they discovered a nicer one on Bleecker Street in Greenwich Village for $375 a month. John was now making about $300 a week, Judy about $200, and the $500 seemed like a fortune. They went out frequently to restaurants or to parties or bowling or drinking after the show. Most of their friends were cast members or others in the *Lampoon* organization, like Doug Kenney, a Harvard graduate and founding editor of the magazine. Many nights they stayed out until 3 or 4 A.M.

John clearly loved the work—acting, the music, being the master of ceremonies, making fun of everything, even death. He was a star in New York and the city was open to him. Famous people came to see *Lemmings*—Dustin Hoffman, singers James Taylor and Carly Simon, Dick Clark, and the Greek actress Melina Mercouri, who liked Belushi so much she went backstage and kissed him half a dozen times after the show. John was young, hip, radical and tuned into the city and the times. President Nixon was snared in the Watergate scandal, and the disclosure that he had secretly tape-recorded his own conspiratorial conversations seemed to legitimize the show's own satiric extremism.

But Hendra was finding that Belushi could be uneven and lazy and had to be watched. He had a number of characters and modes he could fall back on if things started to go flat, and he relied on them too often. If Hendra were not careful, John would steal scenes. When Chris Guest, a versatile musician and a talented mimic, did his James Taylor parody, John would sit on a stool and play a drugged-up bass guitarist, slowly slouching down in his seat in a stupor, on the verge of passing out. The audience loved it. But it was not the point of the sketch, and it drew the attention away from Guest. Hendra told John to cut it way back.

Hendra was aware that there was a fantasy growing among the cast that the show was more than parody, that in fact they had potential as musicians and were on the way to becoming a successful rock group, and that drugs were part of that fantasy.

Hendra had given John a hit of cocaine during a rehearsal, and it quickly became his drug of choice. Hendra had a system for levying what he called a "drug tax" on some of the strait-laced businessmen associated with an underground production who secretly wanted to be accepted as one of the boys. Hendra often asked for money to buy pot for the cast and got a couple of hundred dollars. A few hours later the entire cast would be falling over themselves with, not pot, but as much as a quarter ounce of cocaine.

After a while, Hendra got tired of being the errand boy for drug runs, and other members of the cast had to go get the money and cocaine. They were doing at least some coke nearly every day of the week. To Sean Kelly, Chevy Chase was the driving cocaine force; it was, Kelly felt, probably Chase's greatest contribution to the show.

But it got to be a problem with John. He liked to get high for the performance. Hendra did think John was funnier when he was high on marijuana, but on coke his timing fell off. Hendra started to have run-ins with John about doing coke before the show.

"It's not fair to me or anyone else," Hendra said.

"I can handle it," John replied.

Hendra tried to bribe John. "Look, I'll get coke for you after the show if you don't do it before the show."

It didn't work.

A couple of times John was so drugged up before a show that Garry Goodrow, another cast member, had to hit him hard in the stomach to get him out of his daze.

Kelly was encountering the same problems: John had discovered downers, particularly Quaaludes. He told Kelly that "ludes" were great; it was like being smashed out of your mind on beer—loose but mobile, the perfect antidote to the loud rock concert environment. There were nights when John was so drugged up, his knees so rubbery and speech so slurred, that Kelly was afraid the show would have to be cancelled. Then Kelly or some of the others would walk John around the block, pour coffee down his throat and sober him up.

In the audience one night was Betty Buckley, a lively twenty-six-year-old Texan who was playing in a show on Broadway. She had bought a block of seats and invited ten friends. Buckley had been to the show once before and had loved it: John had been the embodiment of action on stage, piercing and bold. She was anxious to have her friends see the new wonder.

John came out on stage and faked his way through his lines, not even trying to be funny. Buckley was furious. John *was* the show, and if he didn't perform, there was no one else to pick up the slack. Her friends were asking, "How can you think this is funny?" Buckley got up and went backstage. She had never met Belushi.

As John walked by, Buckley grabbed him by the shirt with both her hands and threw him against the wall. She introduced herself and said she was in the musical *Pippin,* which had been a sensation on Broadway for more than a year.

"I'm in a long run, too, and I know it's difficult to give night after night. People come to see *you* and you blew the show off. . . . There are those of us who appreciate it. Do it for us."

John's face lit up. He said he understood. They talked for a bit. Buckley was amazed that he didn't tell her to get lost, that he was big enough to take the criticism.

"I'll be back and bring my friends again," she said.

Several months later Buckley met John at a party. He threw his hands in the air as if he were afraid she might grab him again.

"You remember?" she said.

"How could I forget?"

For months *Lemmings* continued to draw a sellout audience at the Village Gate, and John, having turned into the main attraction, was agitating for a raise. He was a growing thorn in management's side, and Hendra was finally told to get rid of him.

Hendra couldn't believe it. Some people were always willing to save a nickel and lose a buck. Belushi was the star of the show, Hendra argued, and the second act revolved around him. John had created the intricate role for himself. He would be impossible to replace. Hendra refused to fire him. It was Hendra's show; he didn't care how much John irritated the others.

But John was still interested in making more money, so when Simmons decided to have a touring company take *Lemmings* on the road, John was made director and began getting about $700 a week. But they didn't really have the bookings for such an enormous and expensive production. The margin of profit was too small, and Simmons called them home.

John started working on the "National Lampoon Radio Hour," the newest venture in Simmons's growing empire. Judy was also shifted to work on the new radio program. The show had a regular sponsor (Seven-Up—the "Uncola") and was billed as 60 minutes of "mirth, merriment and racial slurs."

One week Sean Kelly was brought in to direct. Kelly was interested in using the show to get under the skin of his class enemies. More important, the times *demanded* it. Watergate was undoing the Nixon presidency. Presidential aides were resigning in disgrace. The taped White House conversations had "gaps." A special prosecutor was hired and fired. To Kelly's mind, a grand comedy skit was being played out right before them, and the "Radio Hour," heard nationally on about 100 stations, was a perfect forum for putting it all in perspective.

On Saturday, December 29, 1973—nine months before Nixon resigned—Kelly ran an "Impeachment Day Celebration," satirizing the official pomp of Inauguration Day.

In one skit John played the unofficial Moral City Father of Wheaton, Illinois, the Reverend Billy Graham, swearing the president out of office in a booming voice cracking with anger: "Goddamn you, Richard Nixon. Richard Nixon, you sonofabitch. Get the hell out of here; you lied your ass off. Fuck off!"

The censors cut the obscenities. Shortly after the broadcast, Seven-Up pulled out, becoming, as Kelly joked around the office, "The Unsponsor." In the fall of 1974, Matty Simmons made John director of the program. John was by now doing more writing, which was part of the *Lampoon* tradition, and as the director he brought in his own people. Judy was finally truly happy. Their schedules coincided, and John seemed more easygoing than ever.

One week John made a trip to Toronto, Canada, where Second City had a troupe, to look over the cast. One member was a tall, handsome twenty-year-old named Dan Aykroyd.

Aykroyd, who had been expelled from a Catholic seminary three years earlier, was a versatile actor—able to learn long complicated scenes and imitate anyone from blue-collar workers to Richard Nixon.

John and Aykroyd met backstage and then went out on stage together to do some quick improvisational work. For Aykroyd, it was magic. He didn't feel defensive toward this stranger, and he was instantly willing to open up his life to Belushi. After the show they went to a few bars and wound up at the 505 Club, an after-hours saloon that Aykroyd managed. It was a run-down place with old furniture, dust and dirt everywhere. They sat for hours and talked.

John offered Aykroyd a job to come work on the "Radio Hour." It would be a start. Aykroyd could get an American work permit, and the job would unquestionably lead to other things in the *Lampoon* organization, which was the cutting edge of humor in America.

Despite being intensely attracted both to John and to working in the States, Aykroyd said that, unfortunately, he had to refuse. He had just signed to do another show in Toronto, and he wanted to honor the commitment.

John said he understood. They exchanged phone numbers, and John went back to New York.

Later that year Aykroyd rode his Harley-Davidson police motorcycle to New York. He loved the road and the bike, the freedom and solitude. It was a nine-hour trip to Greenwich Village. Once there, Aykroyd stopped at a bar and called John.

"Where are you?" John asked.

Aykroyd told him the name of the street and the bar.

"Jesus," John said, "that's a gay bar. In your motorcycle leathers, everyone is likely to get the wrong idea. Wait and I'll be right over."

John went down and bailed Aykroyd out. He spent the night at John and Judy's apartment, sleeping at the foot of their bed. He let John drive his motorcycle around the block and then headed back to Canada. Aykroyd felt he had made an important friend, and as the wind ripped by the bike, he felt fine about the trip.

Late in 1974, Matty Simmons decided it was time for the *Lampoon* to do another stage show. On various recruiting trips, John had infused the *Lampoon* with fresh new talent—a spunky girl from the Second City troupe in Toronto named Gilda Radner, and Harold Ramis and Joe Flaherty from the old Chicago company. Simmons thought it was a shame to have those people doing the "Radio Hour" when they were such wonderful stage performers; and the show was not making money, nor had it been particularly well received. So Simmons launched the *National Lampoon Show,* a cabaret-style revue that played at a few local New York bars and theaters and enjoyed a brief life on the road. John was the director and one of the performers.

Joe Flaherty was uncomfortable with the *Lampoon* style. There were a lot of cheap shots, and John was on a kick of putting down and insulting the audience outright. "All we really care about is your money," John would say, closing the show, "and we don't care about you at all."

One night Flaherty did the "Dead Sullivan" show, impersonating Ed Sullivan hosting a variety show with dead celebrities. He introduced Belushi playing Lenny Bruce.

John came on stage and sat on a toilet, rolled up his shirt sleeve, tied off his arm and pretended to shoot himself up with heroin. Then he fell off the toilet and died.

The audience groaned their disapproval.

John walked off stage and smiled at Flaherty.

"Yeaaaaahhhh," he said with a glint in his eye. Flaherty recognized that look from their days in Chicago: *Screw the audience.* John liked the skit; it would stay.

5

On February 11, 1975, NBC
President Herbert S. Schlosser was in his sixth-floor corner office in the
RCA Building in New York, preparing a memo to the head of NBC
television.

The network had been filling its 11:30 P.M. to 1 A.M. slot on Saturday
night with Johnny Carson reruns. They were stale, and the overexposure
wasn't helping the regular weeknight show. They needed a show that
would make people come home early to watch television on Saturday
night. Schlosser didn't want a revolution; he wanted ratings. His memo
said:

"I would like a thoroughgoing analysis done on a new program concept called 'Saturday Night.' . . . [It] should originate from the RCA
Building in New York City, if possible live. . . . It should be young and
bright. It should have a distinctive look, a distinctive set and a distinctive
sound. We should attempt to use the show to develop the new television
personalities . . . and hire a producer who can do it for the parameters
we establish."

About three o'clock one morning several weeks later, Lorne Michaels, a stylish thirty-year-old television writer, returned to his room at
the Chateau Marmont hotel in Hollywood and found a message asking
him to be in the Polo Lounge at the Beverly Hills Hotel for an early
breakfast with three top NBC executives. Michaels knew that NBC was
looking for a producer for a new television show.

Michaels, a Canadian, had written television comedy for seven years
for a Who's Who of American humor—Woody Allen, Dick Cavett, Joan
Rivers, Phyllis Diller, "Rowan and Martin's Laugh-In," the Burns and
Schreiber comedy hour, Lily Tomlin and Flip Wilson.

At breakfast were the new head of NBC's late-night programming, Dick Ebersol, a young protégé of ABC television sports president Roone Arledge; the longtime, outspoken talent chief for NBC, David W. Tebet; and the new head of NBC programming, Marvin Antonowsky. Antonowsky was among those who had convinced Schlosser that NBC needed a new late-night show directed at younger people. Nielsen data showed there was heavy tuning—channel switching—between 11:30 P.M. and 1 A.M. The audience was looking for something new.

More show-business deals blossom or bust in the several forest green rooms of the Polo Lounge than in any other place in America. The four men huddled at a corner table. Michaels said he knew the ingredients for a late-night show, although he was not sure about the exact combination. It had to be live; there had to be the feeling that anything could happen. This would place it in the tradition of the "Your Show of Shows," the Sid Caesar–Imogene Coca 90-minute Saturday-night show that ran from 1949 to 1954, one of NBC's greatest moments.

He would need a guarantee of twenty shows to get the format down. They would not see *it* until show number ten. He envisioned a permanent repertory company of six to eight actors and actresses; contemporary music, also live, that wasn't being shown on TV; a satirical news segment like "That Was the Week That Was," the British show; parody commercials; short takes by the best new filmmakers; a different host each week, like a magazine cover.

The NBC executives were convinced that Michaels was the right guy at the right time—the needed mix of counterculture and experience. He was invited to make a presentation to the New York programming board.

What Michaels had left unsaid were his personal motives. This show would be a chance to bring a number of ideas together, the beliefs of his generation, a territory that television had only mildly touched. How much would they dare?

NBC flew Michaels to New York in March 1975, and he discovered that he had a natural ally in Schlosser. But then he suggested that Richard Pryor might be one of the hosts, and Schlosser said under no circumstances. Pryor might say "fuck" on air. Schlosser wanted stars like Joe Namath and Rich Little. Michaels said he could get a promise from Pryor. Well, someone suggested, maybe they could have a time delay so anything bad could be deleted. It was not something to get hung up over.

By April 1, they had a deal. Michaels was guaranteed seventeen shows, and that was close enough to twenty. As long as it was live, he could make it work. There would be no tape for the executives and censors to see beforehand; there would be no way they could say, "You can't put *that* on TV." But no one was going to say "fuck" on his show if he could help it. Certain things couldn't be done or said on network TV —that was obvious. Michaels wasn't looking for a guerrilla takeover, just a pirate operation.

Michaels planned six months to start up—three to find the right people and three for them to live together. There would be plenty of time for the first show, but after that only one week to prepare for the next. He interviewed hundreds of writers. One of the first hired was *Lemmings* veteran Chevy Chase, whom Michaels had met in Los Angeles while standing in line for a movie. Chase, who was now older and more savvy, negotiated an $800-a-week salary. It was slightly more than Michaels had budgeted. Chase's contract was for one year; he didn't want to be locked in. And he wanted the option to perform some of his own skits, as he'd done in *Lemmings*.

"No," Michaels said. He was hiring more-experienced actors.

Michaels interviewed Michael O'Donoghue, a former *National Lampoon* editor (1970–74). O'Donoghue specialized in sickness-is-health humor. His *Lampoon* pieces had included "Underwear for the Deaf" and a Vietnamese baby book. O'Donoghue didn't believe that television would ever allow his humor, but he needed the money.

Michaels then signed Anne Beatts, a keen-witted woman—once described as "smart and smart-mouthed"—who lived with O'Donoghue. He also took on his wife, Rosie Shuster, and Alan Zweibel, a twenty-four-year-old stand-up comic who by day sliced meat at a Queens delicatessen. Herb Sargent, an older writer from Hollywood whom Michaels respected, was hired; and Garrett Morris, a thirty-nine-year-old black singer, actor and playwright from New York, was added as an apprentice.

Michaels also turned to two people he'd known from Canada—Dan Aykroyd and the waiflike Gilda Radner, who was one of the most versatile performers he'd ever seen.

Chase and O'Donoghue urged him to hire Belushi. Michaels had seen John with Radner in the "National Lampoon Show" and had found him too hard, too loud, too self-centered. He seemed to Michaels a potentially divisive force. Michaels wanted the humor to be original and warm, not anti-audience. He did not want a mere extension of the *Lampoon*'s bathroom humor. They were going to get enough of that from O'Donoghue.

"Good people are trouble, in life and art," O'Donoghue said, arguing for John.

Michaels agreed to interview Belushi. He was in his office one afternoon juggling budget, planners, set designers, musicians, writers, when John arrived in full beard. Michaels told him he had lots of advocates.

"Television is crap," John said. TV was shallow, mindless, degenerate. He had every cliché line Michaels had ever heard: The network was run by pigs; the censors would never allow anything good; his own TV set was covered with spit.

"Why do you always lead with your asshole?" Michaels asked. He had lived with the Los Angeles, TV-hating, only-film-is-art crowd for years. Some television is good, he said. "Mary Tyler Moore" was good, maybe not for our generation, but it was very good. Phil Silvers as Master Sergeant Ernie Bilko was good; also "The Dick Van Dyke Show" and "Maverick" and the original Jackie Gleason show.

John said those were old shows. Everything on now, everything new, was shit.

"Why are you here?" Michaels asked.

John said he had heard that Michaels might represent something new. But he was skeptical.

"These people I've put together are fucking pros," Michaels replied. "Do you know how hard it would be to make a bad show with these people?" Michaels had the feeling that John wanted to be on the show in spite of everything. He liked John's bravery, even if it was foolish. John was prepared to fight. But Michaels was nervous. John was headstrong and righteous, and he had a split-second temper. Could he muffle these things in front of a live camera? Nonetheless, Michaels invited John to audition.

"You know you'll have to shave off your beard," Michaels said.

No, John said, he wouldn't. He went home to see Judy. "I blew it," he said, and threw things around the apartment. He was insulted that he had to audition. Radner hadn't had to, and neither had Aykroyd.

John had been practicing a mute imitation of a Japanese Samurai warrior for some time. In an old bathrobe, his hair held in a ponytail with a rubber band, he wielded an old closet pole as his sword and grunted and groaned with all conceivable intensity. A week later he showed up at the Fifty-seventh Street audition studio in his Samurai bathrobe. He went on stage and played a Samurai pool hustler—all without a real word, saturating the air with a hundred grunts and garbled, fake but full-blooded Japanese phrases.

Screams of laughter are rare from an audition audience, but they were heard that afternoon, and Michaels's were among them. John had hit a home run and he knew it. There was no way out now for Michaels.

And the repertory company needed a variety of forms and shapes to hang characters on. John would be the beefy one; and maybe, Michaels figured, he was that good.

Ebersol was terrified. He had heard about Belushi's drug use. But Michaels had the authority to hire whom he wanted.

Michaels put together the rest of his comedy troupe—"The Not Ready for Prime Time Players"—with Laraine Newman, with whom he'd worked on a Lily Tomlin TV special, and Jane Curtin, recruited from The Proposition improvisational theater group in Boston.

They were to start work in early July. Michaels insisted there be no advance promotion. There was no way to say it was going to be this crazy, zany new comedy show. Hype would damage their image.

Chase was still bucking for a chance to act, and Michaels was still resisting. As Michaels, Chase and Ebersol were walking out of a restaurant in New York one night after a rainstorm, Chase took off down the street. Ebersol thought he was hailing a cab. Suddenly Chase slipped, his feet flew into the air and he landed in a puddle. He stood up, drenched, and Michaels and Ebersol roared. If he wanted it that much, Michaels decided, Chase could have a chance.

All summer John refused to sign a contract. He had no agent or manager, but he had read the long proposal, a tedious document. It gave NBC everything and guaranteed him little: If he were to be disfigured they could drop him. That was ridiculous. For God's sake. How callous! Corporate greed! Throw the crippled worker out the door! He would have none of it. Pressure mounted. Everyone else had signed.

On October 9, 1975, two days before the first show was to air, NBC sent Belushi an abbreviated, interim agreement, saying that such matters as disability and disfigurement would be worked out in a formal agreement. But NBC could still cancel on four-weeks notice.*

---

* Under the proposal, Belushi would sign a five-year contract. His initial pay would be a weekly $750 per late-night program the first year, going to $1,600 in the fifth year. NBC essentially would own him, permitting only six guest appearances a year on other networks; if "NBC's Saturday Night" (as the show was first called) was cancelled, they could assign him to any prime-time or other daytime show including soap, comedy, variety or quiz; and they could hold him for six months, if the show was cancelled, by paying what would be his basic weekly salary.

The comparison with prime time was stark. If he were assigned to a prime-time show for the same 90 minutes, he would initially get $6,000 per show—eight times as much.

Fifteen minutes before the first show was going on air, John was introduced to Bernie Brillstein, forty-four, who was Michaels's agent-manager. Brillstein's major client was Jim Henson and the Muppets, the puppetlike creatures that were a staple of "Sesame Street," the Public Broadcasting System (PBS) children's program. An executive pleading with John to sign the interim agreement was soon screaming at him.

"Would you sign this contract?" John leaned over and asked Brillstein.

"I designed the fucking contract," Brillstein said. It had a most-favored-nations provision, meaning that all cast members would be treated the same; if anyone got a benefit, all the others would get it.

"You telling me the truth?" John asked, arching an eyebrow.

"Sure," Brillstein said. "Yes, goddamn it. And you can always break it."

"If you manage me," John said, "I'll sign."

Who is this lunatic? Brillstein wondered, but he said okay. He would do anything to get on the air.

Michaels wondered whether the first show was going to work. Comedian George Carlin was the host, and he was involved in a court controversy about a record he had made which contained dirty language. Carlin had been so out of it during rehearsals that week that someone once had had to get an axe to break down his hotel room door. NBC executives were frightened about Carlin and had demanded that he appear in a suit. Carlin wanted to wear a T-shirt. After a lot of foolish arguments it was decided that Carlin would wear a suit and a T-shirt.

Michaels had been unsure how to open the show. He wanted it to look like something that had never been seen on television before in order to assert its identity right off. Using Carlin in the opening would make it the George Carlin show. So Michaels decided to open *cold*—no announcement, no title, no applause, no congratulations, no host, no music, no credits, no clue about what was to come.

At 11:30 P.M. Saturday, October 11, 1975, from studio 8H in NBC's headquarters at 30 Rockefeller Plaza, the camera opened on two men sitting in chairs in an apartment that resembled a setting for a meeting of the Warsaw underground.

"Good evening," said writer and now part-time actor Michael O'Donoghue, playing an English-language instructor.

"Guuuuuuuuud Evvvening," repeated Belushi in a thick European accent, sitting upright, wide-eyed and innocent. He wore an overcoat and a hat with pull-down fur earmuffs.

"Good evening," O'Donoghue said again. "Let us begin. Repeat after me. I would like—"

"I would like—"

"To feed your fingertips—"

John repeated it.

"To the wolverines."

Lots of laughter from the audience.

After more lines, O'Donoghue grabbed his heart, groaned "Ugh!" and fell on the floor, dead of a heart attack.

John, following his instructor, grabbed his heart, shouted "Ugh!" and fell on the floor.

The announcer, veteran Don Pardo, one of the most familiar voices in broadcasting, shouted: "Live from New York! It's Saturday Night!"

Carlin, in his three-piece suit with T-shirt, told several drug jokes in the opening monologue. NBC was delaying the show electronically for only six seconds, making it *almost* live.

After Carlin, Aykroyd did a spoof called "New Dad Insurance." He died and his unhappy family got a new dad, Chevy Chase, the same day. After a commercial, Billy Preston sang his hit "Nothing from Nothing (Leaves Nothing)" and Janis Ian sang "At Seventeen," which had been on the top of the music charts.

Next, there was a skit about that summer's shark mania, which had been triggered by the blockbuster movie *Jaws*. In a parody TV show called "Victims of Sharkbite," Jane Curtin interviewed persons who had been attacked. John, anxious to get on TV, claims to have lost an arm and a leg to a shark, but as he tells his story, the missing limbs flop into view.

After the third commercial break, Chevy Chase was introduced as the anchorman for "Weekend Update," a parody of network news. His broadcast is interrupted by a parody commercial for "Triopenin," an arthritis pain reliever that showed afflicted hands (Chase's) struggling to open the child-proof safety cap. Jim Henson's Muppets had a 5½-minute spot in front of the fourth commercial break, which was followed by a short film. There was one more monologue by Carlin, Preston and Ian each sang another song, and shortly before 1 A.M. Carlin and the cast gathered on stage to wave goodbye behind rolling credits.

Schlosser was watching in Boston and he was a little surprised. He had expected something like Carson's "Tonight" show with a younger look. He called Michaels to mention that he thought it was going to be more of a talk show.

Michaels was not surprised. He had suspected all along that they weren't hearing what he was saying.

All the same, the show was fine, Schlosser said. He especially liked Chevy Chase's "Weekend Update."

The Monday after the show, Dick Ebersol sent a memo to Michaels. "The reaction from the network has been extremely encouraging this morning. . . . *Everybody* is in love with Chevy."

After the first show John told Judy that he was happy. It was, as promised, different TV, even though he was not content with his role or that of the other cast members. They had way too little time on the air. But he raced off; there wasn't much time for anything because the next show had to be put together in a week. Judy noticed that he was using some cocaine, but it made sense since John had to stay up unbelievably long hours.

The second show, on October 18, had singer Paul Simon as host. Michaels had engineered a reunion of Simon and his estranged partner, Art Garfunkel. They sang and embraced, suggesting that old wounds were healed.

John was angry that Michaels had permitted Simon to turn the 90 minutes into a personal concert. Simon and Garfunkel and the other musical guests, Randy Newman and Phoebe Snow, had sung eight songs, three minutes had been allotted to the Muppets, and there had been another film by Albert Brooks. John hadn't been the focus of a sketch.

That Monday, the *New York Times* TV critic, John J. O'Connor, put down the Simon and Garfunkel reunion as a promotion for their separate solo record albums. O'Connor, one of the most respected TV critics in the country, had some harsh words for the show. "It's not enough for the new 'Saturday Night' concept to be transmitted live. Even an offbeat showcase needs quality, an ingredient conspicuously absent from the dreadfully uneven comedy efforts of the new series."

He complained about too many commercials and criticized the parody commercials: "One thoroughly tasteless and insensitive routine used geriatric patients to demonstrate the longevity of certain batteries in heart pacemakers."

Michaels and the others were furious. O'Connor had admitted in the third paragraph that he had not seen the first half-hour.

The day before the third show, David Tebet, the powerful NBC talent chief who was famous for his memos, fired one off to the executives associated with "Saturday Night." "I would like you all to think about going to tape." Although he didn't say so, Tebet was terrified that something disastrous would slip out over the air.

But being live made a big difference to Lorne Michaels. Live was spontaneous, dangerous. He ignored the memo, hoping he had momentum on his side.

For the third show, Rob Reiner was brought in as host. Reiner played Mike (better known as "Meathead"), the liberal live-in son-in-law of Archie Bunker in "All in the Family," the landmark Norman Lear TV series that was number one in the ratings. Midway through the show Reiner came out. "You never know who is going to show up. A guy who just flew in from London. He is a super rock star. He needs no introduction. Ladies and gentlemen, here he is!"

John appeared as Joe Cocker, sounding as though he were gargling sand, creating a physical impression that still amazed Michaels even after so many rehearsals. As he sang, John poured a can of beer down his front, fell on the stage hard, drank more beer on his back and blew it several feet into the air, like a whale. The camera came in for a close-up as the beer went spewing.

In the next skit Reiner was interrupted by Belushi and a number of the other cast members dressed as bees with black-and-yellow-striped costumes and giant bobbing antennae. Reiner acts insulted. "I was told when I came on the show that I would not have to work with the bees. And here they are. . . . How many times do I have to say it? I don't want the damn bees . . . I don't need bees! I'm a major star. I'm on the number-one television show in America."

John had been made to play a bee briefly in the first and second shows and he had hated it, complaining it was a silly costume gag. Now he steps forward. "I'm sorry if you think we're ruining your show, Mr. Reiner," John says sarcastically. "You don't understand. We didn't ask to be bees. You see, you've got Norman Lear and a first-rate writing staff. But this is all they came up with for us!"

John's antennae are swinging wildly, and a hostile, threatening edge has crept into his voice.

"Do you think *we* like *this?*" His antennae are flying and the audience is roaring. "No, Mr. Reiner, we don't have any choice. . . . We're just like you were five years ago, *Mr. Hollywood California number-one-show big shot!* That's right. We're just a bunch of actors looking for a place, that's all. What do you want from us, *Mr. Rob Reiner! Mr. Star!* What did you *expect? The Sting?''* Laughter.

John is so overpowering, so angry, that Reiner, apparently trying to be funny but looking embarrassed, simply apologizes.

The scene that John had put on, of course, meant that the bees would probably be a permanent part of the show, Michaels realized, and John's resistance made it better: here comes Belushi as a bee and he hates it. His true feeling spilled out to reinforce the acting. A backstage tension had been put on the air, and it had worked.

It was also becoming apparent to Michaels that, though they couldn't say "fuck" on television, they could just about say or do anything else. They were pushing NBC's, and television's, acceptable standards to the limit. The NBC Broadcast Standards Department was edgy. Each week Michaels gave them the scripts for the next show, and the censors ruled on what was permissible. They were sensitive about religion, sex and race—the issues most likely to bring floods of negative letters. Michaels and his writers never censored themselves, so they sent up things that were outrageous, sketches that would surely get shot down. One by O'Donoghue concerned the discovery of a rectal cancer named after an NBC lawyer whom O'Donoghue thought had no sense of humor. It was killed, naturally. Michaels wanted the censors to have their victories. The harder Michaels fought and the more he appeared to compromise on the clearly inappropriate material, the more likely the censors would be to let the borderline cases slide by.

Michaels, the censors and the audience knew that things might go too far. That was giving the show its appeal. Maybe this was the week that a four-letter word would slip out, that the establishment's standards of taste would be trampled—*and there would be nothing they could do about it.* The show was a high-wire act for the audience and the executives. It was as if, on Saturday nights at eleven-thirty, the kids came in to take over the studio.

O'Donoghue saw that the first shows were dangerous, not just because of the material but because of possible gaffes. The nervous tension was almost visible in the actors' eyes. There was never enough time during the week to put the show together properly, and the performances were often underrehearsed. O'Donoghue watched the routine develop:

SUNDAY—it was gone, the only day of rest after the show and
    the blowout party routinely held after 1 A.M. and lasting to
    nearly dawn.

MONDAY—meet the host and talk out ideas; generally start planning sketches that night.

TUESDAY—an all-day, all-night writing job.

WEDNESDAY—a 3 P.M. read-through with the cast, host and all the production people; by evening Michaels selected what would be in the show.

THURSDAY AND FRIDAY—work through with the cameras to determine positions for each scene; with luck the sets would have arrived.

SATURDAY—three shows; a 1 P.M. run-through with the cameras, a 7 P.M. dress rehearsal and the 11:30 live show.

Each month they did three shows in a row. The first Saturday of each month NBC ran its 90-minute news magazine, "Weekend."

Nearly everyone was involved in the writing—including Michaels and the actors, particularly Chase, Aykroyd and sometimes Belushi. If there was any extra time, they always chose to work on the writing rather than rehearse. It was a brutal schedule. But O'Donoghue felt that live TV was like touching a battery. They could feel the power and surge.

In late October, Michaels asked Candice Bergen to host. Bergen, a stunning and sophisticated twenty-nine-year-old actress, viewed a tape of the Paul Simon show and loved what she saw. Bergen had grown up in show business (her father was ventriloquist Edgar Bergen), but the industry had never been the creative community she had hoped for; here there seemed something that was not yet tainted.

Bergen and Michaels were sitting in his office early in the week when Belushi and Aykroyd burst in. Belushi's clothes were a mess, and Aykroyd wore a black biker jacket. Michaels introduced them, and they praised her movies, *The Group, Carnal Knowledge,* and some others. Bergen felt like an old lady star, like Gloria Swanson. Still there was something energetic and pure about the two of them.

John and Danny had a sketch they wanted to do with her. John would play Sam Peckinpah (*Bring Me the Head of Alfredo Garcia*), the director who was preoccupied with violence. It was to be a kind of "Beyond Peckinpah." John and Dan were standing, talking about it—you go here and I do this—acting it out, when John advanced on Bergen, grabbed her arms and yanked her up from the couch. "And then the idea . . . ," he said, and moving quickly, he flipped her onto the floor. She found herself on her back and laughing.

"And then Peckinpah gets really frustrated," John explained, and he sat on her, took her head and started bashing it on the floor—one, two, three, four. . . .

Michaels had his head in his hands. Bergen was overwhelmed. John had not really been threatening, but the scene was suffused with vague sexuality.

Michaels did not want to use the "Beyond Peckinpah" sketch that week, but Bergen's affinity for Belushi and Aykroyd was established. They were fearless and unguarded. They sent her presents—little Harley motorcycle gadgets and pins.

As scripts and sketches were developed over the week, Bergen felt it represented the best of the 1960s without the war, violence, menace and politics. She had never been involved in anything quite as compelling.

In Washington, Tom Shales, the young TV critic for the *Washington Post,* had watched the first three shows and saw in them the coming of age for his generation in television. On November 8, 1975, the day the Bergen show was to air, Shales wrote:

"NBC's 'Saturday Night' can boast the freshest satire on commercial TV, but the show is more than that. It is probably the first network series produced by and for the television generation—those late-war and post-war babies who were the first to have TV as a sitter. They loved it in the '50s, hated it in the '60s and now they are trying to take it over in the '70s."

Shales mentioned a "Weekend Update" news parody that had made fun of the handicapped and asked, "Bad taste? Some viewers might think so. But the show's audacity is refreshing in a medium obsessed with the fear of offending anybody."

Michaels was pleased and thought the Bergen show would be even stronger. During her monologue at the beginning, John walked on stage dressed as a bee. Chevy Chase came in and shooed John away, but John came back and put his head on Bergen's shoulder, looking up at her sweetly and innocently. John lifted an eyebrow at the camera and gazed back at Bergen. The genuine affection and his infatuation came through —another backstage reality effectively put on the air.

Bergen was enjoying herself. She parodied a Catherine Deneuve perfume commercial in which the bottle was stuck to her head, and John and Danny revived the spirit of their "Beyond Peckinpah" idea. They had Bergen playing a TV talk-show host, and they chased her around the stage, threw a burlap bag over her and deposited her roughly on the desk.

After the show, David Tebet wrote a memo to Michaels suggesting that Bergen be considered as permanent host. She was a big name, and she could give the show continuity from week to week and create a viewing habit among the TV audience. "I am not saying that is the way to go," Tebet wrote, "but it could be something to think about."

Michaels ignored this suggestion too; he didn't want the same cover on his magazine each week.

On Tuesday, Ebersol dictated a congratulatory memo to the "Saturday Night" staff. He was ecstatic with the audience demographics for the first three shows; they were "fantastically incredible."

"Saturday Night is getting the most attractive audience on television today," Ebersol said, noting that the Simon and Garfunkel and Rob Reiner shows received the highest percentage of eighteen- to forty-nine-year-old men and women of any show on TV those weeks—higher even than Monday Night Football and the five World Series telecasts. Seventy-eight percent of all women aged eighteen to forty-nine watching TV were tuned in, and 75 percent of all men. Eighty-four percent of their viewers were adults.

John was fussing about his back-seat position, and in the pressure-cooker environment Michaels angrily told him to leave if he didn't like it. John wrote out a note to Gary Weis, a filmmaker who did some of the short films for the show: "Could you get me a gram? I'm leaving the show." Weis and John frequently did cocaine together.

"I've just been fired," John told Anne Beatts, the writer. She dragged him off to a nearby bar and pleaded with him to stop being an asshole and apologize. "We fought hard to get you on the show and don't blow it." John relented, but he had to be pushed into Michaels's office to apologize. He was quickly unfired.

The fall of 1975 was one of the best of times for twenty-eight-year-old director Steven Spielberg. *Jaws,* released that summer, was a spectacular success, well on its way to becoming the biggest moneymaker in film history. He had loved the first "Saturday Night" and Belushi's "Victims of Sharkbite." It was like a neighborhood show put on by kids for kids. Spielberg identified with the age group, their politics, their irreverence. He saw the connection with an entire line of television work— "Little Rascals," "Sky King," "Kukla, Fran and Ollie" (the fifties hit puppet show) and even the "Mickey Mouse Club." Spielberg came to New York to meet the players, and at an after-show party at One Fifth Avenue, an art deco bar and restaurant, he was introduced to Belushi.

John seemed almost an amplification of his TV roles. He did not eat with knives, forks or spoons and seemed to lack social grace, but he was raw acting energy.

Spielberg planned his projects years in advance—mulling over each detail of cast, costume, setting, special effects and script. One of his coming movies, he told John, was going to be about a day in December 1941, right after Pearl Harbor, when Los Angeles goes mad with war jitters, suspecting the presence of a Japanese submarine and an imminent air attack. Belushi would be perfect for the Japanese submarine skipper.

Without saying a word, John grabbed a coat rack and hoisted it into the air. Using the hooks as handles for his periscope, he stared intently ahead.

"You want see my Japanese sub skipper?" he asked in Samurai grunts. "Gveet Yaankeeee shipping!" He flashed a look to the side to check Spielberg's reaction.

Spielberg was laughing. Apparently John could do anything. As Spielberg circulated that night, John provided another version of his submarine skipper hell-bent on sinking American ships and the coast of Southern California. He never stepped out of the character.

"If I ever make this movie," Spielberg said at the end of the evening, "you're it." Spielberg returned to California more excited than ever about tackling his first comedy, especially with an actor like Belushi.

6

Michaels brought in Lily Tomlin to host the sixth show, during which Belushi played Beethoven. At the end he did some snuff and got a big laugh. Michaels thought it was very nervy, another backstage reality.

A week after that show, *New York Times* TV critic John O'Connor more or less recanted. "At least 75 percent has proved to be sharply and sometimes wickedly on target. NBC has found itself a source for legitimate pride, a commodity in scarce supply at any network these days. 'Saturday Night' is the most creative and encouraging thing to happen in American TV comedy since 'Your Show of Shows.' "

Lorne Michaels was grateful for the key endorsement, but John was not so happy. The O'Connor review had dwelt on Chase, saying that "one of Mr. Michaels' best performers is one of his writers, Chevy Chase." "Weekend Update" was drawing too much attention, especially a running gag about President Ford's clumsiness in which Chase was always falling down. John had done the original Ford on the *Lampoon* "Radio Hour." O'Connor had also mentioned the sketch in which Chevy had played a woman—with crown, cape and roses—in a beauty contest. John had also played women.

On December 1, *Newsweek* called the show a hit. A picture of Chase and Aykroyd was included and John wasn't mentioned. He complained to Judy that Chase was getting parts that should have gone to him; in fact, John figured, 50 percent of Chase's on-air time was coming out of his time.

With the host, the music guest, the freelance filmmakers, the fucking Muppets (who'd had more than 25 minutes of air time in the first six shows), Chevy's move into performing, and all the other shit, the actors were getting about one-fifth of the camera time, John calculated.

Michaels still wanted comedian Richard Pryor to host. He's going to say "fuck" on the air, Schlosser warned again. Michaels argued that it would make a mockery of their new comedy mantle to veto Pryor. He *was* Mr. New Comedy. They had to have him. Michaels, feeling sure of his leverage, threatened to resign.

Pryor was finally approved, but there would have to be a five-second delay on the live broadcast so NBC censors could bleep out anything offensive. Michaels agreed to bring out John's audition sketch, the Samurai warrior, with Pryor.

"Samurai Hotel" flashed on the screen, December 13, 1975.

John, in Samurai garb, stands behind a very small hotel registration desk throwing mail in the room slots with quick, karatelike motions, yelling unintelligible but loud karate victory shrieks.

Chase, a guest carrying his bags, walks in. "Excuse me, excuse me, I'd like a room for the night, please."

John turns and angrily sputters a long, run-on, mumbo-jumbo speech with Oriental inflection and great seriousness, and in the course of their encounter, embeds the sword in his shoulder ("Oah! Oah!"), lets out a mammoth battle cry, uses the sword as a golf putter, cuts his thumb (*"Aha! Aha! Aha!"*), chalks the tip as if it were a pool cue, hits imaginary balls on the front desk, chalking, hitting, screaming, and finally rings the desk bell and screams, "Poy! Poy! Poy!"

Pryor, in a dark pajama Samurai outfit, scurries in. He and John have a nonsensical screaming match. A matter of honor has somehow come up over who should carry the bags. John and Pryor draw their swords and charge at each other, passing side by side. Pryor sputters, about to explode. John stops him and to prove he means business slashes down the Japanese lamp hanging from a thread above the desk.

Turning to Pryor, John says, "Your Mamasan."

Pryor, his wife or mother clearly insulted, rages, *"My Mamasan?"*

John grunts and nods his head.

Pryor releases an end-of-the-earth primal scream, raising his sword, and cuts the entire front desk in half with one blow.

John shrugs his shoulders and breaks out of character. "Well, I can dig where you're coming from." He grabs Chevy's bags and carries them upstairs.

During the first few months of the show, Judy was gradually easing herself out of her job at the *National Lampoon* and was beginning to help

Deanne Stillman, another writer, and Anne Beatts put together a book called *Titters: The First Collection of Humor by Women*. Beatts was passionately committed to the women's rights movement. "Fear of Fucking" was her contribution to the *Titters* anthology, which was to have a magazine layout.

Judy became the art director, messenger, general organizer and gofer for the project, working out of John and her second-floor Bleecker Street apartment with the material spread all over. Beatts was pushing her 48 hours a day.

O'Donoghue, Beatts's roommate, hated *Titters* and complained to John that women's liberation had robbed them of their girlfriends. They were "Titters Widowers," he stated.

Judy took Saturdays off and usually ate a late breakfast with John about noon—it was often their only time alone during the week—and then went with him to the show and the cast party that followed. Once as they were going to breakfast someone on the street yelled at John, "Hey, it's the bee!" John turned away and, gritting his teeth, said to Judy, "I don't want to be known as that!" The show was passing him by, he said. Chase was writing himself into more and more of the sketches. And even though they were getting about the same amount of air time, Chase was playing parts that spotlighted him—such as the "Update" segment— while John was submerged in gang skits, things like the bees. John said that it was stupefying that success and stardom had come to Chase so fast. He could do many of Chase's parts better, he said, but he was being squeezed out.

Judy also noticed from her times up at the "Saturday Night" office and studio that cocaine use was widespread. Chase seemed to have the most.

Chase was enjoying the sudden fame and the greater availability of cocaine. He felt that drugs were changing his generation the way the Beatles had changed it. It was okay to use drugs—pot, hash and coke. And if you were famous, Chase felt, you could do more drugs. And the show was big; at the least, it was at the top of the minors.

Judy still believed cocaine was the logical drug for all of them. It provided a sense of clearheadedness, of intellectual power. The drug was nonaddictive, and it kept them awake as they wrote, polished and rehearsed into the early morning hours. But it was expensive, and there was never enough of it for John. He bought a gram here and there, spending perhaps $200 a week for two grams.

On December 22, 1975, *New York* magazine, the bible for hip young city dwellers, did a cover story, not on the show, but on Chevy Chase, headlined: AND HEEEEEERE's TV's HOTTEST NEW COMEDY STAR! The magazine announced that the straight, smooth, neatly dressed Chase was becoming a household word, and NBC executives were talking about him as the "first real potential successor" to Johnny Carson. This was after only eight shows.

Michaels immediately sensed a change. The cover story was a stamp of personal success for Chase, and it represented a certain loss of innocence. Other cast members, particularly Belushi, resented it, seeming to interpret it as a sign of personal failure. Chase thought John was the most aggravated, as if Chase's success had somehow been stolen from him. Two years earlier Belushi had been the star of *Lemmings,* with favorable notices from the *New York Times, The New Yorker* and national news magazines, but there had never been a cover story on him. Now Chase had moved ahead of the pack to eclipse them all. Once in Chase's office John gazed at a picture of a woman on Chase's desk. "I got that picture, but it's the one with the donkey dick in her mouth," John said.

Jane Curtin thought that Chase deserved the attention he was getting. The show needed a hook to draw in the audience, and Chase had been developing that presence. His prominence did undercut the intent of a true repertory company, but he was the only one ready to break out.

Curtin was twenty-eight, with wavy brown hair and wholesome, attractive looks. She felt like the outsider on the show. Besides Chase, she was the only cast member who was married, and she felt that gave her more stability. Curtin didn't live only at night, and she was angry when people weren't prepared and deadlines were missed; she was anxious to get home evenings to her husband. Occasionally she envied the fast lifestyle of the others, thinking their ability to cut loose put them more on the edge and helped their performances.

Curtin felt her isolation most strongly with John; they had nothing in common, and their irritation with each other sometimes bordered on hostility. Curtin thought John felt threatened by her, and by all the females on the show. He didn't think the women were funny, and once he had refused to come out of his dressing room to rehearse a sketch that had been written by one of the female writers. He had told Curtin that it was an actor's duty to sabotage bad material, and if he didn't like the way a sketch was written, he would flub the lines or read too softly during dress rehearsal as a sign of protest.

Aykroyd was feeling cooped up and he wanted to get away during the first break after Christmas.

"Have you ever driven across country?" he asked John.

John had not, and he jumped at the chance. Aykroyd felt especially close to John, even more so as they agreed that it was unfair that Chase was getting the lion's share of attention.

They put down a $100 security deposit and were given an Oldsmobile 98 with ripped upholstery to deliver to the West Coast. They added a music system and a citizens' band (CB) radio, which John wired up, though neither he nor Danny knew how to use it.

With great excitement they left New York with the country before them. Aykroyd insisted on doing all the driving since Belushi was inattentive at the wheel. It just wouldn't be relaxing for either of them, he explained.

They modeled their trip on Jack Kerouac, reading aloud from *On the Road* and trying to reenact his experiences, savoring their freedom. In Tennessee, John and Dan were using the CB radio a lot, and since they didn't know the required sign-on and sign-off procedure, they simply treated it like a telephone: "Hey, somebody come in. Who's out there?"

John, whose handle (sign-on name) was "The Screamer," acted like a homosexual truck driver trying to set up a rendezvous at various stops. "Hey, it's The Screamer here," he said in a feminine voice. "I don't know where we are, but I'm looking for some of you fellas. Just where are you? We're going to be at the truck stop in just a few minutes, and I'd like to meet some of you boys."

The truckers weren't amused. One came on to warn in a deep southern accent, "You Yankees, you make sure you know what you're sayin' or we'll run you right off the side of this mountain."

In Little Rock, they stopped at the University of Arkansas and walked around the campus to see whether they would be recognized. John approached some people. No one knew them. Depressed, they got back into the Oldsmobile and headed for New Orleans. "The show's a real flop," John said. "Nobody has seen any of the work. What's it all worth?"

Later they met some girls in a gas station who recognized John, but that was it. At night John and Danny would pull over and sleep in the car or find a cheap hotel.

Aykroyd was anxious to reach California, so he timed the driving so they'd hit Las Vegas when John was asleep in the back; if they stopped, John would want to spend days hitting the town, the slots, the hotels, the shows. The sleazy ambiance would be too much of a temptation. At about 5 A.M. one morning, Las Vegas appeared out of the desert. John was asleep as Dan ran several stoplights. John woke up at dawn with Vegas 50 miles safely behind.

"When do we get to Vegas?" he asked.

"We passed it," Aykroyd said, head down, watching the road. "We're through."

"What?" John asked, stirring and looking about. "What! Wha—! What happened? Where? Why didn't you wake me up? Why didn't we stop?" He shouted and complained that he had been cheated.

Aykroyd just drove on and soon they were in California—barely three and a half days after they had started. They spent a few days and flew back to New York for the next show.

John phoned Joe Flaherty, his former colleague from Second City, for advice. "Have you seen the show?" John asked. He was full of questions about scenes and the cast members.

"John, you know," Flaherty told him, "they're not using you the right way. You're doing these low-key things. Why don't you see if you can do Capote or an impression, or the big stuff, when you work yourself up into a lather and just fall over. Try to play the more aggressive characters. Do something physical."

"Yeah, yeah, yeah," John replied. "You're right. Yeah, I want to do more of that. I just got to get them to fucking write it."

The first show after Christmas, January 10, 1976, featured actor Elliott Gould as the host. John played Brando as Vito, a mafioso Godfather.

Opening on an encounter-group session with Gould as the leader-psychologist, Gould begins, "When we left off at last week's session, Vito was telling us about his feelings toward the Tataglia family. Vito?"

John, gray hair brushed back, wearing a dark, pinstriped, double-breasted suit, is sprawled in his chair, rubbing his chin. "The Tataglia family is moving in on numbers," John says, jaw protruding. "Prostitution, restaurant linen supply, now they want to bring in drugs." As an afterthought he adds casually, "Also they shot my son Santino 56 times."

The Godfather music comes up.

John continues, his teeth set on edge. "The ASPCA is after me about this horse thing. . . ."

Gould says, "Now I want you to act out your feelings about the Tataglia family nonverbally."

"No talking?" John asks. "Do I have to?"

More *Godfather* music, and John pulls out a switchblade, peels a piece of skin off an orange, puts it into his mouth and acts as though it is his teeth. He rises from his chair, swings his arms, makes monstrous growling noises, flashes his orange-peel teeth. It is a perfect parody of the death scene from *The Godfather*. Like Brando, John has a heart attack at the end of the sketch.

The next week John wanted to sing a blues number with Danny; Michaels wanted another bee sketch. They finally reached an accord: John and Dan could do a song together on the January 17, 1976, show, but it had to be done in bees' costumes.

Danny wore a fedora with antennae and sunglasses, and John dressed in his bee costume and wire-rimmed glasses. Danny played the harmonica while John sang, "I'm a King Bee," interrupting the song to do full body flips, landing flat on his back once. He started out singing the blues but slipped gradually into his Joe Cocker voice; it was a big hit with the audience, clearly not because they were talented musicians but because Belushi hurled himself into the part with such vehemence.

John's distress grew. Chase began the "Weekend Update" segment with "I'm Chevy Chase and you're not" on nearly every show; some people were even calling "Saturday Night" the "Chevy Chase Show." Since "Update" ran each week, John and O'Donoghue worked up a solo skit that John could do for it. They wanted an extreme character that John could play to the hilt, take the human engine beyond the red line and blow it apart if necessary. The two worked hard on it, and the night of the March 7 show, Chase said at the end of "Update," "Last week we made the comment that March comes in like a lion and goes out like a lamb. Now to reply is our chief meteorologist, John Belushi."

John, wearing a wig: "Do you know that March behaves differently in other countries? In Norway, for example, March comes in like a *polar bear* and goes out like a *walrus*. Or take the case of Honduras, where March comes in like a *lamb* and goes out like a *salt-marsh harvest mouse*. Let us compare this to the Maldive islands, where March comes in like a *wildebeest* and goes out like an *ant*. On the Malaya Peninsula, where March comes in like a *worm-eating fernbird*. In fact their whole year is like a *worm-eating fernbird*." He starts to pick up steam, fiddling with his notes, squirming in his chair and increasing the tempo. "There is a country where March hops in like a *kangaroo* and stays a *kangaroo* for a while and then becomes a slightly *smaller kangaroo* . . . then it goes out like a wild *dingo*. It's *not* Australia." He yells, "There are nine different countries where March comes in like a *frog* and out like a *golden retriever*. The weird part . . . the weird part . . ."

Overcome with his own reply, John falls backward behind the desk, apparently the victim of a coronary attack.

Still John couldn't steal the spotlight from Chase, whose stock characters and antics were increasingly the show's trademarks. Michaels had Chase do an acrobatic fall for the "cold opening" of almost every show. And Chase's imitations of President Ford had become a staple. Michaels decided to make a pitch to the White House that Ford should good-naturedly join his taunters and host the show himself. It didn't seem that crazy. After all, when Michaels was a writer on "Laugh-In" in 1969, President Richard Nixon had come on and asked the country to "Sock it to me." But with the 1976 campaign underway and the primary season in full swing, Ford's press secretary, Ron Nessen, told Michaels that an appearance by the president would be impossible.

Michaels asked Nessen, a former NBC television correspondent, to take the president's place. Nessen, who loved to perform, accepted.

Some of the cast flew to Washington to visit Ford at the White House, and Ford himself agreed to tape three inserts for the April 17, 1976, show.

"Live, from New York, it's Saturday Night!" Ford said at the beginning of the show, and then he introduced Nessen: "Ladies and Gentlemen, the Press Secretary to the President of the United States."

After Chase said, "I'm Chevy Chase and you're not," the President responded: "I'm Gerald Ford and you're not." In an Oval Office sketch, Nessen played himself to Chase's President Ford. Chase hit a golfball with a tennis racket, stapled one of his own ears to his head, fell over a flag and accidentally signed his own hand.

John had spent much of the week writing and working out his own skit called "The New Army." Michaels included it on the show because it was a chance for John to do something by himself.

The scene opens with John as an Army lieutenant colonel sitting in a recruiting office. A standard Uncle Sam "We Want You" recruiting poster hangs on the wall with the face cut out and replaced by "Star Trek" Captain James T. Kirk. John, wearing a set of stereo headphones and with his feet on the desk, plays an imaginary guitar and wails, "Bum, bum, do-do, dooooow." Suddenly he looks into the camera and yells, "Hi, I'm Lieutenant Colonel Schuman. Hi! Oh, I'm sorry." He removes his headset and lowers his voice. "Hi, I'm Lieutenant Colonel Scott Schuman with a word about today's new Army. Ya know today's Army sure has gone through a lot of changes from when your old man was into it." He looks self-consciously at the camera. "Oh, I'm sorry." He brushes off the top of his desk, which is littered with white powder, some pot and a pack of rolling papers. Shoveling the clutter into his desk drawer, he grabs the butt of a marijuana cigarette, slowly taking one last hit, then leans back casually.

"And now, now it's ah, an all-volunteer Army. I mean, you don't have to be there if you don't want to. I mean, if you don' wan' to, thaas cool. Ah, you have your own lives to lead. You have stuff to do, but so do weee—the best stuff an Army helicopter can carry in from allllll ohh-ver the woooooooooorld. . . . You can even be a paratrooper, and that's the most fun you can have with your pants on. Beleev-you-me, I know, man. So join today's Army. . . ." He starts leaning back in the chair as he talks, raising his eyes to the ceiling and tilting farther back. ". . . because every burst of gunfire has all the colors in the rainbow." And he tumbles over backward behind the desk.

Voice-over: "The New Army—a *joint* venture that wants to join you."

John's skit went well, but the news stories concentrated on Ford, Nessen and Chevy Chase. Nessen and Chase were pictured in *Newsweek,* which said that Nessen had "collaborated with the show's star, Chevy Chase." The gossip that Chase was going to be the next Johnny Carson circulated again. In Monday's *New York Times,* O'Connor said that having the presidential press secretary on might have cost the show something dear—the status of outsider necessary to savage the politicians. It should have fought harder to preserve that, he said.

John agreed. He was lobbying for that great courage they had had in the beginning; there were too many safety plays, he told Michaels. They were betraying themselves.

John pushed for longer, more difficult and complex sketches and, by the April 24 show, was having some luck. Actress Raquel Welch was host. The company did a parody of *One Flew Over the Cuckoo's Nest,* the 1975 movie that won the best picture Academy Award and earned Jack Nicholson and Louise Fletcher Oscars for best actor and best actress. John got the Nicholson role, playing the free-spirit McMurphy in the mental hospital, and Raquel Welch played wicked Nurse Ratched. Everyone had to wear bee costumes, and the skit was called "One Flew Over the Hornet's Nest."

The patients are gathered in a semicircle for the therapy session led by stiff, cold-blooded Ratched. "Ah, look, ah, Nurse Raaaatched," John says, wearing a watch cap on his head, antennae bobbing, stringing out his words as Nicholson did. "I wanna make this as eeeeasy as possible for ya. In a few minutes the Oscars are gonna be on. And I figure I'll be allowed to watch it, ya know whadda meeeean?"

"It might upset the gentlemen if we change the schedule," Welch says. "However, we can vote—majority rules. Who would like to see the Oscars?"

No one responds, and John launches his Nicholson-cheerleader role. "Come on guys, vote. Don't you want to see the Oscars?" He strides jocularly around the circle, a sly look in his eye, cajoling each one. "Come on! Get those hands up, ya loonies, come awwwwhn. Come on, get 'em up there." He lifts Gilda Radner's arm and rests it on the top of her head; she smiles innocently. John turns to Welch: "All right, it's a landslide, look."

"There are twelve patients in this ward," Welch replies. "I only count six hands."

John looks around quizzically. "Whadda ya meeeean? Are you telling me you're counting these vegetables?" He picks up a wooden basket full of vegetables and looks at them dubiously but with resignation. He pulls out a tomato, then a cabbage. "Come on, get those hands up, let's go. . . . Come on, which one of you nuts has got guts. . . . You basket case. Damn!"

Thwarted, John stages an Oscar ceremony in the ward. Gilda starts eating the envelope containing the name of the winner, and John grabs it from her.

"The winner is," he says in mock seriousness, "Louise Fletcher for *One Flew Over the Cuckoo's Nest!*"

Welch is given the award.

"Now listen!" John says, seizing Welch by the neck. "It's mine. It's mine for *Chinatown,* for *The Last Detail, Five Easy Pieces.* That's my Oscar!" He releases her.

"Any violent behavior and I'll be forced to fry your antennae!" Welch says.

"I shoulda got best supporting for *Easy Rider* . . . you know what I mean!"

"Fry him!" Welch yells, and John's antennae are pulled. He becomes catatonic and is led, muttering, from the room.

After their Christmas cross-country trip, Belushi and Aykroyd's friendship deepened. The center of their creative life was a small window-less office tucked behind some file cabinets with a sliding door in the NBC studios at 30 Rockefeller Plaza—a kind of secret clubhouse with a locker-room atmosphere. Some of the secretaries refused to go in, fearful of what they might find growing on the walls. The two spent a large chunk of the week in this room—from late Monday afternoon until scripts were more or less final on Wednesday or Thursday. Aykroyd finally de-manded, and got, shower facilities and bunk beds. John often spent the night. When he went home, Judy saw him only when he came in to sleep and when he got up to go back out.

Gary Weis, the filmmaker who made some of the two- to five-minute films for the show, introduced John to Gary Watkins, a young actor who played bit parts in the show's parody commercials. Watkins could supply cocaine, and John began buying from him on a regular basis, depending on his cash supply. Maybe a gram on Monday to get up for the coming week, perhaps another for Tuesday or Wednesday work and writing ses-sions at night; at times he had one for Saturday's rehearsals and the show itself. Sometimes he bought one for the weekend. Watkins usually came through.

Many of the other members had cocaine during the week, and at first John was able to get a few lines from them. Michaels, Chase, Aykroyd and O'Donoghue often had some. Cocaine was gradually becoming inte-gral to John's life, but he never really had enough money for all he wanted; spending $200 or $300 a week on it meant there was just enough left to live on. If someone offered to share, John would take too much or even take it all. After a while people started denying they had any or simply cut him off.

Once Weis and John were taking a cab together and they found a fat wallet in the back seat with $160 in cash. "Let's take it," John said, proposing they remove the cash and toss the wallet in a trash can. Weis checked the owner's address. It was one of New York's classiest, and Weis proposed that if they returned it along with the credit cards and driver's license, the well-to-do owner would certainly give them more than $160. After a tugging match, John agreed. The owner was thankful. He took back the wallet, gave John $5 and closed the door. John nearly strangled Weis; one and a half grams of cocaine had just been lost, he calculated.

O'Donoghue found that John didn't like to go home and would, in fact, do just about anything to avoid returning to Bleecker Street. John took him to game parlors to play pinball machines or to cheap horror movies in the middle of the afternoon, where they'd eat giant boxes of popcorn. John dragged O'Donoghue into worlds he would not have visited alone, and O'Donoghue became intrigued by the lowest common denominator of American society. A compulsively neat person, O'Donoghue was always picking up and straightening his office. Frequently John came in and destroyed the order in a minute, shifting papers, furniture or pencils or dropping cigarette ashes.

O'Donoghue was also a bit of a dandy, and John loved to paw through his collection of neckties, often filching one. O'Donoghue called him the Bear Monster. Just seeing John's hands touching his beloved neckwear drove O'Donoghue wild. But when O'Donoghue was sick once, John appeared at his apartment with orange juice, sandwiches and new music tapes. John's most annoying traits were also his most lovable —the boyish inquisitiveness, the careless spontaneity and reckless compulsions.

"You know what I love to do?" John once asked. "Get fucked up."

O'Donoghue felt the same way, and they shared many on-duty and off-duty hours together with as much cocaine as they could afford. Once the cast had to do four shows in a row with no break, and the last week, O'Donoghue realized, nearly everyone was taking cocaine to keep going. Mirrors and pictures in the staff offices were off the walls and on the desks and were littered with razor blades, makeshift straws and a fine white residue from the cocaine that had been chopped into powder on the hard glass surfaces.

The show was a giant family in which the members had been picked at random, O'Donoghue thought. Most were funny and creative. They lived, worked and slept together. Belushi was a subject of constant conversation—either because of some monstrous act or flabbergasting kindness.

Lorne Michaels was the switchboard, and he heard nearly everything. In that environment it was easy to see someone fucking up and going under, when it was impossible to see oneself taking that dive. And John seemed to go in and out regularly. He was like a child who needed more of everything—attention, love, scolding, explanations. But he was capable of subtlety. By the end of each week, Michaels had listed on a board all the skits and parts that were ready for the show. Generally there was an average of about 20 to 30 minutes too much, and that meant cutting. Michaels would study the board, shifting, dropping—concentrating on pace and mix. The other cast members regularly came in to lobby him. John came in and massaged Michaels's shoulders, saying nothing. It was always clear what John wanted. Nothing really had to be said.

Michaels kept three or four tickets to the live performance in his desk. "Saturday Night" tickets were the hottest in town, and hundreds of friends, relatives, celebrities, even NBC executives, had to be turned down. But the extra tickets began disappearing, and Michaels discovered that John was taking them out of his desk late at night. He decided to say nothing. Since the demand was so high, it was best to have none and say no to everyone.

On the May 8 show with host Madeline Kahn, the comedy actress, Danny and John played President Nixon and Secretary of State Henry Kissinger at their resignation-eve meeting, when both men had knelt and prayed.

Aykroyd, as Nixon, is in the Oval Office, hunched over, his jaw out, and in a black suit with sleeves three inches too short. His movements are wild, jittery, almost fey.

John, Kissinger, enters. He is wearing a curly black wig, horn-rimmed glasses, a suit and silk tie.

"Mr. President, ah—"

There is loud, long applause.

Belushi: "I, I've just spoken with your lovely daughter and your favorite sons-in-law and, ah, they expressed a deep concern for your vell being, which I, of course, share, and they suggested I come down here to cheer you up."

"You know I'm not a crook, Henry," Aykroyd asserts in a deep, frantic voice. "*You* know that I'm innocent!"

"Vell ummm," John says, nodding.

"I am, Henry! I had nothing to doooo with Watergate, the bugging of Watergate. I had nothing to doooo with the cover-up, nothing to doooo with the break-in of Daniel Ellsberg's psychiatrist's office, nothing to doooo with the guy who was killed in Florida."

"Vut guy was killed in Florida, Mr. Presadunt?"

"You mean you don't know about the young Cuban who was run over by the—never mind! Henry, get down on your knees and pray!" Danny shoves Belushi down by the shoulder, forcing him to his knees on a rug by the side of the desk. "Pray with me! Pray with me!"

"Awe, Mr. Presadunt, please. You've got a big day tomorrow, ah, so vhy don't ve just get into our jammies and go sleepy bye?"

"Yooooou don't want to pray—"

"Vell—"

"Jew boy!"

"Awe, come on, Mr. Presadunt, I don't vant to get into that again, okay? Please? You'll have to excuse me. I've got to go order the Strategic Air Command to disobey all presaduntial orders."

"Right. Right, thanks," Aykroyd says, and as John leaves he almost sings, "Jew boy!"

On the evening of May 17, 1976, hundreds of the key people in television gathered at the Shubert Theater in Los Angeles for the twenty-eighth annual Emmy Awards.

"Saturday Night" received four Emmys—for outstanding comedy-variety series, best comedy writing, best comedy directing, and one to Chevy Chase for best supporting actor for a variety show. Chase accepted the award and fell down.

With four awards, "Saturday Night" had more than one third of the eleven Emmys that went to NBC. They now had a strong hand. But with success certified, Michaels was determined to keep a balance between the contradictory demands. The show had to be *up for grabs* each week, had to be hazardous. Everyone had to feel on the line and under pressure to create. Yet Michaels wanted to keep personal control, and that was becoming more and more difficult. Chase, who was like a brother and something of an equal, had rocketed ahead and was second-guessing everything.

And John was pushing, poking at any and every sore spot, criticizing the show as a cardboard rerun of itself.

John's anger was clear to Tom Burke, a writer for *Rolling Stone* magazine, who had spent several weeks on the set in the early spring. He found John the most openly seditious of the cast members. John really wanted the Muppets off the show forever, and he was willing to shoot or destroy them. Pounding the table, he complained about the stereotyped roles they were falling into—like the bees. "What we are, man, is actors," John told Burke. "And this show's good when we're working together, all of us, in a sketch, as comic actors, playing off each other, with each other, not reading cue cards, like we have to, but memorizing the lines in advance, making eye contact, not dressing like fucking bees! You cannot put an actor in a bee costume and say, well, that funny dress will make up for the weak writing. . . . I hate the fucking bees!

". . . Some of the continuing bits now, we're just jerking off over and over. What I see now is taking the whole show as it is, throwing it out, and coming back with a whole new concept! Get rid of *all* the old standard characters, the stale stuff, catchphrases.

". . . Maybe here we can become total actors. But you can't if the next fucking moment you got to get into a fucking bee costume. I want to burn those fucking bee costumes! We're not little wind-up animals." John said that the cast members, not the guest hosts, were drawing the audiences. ". . . Listen, every one of the players sings great, Gilda, Garrett Morris, Danny, everybody, so instead of bringing in like Esther Phillips [the aging blues singer] why can't one of the *group* sing? If there has to be this host, I'd like to see each one of us doing it in rotation, one week's host is Chevy, next week Gilda, next Laraine, right? The Emmys give us the leverage to carry that. . . ."

O'Donoghue wanted to help John put his acting theories into practice, and he worked with him for a month on a parody of the TV science fiction series "Star Trek." Ironically, "Star Trek" had failed to draw a mass audience during its three-year run on NBC in the late sixties, but the reruns had become a cult.

The skit, called "The Last Voyage of Star Trek," was set for the final show of the season, May 29, 1976. Elliott Gould would again be the host.

At dress rehearsal, John was terrible interpreting William Shatner's Captain James T. Kirk. He had spent hours in makeup to look the part, but he just couldn't get his character to work, or get the lines right. O'Donoghue was worried that the long skit would bomb. He had seen John thrown into the roughest seas before and not drown, but in spite of John's love for "Star Trek" and his familiarity with every nuance, O'Donoghue feared a disaster was in the making. Worse, Chevy Chase was playing Mr. Spock (the Leonard Nimoy character with funny ears). It was a secondary role and Chase was bridling. Throughout rehearsals, he had been trying to move himself to the center. If John slipped, it would be impossible to curb Chevy. "You better pull this off, you sonofabitch," O'Donoghue told John just before he took the stage. "You haven't done it yet."

The scene opens on an elaborate set, a replica of the star ship *U.S.S. Enterprise*. The video screen on the bridge shows an American car chasing the ship. Danny, as chief engineer Scotty, identifies the vehicle in pursuit as a 1968 Chrysler Imperial with tinted windshields, retractable headlights and California license plates, registered to an organization called NBC, apparently the National Biscuit Company.

John, seated in the captain's chair, leans on one elbow.

Judy, who was watching, knew that John was capable of getting the part just right. He had watched the "Star Trek" reruns day after day and had repeated line after line back to the television. He could become Kirk, and now after hours in makeup, he looked like him.

"Captain's log," John says, snapping off his words. "Star date 3615.6. On a routine delivery of medical supplies, we're being chased through space by an automobile three centuries old, owned by a company that manufactures cookies. It would all be trivial if it weren't for this feeling of dread that haunts me, a sense of impending doom."

The captain, out of his seat, orders evasive action, but the *Enterprise* fails to lose the car. Mr. Spock steps forward and begins to question John's decisions.

"Spock!" John shouts authoritatively. "We do not know their intentions. *Spock!* I'm responsible for the lives of 430 crewmen. And *Spock!* I can't take any chances!"

Elliott Gould enters as the head of NBC programming.

"Ladies and gentlemen, due to the low Nielsen ratings, we at NBC have decided, unfortunately, to cancel 'Star Trek.' " John is upset. But Gould tells him he is taking it too hard, being unprofessionally emotional.

"So that's how it is, huh?" John says. "Just me, huh? Well, I've been in tougher spots before. No way. No way am I going to give up. I'm going to go down with the ship." John again takes his seat in the captain's chair, leans on an elbow and works his face into an end-of-the-earth look.

"Captain's log. *Final* entry. We're trying to explore strange new worlds, to seek out civilizations, to *boldly* go where no man has gone before. Except for one television network, we have found intelligence everywhere in the galaxy. Live long and prosper . . . Captain James T. Kirk."

O'Donoghue, off stage, was in ecstasy, almost in tears. Belushi had been brilliant. He had done it perfectly the one time it counted. O'Donoghue was not given to the actor's tradition of hugging other men, but when Belushi walked off the set, O'Donoghue wrapped his arms around him in gratitude and affection.

John and Dan also did a parody of Jackie Gleason and Art Carney in "The Honeymooners" that night. It had been written just the day before as a bee sketch. John enters with a perfect overdone walk, pacing the apartment as Ralph Kramden, bus driver.

"Alice! Alice! I'm home."

From the back room Gilda hollers, "I'll be right out, Ralph!"

John then sits on her knitting needles.

"AaaaaaaHhhhhhhhhh! AaaaaaHhhhhhhhh! Whhhhhhhaaaaaaa! Ahhhhhhhhhh! Whaaaaah!" He runs around the room with the needles in him, an escalating frenzy of Gleason bouncing off the walls. "AaaaaaaHhhhhhhhh! Ahhaaa! Ahhhhaaaa! Alice!"

Gilda comes out. She is a nonchalant, unperturbed wife. "What's the matter, Ralph? What's gotten into you?"

"Hard-e-har-har-har!" John says in a piercing Gleason imitation. Terrific applause. "Hard-e-har-har-har. Alice. You're really funny, *Alice!* You're really a riot, *Alice!* You're going to go places, Alice! You-know-where-you're-going-to-go-Alice?"

"Where?"

"To the moon, Alice!!!!"

"Oh, Ralph, I'm going to go into the bedroom. I feel nauseous."

"Hey, Norton!" John yells for Aykroyd, Ralph's sidekick Ed Norton.

"Hey, Ralphie!" Danny says, strutting through the door. They confer and deduce that Alice's knitting needles and the nausea could mean only one thing—she's pregnant.

Later, when Ralph and Alice are alone, John asks, "Alice, why didn't you tell me we was having a baby?"

"Because, Ralph," Gilda says, "it's not yours. . . . It's Ed Norton's."

"Baby, you're the greatest." He embraces her as the haunting "Honeymooners" theme music comes up.

In Los Angeles, Bernie Brillstein received a call from the office of Paul McCartney, the former Beatle. They wanted John to come to McCartney's thirty-fourth birthday party, June 18, and do his Joe Cocker imitation. They would pay him $6,000. A light went on in Brillstein's head. John was catching on, and $6,000 was a lot of money, particularly for a Cocker imitation, which John could do in his sleep. Lorne Michaels had been telling Brillstein that soon he was going to need a rock-and-roll mentality to represent the "Saturday Night" stars. That meant rock-and-roll prices.

During the summer Michaels took John and Dan to California to the Joshua Tree Inn, a retreat in the desert. Their rooms were small and had no refrigerators or phones. It was a place to settle out and take stock.*

One day at Joshua Tree they all ate some psilocybin mushrooms, a

* The Nielsen ratings were giving the show about a 6.4 (the percentage of TV sets tuned to the show out of *all* the household sets in the country, even those not in use), which translated to about 10 million viewers. Its audience share was about 22 percent of all people watching TV at that time period. That was good for a first season, but eventually they would need about 30 percent to guarantee survival.

psychedelic. Michaels was frightened by the drug, but it turned out to be a good trip. He felt as if he were under a spell, suspended in a state of tranquility and grace.

Belushi arranged a backyard barbecue, which he supervised. There was some cocaine and John did most of it; there was also some pot and he smoked a lot; there was a bottle of tequila and John drank at least half of it; he also took several Quaaludes. Michaels looked on in disgust and wonder. They moved to Michaels's small room. He had a woman with him, but even so, Belushi wouldn't leave until nearly three in the morning.

About 5:30 A.M., Michaels heard a noise in the courtyard by the pool. He went out to his balcony.

There was John in his swimming suit, bouncing on the diving board —up and down, up and down. In one burst he soared up as high as possible, kicked out his feet, landed his ass on the end of the board and flipped over into the water. Michaels looked to his side and saw Dan, also watching John's sunrise theater.

"Albanian oak," Aykroyd said.

"Yes," Michaels replied. Belushi was nonperishable.

Later that summer Aykroyd invited Belushi to Ontario, Canada, to visit his family's farm, which had been in the Aykroyd family for about 150 years. John arrived one afternoon, claiming he had come over the border without a passport or any identification, not even a driver's license.

Danny wanted a motor for their boat that weekend on the lake, and he decided to take one from a nearby marina. But he didn't want to involve John. Breaking the law was a high for Aykroyd, but an American citizen caught stealing in Canada could have real trouble. Not that Aykroyd wouldn't if he were caught, but that was the thrill; living on the brink was a full-time occupation, not just something for the stage. Danny got some bolt cutters and called his friend Speedo, and together they headed down the driveway in an old Buick sedan.

"Where are you going?" asked John, running to the car.

"To get a motor," Danny replied.

"How?"

"We're going to steal it," Danny answered.

"I want to go," John said.

"No."

"I want to help."

Danny couldn't deny John a chance to participate, to enter into his world a little more. So John got into the car and they drove over to the marina. Speedo and John found a motor outside, took the bolt cutters and clipped the bolts on a 50-horsepower Johnson outboard while Danny waited in the getaway car.

John and Speedo were soon racing to the car with their prize, laughing like kids. They jumped in with the motor and Danny sped off. They drank some beer that Danny had brought along. They waterskied all weekend. After the weekend, with considerably more risk—because the marina might have put on alarms, guards or dogs—they returned the motor. That operation compounded the excitement.

All summer there were rumblings that Chevy Chase was going to leave the show. On July 15, 1976, *Rolling Stone* published a long article on the first season of "Saturday Night." Chase was quoted at length about his dissatisfaction with the show, remarking that parts of it had gone "stale." He implied that he might have outgrown it and was ready to move on to writing, performing, directing and producing his own projects.

By August it was official. "I was kind of the thread between the craziness of the program and the straight types in the audience," Chase said as he announced his departure. "But the show gained its own momentum and now it makes its own statement, and it doesn't need any one personality to survive."

Belushi was elated.

When the show resumed in the
fall of 1976, Michaels was worried that Last Year's Sensation might
fizzle, particularly without Chase. One piece of luck was Jimmy Carter's
election victory over Gerald Ford. Chase wouldn't be around to play
Ford, but Aykroyd came up with a penetrating and weirdly acute impersonation of the new president.

The Nixon administration, however, was still satiric bread and but-
ter. On November 13, Aykroyd played Nixon's neurotic persona with
precision, Belushi was a beefy Kissinger and Gilda was Rose Mary
Woods.

Michaels saw this as the heart of the show: Gilda, John and Danny
were a formula that worked in many variations. Talented as John and
Gilda were, it was Aykroyd who really acted, submerging his personality
and carrying the narrative line. He was their Alec Guinness, a utility
player who could do almost anything.

On November 17, *The Washington Post*'s Tom Shales ran a long
piece headlined: CHEVY'S GONE, BUT "SATURDAY NIGHT" LIVES. This
was an important sign to Michaels. And other creative dynamics remained. The writers and cast had effectively won over the original cen-
sor, and NBC had brought in a woman from the Standards Department
who was under orders to crack down. She excised two things from an
"Update" written by O'Donoghue. The first concerned a new branch of
the Catholic Church in which the "host" was supplemented by a "co-
host," the "body of Mike Douglas." Another was about a new venereal
disease appearing in the states where candidate Ronald Reagan had been
campaigning—"spreading conservatism."

The show was taking less and less of John's attention; it was still
hard work, but he was performing skits that other people wrote. John and

Dan shared a writing credit, but Danny found increasingly that John lacked the patience to sit still and think. John had started renting limousines and hitting the New York night life very hard. Soon he was *out* more than *in,* and often Michaels and Aykroyd couldn't find him.

John's salary had made an extraordinary jump to nearly $100,000 a year because of the success of the show, and Judy knew that when he was on a binge, he could spend close to $500 a week on drugs, particularly cocaine. He couldn't afford to do that very often, but he was snorting too many grams a week. The drug was his fuel. Sometimes he would take a hit about a half-hour before the show, and occasionally during the show when off stage. The most cocaine was used during the writing and the postshow party.

Judy saw less and less of him. John felt put upon if she asked him to do the slightest household chore or to conform to any schedule of meals and sleep. She left a note once asking him to take out the laundry. She returned to find a scribbled message, "I can't!"

They had talked about marriage; they loved each other and had lived together for five years. They needed some legal standing with each other. Suppose one of them was in a hospital, unconscious, and the doctors needed a family member to give approval for an operation? Live-in lover wouldn't do. And then there was the question of property, their apartment, insurance.

No decision was made. The show was going full tilt, and John would not sit still to talk or plan. He was driven to become famous. "You can't know. You don't know what it's like to be me," he told her. She thought it was a sad statement. He apparently didn't want to try to explain; he didn't want anyone that close to him. "Things will be better when I'm dead," he said once. She was shocked but let it pass.

Judy raised the issue of cocaine. Wasn't he doing too much? What about all the money? One day John would say, "I'm getting away from drugs," and the next, "I can handle drugs." Judy didn't believe either statement. She knew coke made John less sensitive, and apparently he had to be that way to perform. He feared, sometimes, that people only laughed at him because he looked funny.

Judy was using cocaine with some regularity but mostly during long nights of partying or of staying out late to keep John company in the hope of finding the closeness she wanted. She tried, gently, to gain some control over the cocaine use, and even made some effort to persuade John to hire an accountant, who, she thought, might limit John's access to cash.

But the drugs, the disappearances, the drop-in, drop-out nature of life, the unsureness of everything about their relationship and future upset her. Finally, Judy asked him to leave the apartment, to get out and stay out. Though it was his place also, Judy suspected that his pride would prevail. He walked out just before Thanksgiving.

Judy and her older sister, Pam Jacklin, had a long talk over that weekend. Cocaine was ravaging John, Judy said, and she worried about what it would do to him as a person, not to speak of professionally. He could burn out, he might be arrested, it might damage his creativity. And the money, my God, the money that was being wasted up his nose.

The discussion was painful for the two women. Their father had once had a drinking problem. It had been hidden. Their mother had not wanted to admit it. She had made excuses and called it something else. Her daughters had watched as she was forced eventually to confront it and then deal with the consequences.

Judy saw the frightening parallel. She was not going to repeat their mother's mistake and minister to an addiction for the rest of her life.

Having left Bleecker Street, John went to see Penny Marshall, who was staying at the Sherry Netherland Hotel. Marshall and Cindy Williams had struck it big that year with "Laverne and Shirley," a TV series about two women blue-collar workers in Milwaukee in the 1950s. They were in New York for the Macy's Thanksgiving parade. They had also made a record for Atlantic Records, and the company had set up their suite with the latest in high-tech stereo equipment. John moved in.

Marshall liked John in spite of his regular references to her show as "crap" and "prime-time shit." She called Judy on the phone.

"I got him," Marshall said.

"Keep him," Judy replied.

John stayed for several days, sleeping days, going out nights. When Marshall suggested to him that he cut down on drugs, he screamed, "Don't be my mother!" One of those nights he went to Michaels's loft, got a party going and fell asleep wearing headphones and smoking. A fire started that did considerable damage.

The Monday after Thanksgiving, November 29, 1976, John went to see Dr. Rosenbluth.

Rosenbluth had practiced medicine for seventeen years and had previously run a drug addiction clinic for eight years. He asked John for his personal medical history and stressed the need to be honest and complete. As John spoke, Rosenbluth wrote in John's file:

Smokes 3 packs a day.
Alcohol drinks socially.
Medications: Valium occasionally.
Marijuana 4 to 5 times a week.
Cocaine—snort daily, main habit.
Mescaline—regularly.
Acid—10 to 20 trips.
No heroin.
Amphetamines—four kinds.
Barbiturates (Quaalude habit).

Rosenbluth had then questioned John about the excessive cocaine use and told John he absolutely *had* to stop.

"I give so much pleasure to so many people," John said. "Why can I not get some pleasure for myself? Why do I have to stop?"

"Because you'll kill yourself," Rosenbluth replied.

"My whole life is being conducted for me, schedules are set and I have to be there," he said. It was exhausting and oppressive. Cocaine was relief.

"I want you to see a psychiatrist."

John greeted the doctor's advice with considerable hostility; there was no need and he had no time. The drugs were not that much of a problem: there was no heroin; he wasn't injecting anything. His girlfriend was the most important person in his life, and he wouldn't do anything to hurt her.

"That's why you'd better quit," Rosenbluth said.

"I'm addicted to Quaaludes," John confessed; he needed them to sleep. Rosenbluth wrote him a prescription for 30.

Tom Brokaw and Jane Pauley, then the new cohosts of NBC's early-morning "Today" show, began their day about five-thirty to prepare for a seven o'clock air time. On Thursdays, Belushi would often wander down to their offices, up all night and clearly flying. He would conduct a drug-fueled, machine-gun interrogation of Brokaw: "What's going on? Who's going to be put on the show? What's in the news? Why don't you put me on?"

Brokaw thought John wanted desperately to be taken seriously. On one occasion, Brokaw's children were there to watch the show. John appeared and asked, "Where are they? I want to see them." He went over to them and said, "I like your old man, but he runs too much, gets in shape." (Brokaw was a devout jogger, running every day in Central

Park.) John made a disapproving face. "Too boring!" The kids laughed. Brokaw concluded that John was a lounge act, a 24-hour-a-day, 7-day-a-week rock concert.

John would sit in Pauley's office for an hour after the show ended at nine, joking and hanging around like a high school kid who didn't want to go home. Once he walked her home up Madison Avenue and someone yelled, "Hey, Belushi!" A small crowd gathered, and John launched into a hip rap. He got out a switchblade and in a joking but menacing manner waved it at his side and chased away the crowd.

Each time Pauley saw John, she found herself saying as they parted, "Take care of yourself."

Candice Bergen came to do her third show, the last one before Christmas, December 11, 1976. She had been looking forward to it, but during rehearsals she was shocked by the change from the previous year. Doing a live show, three times a month, had taken a toll. The warmth and openness had dissipated, and in its place there was a cool toughness, especially in John. The pressure had squeezed something vital out of the show and out of the people. They seemed to resent both one another and her. It had become a coke show. Maybe there was no way to get through, week after week, without uppers. Bergen could understand that. Habits that had been scarcely affordable the year before were well within the stars' incomes now.

The writers had come up with an offbeat, ironic skit. Bergen couldn't tell how it was going to turn out, even after several rehearsals.

The "Saturday Night" band plays the opening music. The music stops, but Bergen is not on stage. The camera cuts to the hallway outside her dressing room, number 8H7. Curtin calls through the door, "Candy, they're ready for you. . . . The show has started."

"I really can't do it, Jane," Bergen says from inside, sounding forlorn. "I'm too frightened."

"Candy, you've done the show before and you were great."

"It's different. I'm only here to be close to *him,* Jane."

"Candy, forget him. He's not worth it. No man is. Especially John Belushi."

"I can't forget him, Jane. We've shared so much together. . . . We had something special."

Michaels appears. "I don't understand it. What is this power that Belushi has over women?"

"Candy," Curtin says, "look what you're doing to yourself."

"I don't care, Jane. Oh, if John would at least talk to me."

"He's nothing but an animal," Curtin says (meaning it).

"That's why he bothers me."

"Candy," Jane says, "he's no good. He's had his way with every single woman on this network. . . ."

John enters in a white coat, a red carnation in his lapel, and a black bow tie. His hair is brushed straight back, and he has a terrific makeup job—white face, red lips, jet-black eyebrows. He is smoking a cigarette a la Bogart; it is drooping down, sly. He knocks.

"Go away!" Bergen yells.

"Candy, get out here," he says in perfect Bogart.

Bergen opens the door and gazes at him longingly.

"John? Oh, John."

"Candy, Candy baby, I know how you feel—but it's over."

"It can't be. You're just angry, that's all. Listen, John, I'll do anything, I don't care. What do you want me to do?"

"It's not you, Candy. It's me. How many times do I have to tell ya?" He asks it with the slight Bogey lisp, the paralyzed lip movement, the shrug, the pull on the cigarette. He is the callow, brooding, slightly ruthless antihero.

Michaels and the writers were entranced. John was good, drawing everyone in, making it more credible with each word and movement.

"It's for your own good," he says. "Don't you understand? I'll only hurt you."

"John, can't you think about us?"

"There is no *us,* Candy."

"All you can think about is yourself. One woman hurts you, and you just take it out on the rest of the world. You're a coward. . . ." She hits him and he flinches. "I'm really sorry. I'm really sorry. Did I hurt you?"

"Yes, very much."

"I'm sorry! You know I'd never do anything to hurt you. You're the first man I've ever liked."

"Yes," John replies sarcastically, "and I love you too. That's why I want to get you out there on that stage . . . Bambie."

"Candy," she corrects.

They walk into a fog. "As Time Goes By," from *Casablanca,* starts up from the piano. Belushi and Bergen don fedoras and trench coats.

"I want you out there," John says. "Look, I'm no good at being noble. But it doesn't take much to see that the problems of two little people don't amount to a hill of beans in this crazy world. . . . If you're not out there, you'll regret it . . . maybe not now, maybe not tomorrow, but soon, and for the rest of your life.''

Voice-over: "Last plane to Lisbon now departing."

Bergen: "What about us, John?"

"Well, we'll have Paris—and the Muppets. Well, here's looking at you kid." He gives her a jab on the chin. "Better go." The music picks up.

John turns to Garrett Morris at the piano. "That's enough, Sam. You can close up for the night."

"All right, Mr. Rick."

John turns to Bergen, "Listen, ah, Candy. You do a good show and maybe—just maybe—afterwards, we can have a drink later."

"My place?"

"Fine."

"I don't even know if you're going to show up. You're such a filthy liar; you've never told me the truth. I guess that's why I need you, John. I think this could be the start of a beautiful friendship."

Michaels had always encouraged his cast to use material from their own lives in the show, and this Christmas John had no place to go. In the final skit, Bergen appears on camera:

"Well, it's the last show before Christmas, and after it's over we'll go out and celebrate before heading our separate ways for the holidays. . . . I guess Garrett [the only black] will be going back to Africa. Yes, everybody's going home, everybody except for Belushi. . . . 'Saturday Night' proudly announces 'The Adopt Belushi for Christmas Contest.' . . .''

John appears and sings, "Chestnuts roasting on an open fire" off-key. He addresses the camera. "Hi, I'm John Belushi. You can call me 'Buh-looch' just like my close personal friend Chevy Chase does. You know, it's corny, but I love Christmas. Hey, I'd love to sit around the yule log and play with your daughter. . . . I'm not fussy. I like candied yams, plum puddings, roast goose stuffed with drugs. . . .''

Bergen announces, "If you think you're that special American family, why not write . . . ?"

Bergen and the cast closed with a song about Gary Gilmore, the convicted mass murderer who wanted to be executed, called "Let's Kill Gary Gilmore for Christmas."

Bergen left the studio that morning depressed. The good acting and the skilled writing only made it worse. There was a great deal of talent, but the humanity had been drained out. Drugs, cocaine, was the reason. She would keep a polite distance. She vowed never to host the show again. The cast had come to resemble what they were parodying.

John went to California for a short time before Christmas, and when he returned he went to the old apartment where Judy was still living. He had little money and had no place to go, so he just moved back in. They decided they would visit her thirty-four-year-old brother, Rob, who was a goldsmith in Aspen, Colorado.

John called Rob, who had always been like an older brother. "You've got to help me. I've got to marry Judy." It was not that Judy was pregnant or anything, but he had to do this for her. "I don't want her to be alone," John said. Would Rob find them a place in Aspen for their honeymoon? No mattress on the guest room floor this time. Rob said he probably could find something nice in the ski region for about $50 a day.

John said get a $200-a-day place. Rob was surprised at such extravagance, but he found a beautiful old renovated barn for them.

When they arrived in Colorado, Judy heard the two men discussing a wedding, obviously Judy and John's. But John was being secretive. She tried casually to explain that weddings require planning—blood tests, licenses, rings, a judge or minister.

On the last day of 1976 they made a crash effort to arrange a wedding. Many government offices were closed, and a blizzard was raging, but just before the new year they had it all set. John and Judy were married at 4:55 P.M. on New Year's Eve.

"Saturday Night" was popular among college students, and the writers and cast were often invited to perform on the campus lecture circuit. It was quick money—$1,000 to $2,000 an evening—and Belushi sometimes went with Aykroyd, or with Gary Weis or Michael O'Donoghue.

O'Donoghue liked those evenings with John. They would go to a nearby campus by limousine. Their lecture, usually before a packed house, would begin as O'Donoghue came out and arranged his papers at a podium.

John then appeared and begged for an injection.

"No, John, you've had enough."

After more pleading O'Donoghue would take out a giant syringe and say only this one time, the high will last about an hour and fifteen minutes—the length of the lecture. O'Donoghue would read some jokes and

110

routines that had been censored from the show, and John would usually do a Samurai sketch and a few other routines. A bag of real mail to the show would be set on fire with lighter fluid, and then John would saw the podium in half with a chain saw. On the way back, they played rock-and-roll tapes loud and smoked dope.

During a college lecture early in January, 1977, John jumped off the stage and twisted his knee severely, damaging the cartilage. He was admitted to a hospital, where he had to take pain killers for several days. He was drowsy and upset. Judy brought him some cocaine. He missed the January 15, 1977, show, which was hosted by consumer advocate Ralph Nader.

Lorne Michaels fired and rehired John a number of times. Judy believed the problem was cocaine. There was so much going around the office that everyone's nerves were worn thin. People got wired on coke, made demands, said things they didn't mean, and before too long someone exploded. It was a ritual with Lorne and John.

By late January, John was back for the show. Michaels cast John and himself in the opening. Michaels tells a doctor, "I cannot put Belushi on national television; he's in a coma." Belushi, wearing a bathrobe and three-days growth of beard, is rolled in in a wheelchair, out cold. Michaels walks over to him, looks down in disgust. "Hey, look, I, I can't put this guy on television. I mean, he's got to be awake."

The doctor then says, "I'll be forced to cut off his drugs." Belushi's head snaps up and his eyes pop open. "Live, from New York, it's Saturday Night!" he yells.

It was too real for Judy. She decided once again to try to cut off John's drugs and went to see Gary Watkins, who seemed to be John's principal supplier. Watkins was surprised to see her so steamed up. As John's friend, Judy said, I want you to stop.

Watkins did not think of himself as John's main supplier, and he certainly didn't think of himself as a drug dealer, but he agreed.

But after several days Judy discovered that John had more cocaine, and he admitted to her finally that he'd got it from Watkins. Judy called Watkins. "John's here and he's fucked up. He got the stuff from you."

Watkins didn't deny it.

"What are you trying to do to John?" she shouted.

Watkins didn't feel accountable for John or his actions; he was not forcing John to do anything; John was driven and obsessed all on his own.

Watkins had gone back on his word, and Judy was furious. "I don't want you to sell to John. . . . If you're a friend, don't!"

Watkins thought she was making him the devil. He was not the corner store. "You can't control him," he said. No one could exert that kind of influence on John.

"You've got to stop!" Judy yelled.

"Are you threatening me?"

"Yes," Judy replied. She realized that her anger and vehemence implied that she might take some action, even an extreme one such as going to the police. "Yes, I guess I am." She hung up. She had no intention of going to the authorities, but she hoped she had scared Watkins.

John finally agreed to see a psychiatrist, Dr. Michael S. Aronoff.

One day Judy found a note John had left at their apartment: "Going to Aronoff. I'm going to lick this thing."

But he complained about the long trip uptown. He went off and on for about four months. On April 26, 1977, they went together to see Aronoff. A close friend of Judy's family had just died, and she was upset and broke down during the session. John finally stopped seeing Aronoff, explaining to Judy that he didn't have a problem anymore.

More and more the standout on the "Saturday Night" show, Belushi was becoming the audience's favorite, not the star that Chevy Chase had become but the favorite in his own way—the teddy bear and monster. Mitchell Glazer, a twenty-four-year-old New York writer for *Crawdaddy* magazine, a glossy would-be competitor to *Rolling Stone,* noticed it. Belushi was part of the future. Glazer wanted to do a Belushi cover. John was interested, but he wanted to read some of Glazer's work.

Glazer sent two pieces he'd done, one on George Harrison, and called John again.

Yeah, I've read the articles, John said, and what's this line in one about the "microphones swooped in like gulls" and this one about "low pissed off clouds."

Glazer regretted those lines; they were examples of his weakest writing. John had gone right for them. Glazer tried to explain, but John showed no sympathy.

"I'm going to let a guy who writes like that do an article on me?" he asked, laughing.

Glazer promised he could read the story before it was published.

John said he wanted full approval. He'd talk to Glazer, help him out, but he, John, had to have total control.

Glazer, as any writer would, hated the idea, but without access, he wouldn't have much of a story. He agreed.

"And," John added, "I get approval of the cover picture."

"Okay."

"And approval of the pictures used in the article, all the pictures."

"Okay."

Glazer interviewed some of the people on the "Saturday Night" set. O'Donoghue was the most helpful. Glazer thought O'Donoghue looked like a heroin-lab chemist who sold children on the side.

"What is John Belushi like?" O'Donoghue threw the question back at Glazer. "What you have to remember is that it's that very self-destructive drive, that crazed death-oriented gusto that puts the edge on his performance. It gives him the edge and puts him over the edge."

Glazer couldn't get to John. He kept postponing the interview, dodging Glazer, not returning calls. He seemed annoyed by the suggestion that he should sit still. But one night he called Glazer about 3 A.M. from the NBC offices and urged him to come up with a recorder and lots of tapes. And bring some sandwiches, two sandwiches, John ordered.

Glazer showed up with tapes and sandwiches. As John ate the sandwiches, he said he had decided not to do the interview.

O'Donoghue explained: "You see, John has a phase he's got to work through—the star trip. He's young, probably never had much money, and now he's got limos and all this nose powder. John's got a real Judy Garland personality sometimes; he wants to grab the world and snort it."

Glazer worked on his piece, using snatches of conversations with John and his impressions from hanging around listening, with O'Donoghue as the Greek chorus. The draft was shown to John, who said he wanted O'Donoghue's line about the "nose powder" out; he could never let his parents read something like that. Judy persuaded him to let it stay.

The cover picture was of John with a sly smile, eyebrows up, pointing at a small TV on his shoulder that had a picture of himself with a mock frown. The headline was: THE MOST DANGEROUS MAN ON TV "SATURDAY NIGHT'S" JOHN BELUSHI.

Glazer was now family to John, sometimes father, sometimes son, sometimes errand boy, always John's personal Boswell and historian.

The article, in the small-circulation magazine, marked the first truly individual attention that John had received. He wouldn't let it go. He kept in touch with Glazer with late-night calls and visits.

Michaels took the show to New Orleans during Mardi Gras, where John did a skit from a balcony playing Ricky Mussolini, the twenty-seven-year-old grandson of the Italian Fascist leader. He also played the young Brando of *Streetcar,* in a ripped T-shirt and holding a beer, stumbling around the streets yelling, "Stellaaa! . . . Stellaaaa!"

Later that year, John played a ratings-conscious Soviet leader Leonid Brezhnev, who wanted to be on U.S. television during an upcoming trip—the Johnny Carson Show ("Junny, Junny")—but not with a guest host and *not* during the last fifteen minutes of the show.

At the end of the season Belushi and Aykroyd had a row. Dan was upset that John was not paying attention to his writing. They were splitting a writing credit and $275 more in pay a week. John might drop an idea or talk it out, but then he would disappear and leave Dan to do the work.

"If you're not going to be a writer," Aykroyd finally yelled at him, "then don't take the money, don't waste my time."

"I don't want to be a writer!" John screamed back. "I want to perform. I don't want to write. Keep the money!"

"I don't care about the money!" Danny retorted. "You can have the money, but don't pretend you're a writer. Don't even show up!"

T. Berthiaume

2. Belushi, as Joe Cocker, singing "Lonely at the Bottom of the Barrel" in *Lemmings*.
4. Actress Betty Buckley, who met John while he was acting in *Lemmings* and who saw him the last time he was in New York, about two weeks before he died.

3. Belushi in one of his most famous roles—the mute but passionate Samurai warrior.
5. "I hate the fucking bees," Belushi said, resentful of those gang skits in which he couldn't move to center stage. Shown here are John, Chevy Chase, Gilda Radnor and Michael O'Donoghue as the bees.

6. John and Dan singing and dancing as the
Blues Brothers on "Saturday Night Live."

7. Aykroyd as Nixon and Belushi as Kissinger re-enacting the famous and controversial resignation-eve prayer scene.

8. Writer Don Novello as Father Guido. Novello was doing the real script writing on the wine and diamond caper movie, *Noble Rot*, during the last few months of Belushi's life.

9. Candice Bergen and Belushi play Humphrey Bogart and Ingrid Bergman in a parody of the film classic, *Casablanca*. This was the third time Bergen hosted the show and she vowed it would be her last because the vitality and freshness of the acting had been ruined, she felt, by drugs.

10. Ed Begley, Jr., John's night-life companion during the filming of *Goin' South*, in Mexico, 1977.

11. John with *1941* director Steven Spielberg in 1978.

Jean C. Pigozzi/Archive Pictures Inc.

13

14

15

12. Dan Aykroyd, John, and Penny Marshall, one of the stars of the hit series "Laverne and Shirley."

13. (L to R) Bernie Brillstein and his daughter Leigh, Belushi, Smokey Wendell, Judy Belushi, and John's youngest brother, Billy Belushi, in 1980.

14. (L to R) Belushi, *Goin' South* producer and director Jack Nicholson, actress Amy Irving, and Dan Aykroyd in 1980.

15. Director John Landis during the filming of *Animal House*. Landis became frustrated with Belushi's cocaine use and flushed John's supply down the toilet on at least two occasions.

16. John working out with bodyguard and former world karate champion Bill "Superfoot" Wallace in 1980.

17. Aykroyd on the set of *Neighbors* with director John Avildsen in 1981.

James M. Thiersen/The Washington Post

19   Pictures 19, 20, 21, 23, 24 AP Photo

20

21, 22   L.A. Times photo

18. French director Louis Malle, who planned and had a screenplay written for a movie to star Belushi and Aykroyd that was to be a takeoff of the congressional Abscam scandal, called *Moon Over Miami*. The day Belushi died Malle was trying to contact him to get him to read the screenplay. Aykroyd feared that the part that had been written resembled his partner too closely, but Belushi never got a chance to read it.

19. Producers David Brown and Richard Zanuck, whose earlier work included *Jaws* and *The Sting*, had to monitor every minute of shooting of Belushi's last movie *Neighbors*, fearing a fist-fight between Belushi and director John Avildsen. Screenwriter Larry Gelbart thought the producers naively optimistic and privately referred to them as "the sunshine boys."

20. Frank Price, Columbia Pictures President, whose "hit and run" strategy for marketing and timing the release of *Neighbors* ensured that Columbia made several million dollars on the critical box office flop.

21. Paramount President Michael Eisner, who met with Belushi twice during the last week of the actor's life in an attempt to shift Belushi's $1.85 million contract from *Noble Rot* to *The Joy of Sex*.

22. Michael Ovitz, one of Hollywood's most successful agents, represented Belushi for several years. Two weeks before Belushi's death Ovitz had to get two people from his mail room to help Belushi to his limo because the actor was too high on drugs to walk by himself.

23. Actor Robin Williams visited Chateau Marmont's bungalow 3 the last night of Belushi's life and says that after the experience of March 5, 1982, he turned away from the Hollywood scene and re-evaluated his own life-style.

24. Actor Treat Williams co-starred with Belushi and Aykroyd in Steven Spielberg's comedy disaster, *1941*. Williams loved the Hollywood night life and fast-lane living as much as Belushi.

Nancy Kaye/The Washington Post

25. Belushi claimed in the last week of his life that actor Robert De Niro thought it was a good idea to use real heroin in a drug scene in another movie Belushi wanted to do. De Niro declined to be interviewed.

26. Singer Carly Simon, who found herself both attracted and repelled by the frenzy of Belushi's music, acting, and life.

 Nancy Kaye/The Washington Post

Marcia Resnick

27. Pictures taken by Marcia Resnick in September 1981, six months before Belushi's death.

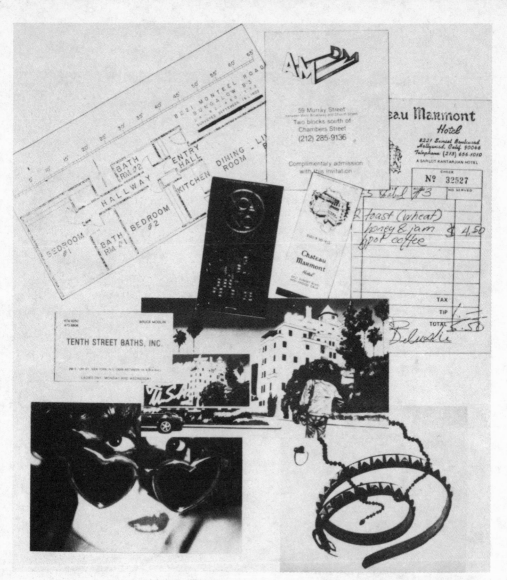

28. Layout of the two-bedroom bungalow number 3 at the Chateau Marmont on Sunset Boulevard where Belushi died: The Rox Club matches where the motto is "Living well is the best revenge"; the breakfast order of wheat toast, honey, jam and coffee that Cathy Smith ordered the morning Belushi died; the AM-PM club in New York where John liked to go in the early morning hours; the Tenth Street Baths or "Schvitz" where he liked to get a massage, steam, and food; a photo of Laurel Rubin, and the belt used to "tie off" John's arm for the injection that killed him.

29. Cathy Smith in late 1982 in Toronto where she was awaiting the grand jury action against her.

Pictures 30, 31, 32, 33 Joanne Rathe/The Boston Herald 30

31, 32, 33

30. Pallbearers at Belushi's funeral: Aykroyd (left); on right, Jimmy Belushi, old Illinois friends Tino Insana and Steve Beshekas, and Billy Belushi.
31. John's mother and brother Jimmy.
32. Friend and music producer Michael Klenfner and "Saturday Night Live" writer Michael O'Donoghue.
33. Bernie Brillstein and Lorne Michaels.

34. Dan Aykroyd at Belushi's grave on Martha's Vineyard where Belushi was buried on Tuesday, March 9, 1982.

Part Two

8

That summer John Landis, then twenty-seven years old, was in New York for the screening of the first picture he had directed, *The Kentucky Fried Movie,* a low-budget, satirical anthology of film and TV spoofs. He was introduced to Belushi at the theater.

"Jesus!" John said, shaking his hand. "You're young. Where are you staying?"

"The Drake."

"I'll see you there later," John said. He turned and walked away.

After the screening, Landis went back to the Drake and waited. Belushi hadn't indicated any specific time, and Landis began to wonder whether he had misunderstood. He wanted to sign John to play Bluto in *National Lampoon's Animal House* and had sent Belushi a script. It was about a naughty-boy fraternity, the Delta "Animal House," which waged war against taste, propriety, deans, grades, women, the local town and the superstraight Omega House. Universal had given Landis the go-ahead to develop the script, but the project, like much of what goes on in Hollywood, was tenuous. Getting a commitment depended on many factors. First, Landis had serious problems with the script. The humor was mean-spirited, like the *National Lampoon* itself. One issue of the magazine had had a cover photo of a puppy with a gun held to its head and the headline: IF YOU DON'T BUY THIS MAGAZINE WE'LL KILL THIS DOG. There were too many shit jokes, tasteless gags, and Landis found some of the humor anti-Semitic, racist and antiwomen. In one scene, a Delta was to put out a campfire by vomiting on it. In another, a beer keg was to fly through the head of a President John Kennedy replica on a homecoming float, emerging at exactly the point of the assassination wound. These things might work for a magazine directed at a small elite, but such sick jokes would not do for a feature film intended for a general audience.

Landis had spent some time with the writers, Doug Kenney, the founding editor and creative engine of the *National Lampoon;* Harold Ramis, a buddy of Belushi's from Second City; and another *Lampoon* writer, Chris Miller.

The writers were testy, and they were trying to be intimidating. But Landis figured that the director could cut what he didn't like, and most important, it was he who would impose the tone.

Universal had wanted Chevy Chase for Otter, the unflappable leader of the Deltas, but Landis wanted a comic actor, none of this "I'm Chevy Chase and you're not." Landis had sabotaged the draft-Chase movement by playing to Chase's ego. Landis had told him that *Animal House* would be an intense group effort. Like "Saturday Night Live," no one would get top billing. Chase turned the part down.

Universal issued an ultimatum: Get Belushi for Bluto or there would be no movie. The *Lampoon* writers had long ago developed the Bluto character with Belushi in mind.

There was a knock on Landis's door. As he was greeting Landis, John dialed room service. Half a dozen shrimp cocktails, he said, some beer, Heineken, and, oh yeah, some margaritas and a few orders of oysters.

Belushi was performing for him, playing Bluto. Okay.

"I got problems with the script," John said. "Bluto is not on the road trip." This was a long scene in which some of the Deltas drive out on an all-night excursion looking for women and booze.

Bluto, Landis said, should not, could not, be in that scene. His character is volcanic. The intensity Bluto embodies couldn't be sustained that long. He can't always be on screen. Landis explained his notion of the character. Bluto was a mixture of Harpo Marx and the Cookie Monster—sweetness and mania, with a voracious appetite for food, trouble and women.

John listened carefully, asked a few more questions, and finally said, "Okay, I'll do it." He asked to borrow $20. Landis gave it to him, saying, "You better pay me back tomorrow." Without saying anything much, John left.

Soon there was another knock at the door. It was room service with about $150 worth of food and drink. Landis laughed, signed the bill and called Sean Daniels, the Universal executive in charge of the movie. "I think we got him."

Two days later Landis was having dinner at a sushi bar in New York. A waiter delivered a paper bag. Perplexed, Landis reached inside and pulled out a tuna fish sandwich. On the other side of the restaurant was John.

It was repayment for the $20. John used to tell Judy that he tested people by borrowing small amounts of money from them—it pushed them, put them out, and it gave him a chance to watch their reaction. Judy never really understood.

John wanted very much to do *Animal House*. He even went so far as to tell Brillstein, "They can't do it without me." Universal approved only a $2.5 million budget for the film, but Brillstein got a $35,000 contract for John, high given the fact that he had no film experience.

There was a part for Aykroyd, as a motorcycle fanatic, and John very much wanted him to take it, but Danny said no. He wanted to write for "Saturday Night Live." "No, no, you do it," he told John. "It's your movie."

Later that summer Brillstein was in his office on Sunset Boulevard in Hollywood when Harry Gittes, a producer who was a close friend of actor Jack Nicholson, called. Nicholson was going to direct and star in a western romance-comedy called *Goin' South*. Gittes had heard that Belushi did a superb Mexican impersonation, and Nicholson wanted him for the small part of a Mexican deputy sheriff. The filming would start in Mexico around the middle of August.

Brillstein, with the growing success of his clients, including the Muppets and most of the "Saturday Night" cast, considered himself king of television, and he was anxious to expand into movies. He subscribed to the old show business motto "Do everything and something will work out."

"My father always wanted to see me on a horse," John told Brillstein. But it was important that he finish filming *Goin' South* in time to start the third season of "Saturday Night" that fall. Brillstein checked with Gittes, who promised they would have John back in New York in time.

John told Judy that *Goin' South* was a good idea; he would have a movie under his belt before *Animal House*. She knew that he was disappointed that "Saturday Night" had not made him a star like Chase. He was impatient for success. Maybe the fast track lay in Hollywood.

John called Steve Beshekas to tell him he was going to do a movie with Nicholson. "Boy, he's a big star, Steve," John said. He admired

Nicholson's renegade style. He had loved playing Nicholson on "Saturday Night" in the *Cuckoo's Nest* takeoff.

On August 16, 1977, Belushi signed a contract for *Goin' South* that gave him $5,000 a week for five weeks, with a $25-per-diem payment plus hotel expenses. Nicholson was delighted though a little surprised that Belushi had accepted a bit part. "What the hell does John Belushi want to do this for?" he asked Gittes.

John was due in Durango, Mexico, a remote town in the central part of the country where a lot of American westerns are made, but he didn't have a passport, tickets or money, and there was confusion about his hotel reservation. Brillstein's office arranged to get a birth certificate from John's mother in Chicago and got him on a plane to Mexico City, where he spent the night. The next afternoon he was dropped off in Durango at a lovely one-story house Nicholson had rented high in the mountains. The house was split into two sections—one for Nicholson and the other for offices and editing rooms. It was the check-in point for everyone arriving on the set. John arrived in bad shape, tired and depressed from the long trip.

Nicholson and Mary Steenburgen, his costar, whom he had rescued from a part-time job as a waitress at a Magic Pan, had already been at work for several weeks. Out on the set Harold Schneider, Gittes's co-producer, got a radio call from one of Nicholson's assistants. There is a big problem at the house, she said, you had better come quickly. Belushi has arrived.

He drove the half-hour to Nicholson's. Schneider, thirty-nine, went way back with the star. He had worked on *Easy Rider* in 1969, and *Drive, He Said,* the only other movie Nicholson had directed. His father, Abe Schneider, had been president, chairman and chief executive officer of Columbia Pictures. He wondered what Belushi, whom he'd never met, had done.

When he arrived, John, in sloppy slept-in clothes, was walking restlessly around the house. Schneider sat down on a stool at the kitchen counter and asked him what was the matter.

"I got to get out of here," he said, avoiding eye contact. He paced. "I got to go. I've got to get back. I can't live here." He had seen the hotel in Durango. "This is suck-o. The hotel is suck-o."

Schneider asked what they could do to help.

John paced some more. "I've got to get out of here."

Why? Schneider asked. He thought John was frightened. Perhaps working on a movie, working with Nicholson, scared him.

"Who needs all this?" John said. He opened a drawer and took out a large kitchen knife. He looked at it and felt the edge. The implication was that he might do something with it.

"Who needs all this?" John said again, and recited a litany of complaints—the long trip, the hotel, his need to leave.

"You got to do what you got to do," Schneider said.

John put the knife down, picked it up again, felt the blade. He seemed to be contemplating something far away.

"Look, John," Schneider said, "if you're doing this and saying you got to go, if you really believe it, do it for yourself. . . . If you're doing this for yourself, fine, I respect you."

John seemed to be listening, but he was moving around uneasily.

"If you're doing it because you think you're going to bring down the movie," Schneider said, "you're kidding yourself."

"Yeah," John said.

"If you think the movie is going to end, you're wrong. We're going to go on." Schneider knew one thing about movies. Once they started, they went forward. The cost of stopping was too great. "The one thing that we won't do is stop."

"What are you going to do?"

"We're going to put the camera here and film and someone is going to say 'Cut and print' without you. We're going on without you. We're going to go on."

"Yeah," John said, his thumb testing the edge of the knife.

Schneider and John talked for an hour and then the scene began to repeat. Schneider felt as if he were giving intensive psychological counseling. It was like talking someone off a ledge while suspecting the guy was not really going to jump. How could Brillstein do this to them? Brillstein should never have let Belushi come to Mexico alone. At least he should have warned them.

John continued to rant: suck-o place, suck-o hotel. Schneider didn't want the situation to blow up, he didn't want John to stab himself or anyone else, and he didn't want Belushi to leave. Nicholson wanted Belushi in the movie.

Gittes arrived. He had been wondering what had been keeping Schneider all afternoon. He took over. John had put down the knife, but he was still recounting his grievances. Gittes didn't think these rather vague complaints called for such a scene. This is all out of proportion, he told John. We're the best in this business; let's act that way. "Maybe you ought to take a nap," Gittes suggested. "You're really acting like an asshole. I'm being really honest. If this goes further, we're in deep shit."

John sat down and fell asleep.

When Nicholson arrived, it was dark. "Belushi is inside and he's a little crazed but is now asleep," Gittes said. Did Nicholson want to let him sleep it off, or should they get him out?

"What is this? A crash pad?" Nicholson asked. "I'm tired." Gittes went into the house, roused John, and told him no one was coming back, not even Nicholson. John got up finally and went outside. Gittes followed right behind.

It was obvious to John that Nicholson was home. Other cars had begun arriving. Gittes was on Belushi's heels when John turned suddenly and shoved him out of his way.

Gittes tensed and started to shake, both frightened and angry. "You better not do that again," he said coldly.

John stepped away and headed for his car, then turned and started back to the house.

Schneider shouted, "Get in the fucking car!"

John hesitated.

"Why the fuck stop?" Schneider shouted. "Go to your hotel, get in your car and go home!"

"That's what I want to do—go home. I've been telling you that for three hours."

Schneider raced forward. John pushed him. "You can shove him, but not me," Schneider said, grabbing John and pushing him against a wall, pinning his neck. "You fucker, who do you think you are?"

Several crew members pulled Schneider off. He was in a rage. "You son of a bitch! Who the fuck do you think you're pushing? Do that again and I'll kill you."

Belushi got in his car and drove off.

Schneider turned to Gittes. "I should have hit him three hours ago."

Late that night John showed up at the house of Bob Westmoreland, the makeup man.

John pounded on his door. "I did it!" he shouted.

Westmoreland let him in. "What?" he asked.

"I hit the producer," John said proudly.

The next day he was contrite. He took Gittes aside. "Hey, I really acted like an asshole," he said. "I'm sorry."

Gittes said, yeah, sure, and he tried to forget. Schneider was still angry.

Nicholson thought Gittes and Schneider should handle the matter. Nicholson, Schneider and some of the others were using lots of cocaine, mostly at night. Given that, Nicholson couldn't really lecture John. And anyway, he was attracted to problems like John. John was as sweet as they came. When Nicholson saw John, he knew he had to say something, but it was John who opened the door by apologizing.

"You ought to kiss their ass," Nicholson said. "If these producers weren't my friends, they would write you out, write your part out. And this would hang around your neck for ten years. If the studio [Paramount] were in charge, you'd be out of here and any career in movies seriously fucked."

Judy flew down to Mexico several days later and rented a small house about twenty minutes from the hotel. Then John got walking pneumonia from working in the hot sun, and a squib firecracker exploded near his hand and he had to be shot up with morphine. When he got home from the set each day, he and Judy would fix themselves drinks and just sit. It was boring; neither of them had much to do. Judy looked at the shooting schedule and realized that John was not going to finish in time for "Saturday Night." John went to Gittes, and Gittes said, yes, absolutely, you'll be done in time.

John made friends with another young actor, Ed Begley, Jr., the son of Ed Begley, a great character actor who had won the 1962 Academy Award for best supporting actor as Boss Finley in *Sweet Bird of Youth.* Like John, Begley, twenty-eight, also had a tiny part in *Goin' South,* and he loved the Mexican nightlife. He drank and used marijuana, cocaine and Quaaludes. Begley and John had some wild times together. On a couple of occasions Judy and John had to drag Begley out of the bars.

Judy returned to New York in September. The filming was not going to be finished in time for the beginning of the third season of "Saturday Night," and John was complaining bitterly that the producers had lied to him. Obviously they had no respect for him or his television work.

John flew back to New York for the opening show, now called "Saturday Night Live," on September 24. Then he flew back to Durango, where his frustration grew. The part was minuscule; there were days of just waiting around, and he had no dialogue with Nicholson in front of the camera. Nicholson and Mary Steenburgen were the movie; John, Begley, the others, were furniture.

John couldn't establish a relationship with Nicholson. Nicholson's house was the center. He had a cook, he gave dinners for the cast and crew, and it was made clear to John that he was to show up only when invited.

After three round trips between New York and Mexico, John had completed his part. He complained to Brillstein that he had felt like an outsider. He liked his own friends; they had no hierarchy, no rules. He was looking forward to making *Animal House* with *his* people—the *Lampoon* crowd.

Landis and Sean Daniels had to find a college campus to use as the set for Faber College since they couldn't afford expensive Hollywood sets. Nearly 50 colleges turned them down until the University of Oregon at Eugene finally consented. Everything would have to be done on location in about 30 days (with 6-day-a-week shooting schedules) if they were to stay within budget.

Barely a week after he had returned home from Mexico, on October 23, John was on a plane to Oregon; the plan was to finish *Animal House* by Thanksgiving. That meant another long commuting period—two long plane rides with inconvenient connections most weeks, bouncing from the Bleecker Street apartment to a house he and Judy were renting in Oregon. John said that drugs were essential just to keep to the schedule, let alone be up for his on-air and on-camera appearances. Judy stayed in Oregon because they couldn't afford the tickets for her to fly back and forth.

Landis wanted to get *Animal House* off on the right note. He had a cast of talented but relatively inexperienced stars, so he arranged for an intensive week of on-location rehearsals in order to build a sense of community. The actors were supposed to participate in fraternity life; Landis had the Deltas paint graffiti on the walls of a house they'd rented as their fraternity.

During these rehearsals, Landis was refining Bluto's character. He took more and more speaking lines from John to force him to use his body. John's face was so expressive that Landis could use it for punctuation—a question mark or exclamation point. When John entered a scene he took it over, and Landis started adjusting the movie around Bluto's entrances and exits.

Landis knew that there was only so much a director could do in rehearsals, so after a week, he began shooting. When he yelled "Action!" there was a tremendous surge in the performers and the crew, and in himself. Often, instead of allowing that energy to dissipate by yelling "Cut!"—losing the moment and wasting time and money to gear up for another take—Landis would scream, "Goddamn it, I'm still rolling! Do it again! Do it again!" Performers and crew scurried back to their positions to start over, the cameras and microphones recording every move. Landis wanted a sense of anarchy, and if the pace slowed, he picked up some object—a pencil or candy bar—and threw it at the actors on camera. He could edit around the flying objects, and it was a way to stir up everyone. Landis knew that if they were going to finish on time, he had to infect everyone with his own turmoil and panic. That meant he had to be *loud* in his directions, convey a feeling of abandon, turn them into college kids.

Landis quickly discovered that John could be lazy and undisciplined. They were rehearsing a cafeteria scene, a perfect vehicle to set up Bluto's insatiable cravings. Landis wanted John to walk down the cafeteria line and load his tray until it was a physical burden. As the camera started, Landis stood to one side shouting: Take that! Put that in your pocket! Pile that on the tray! Eat that now, right there!

John followed each order, loading his pockets and tray, stuffing his mouth with a plate of Jello in one motion.

Bluto sits down at a table with some members of the rival Omega House, who look on in disgust as he attacks the pile of food, picking it up with his hands, squeezing food between his fingers. They call him a pig.

"See," John dares them, raising a finger in dead seriousness, his eyebrows dancing fancifully, "if you can guess what I am now." He fills his mouth with a bowl of mashed potatoes, his cheeks puffing up to the brink. With both hands he suddenly smacks his cheeks together, spewing potatoes all over the Omegas.

"I'm a zit! Get it?"

The Omegas go after him in a fury, chasing him around the cafeteria. John pops up in the middle of the room, yells "*Food fight!*," and the air is filled with flying food.

During another scene—the night break-in at the dean's office—John fell down. "Get up, you fucker!" Landis screamed with the cameras still running. John responded to these loud instructions, his face showing the right amount of disorientation and distress.

Karen Allen, a young actress with some serious theatrical experience, was playing Katy, a mature girl who is skeptical about the goings-on at Delta House, and about the escapades of her Delta boyfriend, Boon. Allen found John astonishingly shy and vulnerable. Rather than being a confident established television star, he seemed nervous about meeting everyone, about fitting in.

She realized that Landis's technique was contributing to *Animal House* an important layer of humor not in the script. The director would fairly fall down himself to get everybody laughing, and then direct the cameraman to roll while everyone was in hysterics. At first this seemed odd to Allen, but then she noticed that everyone had been cast so well that they were really playing aspects of themselves.

When Sean Daniels, Universal's representative on the set, met John for the first time one night, John was wearing a Chicago Black Hawk hockey jersey.

"Hi," John said gruffly, "got the cassette?"

Daniels said he did, a tape of the famous rock song "Shout," which was to be used in the movie.

"Let's go to my room," John said.

John popped the tape into his stereo system and turned the music way too loud. "Okay, I like that," he said, as if it were his decision. In fact, John had nothing to do with music decisions or, for that matter, any other decisions. Daniels barely did.

During the third week of filming, Landis was looking for John for a scheduled scene. He was not on the set, and no one knew where he was. Landis found him smoking pot in the washroom up in a dormitory.

"What are you doing?" Landis asked.

"Getting high," John replied.

"Come here, you fuck!" Landis shouted, and almost dragged him out of the bathroom. It was as if John considered getting high part of the job—like putting on a costume, learning his lines, getting made up or rehearsing. And he wasn't the only one getting high on the set. Karen Allen saw pot all over, and since it was a *Lampoon* project, she wasn't surprised. A little pot probably wouldn't hurt.

There couldn't be a *Lampoon* movie without sex, Landis realized, certainly not a college fraternity film. The script called for several scenes with above-the-waist nudity, the best involving Bluto, who was to take a ladder one night and climb up to the second story of the neighboring sorority house to watch the girls having a pillow fight in their nightgowns. The women were supposed to bare their breasts, and Landis had had some difficulty finding actresses who were willing to do it.

In the Peeping Tom scene, Landis focused on John watching one of the girls undress. To emphasize John's delight, Landis had John break frame and turn to the camera and acknowledge the audience. John turned and smiled, joyfully raised an eyebrow as if half his face were going to fly away, then lowered it and turned back to the girl.

Daniels heard that more and more people were showing up at the screenings of the dailies—the rough, unedited film shot the day before and available to Universal executives in Los Angeles as a sort of progress report. But despite his own enthusiasm for the work they were doing, Daniels knew that the top executives would keep their distance until they had a certified hit and the box office receipts to prove it.

"What are they telling you down in the studio?" John asked him.

It looked good, Daniels said, but that was only his opinion, and he couldn't honestly tell. The Universal executives were pessimistic because they'd had so many recent failures.

"They giving you shit?" John asked. "You just wait. . . . You'll be able to tell them to fuck off."

The villainous and spiteful Dean Wormer finally decides that he's had enough headaches from Delta House and calls some of the fraternity brothers into his office to deliver a scathing lecture about their poor academic performance. Bluto's grade point average was the worst (0.0), and when the dean looks up to see how this bad news is being received, John has two long pencils hanging from his nostrils.

Later, the dean orders the Deltas off campus for cheating on their exams, and back at Delta House everyone is silent and morose.

John knew he had the crucial scene, and he worked hard on memorizing the lines exactly. They were his longest and most difficult. Bluto was going to incite his Delta brothers to action.

"Hey, what's this lying around shit?" Bluto says, coming into Delta House and seeing his brothers so forlorn.

"War's over, man," says Otter (Tim Matheson in place of Chevy Chase).

"What? Over? You say over? *Nothing* is over until *we* decide it is."

Rousing, inspirational, patriotic music is heard.

"Was it over when the Germans bombed Pearl Harbor?"

Otter mouths, "Germans?"

"Hell no," John continues. "And it ain't over now. Because when the going gets tough . . ." he yells, caught, not remembering the end of the saying. He finally adds, ". . . the tough get going! Who's with me? Let's go!"

He runs from the room. No one stirs from the gloom. John pads back in.

"What the fuck happened to the Delta I used to know?" he asks. "Where's the spirit? Where's the guts, huh? This could be the greatest night of our lives, but you're going to let it be the worst." Mocking their cowardice, he says in a high voice, " 'We're afraid to go with you, Bluto. We might get in trouble.' " He shouts at them, "Well, *kiss* my ass from now on! Not *me!* I'm not going to take this. Wormer, he's a dead man!

Marmalard [head of Omega House], dead! Neidermeyer [head of the ROTC unit] . . .''

"Dead!" Otter yells. Bluto is right. All they need, Otter says, is a stupid gesture on somebody's part.

"We're just the guys to do it!" John shouts. "Let's go. *Go, go, go! Charge!*"

This time everyone follows Bluto to wage an attack on the homecoming parade, which includes throwing marbles under the feet of the school's marching ROTC unit, the destruction of the viewing stand where the town mayor and Dean Wormer are sitting, and colorful smoke bombs lobbed into the street, causing panic among the onlookers and turning the parade route into a battleground.

John had to do some of his own stunts in the scene. Dressed in a swashbuckling pirate costume, he is chased up the side of a building onto the roof of a store. Trapped, he finally swings Tarzan-style down to the street to make his getaway. He had taken some coke to get up the nerve.

The filming was finished, but it would be another six months at least before the movie was edited and ready for release. John returned to "Saturday Night Live" full-time. He was becoming closer to Don Novello, the writer who also regularly played Father Guido Sarducci, a Vatican gossip columnist with a routine built around a sweet priest who tried to mesh the twentieth-century world with the church's teachings.

John now had time to prepare for longer, more detailed sketches, and he told Novello about his father's old restaurants. One had been named Olympia Lunch. Novello developed a long skit about a small Greek restaurant with a limited menu and no substitutions. None.

On January 28, 1978, the show opened on a short-order diner with a few swivel stools and fewer customers. John, the management, is in a white shirt, sleeves rolled up, a thin black tie. He has the absent gaze of the assembly-line worker until Jane Curtin orders a tuna salad sandwich.

"Nope," he snaps, order book poised. "No tuna. Cheezbugga? . . . Cheezbugga? Comma, comma, comma . . . we ain't got all day. Cheezbugga? Comma, comma. Whadda ya gonna have?"

Curtin makes a few attempts. No luck. A Coke?

"No Coke," John says. "Pepsi."

French fries?

"No french. Cheaps."

She gives in.

Triumphantly, John orders, "One cheezbugga, one Pepsi, one cheaps!"

He answers the phone to take an order. "Cheezbugga, cheezbugga, cheezbugga, cheezbugga."

Aykroyd, at the grill chewing a toothpick, repeats the order, grabs four patties and slaps them on the grill.

Comedian Robert Klein, the host, comes in to order breakfast.

"No-no-no-no-no—cheezbugga!" John insists. It is not too early in the day for a cheeseburger, he says, pointing to all the others who are eating them.

"Look!" He rattles off "Cheezbugga!" eight times.

Aykroyd thinks John is placing orders and grabs eight pre-made burgers and slaps them on the grill.

Klein relents. "I'll have a cheeseburger."

"One cheezbugga!"

"No cheezbugga," Aykroyd snaps. He is out.

In February, 1978, Jimmy Belushi, then twenty-three, was appearing for the first time as a regular member at Second City in Chicago. He had written a sketch about the reunion of two brothers, "White Horse Tavern," which was drawn from his 1973 visit there with John. Jimmy chose to play the older brother.

The two brothers meet, and Jimmy says, "Give us two shots of white grain alcohol."

"Oh, before I forget," the younger brother says, "Mom and Dad say hi."

"Good," Jimmy replies. "I don't want to talk about it . . . they make me feel guilty. Holidays are the worst. . . . Mom, Mom, I mean I love Mom. Ah, she's a nightmare . . . I used to go to the freezer, get some chocolate ripple ice cream, dish it out, start to eat it. Boom! Here comes Mom. 'Got enough? Going to leave some for the rest of the family?' "

They joke about Mom, criticize her. "Don't ever say I said that," Jimmy says.

The younger brother had just received his degree in English literature.

"English lit don't mean shit," Jimmy says. "A degree's not important; living right and dying right, that's important. . . . See this bar here, Mr. Lit? . . . See that stool right there on the end? Dylan Thomas died right there, man . . . 27 shots of white grain alcohol piled like a Christmas tree. He sat there boom, boom, boom, boom, boom! Went into a coma, went into a hospital across the street and died, man. Sheet over the head, dead gone dead. Right fucking there."

They agree it was a romantic death and toast, "To Dylan Thomas, living right, dying right!"

Jimmy says, "Give me two more shots right fucking here."

The younger brother recites:

"And you, my father, there on the sad height,
Curse, bless, me now with your fierce tears, I
    pray.
Do not go gentle into that good night.
Rage, rage against the dying of the light."

Then Jimmy recites:

"The only seas I saw
Were the see-saw seas . . .
Let me shipwreck in your thighs."

They agree that it takes a ship five hours to wreck itself. Together, drunk:

"He went into a coma
Over to the hospital.
Sheet over the head,
Dead, gone, dead!
Give me two more shots
Right fucking here."

Ernest Hemingway is mentioned. Jimmy says:

"Shotgun in the mouth
Pull the trigger
Brains against the wall."

They recite poems of Virginia Woolf:

"Walk into the ocean
Water in the lungs
Sheet over the head . . ."

Sylvia Plath:

"Head in the Oven
Turn on the gas
Like a chocolate chip cookie. . . ."

"You want some advice?" Jimmy asks. "You're going to die. . . . I'm going to die. I'll probably die in bed."

"Shipwreck," the younger brother says, wishing the older brother to die making love.

Jimmy: "Give me 27 shots right fucking here."

Jimmy received rave reviews in the Chicago papers, and a few weeks later he visited John in New York. He was afraid John would be upset about the sketch because it was close to home. Sitting on the blue couch at the Bleecker Street apartment, he waited for John to turn to the subject.

"Hey," John finally said, "hear you're doing a scene about me?"

"Well, John, it's not about you exactly. It's about Dylan Thomas and the romanticism of suicide."

"That's the last time I take you to a bar."

Tom Schiller, one of the regular writers on "Saturday Night Live," approached Belushi one day to say he had a go-ahead from Michaels to do a short film, and he wanted to do something with an old person. Belushi did a great old man; Schiller wanted a solo performance.

John agreed to spend two days. But he knew something about movies now.

"Did you ever have a production assistant before?" John asked. He had learned about the young people, generally women, who assisted on Hollywood movies, doing anything from getting coffee to helping the production.

"No," Schiller replied.

"You do now," John explained. He suggested that Laila Nabulsi, a friend of his and Judy's, be hired.

"Do you have a trailer for the shooting?" John asked. They would need a place to meet, rest, go over the script and put on makeup. "Farting Room," Nicholson had called it. "If you don't ask for these things, you never get them," John said.

A few days later, they were ready to film. Schiller was astonished at John's zeal; it was how Schiller imagined Marlon Brando. John bowed his head, studied his lines, and in the silence of the trailer, he seemed to be pushing himself into the character.

The scene is a cemetery in Brooklyn. Fresh snow is on the ground; it is pleasantly cold and the air is wonderful. Schiller had set up the camera. Belushi, dressed like an old gray eminence in a heavy, dark coat, arrives with hesitant step at the "Not Ready for Prime Time Cemetery." He stumbles through the gravesites.

"They all thought I'd be the first to go," Belushi says in a deep, raspy voice. "I was one of those 'Live fast, die young, leave a good-looking corpse' types, you know.

"I guess they were wrong. There they are. All of my friends . . ." He points at a grave. "Here's Gilda Radner. Ah, she had her own show on Canadian television for years and years—'The Gilda Radner Show.' She was a button, God bless her. There Laraine is. They say she murdered her DJ husband. . . . Jane Curtin . . . she died of complications during cosmetic surgery. There's Garrett Morris. Garrett left . . . then he died of an overdose of heroin. . . .

"Over here's Chevy Chase. He died right after his first movie with Goldie Hawn.

"Over here's Danny Aykroyd. I bet he loved his Harley too much. They clocked him at 175 miles an hour before the crash. He was a blur. I was called in to identify his body. I recognized him by his webbed toes.

"The 'Saturday Night' show was the best experience of my life," John says. "Now they're all gone, and I miss every one of them. Why me? Why'd I live so long? They're all dead."

He pauses and thinks about it. "I'll tell you why, 'cause I'm a dancer," he says, changing his voice and posture, becoming youthful, dancing over the graves.

John had done it all in one take and had got everything on-the-dot perfect. Schiller felt as if he were working with someone who had been in show business for 40 years. He asked John why he had changed his voice at the end for the line " 'Cause I'm a dancer."

"I like to change the level of reality."

Deep baroque music was added, and the film, "Don't Look Back in Anger," ran March 11, 1978.

Michaels thought that it was prophecy. John would outlast them all.

9

Actress Talia Shire was awakened by the phone early one morning in March 1978.

"Hi. It's John."

"John?"

"John Belushi."

"Do you realize what time it is? It's three-thirty in the morning."

John said he was truly sorry. He hadn't realized it was that late, but he wanted to say how glad he was that the two of them were going to be working together.

Shire said she, too, was looking forward to the movie and suggested they talk later.

By 1978, Shire, thirty-two, had established herself in movies. She had two Academy Award nominations for best supporting actress—one for her role in *The Godfather, Part II* (1974) and the other for *Rocky* (1976), in which she played Sylvester Stallone's shy girlfriend.

Her next movie, *Old Boyfriends,* was her first chance at a leading role. It was built around her part—a recent divorcée who reads her old diaries and goes on a quest to find the three boyfriends who had the greatest influence on her life. Belushi was to play the self-centered high-school flame.

Shire knew Hollywood. She was married to composer David Shire (*Saturday Night Fever*), and director Francis Ford Coppola was her brother. She wanted to get out from under their shadows.

Old Boyfriends seemed to be a perfect vehicle. It was to be the first film directed by Joan Tewkesbury, who had written the screenplay for Robert Altman's controversial country and western musical drama *Nashville* (1975). Tewkesbury was the rising woman in the industry, having started as a script girl only eight years before. *Old Boyfriends* was one of the underdog productions of the year, with a budget of about $2.5 million.

Tewkesbury thought Belushi was ideal for Eric Katz, the man who had never grown out of high school. Sixteen years after his graduation, he is running a tuxedo rental business and making appearances with his rock band at Holiday Inn bars and high school dances. She decided to go meet John.

Tewkesbury was impressed with his presence—fast, quick, bright. It seemed that he could pick a leaf off a tree and do a twenty-minute improvisation with it. She sensed that he didn't have an anchor. If he had, it would curb his talent.

John told Tewkesbury he was excited that Eric played in a rock band and that the script called for him to sing. In spite of the stories she had heard about his drugs, she wanted him, and a deal was worked out. Belushi would get $20,000 for six days of filming.

Shortly before shooting was to begin, Tewkesbury was invited to see a rough cut of *Animal House*. From the first moment John appeared on the screen, she was both impressed and troubled. The movie would be a smash, but Bluto was so strong and fresh that she feared it would overpower the dramatic role she had in mind. John's was to be only a 25-minute segment in the middle of the film.

About a week before shooting, John was in Los Angeles to be fitted for his costumes, and Tewkesbury drove him over to meet Shire, with whom he had had several more late-night phone conversations.

On the way she told John he would have to sing on only two days during the filming. Please don't do any drugs; save your voice.

"I'm not doing anything," John said.

At Shire's house John went right for her two-year-old son Matthew. He petted a house plant, called it a "nice kitty." He called the table a "chair." The kid loved the show.

Shire immediately liked John. She had seen some of his "Saturday Night Live" skits and had noted that he paid careful attention to detail and had precise body and face movements, like a dramatic actor. He hid behind those details. He had a shy, uncertain side. Shire liked his wordless eloquence.

John flew back to be in the "Saturday Night Live" show on March 25. Michaels and the cast, seeing they were about to lose John for the third time that season to another movie, accused him, only half in jest, of "going Hollywood." They kidded him about whether he was going to change his name. They dubbed him Kevin Scott and joked that he was probably going to star in "Grizzly Adams," a TV series about a man and his bear. John didn't think it was funny, and when Aykroyd, the "Weekend Update" anchorman, tried three times to introduce him on the air as "Kevin Scott," John didn't respond. Aykroyd finally yelled "John!" and only then did Belushi do his sketch.

Later in the show, John was cast in another sketch that expressed a general sentiment about him. A husband and wife, Bill Murray and Jane Curtin, are sitting in their living room late at night entertaining a guest. Murray stretches, yawns: "Well, ah, we're glad you could stop by"—he has another fit of yawning—"but it's getting pretty late and we better get to bed now."

John, the guest, couldn't care less. "Don't you have any other records besides these?" he says, flipping through their collection. "I think I'm going to borrow this one."

Curtin, staring at John with a look of torment, produces a blood-curdling scream. Horror music comes up, and an eerie voice-over says: "It came without warning. They were just being polite. They didn't realize that they would be stuck with 'The Thing That Wouldn't Leave.' "

On Monday, April 3, 1978, John arrived in Los Angeles for his first scenes in *Old Boyfriends*. Tewkesbury had arranged to shoot one of the musical scenes first. She knew it was important to John that he put the music together, so she let him pick the musicians and the songs. Above all, she wanted to make him comfortable. Not only was this his first dramatic role, but all the authority figures on the set were women. She did not want John to feel threatened.

Shire was struck by John's confidence. She had grown up around music, and she couldn't believe that John had the nerve to sing off-key on camera. He didn't seem to care, and he was so full of energy that it was effective.

As they did a couple of quick scenes together, John seemed relaxed. He allowed himself to make mistakes, and Shire envied that. John barreled into his scenes, improvising when he flubbed or missed a cue, working around his mistakes as if he had only one chance at it.

"You don't have to talk fast," Tewkesbury said. "This is not 'Saturday Night Live'; we're not going to cut you off after 90 minutes."

The next day was reserved for a night scene, and John wasn't due on the set until dusk. That afternoon Brillstein got a call from Harold Schneider, one of the producers of *Goin' South*. Nicholson was still in postproduction, and he needed Belushi for about twenty minutes to dub two lines into the sound track.

"He needs $100 in cash for expenses," Brillstein told Schneider. "He's got to stay over, and he needs a car and driver." Brillstein was furious at the way John had been treated in Mexico and wanted to give Schneider a hard time.

Schneider reported to Nicholson. "Bullshit," Nicholson said. "I'll do it." A master at imitation, Nicholson dubbed the two lines perfectly. Schneider warned him that they could get into trouble with the unions. They'd get John to come over.

Schneider had been angry with Belushi since their fight in Mexico. The request for $100 and a car was insulting. "Fucking small-change artists," he told Gittes. He promised he would pay them in kind. Schneider sent someone to the bank to get $100 worth of nickels, dimes and quarters. He found the smallest car in the studio, a Subaru, and sent it for John with a woman driver. John arrived and did the dubbing quickly. Schneider handed him his expense money—in a large bag.

John left quietly and went to Brillstein's office, where he burst into tears. He was sure Nicholson had been behind a door laughing. Brillstein was furious. He called Paramount and shouted that they would never ever get John again, for anything. Then he fired off a savage telegram to Schneider, accusing him of unprofessionalism and meanness.

Schneider tacked the telegram up on his wall.

When John arrived on the *Old Boyfriends* set that night on a hillside overlooking Los Angeles, Joan Tewkesbury saw that he was upset and asked him what was wrong. John explained that he'd done some work on *Goin' South* that day. The only reason he'd done the film was to get some experience with his childhood heroes, he said, and they'd let him down.

John went to his trailer, and Talia Shire came by to work on a scene they would do together. John worried. He kept wanting to perfect the sequence and ended by showing his vulnerability. It was as if he was afraid his talent was not enough, Shire thought.

Outside, Tewkesbury set up to shoot the climactic scene between John and Shire. John had humiliated Shire in high school, implying to his friends that he had slept with her. Now she was set to get even.

It was very cold, and the crew was in parkas and thick gloves. Tewkesbury called for John and Shire. The scene was to take place in Shire's car. She was going to seduce John. He had to take off his pants.

Once in the car, John was still nervous. "Please don't make me take my clothes off," he pleaded. Shire was surprised at how sensitive he seemed about his body.

Tewkesbury came over to the car.

"I'm going to have to stand up there with my ass hanging out," John said.

"You're never going to be uncovered," Tewkesbury assured him. His socks would be on, and his shirt would hang down low. She promised him that no one would laugh at him.

The cameras started to roll, with Shire and John crowded into the front seat.

"This time we're really going to go all the way. Come on, Eric, let's get naked."

"Now you're talking," Eric says as they both start fumbling with buttons. She leans over and loosens his belt roughly.

"Hey, hey, hey. Jesus, Di. Take it easy. What's the rush? It's been sixteen years."

"Why should it be any more?"

"You're going through with this, aren't you?" he asks.

"Yes."

"I'm a little bit high," Eric says.

"You going to talk or fuck?"

"This is really heavy for me. . . . Hey, listen, Di, you haven't changed a bit. I mean, you were always the classiest girl in the school. I mean, you know, you were different from the other girls. You had brains. And I respected you for that. . . ."

"Tell me about the other girls. Does it always come so easy for you?"

"Easy?" John asks with a glazed look. "God, well—easy? What do you think I am? A pistol?"

"Eric, come on," Shire says, climbing on top of him. "Beg me, Eric. Beg me. . . ."

John flinches. "Wait a minute. What's happening here? . . . Look, this is a mistake. . . . You shouldn't fuck with people's dreams. . . . Just take me home."

Shire continues to attack him, opening the door. They roll out onto the ground.

"Eric, I'm going to rape you, okay?"

"Okay. God."

"You stay here and let me go get ready for you."

"Okay. God, I can hardly believe it."

Shire goes back to the car, locks the doors and turns on the engine. Eric gets up and bangs on the window as she drives off, leaving him staring after her in his socks and shoes, screaming obscenities. Tewkesbury was pleased with the scene and wrapped up for the night.

When she was completely finished with John's segment she was glad drugs hadn't been an issue. Tewkesbury was sick of drugs. She hated what they were doing to the movie industry, wrecking people, killing timing and the clarity.

She asked John if he had ever thought of not doing drugs for a period of time. "You're terrific straight," she said. "Don't kill yourself, because I want to work with you again some day down the line."

John lifted his eyebrows up and down and smiled. She let it go.

By the spring of 1978, *Animal House* was ready. A test audience was brought in, and 93 percent gave the movie a high rating. That was fantastic, Daniels and Landis agreed, but no matter how carefully test audiences are picked, there is no proof like an audience that has paid their own money. The real test would be a sneak preview.

Universal executives chose the 1,065-seat Century 21 Theater in Denver for the first sneak preview because it was middle America, the heartland, not L.A. or New York. Daniels and Landis flew in, and Landis brought a tape recorder. Daniels hoped just to survive the experience.

The theater darkened. Two freshmen leave Omega House and walk across campus to Delta House. They walk up behind Bluto, standing with a beer in his hand, his head down.

"Excuse me, sir," one of the pledges says. "Is this the Delta House?"

Bluto swings around to face them. He weaves a little, drunk. There is a trickling sound. They all look down. Bluto is urinating on their shoes.

The theater erupted in hysterics.

The movie ran 109 minutes, and at the end an update on each of the characters flashed on the screen. Two Omega members are accounted for:

Gregory Marmalard '63   Nixon White House aide, raped in prison, 1974

Douglas C. Neidermeyer '63   Killed in Vietnam by his own troops

The final shot was of John and a woman in a car:
SENATOR AND MRS. JOHN BLUTARSKY, WASHINGTON, D.C.
The audience applauded.

Daniels raced to the phone in the lobby and called John, who picked up after half a ring.

"They loved it!" Daniels said. It looked like the best preview ever.

The good news was that no one could hear the sound track because of the laughter.

Landis got on the phone, turned on his tape recorder and played some of the audience laughter for John. It was honest laughter, robust. The audience had applauded 35 times and given them a standing ovation at the end. Landis felt as though he had shot the moon.

Dan Aykroyd moved deliberately around his dressing room just before the opening of "Saturday Night Live" on April 22, 1978, near the end of the third season. He had a mania for detail and everything had to be just right. Danny was not simply going to play another role in another sketch. He was going to *become* the character: look, act, even think like him.

He adjusted his tie in the mirror; it was perfect: very thin and conservative, jet black, tied with a small knot close around his neck. The white, crisply starched shirt set the tie off, and the black suit was baggy with narrow lapels and pants legs that brushed the floor. A Timex watch was wrapped around his left wrist. The dark porkpie hat with a black band settled comfortably at a slight angle. Of course, the sunglasses were crucial. They had to be Ray-Bans, model 5022-G15.

Nobody, not even the police, could see through his disguise. He had to pass unnoticed in straight society. The shades hid his stoned, bloodshot eyes. The suit was a neat outer wrapping for an inner madness, a clever diversion, the kind Lenny Bruce used to use. This guy was an outlaw, a renegade junkie who could reach into his pocket at any moment, pull out his harmonica and produce the blues.

In the next dressing room, Belushi was haphazardly throwing on an identical costume. His shirt collar didn't fit properly, and his hat was dark brown instead of black.

At 11:30 P.M., Paul Shaffer, the pianist for the back-up band on "Saturday Night Live," faced the studio camera from a sound booth overlooking the stage. Speaking in a nasal voice with a Brooklyn accent, Shaffer said: "Welcome to 'Rock Concert.'

"In 1969, Marshall Checker, of the Legendary Checker's Records, called me on a new blues act that had been playing in small, funky clubs on Chicago's South Side.

"Today . . . they are no longer an authentic blues act but have managed to become a viable commercial product. So now, let's join Joliet Jake and his silent brother Elwood—the Blues Brothers."

Under the bright studio lights, John and Aykroyd belted out an energetic version of "Hey, Bartender."

John sang, his body in constant motion. He snapped his fingers, grabbed the microphone, unbuttoned his suit coat. Sweat trickled down his face.

Aykroyd stood just behind him to the side, stamping his foot to the music and blowing into a Special 20 harp. Dan was an accomplished player. Occasionally John glanced over his shoulder as Aykroyd blew an especially tight sequence of chords, strong and on key.

Turning the spotlight over to a solo by Aykroyd, John went to the rear of the stage to dance, his arms waving at his sides as he planted his right foot and spun around in circles, then shuffling his feet, then flapping his elbows, keeping time with a clenched fist.

He danced back to the mike and started singing again in his husky voice, out of breath, the words coming out short and quick. His head bobbed up and down with the music as he yelled enthusiastically into the microphone. At the end of the song, John grabbed the mike and delivered a primal scream. Then he and Aykroyd stood silently—looking like CIA agents. There was hearty applause.

Later that night, the Blues Brothers came back on to sing "I Don't Know." John did cartwheels.

The audience loved the performance, but it seemed perplexed. "Saturday Night Live" had a tradition of having some of the biggest names in the music business as their guests—Billy Joel, The Band, Bonnie Raitt, George Harrison. But here were two of the regular cast members dressed in weird costumes booked as the musical guests. Was it a joke? Aykroyd played a mean harp, and Belushi—even though he had a lousy voice—put his heart and soul into singing, and that was the power of the blues. But they were two of the hottest comedians in the country. This couldn't be serious.

One who was deadly serious, however, was John. For about a year he had been in love with the blues—the soulful wails and vibrating voices of black musicians. Ever since he had been introduced to the old blues during the filming of *Animal House,* the music had become an obsession with him. He bought records and took them home, and there with Judy, Mitch Glazer and Laila Nabulsi, he listened hour after hour. The four formed an informal lonely hearts club and listened to Ray Charles, B. B. King, James Brown and others. John would listen for hours, night after night, with the volume so high the air shook.

After one particular session, Glazer said to Laila, "I hate the blues."

"Me too," she said.

But not John. They knew that when he got interested in something, there was no turning him off, and he would find a way to use it. Judy realized that it was like his rock-and-roll obsession in high school.

John and Aykroyd had warmed up the "Saturday Night Live" audience for a year doing various old tunes as the Blues Brothers, until finally, after badgering from John, Lorne Michaels had let them do it on air. John had told Judy and Laila that the Blues Brothers was a way to reestablish his relationship with Aykroyd, who seemed to feel left out since John and Judy had married.

Now, after their successful appearance, John and Dan didn't want to let it go. They got Brillstein to contact Michael Klenfner, a senior vice president at Atlantic Records, to convince him that Belushi and Aykroyd's TV popularity might carry over. A one-record contract was negotiated for $125,000.

Brillstein arranged for the Blues Brothers to appear as the opening act in a nine-night engagement that comedian Steve Martin had scheduled at the Universal Amphitheater in Los Angeles the next fall. They would get only $15,000 for the performances, but Brillstein thought the money was not that important. Much of Martin's fame came from his guest appearances on "Saturday Night Live," and that would almost certainly give the Blues Brothers a friendly L.A. audience to make a live recording. Live would be like a vaudeville show, much more in John and Aykroyd's style than a studio recording.

John took charge and began to assemble the band. He wanted the best available musicians playing behind them so that the Blues Brothers would be taken seriously; it was not to be a comedy show, like *Lemmings;* it was not a lark, like his old high school band or the band in *Old Boyfriends.* John wanted to work with the authentic blues players who had kept the genre alive in the face of the increasing popularity of soul music, jazz, country and western, rock and roll and disco.

The "Saturday Night Live" orchestra had some of the hottest musicians in the country, so John began his search in-house.

The first person he hired was piano player Paul "The Shiv" Shaffer, a solid music arranger, to be the band leader.

Next was the twenty-one-year-old black drummer from the show, Steve "Getdwa" Jordan, a talented graduate of New York City's High School of the Performing Arts.

Then John raided the horn section, hiring two saxophone players, Tom "Bones" Malone and Lou "Blue Lou" Marini, and a trumpet player, Alan "Mr. Fabulous" Rubin.

Finally, John took on a little-known black guitarist from Chicago named Matt "Guitar" Murphy, who had played with such legends as Muddy Waters, Chuck Berry and Little Junior Parker.

Alternating good-natured jokes and hard sell, John got two of the greats, bass player Donald "Duck" Dunn and guitarist Steve "The Colonel" Cropper. Cropper had cowritten "Dock of the Bay" (1968) with Otis Redding.

Judy was concerned that drugs and music were practically synonymous. So much of the rock mystique was wrapped up in the drug culture, and having tested the waters, John was now swimming in them. He would stay up for several days, and it was interfering with their relationship and sex life.

"It's my life-style," he said. He would try sometimes to give up cocaine, but people kept offering it to him. He'd refuse, and they would push. Belushi was no fun just watching others do it; he was funny when he joined in. Cocaine gave him a positiveness about himself; it made everything important and intense.

A cocaine dealer who called himself "David 69" and who had a telephone beeper and traveled around New York on roller skates guaranteed delivery within the hour and charged $125 a gram. John had bought $1,000 worth several times, and it seemed to disappear in less than a week.

Judy was trying to quit cocaine and finding it hard. Their friends kept offering it. She liked the energy that came at first; it was essential for late nights if she was going to stick it through with John until 4, 5, 6 or even 7 A.M. Then she found herself getting anxious and grinding her teeth. Her mouth and skin were dry. She realized that the cocaine gave her energy in the short run; in the long run it robbed her of it. In May 1978 she quit.

John had some free time before the *Animal House* premiere, and he and Judy went up to Martha's Vineyard, an island four miles off the coast of Massachusetts that was a favorite summer retreat for show-business personalities and writers. One July evening they went out with a few friends and wound up at the home of singers James Taylor and Carly Simon. Taylor and Simon, who had separate and extraordinarily successful careers, had married in 1972 and the next year had teamed up for a hit single, "Mockingbird." Taylor, thirty, whose anguished and compassionate songs sometimes told of his two, brief institutionalizations in a mental hospital, was just back for a brief rest in the middle of a long summer tour. Simon was wrestling with her husband's heroin addiction, and she viewed the Belushis as an uninvited and unwelcome party. But if Simon was wary, Taylor was happy. Dreading another all-night binge and the next day's sleep-in, Simon turned inward. John approached her. She knew immediately that he was on cocaine. He began a chest-thumping coke rap, saying that he was worried about Taylor, who, he said, had no control over his drug habit. Not me, John said, I have control and I want to help. He was going to exert the same good influence on Taylor as he did on himself. And Taylor was not going to be able to live with himself if he didn't go back to making the great music he used to make, like "Fire and Rain."

Simon didn't attempt to say anything because John wouldn't be listening. They never did when they were on drugs. They only wanted to talk. And John was saying Simon was a saint—tolerant, understanding. Simon knew that he was buttering her up, that he knew what she wanted to hear. He had a program for saving her husband. Drugs were bad for anyone, John said, but they unleashed something unique that helped a performer, and the key was to find some way to retain that without being destructive. He didn't say how that was going to work, but he implied it was a matter of personal discipline. Such as he practiced; he was high because he wanted to be.

Simon walked out to the sun porch to greet Judy, whom she barely knew. Judy's hip clothes and attitude seemed to say, "I go as fast as John. Watch out. Don't touch me." As they talked, however, it became clear that neither of them liked the direction the evening was heading.

"I've tried doing everything," Judy said in her fast, peppery, high-pitched voice, shaking her head from side to side. "I've tried doing drugs with him. I've tried not doing drugs with him. I've tried going to a shrink and not going to a shrink. We tried going to a shrink together, and we've tried going to a shrink separately."

Simon burst into tears. If Judy, who seemed willing to try anything to make her relationship with John work, couldn't succeed, Simon had no chance.

John and Judy returned to New York to attend the *Animal House* premiere. No more low-budget celebrations; this was the big time, and Hollywood knew how to kick off a picture with a splash. Universal invited Brillstein to the premiere in New York. They sent him a first-class airplane ticket, provided him with a limousine and gave him a suite.

Not everyone was optimistic. The day before the premiere, Sean Daniels talked with the president of Universal, Ned Tanen. The movie previewed well, Tanen said, but it opens tomorrow, and I think you should probably decide which building to jump from.

The day of the premiere, July 28, 1978, at 9:05 A.M., Landis wrote a note to his star: "John, I love you. You bless my movie and my life. Thank you."

Before the evening premiere, John and Brillstein took a walk down Fifth Avenue. Brillstein wasn't sure if they were in for a big disappointment. Things didn't turn out well in show business that often. But John seemed on top of the world as they gazed at the windows of the famous shops. John wanted some fancy new boots or shoes. Brillstein said he would buy him a pair, and they decided on two pairs of expensive Bally shoes from Switzerland. John was in good shape, and he looked handsome in his full growth of summer beard. The two heavy, bearded men looked almost like father and son. Brillstein felt that close to John.

At the premiere John got up from his seat, wandered into the lobby and told Daniels and Brillstein that it wasn't going over as well as he had expected.

New York premiere audiences were notoriously aloof, they reminded him.

"Wait till we get to Chicago with this," John said to Brillstein and Daniels, reassuring himself as much as them. "Best comedy city. New York—they're all pussies."

The next day the *New York Times* had cool praise in a short, seven-paragraph review: " 'Animal House' is by no means one long howl, but it's often very funny, with gags that are effective in a dependable, all-purpose way."

They went on to Chicago, and John took Sean Daniels on an all-night tour of his favorite bars, bands, old haunts. John was supposed to be up about 6:45 A.M. the next morning for the early TV shows. When Daniels called his room in the Whitehall Hotel, the phone was off the hook. The door was chained and John didn't answer. Daniels had the hotel staff take the door off its hinges. John was asleep, but they dragged him into the shower and onto the shows. And he was right; the reception was more friendly all around.

Within a week *Animal House* had opened at hundreds of theaters across the country. The reviewers showed grudging respect. *Newsweek* said it was a "panty raid on respectability . . . low humor of a high order." The *Los Angeles Times* arts editor Charles Champlin found the movie "paradoxically innocent and even endearing." And John was "the principal figure, the most mastodontal of the animals but, in the prevailing spirit of the piece, oddly likeable." The *Washington Post*'s Gary Arnold saw it as John's movie: "John Belushi gets what could be a phenomenal movie career off to a soaring low-comedy start. . . . Belushi's sensational impact may obscure the movie's abundance of fresh faces and adept comic performances."

Young people began flocking to the movie. Box-office receipts climbed to more than $1 million a day.

John decided he needed a rest, and on September 1, 1978, he and Landis checked into La Costa, the famous health and weight-reduction spa outside San Diego. John took the health regimen seriously—the herbal wrap, the $13.80 massage and $13.80 facial. But he had a cache of fresh cocaine with him, and Landis discovered it and threw it out. John complained bitterly. A thousand dollars' worth of coke had just been wasted.

One night, John and Landis ran into actor William Holden, who was also staying at La Costa. The three sat down for their 800-calorie, mostly vegetable dinner. Holden, who had won an Academy Award for best actor in *Stalag 17* (1953) and had been nominated for *Network,* looked thin and seemed angry and frazzled about the press and reporters.

"You know they're going to get you," Holden said. "You know what they are? They're vampires. You know what we are? We're in our homes with garlic around the windows and hoping it will work."

Being a star, Holden said, is transitory. He had been up, and then down, and up again, then down again, and then up once more. Hollywood was a mess. John loved the speech.

"They're bloodsuckers," Holden said. "They'll fuck you." Everyone in show business needed something on the outside to retain sanity. Holden said he had his co-ownership of the 1,260-acre Mount Kenya Safari Club, his hideaway. When things got fucked, he said, "I go to Africa."

John hung on Holden's words.

"You have to take it for what it's worth. If they say you're a genius, don't believe it." He returned to the press. "They'll hate you if you die in your sleep. You know why?"

Neither Landis nor John had an answer.

"Because it's bad copy!" *

* Holden was found dead in his Santa Monica apartment on November 17, 1981, after bleeding to death when he fell and injured his head. Thomas T. Noguchi, Los Angeles's controversial "coroner of the stars," said the next day that Holden had alcohol in his blood equivalent to ten drinks.

Since the successful Blues Brothers performance on the show, John and Dan had talked about expanding to some five-minute films for the show—the Blues Brothers waterskiing or at the Beverly Hills Hotel, in full uniform, shades, dark suits.

In Canada that summer, Aykroyd expanded the idea to a full-length Blues Brothers movie. The brothers, Jake (John) and Elwood (Aykroyd), would round up their old band in Chicago to give a benefit concert to save the Catholic orphanage where they had grown up. Aykroyd described his idea to John, who called Sean Daniels at Universal.

Daniels talked to his superiors. He knew it would be virtually impossible for the studio to refuse. *Animal House* was the number-one movie in the country.

Word came from the top: Make *The Blues Brothers*. Daniels called Brillstein. It was settled on the phone.

In New York, Belushi and Aykroyd were gathering their band to begin rehearsing for the Los Angeles concerts. Steve Cropper, the guitarist, flew to New York and went straight to the recording studio where the now seven-member band, with John and Aykroyd, were practicing.

Duck Dunn met him outside. It's chaos in there, he said. John and Danny have all the best intentions but they really don't know the music. They're going to need a lot of help.

Cropper and Dunn knew that John wanted to do the songs the way they had been sung in the original versions. So they coached him, suggesting where the words should fall within the beat in "Soul Man," how long to draw out a note, how loud.

Before the opening concert, the Blues Brothers moved rehearsals out to Los Angeles, and saxophonist Tom "Triple Scale" Scott was asked to join the band. Scott was a soft-spoken man with short sandy hair who had gotten his nickname because, it was said, he was paid triple union scale, though in fact he got more. He had played with superstars George Harrison, Paul McCartney, Joni Mitchell and Steely Dan.

On Monday, September 9, 1978, at 8:30 P.M., the Blues Brothers opened before a capacity crowd at the Universal Amphitheater. The band wore sunglasses with black rims, and John and Dan were in full Blues Brothers regalia.

As the band did a hard-driving version of Otis Redding's "I Can't Turn You Loose," Belushi and Aykroyd strolled coolly out to the screams of 5,000 fans, who jumped to their feet. Aykroyd had a briefcase handcuffed to his wrist. Belushi, twirling a key on a long chain, walked over and unlocked it. Aykroyd pulled out his harmonica.

Bernie Brillstein saw that they were stealing the show from Steve Martin. They played a 40-minute set, and the audience seemed transformed. And it was John who had choreographed the dance routines and had supervised the lighting. He had told the band that there were to be no drugs.

Backstage after the performance, drummer Steve Jordan felt like a star-struck kid. They had rocked the roof off. The band members were hugging each other and accepting champagne from Mick Jagger, Linda Ronstadt, Joe Cocker, Jackson Browne, even Walter Matthau. Jordan went outside, looked at the sky, and laughed with joy.

Tom Scott was backstage after a performance later that week when a call came for John and Dan. It was the office of Hugh Hefner, the head of the *Playboy* magazine empire, inviting them to a party at the Playboy mansion that night.

Was the band invited?

No.

We are the Blues *Brothers,* they answered; the band must be invited also.

The band was not invited.

In that case, John and Dan said, we will not be coming.

Scott loved the feeling of a musical brotherhood come alive. John and Danny, absorbed by their roles, addressed each other as Elwood and Jake in private, taking on their outlaw identities. John loved his rock-star fantasy, and the role of Jake made it come true. It was not just a part-time stage show anymore. When John put on his black suit, shades and porkpie hat, he *was* a rock star.

Brillstein met John's parents when they came to Los Angeles for the Blues Brothers concerts. Agnes Belushi appeared backstage one night with that look mothers get, as if to say "I'm John Belushi's mother." A typical stage mom, Brillstein figured. She acted as if John were an eight-year-old who had just tap-danced in an amateur show. She seemed to take the bows and draw attention to herself. And it was clear John ran from her.

Soon Brillstein's duties included handling John's mother. She called Brillstein's office trying to find John, who regularly asked Brillstein to call her and say everything was fine, even if she called while he was in the office. Perhaps John felt pressure or guilt, Brillstein thought.

It didn't take long for Agnes Belushi to get to know Brillstein's office and the many services his staff could provide. She started asking for tickets and travel service. John said to go ahead; he would pay.

Adam Belushi was less intense, a quiet, old-country gentleman. He usually had two questions: "How's John doing?" and "Is he a good boy?" Brillstein was always enthusiastic and optimistic.

10

During the several years after their encounter at One Fifth Avenue during the first year of "Saturday Night," Steven Spielberg and Belushi had kept in touch. When Spielberg's *Close Encounters of the Third Kind* was released, John was enchanted by it and took the film as a kind of religion. When *Animal House* was released, the two became a mutual admiration society. Spielberg found *Animal House* touching and sweet. There was a softness in the power of the humor. He wanted to capture the Bluto character and improve on it. Spielberg had committed to do the Japanese-attack–Los Angeles movie, now called *1941*, but now he doubted that it would be proper to have a Caucasian play the Japanese sub skipper.

Spielberg had another part in mind for John: Wild Bill Kelso, a crazy P-40 bomber pilot determined to shoot down the first Japanese plane over America; Bluto in aviation goggles. Spielberg could see John jumping on a chair. Instead of yelling "Food Fight!," it would be *"Jaaaaaaaps!!!!!"*

As the box-office receipts jumped for *Animal House,* so did the price of getting John. The studios that were bankrolling the project, Columbia and Universal, offered $350,000.

Brillstein liked the money, but he argued against the project. Spielberg had never done comedy, he said to John, and the script was not really that funny.

John never had a second thought. "I can't turn down Spielberg." Besides, $350,000 was his first big money.

The future looked very fine. John and Judy had moved out of the Bleecker Street apartment into a house at 60 Morton Street in Greenwich Village; the rent was $1,650 a month. John and Danny decided they needed an office for their business dealings. They rented some space on the seventh floor of a building at 150 Fifth Avenue in New York, hired a secretary, installed a few phones, added a stereo system and a couple of typewriters, put some of Judy's art work on the walls. John's incorporated business was called Phantom, and Dan's, Black Rhino.

One night a few weeks after the deal for *1941* was set, Spielberg went to see Belushi and Aykroyd in Los Angeles.

"I want you to meet Sergeant Tree, tank commander," John said, pushing Aykroyd forward for the part of the gung-ho superpatriotic Army sergeant who plants an artillery gun on the lawn of a private home by the sea. Aykroyd spun out information about ammunition and guns, high-technology background on tanks and so forth.

Spielberg was sold, even annoyed that he hadn't seen the possibility himself. Aykroyd was signed; it would be his first movie.

Soon afterward, Spielberg went to New York to begin rehearsals with John. John took him to his soundproof vault on Morton Street. Whoosh. He closed the door and cranked up the music. An overpowering sound descended on them. On the floor was a crust of bread, a decayed pastrami sandwich, some candy bars and assorted wrappers. Spielberg, who loved classical music, tolerated John's barely audible lecture on rock music and its importance in his life.

But Spielberg was attracted to John's boyishness, the waves of expression that passed over his face. He found them truthful and direct. "I'm getting $350,000," John said. "I can't fucking believe it. I've made it." He could help his family, and he could buy new and better stereo equipment.

Spielberg felt good; it was the first time an actor had thanked him for a deal. He tried, gently, to turn the conversation to the film. John deflected it, changing the music, turning it up. He played blues records and tapes for about 45 minutes.

Finally Spielberg asked John to tell him what he liked and disliked about Wild Bill Kelso.

"We'll work it out on the set," John insisted. "I'm best there. I'm fast. I like to improvise. I won't let you down."

Several weeks later in Los Angeles, Spielberg took John to a hangar in Burbank in which a hundred or so people were constructing planes and sets. John was seeing for the first time what elaborate and expensive filmmaking involved. He walked around, saying little. Finally, he paused. "Gee, you're making a real Hollywood movie."

"Yeah," Spielberg said. "We build it up and then destroy it." He was touched by John's innocence.

The October 2, 1978, *Newsweek* had a long story about college campuses swept by Roman toga parties modeled on the Delta gathering in *Animal House*. "Be it at Yale or at the University of Arizona, Oregon or Ole Miss, the cry of 'To-ga! To-ga! To-ga! To-ga!' is rumbling up from the commons tables and out across the campus green."

That same week Jack Nicholson's *Goin' South,* John's first film, was released, almost a year after he had gone to Mexico. John appeared for less than three minutes in the final version.

The reviews were mostly negative, dismissing the film as romantic fluff, and many critics mentioned that they wished there'd been more Belushi; *Newsweek:* "A little less coyness, and a lot more John Belushi . . . would have helped." Many referred indirectly to drugs. *Time* remarked on Nicholson's "somewhat stoned eyes." *The New Yorker* noted that Nicholson "talks as if he needed to blow his nose—this must be his idea of a funny voice." *New York* referred to Nicholson's "peculiar nasal voice and fogged manner."

For Gary Arnold of the *Washington Post,* the movie was "Nicholson's embarrassment . . . another director would have said, 'Enough' and advised him to put a lid on all the smirking, winking, strutting, grinning, leering, tongue-wagging, squinting, growling, cackling and scratching . . . most of his lines are spoken with a peculiar cold in the nodze."

In the most favorable review, Charles Champlin in the *Los Angeles Times* wrote: "Somewhat confusingly, Nicholson plays the whole role like the before half of a Dristan commercial, with nasal passages blocked. Why, I don't know, and don't care to ask."

John was back in New York for the opening show of the fourth season of "Saturday Night Live" on October 7, 1978.

Lorne Michaels was beginning to be alarmed. His stars were starting to slip out of his hands. Laraine Newman had made her first movie, *American Hot Wax;* Billy Murray was reading a script for his first movie, *Meatballs;* Gilda Radner had scores of film offers; Garrett Morris was considering a show on Broadway; and John and Dan were going to be flying back and forth to California working on *1941.* It was all changing. On the season's first show, the evidence was in abundance: The host was New York Mayor Ed Koch; the musical guests were the Rolling Stones, making their first live television appearance in over a decade; the audience included the new NBC president and chief executive officer, Fred Silverman, accompanied by an entourage of network executives; Atlantic

Recording President Ahmet Ertegun; Spielberg; and former hosts Steve Martin and Paul Simon.

John had assumed the mantle of the bad boy. He was complaining to Brillstein that he was tired of Michaels, whom he began calling the "Canadian Jewish intellectual." With the success of *Animal House,* Michaels saw that John had exceeded the boundaries not only of the show—he was better known than "Saturday Night Live"—but of NBC and maybe television.

Belushi was heading for the door, Michaels could see that.

On October 16, 1978, John Belushi's face was spread over America, staring defiantly and confidently over his toga from the October 23 cover of *Newsweek* under the headline: COLLEGE HUMOR COMES BACK. *Newsweek,* which reserves its cover space for presidents, prime ministers, corporate heads and the biggest names in show business, was announcing to Main Street and Park Avenue that John Belushi "has now become—surprise of surprises—a star."

The five-page story included a picture of John as Cardinal Wolsey from the Shawnee Theater's *Anne of the Thousand Days;* his high school yearbook picture, accompanied by a list of his accomplishments (Class Council, Forensics, Thespians, Choir, Football, Key Club, Homecoming King); a picture with Judy; and as a samurai on "Saturday Night Live." The potato-spitting scene from *Animal House* was inevitable. "Bluto is irresistible," *Newsweek* said. "Eleven years ago, in 'The Graduate,' Dustin Hoffman proved that a movie leading man need not be tall, chiseled and dashing. Now John Belushi has demonstrated that he can even be a slob."

Interpreting the "new college humor" as a backlash against the seriousness of the 1960s, John was quoted: "My characters say it's okay to screw up. People don't have to be perfect. They don't have to be real smart. They don't have to follow the rules. They can have fun. Most movies today make people feel inadequate. I don't do that."

"Belushi is a rarity among comedians," *Newsweek* said. "What you see on stage is also what you see off. He is a bundle of conflicting emotions. Yes, he wants success, money and stardom, but the punky kid in him recoils at the prospect of it all. Belushi enjoys operating at full throttle, on the edge, and he knows very well that his manic style has helped get him where he is."

John Landis was quoted: "He abuses his body in ways that would kill bulls. . . . If he doesn't burn himself out, his potential is unlimited."

By then *Animal House* had taken in $60 million on Universal's initial $2.7 million cost.

Brillstein was wide-eyed. Thom Mount, head of Universal, called to ask him to breakfast. His message was simple: John was going to be a big star and Universal had big plans for him. Mount and Brillstein went to see the head of business affairs at Universal.

Okay, Brillstein said, a discussion of the future might begin with the past. Why not agree to give John some retroactive percentage of the *Animal House* profits—perhaps one or 2 percentage points? After all, the big stars normally got 5 to 10 such profit points. He reminded them that John had been paid only $35,000—peanuts by big movie standards—and Universal was going to make millions, tens of millions. And he had heard, reliably, that Landis was going to get a retroactive percentage of the profits that would be worth hundreds of thousands, even millions.

Universal wouldn't budge.

How about a bonus? Brillstein asked.

That was feasible, but Mount wanted to sign John to a three-picture deal and guarantee $350,000 for the first (already set with Spielberg's *1941*), $500,000 for the second (which was the Blues Brothers movie), and $750,000 for the third. Brillstein said okay, but he wondered about the bonus. No one wanted to mention a figure.

"I'll go out for ten minutes and give me your best shot." Brillstein walked out of the room. He called John. John had only one suggestion: Get the bonus check today.

Brillstein went back in.

Two hundred and fifty thousand dollars, Mount said. Brillstein said only if they turned over the check that day.

Universal agreed, and the three-picture deal was formally announced in a press release, without a mention of money. Brillstein had secured a total of $1.8 million for John, and the last sentence of the release said, "Bernie Brillstein will serve as executive producer on the three films to be developed with Belushi." Executive producer meant Brillstein would get paid and have no real responsibility. It was his pay for delivering Belushi.

John called Judy's brother, Rob Jacklin, who was still working as a goldsmith in Colorado. "I want to do something for Mom and Dad. I want to buy them a ranch. I've got the money. I'll pay your expenses if you go around and look for a place."

Rob began a search. He finally found a five-acre place in Julian,

California, about an hour outside San Diego. It cost $129,000, for which John put some money down and took out a mortgage.

Sean Daniels, who had been promoted to a vice president at Universal after the success of *Animal House,* began to notice a change in the public's attitude toward John. Before, he had been the hip, irreverent, late-night comedian. Now he was Bluto. People shouted at him on the streets: "Hey, Bluto, want something to eat?" or, "Hey, Bluto, break a beer bottle over your head!" He stopped traffic, heads turned.

Animal House was becoming a part of the culture. Food fights erupted on college campuses. One day Daniels showed John a copy of a memo put out by the dean to all Rutgers students:

Dear Student:
    There have been two "food fights" during the past week at the Brower Commons. These activities are seriously damaging to the budget of the Brower Commons which is supported solely by the students board fee, destructive of staff morale, and dangerous to the safety of students and staff in the area.
    ANY STUDENT IDENTIFIED AS PARTICIPANTS IN A "FOOD FIGHT" WILL BE REFERRED TO THE RUTGERS COLLEGE JUDICIAL COUNCIL FOR APPROPRIATE DISCIPLINARY ACTION.

John laughed heartily.

One night in New York, John knocked on the door of Karen Allen's apartment. It was about midnight, and he wanted company. They went walking and stopped at a bar with a blues band. John wound up on stage performing.

On the way back to Allen's, John talked about fame and success. Allen, who had drawn considerably less attention for her role in *Animal House,* sensed anyhow that John was disappointed, that the sudden recognition and money were doing him more damage than good. John said fame wasn't what he had been led to believe. The disappointment carried over to people, he said. One day you're nothing to someone, and the next day they want to be your best friend. So there was an awful breakdown in relations with people—new people, old people. And he wondered if it was worth it.

John flew out to California in late October to begin filming *1941.* Spielberg was aware that *1941* was a movie with no center, and he was nervous. He was going in too many directions at once; he had to focus on a giant dance scene in a USO dance hall, a street brawl on Hollywood Boulevard, a house that falls off a cliff into the ocean, a gigantic ferris wheel rolling down a pier and into the ocean.

He found John unusual to direct. Belushi never fully mastered his lines in advance. It took him a few minutes in front of the camera to get his character warmed up. If Spielberg shot six takes of a scene, John would be very different each time. But Spielberg soon realized that he had to keep the camera going a minute more than the scene called for because John would always throw something in. The improvised material was often better than the script, and then Spielberg wanted it polished. "Good, I like that. Do it in the scene," he'd say, and they'd do another take.

Spielberg was struck by the warmth between Belushi and Aykroyd. They were not equals. It was more like Muhammad Ali and his manager. Dan took a back seat willingly. Spielberg thought of them as foxhole buddies, protecting each other's flanks, sharing C-rations, dying together.

He knew John was using drugs. Belushi was often asleep in his private trailer, and people were afraid to wake him up if he had to do a scene. Spielberg woke him on one occasion, and John sat up and said he'd had a bad dream about Judy. There were tears in his eyes. It was obviously a bad day on drugs, Spielberg concluded. He didn't lecture John, but he did talk to Aykroyd about it. Dan was protective.

Michael Dare, a twenty-seven-year-old native of Los Angeles, a photographer and a would-be scriptwriter and musician, was home in his small bungalow on Hayworth in West Hollywood one night when there was a knock at the door. It was Belushi, whom Dare had never met. But the countenance was unmistakable: John's eyebrows were a ticket of admission.

Belushi came in and explained that he had just smoked a marijuana cigarette with a friend who said he had got it from Dare. "Here," John said, taking out a roll of hundred-dollar bills. "Take all this and get me what you can . . . peel off a bunch of this and see what you can do." He said he was more interested in cocaine than marijuana.

Dare took more than $1,000 and got about half an ounce of coke, which they shared.

Throughout the filming of *1941*, John visited Dare's place regularly. He would appear at the door any time of the day or night. Dare generally had something, and if he didn't, he knew how to get it fast. At times Dare got as much as an ounce of cocaine for John; the price was $2,000 to $2,500, depending on the quality and availability. Dare didn't think of himself as a dealer; he was a facilitator, the master of ceremonies. He wasn't in it to make money; he liked having John in his house, and he was proud that John considered him a friend. His place became a party center, with John supplying the money and Dare the drugs. John showed off—"Look how much I can do"—and would sometimes take a gram, pour it onto his hand and snort it all up at once.

Several times John took about a quarter of an ounce—$500 to $600 worth—and laid it out in a single line, several feet long, on an upturned mirror. Then he would challenge someone to start at the other end. Each, finger over one nostril and a straw stuck up the other, raced to the center. Usually John won.

Dare played the piano, and often John played the guitar. At other times John would just come and sit bleary-eyed in the middle of the living room, listening to Dare's record collection for hours, without saying much of anything. When Dare tried to engage John, he showed no interest. Dare wanted him to consider a role in some movies that he planned to write, including one role as the Pope. John didn't pay much attention. He just wanted more drugs.

Dare moved his operation to a bigger house, a crumbling four-bedroom place on Poinsettia in West Hollywood. Because Belushi was in regular attendance, and because he contributed a fair amount of cash, Dare found more sources of drugs and more customers. He started calling himself Captain Preemo, "the best," after the old 1960s drug term. In a little room under the staircase, Dare posted a big "Captain Preemo's" sign and wrote out the menu of drugs that were available:

- Afghanistan hash.
- Hash cookies made with chocolate, supplied to Dare by the dozen in labeled packages.
- Peruvian flake cocaine, chips of coke that looked like mother of pearl; one gram filled two one-gram bottles.
- Bolivian rock cocaine, solid as a rock and pure.
- Bubble gum cocaine, a slightly pink substance that smelled like Double Bubble gum.
- Colombian marijuana at $50 an ounce.
- Thai sticks; marijuana leaves from Thailand wrapped around sticks—the finest pot available and hard to get—at $150 an ounce.
- California Sinsemilla, without seeds.

- Mexican marijuana, with little seeds.
- Hawaiian marijuana.
- Mushrooms; large bags were available.
- A $10 drug grab bag, a basket containing a varied mixture so the buyer did not know what he or she would get for the money.

After a while, Dare had more than 100 regular customers, and Captain Preemo's had become a kind of Hollywood drug Algonquin Hotel roundtable. Dare was taking in about $5,000 a week.

Dare was eventually busted by the police but not convicted.

Back in New York, Michaels had a female impersonation for John for the November 11 show. He knew John hated to play women, but he had a classic John couldn't turn down. A month earlier, actress Elizabeth Taylor, wife of the Republican senatorial candidate of Virginia, John W. Warner, had choked on a chicken bone. Bill Murray, who had joined the cast during the second season, opens his "Celebrity Corner" on "Weekend Update" with a glowing introduction to "the greatest actress that's ever lived."

Murray turns to address Belushi, who fills the big screen behind the news desk. Belushi is wearing a black beehive wig and a black lace dress. Diamond earrings hang down almost to his shoulders, and a diamond brooch is pinned to his dress. Slouching in his chair, grossly overweight, he is ripping into a piece of chicken, smacking his chops and occasionally licking his fingers.

Murray: "Liz, how does it feel to be Mrs. Almost, Too-soon-to-tell, Senator-Elect Warner, anyway?"

Belushi barely looks up. "Very exciting, Bill. I'm looking forward to being a Washington hostess." He turns back to the chicken, looking like a female version of Bluto.

Murray: "They tell me that—we've heard that you promised that if John won the election, you'd go on a diet from your present weight of 167 pounds down to 120. Is that true?"

"That's right. I'm going to start on a strict diet—nothing but chicken." He waves a breast.

"That sounds great, Liz. . . . I don't care how much you weigh, just so your cheeks don't puff up over those beautiful violet eyes that I've been in love with since *National Velvet*."

Belushi looks up, too busy eating to reply, and nods his agreement. He licks his fingers, his mouth full of chicken. "Thank y—" He starts coughing, unable to finish his sentence. The cough gets worse. His face turns red. He is panicky, eyes bulging, and he can't stop.

Murray seems not to notice. What about your career? Will there be a "Cleopatra II"?

Belushi can't answer. He is gagging, his hands to his throat, gasping for breath, his body shaking with convulsions.

Murray: "Well, thank you so much, Liz. It's been a real pleasure having you on 'Celebrity Corner.' "

John gives a huge, deep cough, and a chicken bone pops out of his mouth. He looks at it—a little surprised—shrugs, swallows, waves at the camera, and starts eating again.

After the show, John and Danny invited the musical guests, the Grateful Dead, some of the cast and their friends to stop by for a post-show party at a private bar they had at the corner of Dominick Street and Hudson. Danny had discovered the place, an old seamen's bar, and he had intended to store his Harley there, but when John came down for a visit, he had fallen in love with it. They had decided to clean it out, put in a jukebox, stock it with liquor, and call it the Blues Bar. It would be a clubhouse for them, a hideout to which they could invite their friends and where they could get away from the public. Everything would be free, so they wouldn't need a liquor license and they could stay open as long as they wanted.

Mitch Glazer, who had written the 1977 *Crawdaddy* article on John, stopped by for the opening. It was packed with some of the hottest names in show business. Keith Richards, of the Rolling Stones, and director Francis Ford Coppola stood behind the bar filling orders.

Back in Los Angeles on the set of *1941,* Kathleen Kennedy, one of Spielberg's assistants, saw that her boss was trying to use Aykroyd as a lever on John. It was clear that if Dan couldn't influence John, certainly Spielberg could not. Kennedy talked to Aykroyd about John's drugs, and it was clear to her that Aykroyd was scared to death.

It was Kennedy's first movie, but she had already learned the business's motto: "Do what you have to do to get the movie made."

On December 5, John arrived on the set an hour and a half late, delivered by Lauren Hutton, the model-turned-movie-star. John was so drugged up that he nearly rolled out of the car onto the ground. Spielberg was angry and might not have said anything, but John had also been late the day before.

Spielberg went to John's trailer.

"I'm sorry," John said.

"You can do this to anyone else," Spielberg said, "but you can't do it to me." No one had ever shown up late on one of his sets in this condition. He had paid Richard Dreyfuss less than $350,000 for *Close Encounters,* he told John. "For $350,000 you're going to show up."

Spielberg summoned Janet Healy, the twenty-nine-year-old associate producer, and ordered her to watch John. She was to babysit him, make sure he was on time in the morning.

Healy gave Spielberg a blank stare but said okay. She walked over to John's trailer, where Hutton was trying to help John learn his lines for the day. Hutton soon left, and John made it through the scheduled scenes. Later Healy drove him to the house of Ron Wood, the Rolling Stones guitarist.

Healy found taking care of John on a daily basis quite pleasant. She made sure he was on time, saw to routine calls, helped him learn his lines, and handled the moves as he shifted in and out of hotels in search of privacy. He seemed to be using too much cocaine. As she grew closer to him she realized that he took coke every few hours. It was routine: a few snorts of coke and Belushi had an hour of good work or wakefulness, then a so-so hour, then he took a dive, and unless he had some more, he faded out. Coke explained why he couldn't memorize his lines. But Healy didn't find John's drug use unusual compared to that of some other members of the cast and production crew. She counted twenty-five people on the set who used cocaine at times.

Healy sometimes traveled with John at night as he made his rounds to clubs, parties, music gatherings. One night she went with him and Dan to a studio where the Rolling Stones were holding a private jam session. There were only about half a dozen people in a very small room, and she was impressed to be in such exclusive company. She and John danced until about 3 A.M. When she left, John followed her outside. He wondered why she was leaving so early and why she had not said goodbye.

"I didn't want to say goodbye," she answered, "because you'd talk me into staying."

John laughed and walked back inside.

One night John and Dan had a fight. It wasn't clear to Healy what had triggered it, but the blowup cast a dark cloud over them both. They were upset that they were upset with each other. Healy was reminded of an old married couple.

One morning about 4 A.M., John had had so much cocaine that he couldn't get to sleep. He called his friend, actress Betty Buckley, who was now the stepmother in the TV series "Eight Is Enough."

Buckley could sympathize. She and John had traveled far since they'd met backstage at *Lemmings,* where she had pushed him against the wall. Back then they smoked an occasional joint together because it was the hip thing to do. Fame and money had come so suddenly for them both. Projects got bigger, expectations increased, and the drugs got more expensive and insidious. Sniffing cocaine gave her exciting and surreal impressions; it was like living in a dreamscape.

One day Buckley took a look at herself. I'm in physical pain, she thought. I'm hurting myself. It was time to decide. She got professional help and went cold turkey. It had taken an extraordinary amount of discipline. But she had been off drugs for some time.

I've been up all night doing too much coke, John told her, and I have to be at work at 7 A.M. and I can't get to sleep. What should I do? He sounded panicky.

Buckley told him to drink some warm milk and then heat up a salt-water solution and inhale it gently to flush out his nostrils. Then take a hot bath. She told him to call back if that didn't work.

Half an hour later John called.

So Buckley talked to him for an hour and gave him the "life is worth living" rap, and the next day John made it to the set.

John's comrade in arms for the Hollywood nightlife was Treat Williams, who was playing Sitarski, the girl-chasing soldier in *1941.* Williams, who had starred as the hippie Berger in the movie musical *Hair,* was twenty-six years old and had just broken up with his girlfriend. Treat and John had access to everything—tickets, parties, women. With so many stars and special effects, there were days spent waiting in their trailers, on call. So they took more and more cocaine, particularly during night shooting.

"These drugs, man," John once said to Williams, "you know, I got to stop." But he didn't.

One night John called him about 4 A.M. "Treat . . . John."

"How are you?" Williams asked.

"Fucked up, man."

"Get some sleep," Williams suggested. "Anything I can do for you?"

"No," John said.

Williams figured that John needed to make contact with someone, to come down and touch base. It wasn't quite right, though. It was too late, too intense. John was putting away too many good times. But they were young, and everyone knew coke was okay—nonaddictive and just an energy burst.

In December, Atlantic Records released "Briefcase Full of Blues," a collection of ten songs recorded live from the Blues Brothers Amphitheater concerts. John had put up some of his *Animal House* bonus money temporarily to get the record produced because Atlantic had been slow coming up with cash. But he believed in the project, and so did Judy.

Atlantic executives wanted the names of Belushi and Aykroyd on the album cover, but John and Danny had insisted that Jake and Elwood Blues be credited for everything and that a small "special thanks to Dan Aykroyd and John Belushi" be included on the back.

Within five days of its release, all 50,000 copies were sold. Atlantic was so backed up with orders that it had to go to other production plants to make more copies. It turned out to be the fastest-breaking album Atlantic had ever had, and within several more weeks it had been certified platinum, with sales in excess of one million.

In Los Angeles, John took the record over to Captain Preemo's, put it on and silently lip-sang the entire album for a half-dozen of Dare's friends and customers.

On New Year's Eve, Bill Graham, the most successful rock promoter in the country, was staging one of his famous musical events: the closing of San Francisco's Winterland Colosseum, site of some of the most outrageous rock concerts in America. Graham had lined up the San Francisco staples—the Grateful Dead and Jefferson Starship—along with the New Riders of the Purple Sage and the Blues Brothers.

Bass player Duck Dunn and his wife June were standing around backstage before the Blues Brothers set. It was a madhouse. There was no room for the band to move or sit, no place for their guests. Everywhere Dunn looked he saw wall-to-wall strangers—groupies, Hell's Angels, the stage crew and a swarm of spaced-out people.

Dunn knew that John was thrilled to be on the same ticket with the Grateful Dead—one of America's most enduring bands from San Francisco's psychedelic era. It proved that the Blues Brothers were more than just a novelty act.

John told Dunn to watch out for the strangers and not to eat or drink *anything*. There were rumors that everything was being mixed with LSD. People were spiking the champagne with drugs by sticking hypodermic needles through the corks, and the word was out: If you don't want to trip, steer clear of people you don't know.

Dunn watched as John, worried that someone was going to get dosed with acid, warned the other band members. Thousands of people were on their feet roaring when the Blues Brothers band started playing. Then John and Dan walked on stage and the crowd started to wail. Even the Deadheads—people so devoted to the Grateful Dead that they rarely bothered to listen to anything else—were up and dancing in the aisles. Dunn had never had a reception like it.

John and Danny's dance moves were rusty, Dunn thought, and the band had not played together in a long time and could have been tighter, but it didn't seem to matter.

They finished the set and Dunn walked off the stage. He unhooked his guitar strap and saw John, covered with sweat, reach out and accept a glass of champagne. He downed it in a gulp, then was lost in the crowd.

A short while later, John was back at Dunn's side. "Guess what?" he said, taking ahold of Dunn's arm. "I've been dosed. Stay with me and take care of me." Dunn and his wife and Judy stuck close to John all night.

When the concert was over they went to a party at the Fulton Street mansion of the Jefferson Starship. Someone was at the door pointing the way to the cookies laced with psychedelic mushrooms.

John didn't seem in the least bit concerned that he was on acid. In fact, he was as calm, friendly and wide awake as Dunn had ever seen him.

"God. Isn't everybody dressed nice?" John asked.

"John," Dunn laughed, "you should take more acid instead of coke."

The next day, January 2, 1979, John and Judy flew back to Los Angeles to continue shooting *1941*. Two weeks later they went to see Bernie Brillstein to discuss an invitation from New Orleans for John to be the grand marshal of the Mardi Gras celebration; the city promised to provide Lear jets to fly in friends and family and pay for eight hotel rooms. John decided eventually to decline—his schedule was crammed enough—but the offer seemed to impress him.

On Friday night, the nineteenth, Judy started pressuring John a little more on his drugs. He gave his standard argument: "You've got to understand. It's my life-style." Judy said it couldn't continue. They stayed up all night discussing their future.

With the new year Judy had begun to keep a daily diary, anticipating a period of uncertainty and turmoil. On January 20 she wrote: "John and I are still talking. New understandings. We cancel dinner with Penny

[Marshall] and Rob [Reiner] so we can continue to talk. . . . We begin to realize how long we've been out of touch and what we both want is still the same although we've been on separate paths. Reached out just in time."

The following day, they canceled an early flight to New York and slept late. They watched the Super Bowl together and took an 8:30 P.M. plane to New York. "Talk the entire plane ride," Judy wrote later in her diary. "Arrive 6 A.M. I sleep for four hours. When I wake up we resume our talks. There is so much to uncover, digest and share."

Judy, her anger dissipated, and glad that John was listening, had finally formulated her position on the drugs, telling John, "If it's your life-style, then I don't think we can live together and have a successful marriage because it causes too many problems between us."

Finally John said, "I don't need the drugs. It doesn't have to be my life-style. I'll change."

Judy sensed that he was acting out of panic, but there did seem to be a new resolve. On January 23 she wrote: "Now we see New Year's Eve and the talks as the beginning of having fun together again."

The next day, John's thirtieth birthday, they had dinner at home alone. That day the Blues Brothers record album hit Number 1 on the charts.

On February 16, Judy entered in her diary: "Did some coke—not much—his first feeling was that he could do it differently—not every day." Cocaine in small amounts didn't work, however, and the following Friday, February 23, the Rolling Stones lead guitarist Keith Richards showed up in town, and John went out with him and stayed very late, taking cocaine much of the night.

Lorne Michaels had something close to a mutiny on his hands when John stumbled in shortly before dress rehearsal the next day, barely able to function. Belushi's inattention was beyond any acceptable limit for any boss, even Michaels. The show wasn't important to John anymore; he didn't care.

John closed his eyes and moaned, saying he wouldn't be able to go on. Michaels called an NBC doctor, who came down to examine John. His lungs were full of fluid, the doctor told Michaels. If John performed, it would be at great risk to his health. In fact, the doctor said, there was a "50–50 chance he'll die."

It sounded melodramatic. "I can live with those odds," Michaels said angrily.

For the next couple of hours they fed John coffee and prepared him for the show. Jane Curtin was infuriated by the scene, though she was used to people arriving in various states of consciousness. John should have been disciplined years ago, back when the show first began.

John got dressed in a suit and tie, and just before the show he was plopped down behind a desk to do the cold opening with Curtin, Gilda Radner and guest host Kate Jackson, the beautiful private detective from "Charlie's Angels." At 11:30 P.M., 28 million television sets—the largest audience of the season—were tuned in.

"Hello, Angels," a voice says from a telephone speaker on the desk in front of John. "You all have heard of Freddie Silverman" [the new head of NBC and former program chief of ABC; John was playing him on the show].

The Angels turn to address John. "Sorry things are going so badly at NBC, Freddie."

"You see," John says, "I'm not really working for NBC. . . . I never stopped working for ABC. . . . Fact is, I'm ABC's head of covert operations. . . . You see, the plan is for me to destroy NBC."

Michaels, watching from under the bleachers by the door to the control room, saw that John could barely talk.

Judy's diary entry for the next day: "John trouble." He was off on a binge for several days. Judy didn't make any diary entries during those days; living them was bad enough.

Within a few days John was back home and they took a plane to Los Angeles for a huge record promotion convention at the Century Plaza Hotel. John and Danny were given a great reception and three standing ovations. Later John and Judy went up to a record company's suite. "Champagne and coke for everyone," Judy wrote in her diary that night. That included herself, and she realized it was harder than she had expected to abstain; it was so available, it provided such a rush and so many potent feelings.

On Tuesday, March 6, John and Judy flew back to New York for the next day's read-through for the show. John was late and everyone was angry. John reported this to Judy, who reenforced his feelings that Lorne Michaels and the others had no sympathy for John and his other projects. It was unfair, she felt, because his success in movies and music had had a tremendous spillover effect. John's visibility elsewhere had helped the show and all of them.

On Sunday, March 11, John and Judy took a 6 P.M. flight to Los Angeles for '41. They went to a bungalow at the Beverly Hills Hotel. John was weary and jet-lagged. The next day he had a 7 A.M. call, and he worked until almost five in the evening. On Tuesday they caught the ten o'clock red-eye to New York for Wednesday's "Saturday Night" read-through.

John was so tired that he didn't go to the screening of *Old Boyfriends* that Wednesday night. Judy went with Mitch Glazer, and they came back to report to John. He was great, they told him, but the movie was badly made.

On the next show, hosted by actress Margot Kidder (Lois Lane in *Superman*), John did an impersonation of the missing, and presumed dead, labor leader Jimmy Hoffa. The next day he flew alone to Los Angeles while Judy stayed in New York. It was the first time she and John had been apart since early December. She felt sad and wrote John a letter saying she was uncertain but hopeful about their future.

On Monday, March 19, she wrote in her diary: "John phoned about six times today. It's raining in LA so he didn't work. That's hard on him. He doesn't know what to do. Goes to Ron Wood's. Wakes me twice during night. Each time more depressed, finally feels better."

Judy flew out to Los Angeles that Friday and discovered that John had been doing coke. She asked why. He sent her flowers with a note. Later that day he complained about a bad earache. On Saturday, March 24, a drug dealer who looked like a cowboy came by. Judy warned John, and the dealer got mad at her. Bobby Keyes, the saxophonist for the New Barbarians, Keith Richards' spin-off from the Rolling Stones, came by. Judy went to bed and awoke at seven-thirty the next morning. John, Keyes and the dealer were still up watching television. After they left Judy got very angry. John had a week off, and she insisted they get out of Los Angeles. He finally agreed, and they drove down to Palm Springs and got a room at Two Bunch Palms for two days. One afternoon they went to see *The Deer Hunter,* in which Robert De Niro plays a Vietnam veteran haunted by his war experiences. John loved the movie, the intense and powerful scenes of American prisoners of war being forced to play Russian roulette with loaded revolvers. Chagrined, he asked Judy, "Why don't I see scripts like that?"

Over the next section of her diary, Judy wrote: "*1941* is taking too long. There's too much time in LA, too much traveling, too many drugs. . . . Too many things to deal with at once. Can't keep daily, weekly, even monthly diary. Times too turbulent. Feelings too uncertain to put down."

11

Old *Boyfriends* finally opened in New York City and did well the first weekend. AVCO Embassy Pictures, which had put up much of the money, quickly learned that audiences were lining up to see what they thought was Belushi's new film. When people discovered he had only a short segment in the middle of someone else's movie, many got angry and some audiences erupted in boos and catcalls. People coming out of the theater dragged away those who were lined up, and attendance fell drastically.

AVCO had to move fast. They put Belushi's name to the forefront of the advertising and promotional efforts to grab his fans fast. The initial ads had spotlighted Shire and had given small mention to the three boy-friends, including John. The new ads treated Shire and John as equals. When the movie opened in Los Angeles, the promotional posters showed a pensive Shire and John singing at a microphone. The headline ran: "John Belushi's still singing the blues. Talia Shire's still carrying the torch—but this time he's the one who is going to get burned."

Tewkesbury and the producers were furious, arguing that it was misleading and that it would bring in Belushi fans for the wrong reason and drive away those who were interested in a drama about a woman searching out her past. But AVCO had its way.

Soon after the movie opened, Tewkesbury went to a neighborhood theater in Westwood, a posh part of Los Angeles, to hang around the long line forming for the late show and note the reactions of those leaving the early show.

Suddenly a young man approached the ticket window. It was absolutely the worst movie he had ever seen, he said, and he demanded his money back. It was not at all what he had expected from the advertising, and he explained in rapturous detail how rotten the movie was. Tewkesbury felt sick. Coproducer Michele Rappaport went over and gave the young man a refund.

The reviewers seemed stumped by John's place in the picture. He was too comic and entertaining to be resented, let alone despised, as a character in a revenge movie.

John was furious at what he heard and read. To Judy's knowledge he had never seen the final product and he felt exploited. The investors in the film, which finally had cost $3 million to make, lost about $1.8 million as the movie died.

John's ear continued to bother him, and in the first week of April, his doctor told him he shouldn't fly. That meant he couldn't return to New York for the "Saturday Night Live" show that week.

On April 4, 1979, John sent a telegram: "To cast and crew of Saturday Night Live and some of the writers. Sorry I can't be on the show this week. I feel okay but my ear is infected. . . . I can't fly. . . . A lot of doctor's orders. I'm working on a film piece, hopefully for this Saturday. If I can't fly by Saturday I'll start driving. . . . I miss almost all of you. . . . Love John."

John told Spielberg they were giving him hell for not showing up, charging that he was "going Hollywood." He was worried that he might be fired because Lorne Michaels didn't believe the ear infection story, and John didn't want to lose his roots, which were with the show.

Spielberg said they could do a remote hookup from California and put on some skits; he would be willing to direct it.

John arranged for several dozen women in bathing suits to sit with him beside Spielberg's swimming pool. The camera started close, and John began by saying he was sorry and couldn't make it because of an earache. The camera then pulled back and gradually revealed all the women who were gawking over him, massaging him and waiting on him.

Spielberg's girlfriend had a fit when the sequence was shot at their house. "It's only a movie," Spielberg said to her. "We're going to save John's job."

But Michaels, who wanted as little as possible to do with Hollywood, didn't use it.

As the end of shooting *1941* approached, Spielberg was jittery and wasn't hiding it. He told a *Time* reporter, "Comedy is not my forte. I don't know how this movie will come out. And yes, I'm scared." But he hoped for, and described the movie in progress as, "a celebration of paranoia." He really had loved the script, perhaps too much. "I was leery. When a script is so funny that you gag, that's really the kiss of death because it usually doesn't film that way. . . .

"The most expensive habit in the world is celluloid, not heroin, and I need a fix every few years."

Spielberg ran around the set, repeating, "If you're having this much fun making a movie, something must be wrong."

On April 20, Keith Richards, who had been arrested in Canada for possessing heroin with intent to sell, was giving a benefit concert in Toronto with the Barbarians as part of the court's sentence. John wanted to go to show solidarity. Judy discovered that John had a good deal of coke, and she took it away from him. They had a terrible fight, and John went off alone to Canada. Judy went to Key West for a day.

She realized that her antidrug stand was increasingly inconsistent and hypocritical. She was still doing drugs herself too often. She decided she needed help.

On April 26 she wrote in her diary: "I decided to see a psychiatrist, go several days a week, best to help me find a way to work things out, talk a lot about coke, desire to work through these times is strong. . . . Will we ever deal with these things better?"

With *1941* filming finished, John was back in New York, spending lots of time at the Tenth Street Baths, or *schvitz*. John and other regulars followed a routine: a few minutes on one of the three tiers of benches in the small steam room, a *pleitze* (a vigorous scrub and wash with hand-held oak-leaf brooms), a cold swim and then back again to the steam room.

Afterward John would find one of the old cots lined up in rows, preferably one off to the side in darkness, and sleep for hours. He loved the *schvitz,* particularly after a night of drugs.

John became friendly with a regular at the baths, a thirty-one-year-old boyish-looking drug dealer named Mark Hertzan. Hertzan was involved in a sophisticated drug-smuggling ring that brought cocaine and marijuana into the United States in specially built boats that had secret hiding places.

One day about 5 P.M. John called Mitch Glazer over to Morton Street. He explained that he wanted to do a movie based on Hertzan's life of drug dealing. The title was going to be "Kingpin," and he would play the lead. Hertzan had agreed to cooperate fully as long as his identity was kept secret. Glazer and Hertzan could go to work at once. Hertzan had made millions from his drug trade, investing in a 250-acre farm in Upstate New York and a horse-breeding enterprise in Kentucky.

John called Brillstein in Los Angeles to outline the idea. "The guy is a big drug dealer, has money and horses," John said. "Lives two completely different lives." He said that the guy wanted to stay completely in the background though they might have to make a rights deal with him someday. "But you don't want to meet him and don't put it in writing."

Brillstein liked the story and figured he could sell any Belushi movie idea. He contacted Sean Daniels at Universal. On April 27, Universal made a deal with Glazer to write the "Kingpin" screenplay: $7,500 on signing and $7,500 for the treatment, with escalating payments for the finished screenplay and more if the movie was made. On May 25, Universal signed the deal with John, paying him $7,500 for the idea and guaranteeing $100,000 if the movie was made. His deal as the star was unresolved pending completion of the script. John had assured Daniels it was based on the real life of a real drug dealer who was a kingpin.

Judy was wary of Hertzan. He was married and had a young son, but he was clearly a man who felt that wives should stay home. One night when Hertzan was over, he and John talked about making Hertzan an associate producer. No, Hertzan said; it would bring him to the attention of the police. But he could go to the movie set and watch, he said, and he had only one request—his own trailer so he could bring girls there. "I want to do this movie," Hertzan said to John and Judy. "I want to do something else other than just make money on drugs. I want something for my son to be proud of."

Another night Judy came home, and Hertzan and a friend, known only as Crazy Louie, said John had taken a lot of Percodan pills, a highly addictive pain killer, and was asleep. Judy was worried. They couldn't wake him. She felt a rush of fury and fear. They continued trying to wake John, but he didn't stir. Hertzan and Crazy Louie carried him to the shower. Judy was certain that John was going to die, he was so lifeless. The shower revived him, and he began throwing up violently. They took him back to bed. Hertzan gave Judy the impression that John had been talking about suicide. She went upstairs to the kitchen and hid all the sharp knives. Hertzan and Louie finally left, and Judy went down to the bedroom and found John awake.

"Are you talking about killing yourself?"

"I just want to fuck my wife," John said. So they made love and he fell asleep. The next day he was fine.

Glazer and Hertzan spent lots of time together, and eventually

Glazer finished a 139-page screenplay. The Hertzan character was named Jack Kyle. John mentioned the project to Spielberg, but Spielberg declined. He didn't think anyone would like such a movie. Drugs were like sports: people would rather participate than watch.

John sounded out Landis to see if he wanted to direct.

"You got this problem," Landis said. "You're going to make a fucking hero out of a drug runner. I don't like the idea of glorifying it."

"It's just marijuana in the screenplay," John said.

"No," Landis replied.

John tried others, but he couldn't find anyone who was interested in directing his movie.

The regular party following the May 19 show, hosted by Maureen Stapleton, was the first time in a year that John and Judy didn't take drugs afterward. The next day they slept late and felt great. John had a new Mercedes delivered to Judy for her birthday; it was four months late, but she loved the car. On Monday she awoke at 7 A.M. and John was not there. She was worried and felt she had been stupid to think that things were getting better. Upstairs she found notes saying he had gone to the *schvitz* and NBC. She called both. He wasn't at either. A few hours later he called to say he was sleeping in his office and that everything was fine.

On Saturday, June 2, John and Judy flew to the Vineyard, where they rented a house on Lambert's Cove. It was a short rest, and on June 15, John and Judy flew back to New York so that John could deliver what he called his "Farewell Address" to the Blues Brothers band. He was no longer going to be their leader, John said. The Blues Brothers had become too big with the upcoming movie. It would be Universal Studio, not Phantom, running the show. Producer Bob Weiss and director John Landis were now in charge.

That night Judy wrote in her diary: "I'm disappointed because they did coke. It must not be this way in Chicago [for the filming of the movie]. I still haven't done any since the show ended." That had been three weeks earlier.

Back at Martha's Vineyard, the weather was beautiful. John and Judy relaxed, went to some parties, dug for oysters. On June 28 she wrote: "John and I are enjoying being alone. He's much more alive without cocaine. . . . I'm getting nervous about going to Chicago." On July 1 they flew to Chicago.

•   •

Aykroyd was having a great time with John in Chicago. The Blues Brothers were taking over the city. Everyone, from Mayor Jane Byrne to passersby in the street, lent support.

One of the first things John did was grab Danny, hop in the car, and track down his old landlady from the Universal Life Coffee House, home of the small comedy troupe he had formed nine years earlier.

"You remember me?" he asked her.

"Ah! Mr. Belushi!"

"I still owe you for a month's rent," John said, reminding her that he had skipped out on it when he went to Second City. "I want to make sure you get it," he said, and paid the hundred dollars.

John and Aykroyd were spending a good deal of time at Second City, often showing up for the improvisational hour. One night they went exploring, looking to see what had happened to the old Sneak Joint, the little bar in a yellow house that used to be a hangout for the cast. It was boarded up. They peeked in the windows and saw that the bar fixtures were still there.

John and Danny both loved the idea of having their own bar, like Rick's Café, Humphrey Bogart's place in *Casablanca,* or like their bar in New York. They signed a six-month lease for $500 a month. Aykroyd bought a 1962 jukebox, and John stocked it with some classic 45s. They got a pool table, a pinball machine, some Dixie cups, a styrofoam ice chest and a stock of liquor and opened the doors. John hired Steve Beshekas, his old friend from the College of DuPage and the West Compass Players, now a refrigerator repairman, to manage the bar.

John and Judy continued to make occasional weekend trips to the Vineyard. The island was a sanctuary, quiet and removed, and they decided to look for a house to buy. They had the money now; the Blues Brothers record had earned John about $1 million. It would be the first home they would own.

The home of former Secretary of Defense Robert McNamara, one of the best on the island, was for sale. It was a modern, four-bedroom, one-story house situated on a tall bluff overlooking some of the most spectacular beaches of the south shore. The property consisted of 8.5 acres and shared a 1,900-foot private beach front that had been known as "Jungle Beach" until 1972, when McNamara and his neighbors had closed off a section.

John and Judy joked that they would probably find a bomb shelter, machine-gun nests and hidden microphones in the beautiful, remote, natural-colored structure. In late August 1979, they decided to buy it for

$425,000. "Shit," John told Judy, "the press won't be able to pass this up—the opportunity to mention McNamara and Belushi in the same sentence." He was right. It made most of the newspapers.

Belushi and Aykroyd were struggling with an important career decision. *The Blues Brothers* movie was going to take longer than anticipated. They were due back for the fifth season of "Saturday Night Live," and they dreaded the prospect of commuting every week. After 87 shows in four years, they were both tired. It had been a steady, grueling climb up the rating ladder, from an average 6.4 Nielsen and 22 percent audience share the first season to their current 13.1 and 39 percent share. Advertising rates had gone from $9,500 per 30-second spot in 1975 to a hefty $22,000 per spot the fourth season.

John told Brillstein, "I can't do this anymore. I'm going to burn out. I won't know if it's Monday or Friday."

Aykroyd agreed that there was no way they could do both the movie and the show.

In September 1979, a month before the show was to begin, they announced they were not returning.

John said in a statement, "Sometimes success can be very bittersweet."

Once in Chicago about midway through the filming of *The Blues Brothers,* John said he needed a shot of speed, an amphetamine, to rehearse for a dance routine; it would help him go all out. Lyda, the Blues Brothers road manager and John's personal caretaker, went with John and Judy to the apartment of Del Close, the Second City director who had had various addictions, including speed, heroin, Valium and alcohol.

John liked going to Close's, Lyda knew, because Close was very familiar with handling the needle and could inject John in his ass like a professional—quick and with no pain. "That's the only way to take it," John told Lyda. Having once done it that way himself, Lyda agreed.

Judy wanted to try it. Speed was not a worry with John, she felt. It was only cocaine. So Close gave them both a shot. Judy was surprised at how easy it was.

"Junkies give the best shots," Close said.

On Thursday, October 4, John, Judy, Aykroyd and Carrie Fisher took a chartered jet to the Vineyard for a long weekend. John and Judy were excited to be back on the island. It was now home, and they went exploring their new house, discovering closets, storage space and other things. On Saturday, Danny and Carrie took some acid and were roaring.

John and Judy walked around their property and made love on the cliff outside. John's back was bothering him, and he was heavier than she'd ever seen him. She'd been hesitant to bring it up, but John looked stuffed, his stomach like a giant, taut beach ball. Finally, she decided to broach the subject—wouldn't it be tough when he had to sing and dance hard for the filming? He agreed it would be and said he wanted to do something to lose weight. But that night they went for a big dinner.

John decided not to reopen Jungle Beach to the nudists who had used it before McNamara had closed it off. Several friends had expected something very different from John and were upset. But John felt that people were harassing him, and one day he went out on the lawn and screamed, "I didn't kill the Vietnamese; I didn't bomb secretly!" He decided to get rid of the place and had his accountant, Mark Lipsky, put it quietly on the market.

Judy got a call from Lipsky saying that former President Richard Nixon was looking for a place on the Vineyard and what did they think.

"We can't even let him look," Judy said.

"Suppose he meets the price?" Lipsky asked.

"No," Judy said. She checked with John, who agreed that selling to Nixon would be too much of a betrayal. Shortly after, they took the house off the market.

While Belushi and Aykroyd were filming *The Blues Brothers,* Steven Spielberg was doing the postproduction work on *1941* and was wondering more than ever what he'd gotten himself into. The normal uncertainty any director feels before the release of a movie had turned to fear. An unenthusiastic preview of *1941* in Dallas seemed to confirm the worst, and Spielberg delayed the scheduled release of the movie for six weeks until December so that he could shorten some of the scenes.

The December 9 *New York Times* carried a long article, headlined: WILL "1941" MAKE SPIELBERG A BILLION-DOLLAR BABY?, noting that if it were a big box-office hit, his three-movie total might reach $1 billion. "I'll spend the rest of my life disowning this movie," Spielberg was quoted as saying. But he'd gotten hooked on the characters, he said, particularly Belushi's.

Spielberg made sure he would not be around for the Hollywood opening on December 14. He left for a vacation in Hawaii.

The night of the fourteenth, John, Judy, Aykroyd and Penny Marshall, who had a cameo in the movie, rented a 1941 car and dressed for the premiere in forties clothes. To quiet their nerves they passed around a joint on the way to the Cinerama Dome Theater. It was a charity benefit performance and had an older audience.

The house lights dimmed. On a beach a woman disrobes and dives into the ocean to swim. Deep, foreboding *Jaws* shark music signals danger. It was a sight gag—a parody of the opening shot in *Jaws*. Rather than a shark, a Japanese submarine surfaces and lifts the naked woman out of the water on its periscope.

Judy thought it was funny, but there was scarcely a chuckle from the audience. It was a deadly two hours, and when they walked back to the car afterward, they were furious. John was in despair, afraid the movie would ruin his career.

The reviews were unpleasant.

Newsweek headlined it: SPIELBERG'S MISGUIDED MISSILE. David Ansen called it "spectacularly unfunny . . . like the most extravagant Erector set a kid has ever had to play with . . . a tedious John Belushi wears out his welcome early on."

The *Washington Post*'s Gary Arnold, under the headline DAZE OF THE YEAR, called the movie "a hectic, smug, self-destructive farce . . . an appalling waste of filmmaking and performing resources . . . pointless . . . hateful . . . [an] artistic disgrace."

Nearly every critic pointed to the $26-million budget, one of the most expensive comedies ever made, and some inaccurately reported that it was $30 to $40 million. Spielberg, who was thirty-two, was portrayed in the press as a spoiled child who would be allowed by the studios to make a movie about anything—toilet paper, or Henry Kissinger's memoirs if he wanted.

When Spielberg returned from Hawaii, John and Aykroyd showed up at his house.

"Fuck the critics," John said, launching into a half-time pep talk. The movie was important, he said, and the public likes it; the critics were gunning for all of us. The reviews were about the budget.

"Yeah, man," Aykroyd said. "We got $25 million in"—the then-current gross.

"It's got so much stuff in it," John added, "so much up on the screen, the fucking critics can't sort it out."

Spielberg felt he had let them down, but he was touched by their support. He knew the movie was not funny enough. The audience was looking for something more hilarious than *Animal House;* it had been advertised and presented that way, with pictures of John chomping a cigar in his airplane. John and Dan hadn't been in enough scenes, Spielberg concluded. The movie was too noisy. There was no real center—no shark, no Richard Dreyfuss—to focus it around. Spielberg thought he had learned something and would do better next time.

Spielberg still knew the importance of a good script; it was the only way to get a movie off on the right foot. He read them carefully as he cast around for new projects, nurturing his own ideas but following what was circulating among the agents, producers, writers and studios. Two years earlier he had read a script called *Continental Divide,* by an unknown, Lawrence Kasdan. Kasdan had been working in the advertising business for five years, writing at home at night and at the office during the day.

Spielberg liked what Kasdan had done with *Continental Divide.* It reminded him of the Spencer Tracy–Katharine Hepburn classics (*Woman of the Year, Adam's Rib*). *Divide* put a modern twist on a standard romance comedy: man and woman hate each other's guts in the first half of the story and then can't live apart in the second. A famous muckraking columnist named Ernie Souchak, modeled on Chicago newspaperman Mike Royko, goes to Colorado to interview Nell Porter, a beautiful but reclusive bird specialist. At the end they get married, an old solution, but agree to live apart, a new solution—Ernie in the city, Nell in the mountains—with a pledge to visit each other regularly.

Spielberg wasn't committed to direct it himself. Despite the failure of *1941,* he took the script to Universal. His interest made the script hot, and three other studios bid for it. Universal came out on top, paying $150,000 for what was basically Kasdan's first screenplay, plus another $100,000 in promised bonuses if the picture was made. (Spielberg was so impressed with Kasdan that he hired him to write the screenplay for another development project, *Raiders of the Lost Ark.*)

In early 1980, soon after the release of *1941,* Spielberg slipped a copy of the *Continental Divide* script to Belushi, saying, "You're the most original comedian to come along since Lou Costello." If John lost weight, it might be a serious romantic role for him.

John read it and called Spielberg. I hate you for giving it to me, but "I'm Souchak." As John talked further he said, "I can't play him." Then for an hour he alternated: I want to play him, I need to play him, I'm afraid, I hate it, I can't.

Spielberg wanted to bring in two of his best friends, Matthew Robbins and Hal Barwood, to direct and produce. Robbins and Barwood had cowritten Spielberg's *Sugarland Express* and written and directed (Robbins) and produced (Barwood) *Corvette Summer* (1978). Spielberg thought that both men had bright futures.

John agreed to come to a meeting at Spielberg's Coldwater Canyon house after dinner one night. Robbins, Barwood and Spielberg were watching an old 16 mm movie when John and Judy arrived. John did not sit down.

Spielberg introduced everyone, thinking that the three of them would interview John. Such meetings were normally run by the director.

"I'm from Chicago," John said, half bellowing. "I am Souchak. I *am* this guy. I know Mike Royko."

He went to the bar and poured himself a Jack Daniels. He then took orders aggressively, forcing drinks on the others. Spielberg suspected that John was drunk. Robbins suspected drugs. Judy seemed wan and miserable. She hung far in the background.

Royko, John emphasized, is the pulse taker of the real Chicago. He knew John's family from the Chicago restaurant business. John had met Royko years ago and had seen him occasionally when he was working with Second City in Chicago, and they were now friends.

Robbins looked John over closely: He was dexterous but grossly overweight. Robbins couldn't envision a beautiful leading lady wrapping her arms around that body and bringing her lips to that cheek.

But John was turning the meeting into a kind of performance. "You've got to let me do this part, man," John said, more to Spielberg than anyone. "It's my life. I know Chicago. I've been to every street corner as a kid."

Robbins brought up the love story, which was what he liked about the script. My concept, he said, is of two intense, equal professionals absorbed totally by their careers. The attraction is that they are very alike even though they seem to be opposites.

"I got to play it," John said. He offered more drinks.

No one wanted one.

John asked Robbins what he had directed, what were his screen credits?

Spielberg felt his skin crawl. Robbins fell silent; Barwood had nothing to say; Judy seemed to step further back.

John made a joke about his daily growth of heavy beard. Maybe he'd have to shave two or three times a day so the camera wouldn't catch his five-o'clock shadow.

Somehow Jack Nicholson's name came up.

"Jack treated me like shit on *Goin' South,*" John said. "I hate him.

If I see him, I'll punch him." John slammed his fist on the pool table and then into his other hand like a baseball catcher pounding his mitt. "I'm going to punch out that sonofabitch Jack Nicholson when I see him next," John shouted. "They really fucked me over," he said, moving closer and glaring at Robbins.

Robbins, a much smaller man, was frightened and pretty certain he didn't want to direct this man. What a power move, what a "don't fuck with me" warning. He agreed with Spielberg that the authority of the director was important and that it must prevail. A director needed autonomy if a movie was to have a coherent point of view. And here was a living, heavy-breathing wildman in front of them, roving about, promising to disfigure Jack Nicholson permanently.

Yet another part of Robbins, the creative eye, was still busily acquainting himself with what John could do. There was something intriguing about the idea of trying to bring this guy under control. The stumbling block would be finding a leading lady who could make it credible that she found Belushi attractive. John was in a kind of agony, wedded to the idea of breaking out of the Bluto role, but also terrified. Robbins studied John's shape some more. It would be a challenge.

Judy, seeing that John was out of hand, went over to him and put her arm around him and began to coax him out the door. Everyone said abrupt goodbyes, and John and Judy left. They'd been there nearly two hours.

Spielberg turned to his friends, made excuses and offered apologies. A lot of it was alarming. He had never seen John like that. It was as if you had looked inside someone and had seen the self-doubt and insecurity too clearly.

Barwood answered that he had never seen such a revealing and self-destructive performance. The monologue had been an audition *not* to get the job; John had come to lose the part.

For Ned Tanen, the president of Universal Pictures, the basic issue was Spielberg. Would he direct? What did he want? Spielberg's indecision lay over everything. Tanen had several meetings with Robbins, Barwood and Kasdan about the casting. Tanen explained that they had to have the right match between the male and female stars, whether it was Belushi or not. As dozens of names were mentioned, Kasdan, who was new to such matters, concluded that it was all about levels of stars, getting the most famous name and face.

Tanen blamed the star syndrome on the theater owners. As the head of the studio, his job was to look ahead to when he had to take the movie out and sell it.

Robbins and Barwood were still in love with the script and wanted to do the movie. Thus began a prolonged, star-studded mating game that drove them all nearly crazy. Belushi was on hold, but it looked as though they could get Richard Dreyfuss. That fell through. Peter Falk was in and out. Next George Segal. Elliott Gould was set and fell through. Universal talked to Dustin Hoffman, but that was as far as they got. A Jill Clayburgh–Robert DeNiro matchup backfired. Julie Christie didn't work out. Then Al Pacino fell through also. There was talk of Barbra Streisand playing the Souchak role and Robert Redford the bird lover. Kate Jackson's name was mentioned. Robbins and Barwood, disenchanted with the star process, finally backed out of the project.

This apparently was what Tanen had wanted. Spielberg was his solid choice, but Spielberg's ambivalence became only more apparent with time.

Meanwhile, Brillstein heard that Universal was offering the script around to others. He called Sean Daniels at Universal and threatened him: "You've got major trouble if that happens, and if it does, you'll be looking for Belushi the rest of your life."

John then began applying pressure on Universal. Spielberg, great as he is, is not essential, he said. Get a director and a female lead, John said, and I'll make the movie.

So Universal bought out Spielberg's right to direct for $100,000 and 5 percent of possible profits. Spielberg would be listed as an executive producer along with Brillstein.

Universal hired Michael Apted, a thirty-eight-year-old English director who had just finished *Coal Miner's Daughter,* a film about country music queen Loretta Lynn.

When Apted went to talk to John, however, he found John wanted to be wooed. It was almost as if he was testing Apted's nerve and patience. But John soon agreed, and the deal was signed, giving him $850,000.

One night John and his new drug enforcer Smokey Wendell went out in a limousine in New York. John was looking for drugs. He never gave an address to the driver, simply ordering, "Go straight, now turn left . . . turn right here! . . . Stop at this corner." When they got to a destination, Smokey insisted on going with him as John pounded on doors and wildly rang buzzers. He had had no luck after seven stops.

After working with John for several weeks, Smokey had tried to find out what the hell was going on. He and John were in the living room at Morton Street. "Why do you take drugs?" he asked.

"Because they're there."

"Come on," Smokey said. "I don't understand when someone like you has all this going for himself. . . . Why do you have to rely on drugs?"

"Basically, it's the pressure," John answered. "Whatever you do as a person to maintain patience and stay alert—the people in this business rely on drugs to do that."

"That doesn't make sense to me," Smokey said. "By doing what you're saying, you've got to realize how it's endangering your ability to function. Like alcoholism."

"Alcohol and drugs are different things," John said with disgust.

"You use this, you use that," Smokey said, "and you use everything. What happens when you reach this plateau and don't get that snap, that buzz? When you get to that level and have tried every drug, at every level? What happens then?"

John pondered for a moment and said, "I don't know. . . . I guess you'd just go crazy." He then got up uneasily and went to the kitchen.

In the spring of 1980, as preparations were being made for the Blues Brothers' elaborate 22-show, 13-city nationwide concert tour, scheduled to coincide with the release of the movie that summer, Morris Lyda made arrangements for John to have voice lessons with a vocal therapist who was going to show him techniques to save his voice when he ran into problems and give him tips on how to improve his vocal strength. When John skipped the appointment, Lyda asked, "Don't you even want to attempt to do things right?"

"I just don't want to go," John said. "I've been doing this for years, and I've never had any problems before."

Lyda said this was different. These would be long shows with no time to rest his voice in between.

"You work for me because I pay you to. Do it my way," John said.

"You pay me to do things right, not to fuck things up." Lyda told John he was quitting, and he left town two days before rehearsals were to begin on June 8. A few days later Brillstein called. "Morris, you're right and John's wrong. But your timing is all fucked up, and you did it all wrong."

"You know that he needs it," Lyda said. "John just doesn't want it in the newspapers that he went to a vocal doctor." Lyda hung up.

The band members called, evidently at John's urging. Lyda finally took back his job, but he decided to stay in the background and avoid direct contact with John.

Paul Shaffer, the pianist and bandleader, was also worried about John's voice. John had decided not to have a warmup band for the concerts, and that meant the Blues Brothers would have to play a much longer show—two hours—and more songs had to be added to their repertory. Shaffer knew the schedule would be rough enough on John's voice; if he did coke, it would be that much tougher. John was not doing any TV interviews and gave his reason: "What are they going to see? An insecure guy with a drug problem."

John decided there was one song he especially wanted to sing on the tour—"Guilty," by Randy Newman, a cynical singer-songwriter whose 1977 "Short People" was a controversial hit. During rehearsals, using his raspy Joe Cocker imitation, John started practicing "Guilty," a song about a fuckup who is lost, riddled with self-doubt, booze and cocaine. He sang the last three lines:

> "You know I just can't stand myself.
> It takes a whole lot of medicine, darlin',
> for me to pretend that I'm somebody else."

Each time John put down the microphone after doing the song, he was clearly wrung out. Lyda had wondered all along if John was man enough to sing it and had previously told him so. It seemed almost like self-punishment, and the intensity John gave the song left a deep impression on many of those closest to him, including Judy, Aykroyd and Brillstein. For Landis, the song told too much of the John Belushi story.

Just before the opening of *The Blues Brothers* movie, Landis was deeply worried. The critics were gunning for him. Universal was going all out with the promotion—buttons, T-shirts, even a Blues Brothers book done by Judy and John's old friend Tino Insano, giving fictionalized biographies of Jake and Elwood. Mitch Glazer was doing a paperback novelization. A toy replica of the Bluesmobile, the black-and-white former police car used by John and Aykroyd in the film, was being produced. Massive radio and television advertising was being coordinated for both the movie and the sound-track album, which was going to flood the stores.

Landis found all this mildly frightening. In addition the movie was coming out up against the long-awaited *Star Wars* sequel, *The Empire Strikes Back*.

When the theater owners saw that *The Blues Brothers* was more than two and one-half hours and had an intermission, they rebelled. Long movies meant fewer showings and no midnight shows on Friday and Saturday nights. Universal ordered Landis to cut about 20 minutes, bringing the film down to two hours and 10 minutes. He didn't have much time, and he felt like a butcher.

Some theater owners said it was a "black movie." One owner told Landis that he wouldn't book it in his theater in a fancy part of Los Angeles because it would bring in blacks, the originators of the blues. Landis was shocked by the racism, but he knew he would have to work with these people again, so he kept his mouth shut.

John and Danny went on the "Today" show to promote *The Blues Brothers*. Before going on the air, however, John told host Tom Brokaw that he was going to talk mostly about the sound-track album rather than the movie itself. "We got to push the album, because that's where the bread is."

They got a fixed royalty on each record sold of nearly $1, whereas the studio would get millions on the movie before he got any portion of the profits, other than the $500,000 he had been paid up front.

Charles Champlin was out with the first review in the *Los Angeles Times* under the headline "Blues": A $30-Million Wreck, Minus Laughs. "The ruthless joke around Hollywood has been that the 'Blues Brothers' should have been called '1942,' homage to the earlier work which similarly suffered from swollen glands. . . ."

In the *New York Times,* Janet Maslin termed it "a bloated saga." *Washington Post* reviewer Gary Arnold fingered Landis as the culprit, responsible for a "ponderous comic monstrosity. . . . Belushi lowers his shades once near the end, supposedly a dynamite jest but actually a confirmation of the obvious: Never, never, never should anyone, especially a performer with expressive eyes, be allowed the imbecilic drollery of concealing them from a motion picture audience."

The *New York Times* later featured *The Blues Brothers* in two stories about recent films—including Spielberg's *1941*—headlined: The Golden Age of Junk, and Why Hollywood Breeds Self-Indulgence.

Landis was instantly defensive, claiming the bad reviews were an attack on the $27-million cost, $11 million over the original budget. Later on, he admitted that the movie didn't have enough plot or character; it was a quirky idea that had not been well executed. Other times he thought, really, it was a fine movie with a stark realism that looked good on the big screen. In any case, Landis thought Aykroyd had carried both the film and John, but that that had not been enough. Dan, so easy and comfortable before a TV camera, had tightened up. But the real story of the movie had been John's drugs, which had infected the production.

While preparing for the Blues Brothers tour, John had been spending lots of money, particularly on limousines. He was ordering one and keeping it for two days straight, wasting thousands of dollars a week. Judy and Mark Lipsky, their accountant, had been trying for a month and a half to get John to cut back. When Lipsky mentioned it to John, he advanced on him, grabbed his necktie and threatened him. Another time Lipsky told Judy that John was going overboard. That night John called Lipsky at home and screamed at him, cursing him out for meddling and causing trouble.

John's response to the negative reception of *The Blues Brothers* was a drug binge, and Lipsky was choking off the cash, giving him the third degree each time he wanted money. What is it for? Do you really need that much?

One day toward the end of June, John appeared at Lipsky's Fifth Avenue offices around lunchtime. Lipsky was out, but Shirley Sergent, his assistant, got word that John was in Lipsky's office demanding cash. She went in. Dressed in khaki pants with his shirt hanging out, John was lying on Lipsky's office couch, a hat pulled down over his eyes. He sat up and demanded $1,000. Sergent stalled.

"It's my money," John said, rising up and grabbing her arm, squeezing hard. "I want it!"

"Let go of my arm," she said, jerking it away. "I know it's your money, but you can't have it now because Mark's not here to approve it. You'll have to sit here and wait for Mark." She walked out, and Lipsky came back ten minutes later. Sergent pulled him into another office and explained that John was waiting for money, camped in his office.

"I feel I shouldn't give it to him," Lipsky said. "I know what he's going to do with it." Lipsky was tired of John's repeated claims of self-knowledge and self-control: "Don't worry, don't worry. I know what I'm doing, I know what I'm doing." John often had no idea what he was doing. Lipsky's resolve increased when he entered his office. John was almost out cold on the couch. When he rose he was wobbly, drugged up and telling Lipsky he didn't want any shit.

Just then Lipsky's secretary buzzed and said Judy was on the phone. Lipsky left to take the call down the hall. Judy said John was really messed up and to "please, please" not give him any money.

Lipsky returned to his office. John repeated his demand. $1,000. Cash. Now. Lipsky shook his head no.

John stepped forward and threatened to wreck the entire office or drag the money out of Lipsky himself. He shoved a chair around violently and sent it crashing down at Lipsky's feet. John moved closer. John seemed capable of anything, and Lipsky decided there was no choice. He got the money.

As John was leaving he shouted, "You are no longer my accountant. I'm pulling all my money out! Fuck you, Mark."

"Fuck you!" Lipsky shot back.

A few weeks later John apologized, saying, "Hey, I'm sorry about what happened in the office the other day."

When the tour was about to begin, John snapped out of his binge. Smokey could see that with a new task before him, John was taking things much more seriously. He made an antidrug speech to laughter and suspicious gazes of the band members. "If you're wired, you're fired!" he told them, explaining that it was their job to give the people in each and every city what they paid for, and more. Too much was at stake, he said, to use drugs.

The movie and concert tour opened in Chicago on the same day, Friday, June 27, 1980, to enthusiastic, capacity crowds. Gene Siskel, the *Chicago Tribune* film critic, interviewed John and Aykroyd at the Pump Room in the Ambassador Hotel.

"I'm not envious of Danny," Belushi said. "But I have real admiration for his writing skill and his intellect. Envy, no, but I wish I could be as good a writer as he is."

"But, John, you're just lazy," Aykroyd said, and he told Siskel, "He's a good writer. He knows structure, he knows scripts, he knows comedy, he knows running order, he knows all those things. . . . My attitude is that I've hooked up with a very big American star and I'm in his workshop."

After concerts in Philadelphia, New York and Washington, D.C., the tour moved to upstate New York over the Fourth of July weekend. There, Smokey took John and Judy to his family's farm outside Cooperstown, New York. John went fishing with Smokey's thirteen-year-old nephew, hunted and visited the Baseball Hall of Fame. He lingered like a kid by the plaque to Ernie Banks, the famous Chicago Cubs shortstop. Smokey bought John a baseball that had been signed by Banks, and John was touched. "It's great to be alive," John said.

Smokey was glad to see that the routine and responsibility of touring had forced some self-restraint in John. But some members of the band thought things were being carried too far. It had gotten to the point where Duck Dunn and Steve Cropper were afraid even to be caught in a hotel bar having a drink after the show. And Dunn was told to stop keeping a bottle of Russian vodka behind stage during the performance.

Dunn found this holier-than-thou attitude part of the effort to shield John, to keep him away from the rest of the band and drugs. Hell, Dunn had never even done any coke until he had met John and joined the Blues Brothers. If John was going to go out and go crazy—and there were still the little isolated incidents, though nothing major—Dunn figured it would be better to have him with a member of the band who could watch out for him.

On July 13 the Blues Brothers played a concert in the Dallas Convention Center. Afterward, John and some of the band members gathered in a hotel room. Smokey noticed that cocaine was being passed around.

"Give me some of that," John said.

Smokey froze, and the three band members in the room stopped in their tracks.

"Come on," John said, "give me the blow."

"Don't you listen to him," Smokey said.

John assumed the role of boss. *He* was paying everybody's salary and *he* wanted the cocaine.

Smokey snatched the cocaine from the table.

John made a tight fist and moved back as if he were going to slug Smokey.

"Since when were you a quarterback?" Smokey said, smiling. "You got a football there?"

John dropped his fist. "I don't believe I was going to hit you."

The two walked out of the room and down the hall. Tears were running down John's face.

"I'm sorry, so sorry, man," John said. "That will never happen again." They walked and embraced. "That was quick—a good line." John started to reminisce about football; he used to have a good line himself at the line of scrimmage. Looking at the player across from him, he'd say, "When the ball is snapped, you'll hear your nose break." The intimidation often worked, and John said he would have control for the entire game.

Smokey thought that John hovered between extremes of self-confidence, at times arrogance, and deep fears—about the music, the tour, the movies, his career, Judy, friendships, himself. One moment he would dodge Smokey; the next he would seek his company. Frequently in the morning about five, John would wake him up to play gin rummy, go for a drive, a walk, or just sit and watch television. John needed companionship. He was a night wanderer, aggravating one moment, endearing the next.

12

On Saturday, July 19, the band flew into Los Angeles for the last leg of their tour, a grueling seven-night stand at the Universal Amphitheater, where the Blues Brothers had given their first public performance 22 months before. Tom Scott had noticed some changes in John over those many months and most of them were not good. In private, John was playing rock star. On stage, he was lapsing into John Belushi and the old Cocker routine—more physical, less musical; there was less of Jake. Scott thought the role of Jake had promise, but John was screaming into the microphone, not singing. By L.A., he had lost his voice.

Scott had a house in L.A., but the rest of the band was holed up at the Sheraton Universal, while John and Danny were in bungalows at the Beverly Hills Hotel. And John had started taking a limousine to the concerts instead of riding in the bus with the band. They had come a long way from the night when Belushi wouldn't go to Hugh Hefner's party unless the band was invited.

During rehearsals before the L.A. concerts, Scott had talked to drummer Steve Jordan, who told him that he had demanded $1,000 a week more than the other members and that John had agreed to it. Scott was furious. They were supposed to be paid the same. He told the other band members he was going to demand that his equal-pay agreement be honored. They asked Scott to represent them, but he refused; he was going to get his, and he would let them know the outcome.

Lipsky told Scott that he knew nothing about John's arrangement with Jordan. Judy was asked. She knew nothing about it either. Scott was not surprised. John loved to exercise power. Scott said he would quit unless he received an extra $10,000 to bring him in line with Jordan.

He got it and then told the other band members, but none of them protested. Scott knew that some of them felt that John held the key to their futures—the possibility of another movie, more albums. None of them wanted to rock the boat.

One night, John and Smokey went up to the home of Ringo Starr, the former Beatle. Smokey was told to wait outside. He got bored and walked around the back and found his way inside the house. John, Ringo and Ron Wood of the Rolling Stones were sitting talking.

"Oh my God!" John screamed. "Oh my God, it's him! Not him!" He put on a skit, pretending Smokey was a cop or some past tormentor.

Ringo was set to run until John explained.

"You scared the shit out of me," Ringo said, not sure it was funny.

Smokey knew that Los Angeles meant temptations for John, but he was being pretty good. And Judy was relieved that John was taking a more moderate course and avoiding drugs of his own free will, maybe not entirely but more often than not. During one of the Amphitheater concerts, someone in the audience yelled up to John, "What about drugs?"

"Stay away from them," Belushi said into the microphone. "They're bad." Judy knew that for the moment he meant it. John was taking oxygen after the shows to help his voice, but by the third night his voice was fried—not from cocaine or drugs but from overuse and the tension of the tour, which they were calling appropriately "The Road to Ruin" summer tour.

One night at the Beverly Hills Hotel, John and Smokey ran into actor Tony Curtis, who invited John, Judy, Steve Beshekas and Smokey to a bungalow, where some cocaine was laid out.

"Remember what your doctor said about your valve," Smokey said, referring to John's nose. He could see that John was wavering, but he did in the end decline.

Out in the living room, they began talking about someone in the movie business who had recently died.

"Fuck it," Curtis said. "One less guy I have to compete with. . . . The movie business is a cutthroat business! This business of getting a script is fucked. You got to get to them before they get to you." At that, Curtis put on a big white hat, jumped over a coffee table, and stormed out the door.

John made it through the last concert, and on the way over to a midnight celebration party at the Tony Duquette Studios, he was excited and relieved. Whether it was the release of tension, the screwdriver he was drinking or something else, John got sick in the limousine and started to cough and gag.

Smokey yelled to the driver to stop, dragged John from the car, cleaned out his mouth and started mouth-to-mouth resuscitation. John's breathing passage was finally cleared and he sat up, dazed but okay. They drove back to the hotel and he changed his clothes.

Later at the party, John played celebrity host to the crowd of stars, moving around rapidly, accepting and offering congratulations.

Penny Marshall saw someone drop a vial of cocaine in John's pocket. Smokey saw it too and went over and had John lift his arms while he searched and got it. Someone else passed another packet in a handshake, and Smokey retrieved that one. No fewer than five more people passed or dropped vials or packets in John's pocket—a standard Los Angeles way of sending best wishes, Smokey figured. When another vial was passed in a handshake, John apparently thought Smokey hadn't noticed and headed to the washroom and closed the door. Smokey, passing John's brother Jimmy, who was standing outside, charged in after John. It was a small room meant for only one person.

"Come on," John said, "just let me have a little."

Smokey seized the vial and held it tight.

"I've been real good. Please," John begged.

Smokey said that he wouldn't allow any drugs until his assignment was over, and the tour was not technically finished—there was just this last party.

"It's past midnight," John argued, and added snidely, "You got your check."

Smokey held his fist in the air, kept it there a moment, then plunged it into the toilet.

"Oh, oh, oh! No, no, no!" John screamed. "I will never forgive you. I'll never forget." He buried his head in his arms in despair.

Jimmy Belushi, outside the door, was wondering what all the noise and commotion were about.

Smokey walked out, slipped through the crowd and walked up to the man—a magazine reporter—who had given John the vial and handed it back. John raced up.

"How did you do that?"

Smokey told him the vial had been in his other hand.

After a few hours they went back to the Beverly Hills bungalow. John lit up a cigarette and lay down on the bed to relax and unwind. He looked enormous; his weight was up to 245. The adrenalin was still flowing fast, but he seemed subdued. He looked at Smokey.

"I asked you to give me a break, and you wouldn't even give me one," John said. He didn't seem angry, rather more astounded. He chuckled. Well, he said, he had arranged for a $2,000 bonus for Smokey, plus a video recording machine and a ten-day, all-expenses paid vacation at the Bel-Air Hotel for Smokey and his wife, Deborah.

Later that night Smokey awoke in the bungalow and heard John in the kitchen. After John had a sandwich and a glass of milk, Smokey followed him back into the bedroom, where Judy was asleep on one side of the king-size bed, a pillow over her head, the way she usually slept, to drown out John's snoring. John propped himself up on the other side of the bed.

"You know, this is a strange business. Have you ever stopped to think about it?"

"In what way?" Smokey asked.

"Well, you work so hard in the early years . . . you struggle hard. You go without."

"Yeah," Smokey said. "You pay your dues."

"Then the time comes when you make it—you're the star," John said derisively. "Then all of a sudden everyone is doing it for you. You're directed. People are doing it for you. . . ."

"*Animal House* hit," Smokey said.

"Yes," John said, "and then I was a millionaire. The rough living, going without was over. Then I had all these friends, going to all these parties. All of the deals. It was getting very scary because it was happening so fast. I had more money than I knew what to do with." John paused. "It gets worse as it gets better. That's it . . . I'm talking to you, sitting here. I never thought I could afford a place like this. . . . What happens, you get caught up in this business and the drugs are inevitable. They were here before me and will be here after me."

"What are you trying to say?" Smokey asked.

"I'm going to be on my own. . . . I'm uneasy. There is that little scare inside."

"Whenever you get that, you can call me. Just call me. Okay?"

"Yeah," John said.

Smokey nodded. It had at times seemed as if John were falling and there were no bottom. But it hadn't all been screaming self-indulgence and nasty confrontations. There had been many elegant refusals and moments of self-awareness and honesty for John. John rebelled at authority; yet he had hired an ex–Secret Service agent to watch his every move. At times they had fought like hell, but at the end of the tour there were, of all things, goodwill, a bonus, video equipment and a vacation at the Bel-Air for the enforcer. Smokey left the next morning for his holiday.

A week later John and Judy went to Europe together. They stayed in a remote castle in Scotland, and John did little but sleep for five days. Then they continued to the South of France and visited a grand house in the mountains that Michael O'Donoghue, his friend, writer Carol Cald-well, and another writer named Nelson Lyon and his friend Viviane were renting.

At the end of August, John and Judy arrived in Venice. One after-noon they took a gondola ride and came back to their hotel room. The phone rang. John took the call while Judy was in the bathroom. It was Brillstein. The call took a long time.

"Hey, you ready to go?" John said to her afterward. She could tell something had happened.

"Doug Kenney's dead," John said finally. It had happened in Hawaii on a cliff; he fell, or was pushed, or jumped. No one was sure.

The hotel room suddenly seemed terribly small and confining to Judy.

"I just feel terrible that we never made up," John said. His face was grim and hard. He said he felt that Kenney, a founder of the *Lampoon* and coauthor of *Animal House,* had been trying to get John Landis away for his own movie and had tried to sabotage *The Blues Brothers*. John and Kenney had fought about it, bitter, harsh words, as if they couldn't find a way to divide up the *Animal House* success.

"This goddamn business," John said. "I'm not going to let it inter-fere with friendships anymore."

John called Lucy Fisher, the thirty-one-year-old head of production at Francis Ford Coppola's Zoetrope Studio. She had been Kenney's best friend.

Fisher had met John in 1975 when he was starting "Saturday Night" and she was a script reader at United Artists. Both she and Kenney loved John: he was kind, smart and not yet famous. Kenney used to call Judy the "East Coast Lucy Fisher," claiming that Judy and Fisher were alike —the mother confessors and big sisters on their respective coasts.

Fisher and John shared their grief and anguish, their conviction that neither of them had done enough. John wanted to be forgiven and was deeply upset about his own behavior. The things he'd said about Kenney were bullshit, he said. He hadn't meant a single one. Fisher knew that John was telling her the things he wanted to say to Kenney. Cocaine had helped kill Kenney, she felt. Kenney would get coked out and lose his judgment and then later see himself and what he'd done. Then he would get angry and feel he was a failure.

She and John marveled at how all the success and money and genius had turned into a failure for Kenney. It wasn't what it was supposed to be. Being on top often made you feel like shit. Fisher recalled that when someone once had asked Kenney about all the fame and money, he had replied, "It doesn't make you feel better at all. Not even the first five minutes when you walk into a party and don't know anyone."

It was too easy to get swallowed up in Hollywood, they agreed. John expressed his sorrow again.

"It's okay," Fisher said. "It's okay." She resolved to keep the channel to John open.

John and Judy moved on to Germany to a film festival, but the rest of the trip wasn't the same and they wanted it to end. The first bright light of their generation who was a close friend—and should have been closer—was gone. Kenney had been thirty-three.

In September 1980, soon after he returned from Europe, John decided to get a physical trainer to help him lose weight. He hired Bill "Superfoot" Wallace, the world champion (1974–80) of full contact karate, the variety that allows knockouts. Wallace had 13 knockouts in his last 23 matches. A thin, unassuming thirty-four, at five feet eleven, 165 pounds, Wallace had run a karate school for Elvis Presley for two years in the seventies and had helped John on the Blues Brothers concert tour that summer. John explained that this time it was serious and he had only a month left to get his weight down for the filming of *Continental Divide*. Wallace moved into Morton Street. They began a rigorous physical regimen.

Michael Apted was having problems finding a costar. Many agents refused to send the script to their female superstar clients, feeling it would be too embarrassing for any of them to play in a romance opposite Belushi.

But John, shaken by the attacks on *1941* and *The Blues Brothers,* was firm in his desire to do *Continental Divide*. It was clear that "Saturday Night Live" on the big screen, his latest movies, were not working for his career.

Apted finally found Blair Brown, a little-known actress who had just finished a starring role in *Altered States,* a Ken Russell science-fiction film that had not yet been released. A beautiful, almost brassy woman with a background in classical theater, Brown looked like a cross between a young Jacqueline Kennedy Onassis and Katharine Hepburn. She had auburn hair, near perfect teeth and a comfortable, disarming presence. She also had an air of upper-class irreverence and fearlessness. She had been raised near Washington, D.C., where her father had worked for the CIA.

Brown jumped at the offer. She was a fan of "Saturday Night Live" and was intrigued that the male lead wasn't a beauty.

Apted began rehearsals in his Los Angeles office at Universal a couple of weeks before filming was to begin. John was about 45 minutes late for the first meeting, and Apted took him aside and warned him not to be late again.

Brown found Belushi all nerves; he also seemed bored and never really focused on her and, at first, seemed to regard the material as if it were going to be a snap. Brown tried to make herself seem approachable through strong eye contact with John, but he remained aloof. They read some lines, but she had the feeling that John would have liked to leave. As they rehearsed over several days, Brown saw that John had a way of keeping her off balance. If she approached something seriously, he would try to cover it with a laugh. But if she tried to lighten it up, he would hit her with a serious side. The remoteness remained, and she felt more and more on the outside.

Brown's boyfriend, Richard Jordan, had been one of the costars in *Old Boyfriends,* and she knew that most male stars sat well on their power. She was nervous, wondering what she was up against.

Carrie Fisher, who had played John's spurned fiancée in *The Blues Brothers,* went out with John several days before he was supposed to go to Colorado to begin the filming. She was pleased to see that he was losing weight, and he had apparently been off drugs for three months. They went to the Imperial Gardens restaurant in Hollywood and joined a small dinner party that included actor Robert De Niro. Fisher was the only woman in the group.

John urged them all to join him at On the Rox, a small private club above the famous Roxy Nightclub at 9009 Sunset Boulevard. On the Rox, which was nothing more than a living room with a bar at one end, was owned by record producer and movie director (*Up in Smoke*) Lou Adler. It was John's favorite hideout in Los Angeles, a place where he and his famous friends could enjoy a few drinks and something to eat away from their fans. The club motto, printed in raised letters on the back of its matches, was "Living well is the best revenge."

John piled everyone into his limousine. Fisher was enjoying being part of the boys' night out. There was a large crowd at On the Rox, which was unusual, and she lost John for a few minutes in the small, crowded room, but soon he reappeared.

"I just did a hit of coke," he said, staring at her uneasily as if to say, "Oh my God, I can't control it." Fisher stood there, haunted. There was such emotion in his voice and gaze. She couldn't believe that the last months had been for nothing. Even worse, it was the first time she had ever seen him afraid.

John's gaze was an addict's. She knew it from her father. For the first time she realized that John might die; she realized it because *he* seemed to realize it.

"John," she said forcefully, "leave with me now. It doesn't matter. Let's go."

"No," he said.

Fisher thought it was hopeless and wanted to spare them both a confrontation. At 95 pounds and five feet one, she didn't stand a chance of dragging Belushi out. He held his ground and she left.

The next morning, Apted showed up at John's bungalow at the Beverly Hills Hotel for a nine-thirty meeting, and John was not there. Apted waited. About an hour later John arrived. He looked as if he had been up all night.

"We've got to see Bernie," John said, pointing to Brillstein's house across the street on Crescent Drive. "I can't do it."

Even though they were scheduled to leave for Colorado in three days, John said he was dropping out of the movie.

Apted called Sean Daniels and told him to meet them at Brillstein's. It was an emergency.

Within a half-hour Brillstein, Apted and Daniels were sitting down with John. He got up and helped himself to a beer from Brillstein's refrigerator. It was now about 11 A.M.

"I can't do it," John said. He didn't know how to do this kind of part. He was out of his depth. He knew it, everyone knew it. This was *not* him. In fact, he was *not* Ernie Souchak, *not* Spencer Tracy, *not* a plausible romantic hero. It was all wrong and he was out.

Apted saw that John had had a complete loss of nerve. John was not attacking anyone other than himself. He was saying it was his failing;

better to pull back at the edge of the cliff. Apted felt no indignation, only alarm.

"We're all friends," Daniels said. "Let's talk about it." There was no possible strategy other than to let this meeting take its course. John was not threatening; there were none of the usual heated "fuck you's."

John paced about the room, sitting down and then jumping up again, trying to explain his anxiety. He said he had been up all night worrying about it.

Apted was concerned that no matter what happened now, they were in trouble. Even if they got him back on track, Apted thought he'd have to be in John's pocket 24 hours a day.

Let's go out on the patio, Brillstein said to John. The two sat overlooking the pool. Brillstein knew that John didn't like to work with strangers. There was no Danny, no familiar writer, no one from "Saturday Night Live" on this movie.

"I don't know," John said. "Look, we took a chance on *1941* and look what we got. . . ." John said he liked Apted, but he was uncomfortable with Blair Brown. She was intimidating. Did she know what she was doing? He knew something about the chemistry of comedy and with audiences, but he didn't understand this sort of relationship with a woman. John, Brillstein knew, had a big problem with women; he always had. Brillstein pushed. They had a contract. Hundreds of people had been hired, were being paid. There were sets and locations. There was no choice. If it didn't work out, it would not be the end of the world. Apted was one of the greats. Blair Brown had a terrific reputation. The script had practically become a Hollywood legend.

John finally agreed.

In October, when John arrived in Canon City, Colorado, 90 miles south of Denver and in the shadow of the legendary 14,000-foot Pikes Peak, he had with him Judy, Bill Wallace and Smokey Wendell. They arrived at night, and Wallace suggested that he and John go for a run since they had been sitting all day. It was dark, so they had Smokey follow them in a car. The atmosphere was thin in the foothills of the Rockies, and after about a mile John gave out. But he proved determined to live on a strict regimen. Judy had rented a big house for them, and a helicopter was to come each morning to pick John up on the lawn and take him to the set, high in the snow-capped mountains. Smokey would get John up at six o'clock and make breakfast—puffed rice, black coffee with Sweet 'n Low, cantaloupe and skim milk. John was silent as he ate his food. He had lost 40 pounds for the part, down to 199, and was healthier than Smokey had ever seen him.

The scheduled scenes during the first week were outdoors—mountain climbing and episodes outside Nell Porter's cabin, where she lived alone. The newspaper portions were to be done in Chicago, and after that the love scenes between John and Blair would be shot on the Universal lot in Los Angeles.

Brown found John still distant. He didn't enjoy the outdoors. Nearly everyone was stocking up on equipment from L.L. Bean catalogues, but John seemed obsessed with weight loss and exercise, mostly indoors.

Brown found Judy nervous, thin and strung out. At first she thought Judy must be a doper, but she soon learned that it was merely shyness. Judy was also clearly bearing most of the burden for John's personality and abuses.

Apted saw that the right feeling was not developing between his costars. The film hinged on the degree of unspoken empathy that the two had for each other—touch, eyes, voice inflections. And that depended on a balance, a like-mindedness and harmony—a natural affection. Apted couldn't wrestle it out of them. And neither of them could get the upper hand. Apted took Brown aside and said, Don't take any shit from him. John may try to flex his muscles in all kinds of ways.

Not long after this, Brown went to her trailer and found some workmen moving her things out. She asked what was going on.

One of them said Belushi wanted to switch trailers. He liked this one better.

She told them to stop and never heard anything more about it.

But John was staying away from drugs and refused when crew members offered them to him. "I can't believe I turned it down," he said to Wallace.

Getting up and making it to the set in the mountains on time was difficult. John was generally a few minutes late. Once he kept everyone waiting in the freezing cold for nearly an hour, and when Apted complained, Belushi reminded him: "I'm a sleazy nightclub act. I work at night."

Apted decided that it would be foolhardy to push too hard. He had rarely seen anyone punish himself as much as John.

The dailies—the unedited film from the day before—were shown twice, once for Belushi and again for everybody else. Apted tried to guide John. And he explained that constructing a character like Souchak was a slow, businesslike job: like building a brick wall, it was one brick at a time. Each line, each scene, did not have to pay off immediately. John was racing for the laugh or to the tag line. What was needed was subtlety, and that took patience. It was important to let his character grow. John seemed intrigued and alarmed.

He was also proud of his weight loss. Joel Briskin, Brillstein's adjutant, came to visit the set and went to John's room.

"You know what these are? See these?" John announced. He was holding his face up. "You know what they are? *Cheekbones*."

Briskin had rarely seen John so happy and proud.

By mid-November they had finished the Colorado shooting, and everyone flew to Chicago for the newsroom and outdoor city scenes.

"Oh Chicago," John said with a smile as the plane descended. "Let's go to the bar," he said to Smokey.

Smokey knew that almost nothing could test John's restraint more than the Blues Bar, so he watched closely when they entered. A number of John's old friends were there.

While John was playing pool, Smokey saw someone stick a little packet inside the pipe of an old potbellied stove once used for heat. He went over and took the packet. Soon John was reaching up inside the pipe. He found nothing. Smokey found drugs in the washroom and inside the pinball machine and removed them.

Unsuccessful at making a score, John got drunk. Smokey took him to the hotel. In the penthouse that Frank Sinatra often used, John had a video tape of *Triumph of the Will,* the propaganda film of the 1934 Nuremberg Nazi party rally made with 40 cameramen by Leni Riefenstahl. He watched it over and over again, spellbound.

John was also showing an interest in Napoleon and was reading about him. Judy noticed that he had picked up some of Bonaparte's alleged mannerisms. Once she awakened and John was talking in his sleep, saying intelligibly, "I ride at the head of my men. I will ride a white horse!"

Apted was increasingly concerned as he watched John slipping into his natural environment. The three weeks of Chicago work consisted mostly of basic street shots to create a feel for the city. John was coasting, a returned hero; on the streets he created quite a commotion. *"Hey, Belushi!"* they shouted at him, as if he belonged to them. There were new clubs for John to see, new bands to check out, old friends to visit. Apted was aware of the pressures on John: come back to Chicago; come back fully, in the old way; join the urban festivities.

At least John was not disappearing, so the binges were not so bad. But Apted was shocked by how fast John put weight back on. He was blowing up. The scenes were not being shot in sequence, and if John ballooned up, the continuity would be destroyed. Apted was worried that this might affect the love story. It was a question not only of Brown's reaction to John, but of John's to himself. John's weight was as much a psychological as a physical burden, and as he got fatter, he would loathe himself more.

Blair Brown was unhappy in Chicago. John took her to the Pump Room with Bernie Brillstein and then abandoned them both. On another occasion, they went out with Mike Royko, who beamed at John as if he were his son. Brown felt it was urgent that they get down to acting. She tried to get more out of the scenes, to give them some depth. There clearly was a powerful actor inside John, but only he could let it out, no matter how much she tried to help. She suggested more and more takes of each scene to give him more opportunities. The problem was to find the tone.

Apted was trying to extinguish some of the standard Belushi humor, telling John, "No eyebrows." John said he didn't think there were enough jokes in the script. His notion of intimacy was to grab Brown's arm and wrestle her. Every now and then, when they shared a laugh, she felt that he had let her in. But mostly she thought of him as a bear, not a romantic partner.

The script called for a love scene, in bed, in a hotel room. They were to be nude under the covers. John was very nervous preparing for the shooting and kept making jokes, trying to get them to remember all the known names for the male sex organ. They came up with many— "the hose of horror," "Mr. Wiggly's dick," and "one-eyed snake in a turtleneck." Brown didn't mind the conversation, but she thought it was an inappropriate prelude to a love scene.

Bill Wallace was not having a good time in Chicago. John had abandoned him one night for five hours with "I'll be right back." He thought about quitting. But on his birthday, December 1, his parents came in from Indiana, and John made amends. He took them all to the Pump Room, had a magician perform, and arranged for a limousine to take them to the Second City show, where they had a table with John and some friends and family.

In early December the enterprise moved to Los Angeles and the Universal lot. Apted had just the two of them—just John and Blair—for almost three weeks of interior shots. These were the central love scenes which took place in Nell Porter's remote cabin—their meeting, seduction, love.

Apted thought John was improving. He had started losing weight again, and he had begun to show that he could handle words, learn the dialogue and relate to his costar.

Brown thought John had warmed up to her some and could show some affection, even if it was more like brother-to-sister. At least he was playing a man to her woman. Perhaps the editing could fit it all together.

One day John took Smokey with him to Chevy Chase's house in Pacific Palisades. Chase was surprised to see Belushi and realized the visit was a peace mission, an effort by John to apologize indirectly for a remark he had made in the men's room at One Fifth Avenue several years ago, after a "Saturday Night Live" show. "I make more money in movies than you, *boy,*" John had said. Chase had by then left the show to make movies, and John was on the crest of *Animal House.*

Chase found John contrite. John mentioned that he was doing a romantic comedy, exactly what Chase had done with Goldie Hawn in *Foul Play* and *Seems Like Old Times.* John was full of questions for Chase, and he left on a pleasant note. Chase didn't think they'd ever be friends, but at least, it seemed, the feud was over.

John was getting per diem payments from the studio that amounted to $2,000 a week. He and Judy took half in cash, and the other $1,000 went back to their accountant, Mark Lipsky. With no drug purchases, $1,000 a week in cash was more than was needed, so Judy socked away several hundred dollars or more each week in drawers, clothes pockets and other hiding places.

Before Christmas she rounded up about $1,000 from her various hiding spots to go shopping. When she got back, she decided to see how much more she could pull together and found another $1,000 in various places. The money seemed endless.

That New Year's Eve John and Judy had a party to celebrate their fourth wedding anniversary. One of the guests was Ed Begley, Jr., who had played a bit part with John in *Goin' South* three years earlier. Since then Begley had given up alcohol and drugs. One of the other guests was drugged up. John gazed at him and asked Begley, "Did I look like that?"

"Yes," Begley said, "we all did."

Later John took Begley aside and said, "Let's smoke a joint."

"If you take a joint," Begley said, "why not a Valium, if a Valium, why not a quarter of a 'lude, and why not a full 'lude and . . ."

"Begley, Begley!" John said. "Come on. It's just some pot."

"It's all or nothing for me," Begley said. He felt he was an addictive personality who would go overboard on whatever he did. "No in between for me. If it works for you, let me know."

13

By the end of 1980, producer Richard D. Zanuck was on the verge of proving an important point. Zanuck, with his handsome, beachboy looks intact at forty-six, was back at 20th Century–Fox, the studio his father, the legendary Darryl F. Zanuck, had helped create. Ten years earlier Zanuck had been fired as head of Fox in one of those nasty, public, movie-business tantrums. He had teamed up with his friend and Number 2 at Fox, David Brown, and they had produced two of the most financially successful movies of all time, *The Sting* (1973) and *Jaws* (1975), for Universal Studios. Now, Zanuck and Brown had returned triumphant with an independent-producer deal that allowed them to make the movies they wanted to make.

Zanuck was looking forward to finding some topical or controversial movies, in his father's tradition. A short, dark comic novel by Thomas Berger called *Neighbors* had caught his eye. It had a front-page review in the *New York Times Book Review*. The novel brought a kind of *Catch-22* view to suburban neighborliness. Earl Keese, a forty-nine-year-old property-owning model citizen, is the central figure. A younger couple move in next door and quickly become Keese's ubiquitous tormentors, testing him, forcing him to confront his drab existence, and finally liberating him.

David Brown, the sixty-four-year-old husband of *Cosmopolitan* editor Helen Gurley Brown and the New York half of the Zanuck/Brown company, was a debonair man with a large mustache and a vital, outgoing manner. He too thought *Neighbors* might be a good first project back at Fox. When he and Zanuck approached Berger's agent, they found that they were one step behind superagent Irving P. "Swifty" Lazar, who also was in deadly pursuit of the movie rights. At seventy-three, Lazar still could move faster than anyone. He was agent for a broad spectrum of authors from Irwin Shaw to Richard Nixon.

With Lazar after *Neighbors,* Zanuck and Brown realized that they risked getting into a bidding war. They discussed the matter with him and agreed to buy it together: Zanuck and Brown would produce the movie, and Lazar would be executive producer, his reward for being there first.

John G. Avildsen, who had won the best director Academy Award in 1977 for the boxing movie *Rocky,* inquired about the movie rights to *Neighbors* and learned they had been sold. Avildsen, a small forty-four-year-old New Yorker, contacted Zanuck and Brown.

Zanuck and Brown were impressed with Avildsen's background. Besides winning the Oscar for *Rocky,* he had directed the low-budget hit *Joe* (1970), about a hard-hat bigot, and *Save the Tiger* (1973), for which Jack Lemmon won the best actor Oscar. They made a tentative deal for him to direct and agreed to a first meeting at his office in New York.

Zanuck brought his wife, Lili, to the meeting. A short, red-haired woman with an explosive personality, she had important input on the creative decisions. Avildsen had several "No Smoking" signs around his office, and Lili, who wanted to light up, found the two-hour meeting an endurance test. As they got into a limousine after the meeting, she turned to her husband and asked, "Jesus Christ, do you think this guy is right for this picture? I don't know whether I trust anybody with comedy who is so fucking rigid."

In fact Avildsen, who had a reputation for pulling in a good performance from a star when the chemistry was right, had a checkered career in Hollywood. He had been fired as director of John Travolta's *Saturday Night Fever* because he wanted to put an uplifting ending on the movie. Burt Reynolds had picked him up by the neck and threatened to break it during the filming of *W.W. and the Dixie Dancekings* (1975). And when Avildsen had refused to make the changes that MGM wanted on *The Formula* (1980), the studio had taken the picture away and hired someone else to edit the final version. But on balance, Zanuck and Brown thought that Avildsen's strong credits far outweighed any of this. They liked him. He seemed thoughtful and unassuming, a rather mild character.

They already had one fiery person on the movie, screenwriter Larry Gelbart, the fifty-two-year-old veteran comedy writer and creator of the television series "M*A*S*H." Gelbart was one of the best writers in the business, but he was very outspoken and had a cutting wit. He was a perfectionist who didn't like it when strong producers, directors and stars had the upper hand. But he had a first draft and several revisions of *Neighbors* finished by the end of 1980, and both Zanuck and Brown thought it was a very funny adaptation.

When Gelbart and Avildsen were introduced, Gelbart asked Avildsen for an example of a good, funny movie.

The Blues Brothers, Avildsen said.

Gelbart went to see it, and afterward, he felt like crying. The movie was awful, it was simply not funny, and there was almost no dialogue. Gelbart had a much more lethal notion of comedy. The dark bite in Berger's *Neighbors* needed a sophisticated translation for the screen. He went to Brown and argued that Avildsen was the wrong man, a director with no real experience in comedy. It was a mismatch.

Brown held firm. Once they had made a decision, he and Zanuck stuck to it. This was a rule they had. Over the years they had heard many pronouncements of doom, but they thought it was important to set a course and stay with it. Loyalty was their vice, and certainly a screenwriter wasn't going to talk them into dumping their director.

Gelbart couldn't believe the producers would go ahead. He had never seen such optimists, and he called Zanuck and Brown the "sunshine boys" behind their backs.

Zanuck, Brown and Avildsen turned to the more vital question of casting. Zanuck and Brown had a developmental deal of several hundred thousand dollars with Fox, which meant the studio was not yet committed to make the movie. The absence of a big star put the producers on shaky ground. But this was their first effort under the new agreement, and the "Welcome Back Dick and David" signs were still up. No way, they concluded, could the studio say no.

The person who could say no was Sherry Lansing, the thirty-seven-year-old president of 20th Century–Fox and the first woman to head a major studio. A former model and actress, Lansing had taken over the reins at Fox after a phenomenally successful career at Columbia, where she had been the senior production executive for *The China Syndrome* and *Kramer vs. Kramer.*

Lansing saw *Neighbors* as a comedy that would require skillful directing and brilliant casting. She liked Avildsen's other work, but she knew of nothing to suggest he had a sense of humor. To be successful, a black comedy like *Neighbors* would have to be tongue-in-cheek and brutally satirical, like *Dr. Strangelove,* the 1964 Peter Sellers movie.

Though she had doubts about Avildsen, the script was okay. And the budget was about $8.5 million, within the acceptable range. She told Zanuck and Brown that the movie would likely get a go-ahead with a good cast. Her list of candidates included Dustin Hoffman, Richard Pryor, Gene Wilder, Bill Murray, Belushi and Aykroyd.

On January 5, 1981, Zanuck and Brown had lunch with her at Bruno's Ristorante on Santa Monica. They had been unable to secure any of the stars on her list, and she began to hesitate. The script was "very special," she said.

Brown knew that "special" meant some people had concluded it would not make money. Zanuck argued that *Neighbors* was never conceived as a star vehicle.

"I'll let you know, real soon," Lansing said at the end of the lunch; a final decision had not been made. Zanuck and Brown still thought it was in the bag.

The weekend of January 31, 1981, Lansing called Zanuck at his home. Fox is *not* going to make *Neighbors,* she said. My people voted no. "They don't think it's funny."

Who? he asked.

My people, she said.

"Sherry, this is a shock," Zanuck said. "How is this going to look! It's our first picture, and you're going to say no? You're paying us a lot of dough, for Christ sake."

Lansing wouldn't budge. She'd make a potentially unprofitable movie if she believed in it, but after having read the script almost ten times, she had no faith in *Neighbors.*

Zanuck called Brown. Both were furious. Fox was clearly run by know-nothing amateurs, and this was a personal humiliation for them. Their contract with Fox was very strong. If Fox "passed" on one of their projects, they could take it someplace else (called "turnaround") without having to wait. Not only did they want to take the movie to another studio—they almost had to.

Frank Price, head of Columbia studios and a Jack Lemmon look-alike, was having a fair year thanks to the success of movies like *The Blue Lagoon* with Brooke Shields. Price had kept things together at Columbia following the check-forging scandal involving former Columbia head David Begelman.

Price, fifty, had spent twenty years as a television writer, producer and executive at Universal before he had been brought in to provide stability to Columbia. He was very anxious to prove himself, so in early February, when Zanuck called to say that *Neighbors* was on turnaround, Price moved quickly. In the movie business sweepstakes, Zanuck and Brown were important. Not everything they did was a hit—no one had a perfect record—but their record was among the best, and Price wanted to be in business with them. Sometimes, he realized, it was necessary to do one movie with someone to establish the relationship. It might not be until the second or third film that the relationship paid off with a runaway hit.

Price invited Zanuck to his large red-brick house on Doheny Road in Beverly Hills on Tuesday, February 10, at 4:30 P.M. Meetings at home were only for the most important business, matters best kept private.

They settled into a long conversation about the movie. "Can you do it for Christmas?" Price asked.

Zanuck said yes. Gelbart's script was brilliant. And John Avildsen was already in as director.

Is he right? Price asked. It seemed unusual to have somebody like that with no real comedy record.

Zanuck said it was settled.

Okay, Price said. He liked the script, though the movie violated a number of rules. Dark comedy had not been done that often, or that successfully.

Zanuck said they could make it work, they would try their damndest. He liked Price. Compared to Lansing, he was the other side of the moon —the light side. He was a real professional.

Pending a few budget and other details, Price said Columbia would do the picture. He liked to make decisions, and this one was easy. The next day, he had a check for $400,000 sent to 20th Century–Fox to cover their developmental costs. The movie was now Columbia's. Nine days later, February 20, Price called a nine o'clock breakfast meeting with Zanuck and Brown at the fashionable Bel-Air Hotel.

"Let's talk about casting," Price said, moving right to the point.

After a year of not keeping a diary, Judy resolved to start one in 1981. Her first entry, January 3, said: "1980 turned out to be a year packed with events. Often I regretted not keeping up with my writing, but . . . it always seemed there was so much to tell, too much to even begin. So I will leave thoughts of 1980 behind for now and begin anew and fresh with 1981."

Jimmy Belushi's wife, Sandy, was pregnant, and Judy had recently seen both of them. On January 4 Judy wrote, "Tonight I'm upset. I tried to talk to John about the physical and emotional changes women go through when pregnant. . . . But I feel he doesn't understand. He's not totally insensitive and yet he doesn't truly accept the idea that the physical changes a woman undergoes could cause emotional imbalance. I realize there is much more involved. . . . Here I am 30 and thinking about children. Shall I have a baby? I think about it a lot. . . . Does this fit in my life? Our lives? How will it change things, etc., etc.''

Judy and John talked about children, but his position was ambivalent, and she figured that she had enough on her hands. For the moment John was plenty.

During the first months of 1981, with *Continental Divide* finished, Judy thought John was doing pretty well with drugs. Smokey was still keeping a watchful eye. Judy and John had tickets for a play one night, and John had gone out and not come home. After several hours, Smokey phoned the hospitals and couldn't find him. At six in the morning, John called. "I don't know what happened," he told Judy. "I don't know where I got the coke."

Still, there had been no binges for nearly nine months, and Judy was holding her breath. Without Wallace's physical regimen, and without the demands of another movie project, John was apt to fall into old habits.

They celebrated John's thirty-second birthday that January 24 with Michael O'Donoghue and his friend, writer Carol Caldwell. Smokey arranged for a limousine and went with them to Radio City Music Hall, where Francis Ford Coppola was showing a reconstruction of one of the most famous silent films, Abel Gance's 1927 epic *Napoleon*. The movie was four and a half hours long. John loved the Napoleonic myth, had played Bonaparte on "Saturday Night Live" and had read a lot about him.

Smokey thought John looked good that evening in his gray pants, plaid shirt and tweed jacket; Smokey liked to see John with his spirits up. In the limousine, John directed the driver to a punk music club that was opening that night. He had two bottles of champagne. John, Smokey thought, acted like the mayor of whatever city he was in.

"This is going to be a problem," Judy said to Smokey when they entered the club. New York's punk elite—hair standing on end, dyed bright, shocking colors with safety-pin jewelry, chains and leather clothes —muscled their way around the large room. There was a loud band and a crowded bar.

Smokey went into his Secret Service mode. John was like a candidate in that crowd, pressing flesh. He started on gin and tonic and switched to Jack Daniels. Smokey knew that John had had almost nothing to eat, and the alcohol was bound to go straight to his head. Everything, everyone had to be watched.

A woman approached John and suggested they go upstairs. He was off, zigzagging through the crowd. Smokey trailed them. They climbed the stairs to a windowless room. The woman climbed onto a bed. John stood by the entrance.

"You know I'm coming in," Smokey said.

John hesitated. "Well, I'm not going in." He turned and walked down a hall, went into the men's room and stepped up to a urinal. A few men were in a corner, snorting cocaine. Smokey stepped up to the urinal next to John.

"You never let up for a minute, do you?" John snapped.

"What do you mean?"

"Fuck you!" John shouted, and raced out.

Downstairs, John drank more Jack Daniels. He was on the loose, searching the crowd for drugs, or for a friendly face, or trouble, or whatever. He was replaying the first meeting a year earlier with Smokey. It would be a test: John finds the drugs; Smokey tries to get a step ahead, figure the angles, find the hiding places. It wasn't so much the drugs or alcohol as it was the desire to cast off the restraint, Smokey concluded. John was like a defiant child. Smokey didn't want to aggravate him.

"We got to get out of here," said O'Donoghue. He would go look for Judy.

John got out on the dance floor and started some Blues Brothers steps. The crowd gathered to watch.

O'Donoghue, Judy and Caldwell went to the limousine.

"Come, let's go," Smokey said to John. John's favorites—French bread, egg salad—were waiting at home.

"Yeah, yeah," John said. "Who needs these people."

"Hey, John," a young man shouted from the crowd. "How you doing? I've followed your act for years."

"What of it?"

"You're a great actor," the man said. He was obviously just a fan, but Smokey saw John adopt a particularly belligerent posture.

"Yeah," John said.

"Did you actually do those flips?" the man asked, referring to John's flips in *The Blues Brothers*.

"I'm fast on my feet," John said. "I'm a karate expert."

The stranger said he, too, was fast.

"Fuck you!" John shouted. "I'm faster." He went into a karate stance. The stranger followed. Smokey tried to get between them.

"I've got my wife, Judy, in the car," John said.

"I've heard of her."

"What you heard about her is not true," John replied. "They never went to bed."

Smokey was astonished. John was crazy drunk, making no sense.

"This guy is a killer," John said, pointing at Smokey and throwing the problem of the stranger his way. Smokey backed away and guided John outside.

"What the hell was that about Judy?" Smokey asked.

"It's between us," John replied.

In the limousine, the others were drinking champagne. "I'm tired of you fooling around," John said to Judy.

She threw her glass of champagne in his face.

John leapt out of the car and ran toward the club. Smokey followed and grabbed John in a full body embrace, locking his arms at his side.

"Let me celebrate my birthday!" John yelled. He broke loose, turned and clutched Smokey's jacket. "You piss me off," he said. "Don't ever grab me again—never, never!"

Smokey nodded. They walked to the car. Before they had driven the four blocks to Morton Street, John had passed out. Smokey carried him inside, undressed him and put him into bed.

Smokey felt it was time to leave. Life with John had taken its toll—the months on 24-hour call, staying up all night, traveling nonstop or without notice. Smokey felt run down and sick. On a weekend of rest, he sent a telegram to John and Brillstein to say he could no longer work for John.

Shortly after that, John called Smokey. "I got your telegram here," he said. "It's cool. I owe you my life. If it hadn't been for you, I'd not be around. You've saved my life on more than one occasion. You've kept me and Judy together."

Smokey was moved, and on March 10, in a moment of emotion, he scrawled a note:

> I am very happy to hear from you, that you really are up in spirits. Also hearing from you that you feel you have me to thank for your life being together—it really made me feel very proud.
>
> So when I am back in shape in two or three months, we can do it again, that is if you feel you'll want me back to be with you. I know that so many months on, shall we say "sick leave" (that sounds strange) maybe you'll feel you won't need me.

Anyway that will be up to you, John. As for me I would like to
just pick up again like nothing happened to me. Think about it.
Smokey.

John and Brillstein had also brought in Hollywood's hottest young
agent to help negotiate movie deals. He was Michael Ovitz, thirty-four,
the head of Creative Artists Agency, which was only five years old.

Ovitz, high voltage all the way, represented such stars as Robert
Redford, Dustin Hoffman and Paul Newman. Ovitz was contacted about
Neighbors, and he raised Belushi's name for the part of the obnoxious
neighbor. And along with John, there was always the possibility of getting
Aykroyd.

One day, later in March, John went to see Avildsen at his office in
New York. He took one look at the "No Smoking" sign on Avildsen's
desk and lit up a cigarette. Avildsen smiled. It was childish but charming.
He had seen John in *Lemmings* and had followed his career. He was
clearly a good actor; he had technical skill and did great impersonations,
extracting the essence of a character and drawing out the recognizable
elements—a walk, eye or hand movements, the voice.

"I have an unusual idea for this movie," Avildsen said. "You should
play Earl Keese," the older, established neighbor, the victim.

"I think I'm the other guy," John said, referring to Vic, the neighbor
who moves in next door.

"You've played him," Avildsen said.

That was the point, John said. He could do it naturally, with greater
ease.

No, no, Avildsen said. Vic was the predictable, stock role for John.
It would be great to try something new, something *not easy.*

John seemed willing to think about it and took the script to Aykroyd.
"I want you to do it," John said, and explained that they could film
somewhere in the New York area—possibly Staten Island—and com-
mute from home. Aykroyd agreed that switching roles, breaking out of
their stereotypes, was an interesting idea.

Frank Price liked the idea of Belushi and Aykroyd. Like Columbia's
new relationship with Zanuck and Brown, a deal with Belushi and Aykroyd had to be viewed with an eye to the future—what movie deals might
come at some later time—rather than just for the one, immediate project.
Belushi and Aykroyd had an incredible future, Price felt. No one could
match them. So Price okayed a deal guaranteeing John $1,250,000—the
most he had ever been paid for a movie.

Avildsen was worried about John and drugs, so he told Brown, the producer who was going to oversee the production, that he was going to talk to John about it.

Brown said that he and Zanuck had already checked out the rumors, and they had learned that John had been clean on *Continental Divide*.

Avildsen persisted. Uncontrolled drug use could be a nightmare on a movie, and he had to find out for himself.

"God," Brown warned. "We got Belushi; now don't go blow it."

In his next meeting with John, Avildsen gently steered the conversation to drugs.

"I used to do a lot of the stuff, and I don't any more," John volunteered. "I didn't on *Continental Divide*." He was convincing.

Avildsen had seen a number of stars wrestle with success. He could see the stress reflected in John's behavior, his face. There seemed to be two fairly well-defined sides to him. There was the person full of ambition and good intentions. There also was the side that was almost embarrassed by those constructive and creative drives. That side exuded cynicism, indifference, destructive feelings, punkness.

Screenwriter Gelbart agreed to go to New York and meet with Avildsen, Belushi and Aykroyd to go over the script. The afternoon of Tuesday, March 17, Gelbart picked up Avildsen and they went to the Phantom offices.

It hadn't yet been decided which neighbor John would play, so Avildsen suggested that they go through the script twice, with John and Aykroyd switching roles each time. As they proceeded, Gelbart could see that neither Aykroyd nor John stuck to what was on the page. They were just itching to improvise, impose their own ideas, change the dialogue; they even made suggestions about scene and structure.

Gelbart was astonished by Belushi. He was a terrible reader and acted like a kid with homework that he didn't want to do. He made repeated mistakes. He was also smoking marijuana and offering it around. John left the readings a couple of times, and when he came back it seemed as though he was more withdrawn than before. Gelbart was sure he was taking something stronger when he was out of the room.

After about two hours, John was in even worse shape than when they had started. Gelbart sat quietly, simmering. They were all meddling with his script. The words—those precise words—had taken months to write, and these people were altering them impulsively, never really looking for the reading he had intended. But he held his tongue.

"Are you going to be there when we do it?" John asked.

Gelbart said he wasn't sure. He figured that the question was asked not because they might want his help during the filming, but because they were going to do what they wanted regardless, and John was wondering if they were going to have to contend with the screenwriter on the set.

When they finished, Gelbart and Avildsen left together. Gelbart felt it had been a horror show, and Avildsen was as much a part of the problem as the two stars.

"We've got a big problem here," Gelbart said, referring not to the marijuana, but to what John obviously was doing when he left the room. "He's using drugs. . . . How are you going to handle this, working with a guy on drugs?"

"I can handle it," Avildsen replied.

The next day, Gelbart and Avildsen went up to Phantom for another afternoon of script readings. It was a repeat of the day before, only worse. John acted as though he were twenty drinks ahead of everybody. And they were all tangling with Gelbart's script, carelessly and thoughtlessly. By the end of the afternoon, Gelbart was enraged. He went over to Wally's Bar on West Forty-ninth Street, took a seat by himself and downed a few drinks.

Gelbart had been writing all his adult life, going back to radio with the "Maxwell House Coffee Time." He was also working with Dustin Hoffman on a movie called *Tootsie,* and he was having problems with that script. But *Neighbors* was heading for disaster. He called Zanuck and Brown in California. The producers each got on an extension.

"You've got a problem. Belushi was flying," Gelbart said. And, Gelbart added, Avildsen is not funny.

But both Belushi and Aykroyd *are* funny, the producers insisted.

Still the sunshine boys, Gelbart thought. A ghastly decision on the director, he said. Trouble everywhere, he added, half slurring his own words.

Zanuck and Brown glanced knowingly at each other from across the office. Brown took an imaginary bottle in his hand, tilted his head back and tipped it into his open mouth.

Zanuck smiled and nodded. Gelbart himself was in the bag and sounded very depressed.

Gelbart recounted the horrors of the last two afternoons: Everyone was going to fuck up the picture.

Zanuck felt the drug warning was secondary; what really was bothering Gelbart was that they were tampering with the script. It was nice to know these things, but there was very little they, as producers, could do.

They had to start filming the next month in order to meet the Christmas release promised to Frank Price. The last thing they wanted to hear was that they were heading for calamity with a dope addict.

Zanuck and Brown knew that the screenwriter was no longer that important. Fuck him, they figured; they had been warned that he was a prima donna. Avildsen, Belushi and Aykroyd seemed to be getting along very well. The director and the stars—that's all that counted now.

Zanuck and Brown felt they knew how to deal with Gelbart: Treat him seriously but pacify him, and be firm.

—"Larry, maybe you're exaggerating. . . ."

—"Larry, you're upset because they're changing some of the stuff. . . ."

—"We've got to get on with the picture. . . ."

—"Thank you, thank you, for going to New York. . . . Complete your part and come home. . . . Everyone has the best intentions. . . ."

Gelbart said that no one could tell him what was funny; that was his job. This movie was not going to be funny.

Thank you, thank you, thank you, both producers said.

Gelbart finally hung up, promising to return to California.

"Jesus, get me a drink," Brown said to his partner. "Here's a drunk telling us the other guy is a dope fiend."

Aykroyd was worried that the script needed a lot of work. The dark jokes in Berger's book might not work well on the screen. Avildsen seemed to agree. Since Aykroyd, John and Avildsen were members of the Writers Guild, they set about doing a rewrite. John deferred to Aykroyd on most of the writing but was concerned that there was less than a month before the scheduled start date of April 20.

They all finally agreed that John should play Earl Keese—the stuffed shirt, the uptight suburbanite. Aykroyd was to be his new neighbor. Now they had to find actresses for the wives.

Penny Marshall of TV's "Laverne and Shirley" auditioned for the part of John's wife, Enid. She wasn't chosen and called John to ask why, knowing he had a veto.

"It's wrong for you," he said.

"Why?" she asked.

"I have to leave you. At the end I have to leave you and burn the house down. They [the audience] will like you, and I can't have that."

There wasn't much for Marshall to say. John was such a strange mixture of self-awareness and self-deception. Once John had given Marshall's teenage daughter Tracy an antidrug lecture. He had done it directly and with love. He had used himself as an example.

"Don't do this shit," he had said. "You'll turn out like *this,* like *me*." And he waved a finger at himself.

Instead of Marshall, John wanted Kathryn Walker, a serious actress and the former girlfriend of *National Lampoon* founder Doug Kenney, to play Enid. Since Kenney's death, John had reached out to her and was helping to promote her career. She took the part.

For Aykroyd's wife, Ramona, they picked Cathy Moriarty, a beautiful young actress with a raw, husky voice who had played Robert De Niro's wife in *Raging Bull.*

Zanuck and his wife, Lili, went to New York for the first full day of rehearsals on Monday, April 6. The mood was wonderful. There seemed to be a good feeling among John, Aykroyd, Walker and Moriarty. Gelbart's warnings seemed unfounded. John was sober. It was touching the way Aykroyd got up—in the middle of reading his lines and without missing a beat—to get a tissue for John to blow his nose.

Brown wanted to make sure that the screenwriter was kept informed, so afterward he phoned Gelbart in Los Angeles. There are minor changes being made, he said, and you're not going to be happy with them.

Gelbart grumbled knowingly.

Brown's job was to keep things moving, keeping informed and ahead of any problem. That meant spending lots of time with the key players. Brown could see that John was committed to a good, thorough job. He knew movies and clearly cared, often about things that were not his responsibility.

"David," John said one day, "I want to know every fucking thing that is going on." John considered it his movie and took an interest in the most obscure details, even threatening, briefly, not to do the film if they couldn't get his favorite sound man—Bill Kaplan. But Kaplan worked out of Los Angeles and was discouraged by the New York unions.

In the same vein, Brillstein told Brown, "One peculiar thing—he's got to know everything and I mean *everything*. . . . You're getting along fine. He likes you. But don't ever lie to him. He'll find out, and then you'll have a real problem."

Avildsen and Aykroyd were making progress on their rewrite, but on April 11 the Writers Guild called a strike. A copy of the shooting script would have to be registered immediately with the guild to ensure that no member did any writing during the strike. Avildsen and Aykroyd put their names on the rewritten script as coauthors along with Gelbart.

Brown called Gelbart. Look, Larry, he explained, I was so incensed that I just ripped the title page out before registering the script, so it was registered without any writer's name.

Gelbart was outraged. Now he might lose his writing credit. He called Avildsen's agent to complain and started keeping a detailed diary on the project in case he wanted to file a formal protest with the guild.

Several nights later Brown was at home in his vast triplex overlooking Central Park when John called. He wanted to stop by, making it sound at first as if he wanted to pay a casual visit. Brown tried to find out more.

It's urgent and important, John finally said, his tone changing. They had to talk tonight. Aykroyd wanted to talk too. Brown arranged to meet them at a small restaurant in Greenwich Village.

At the restaurant John was very agitated. We have to get a new director, he said. The rehearsals had not gone well. John presented a long grievance list: Avildsen wants to shoot the movie in the exact sequence of the script itself, like a play. Everyone knows that's not advisable—to do just one scene in a room, then move to the next room and have to spend hours setting up the sound equipment, lights and cameras, and then go back to the first room, and again wait hours to set up. It was better, they all knew—less costly, less time-consuming—to shoot all the living room scenes at one time, then all the kitchen scenes, then all the bedroom scenes, instead of jumping back and forth all over the goddamn house. Fucking crazy. Some fucking notion of the movie flowing like a stage play, John said.

Brown wanted to get to the bottom of this.

John explained how he and Aykroyd worked. They'd do a scene, let the camera keep rolling, throw in a little spontaneity, improvise. Avildsen would have little or none of that, even in rehearsal. He was fucking rigid, "a little Hitler."

John was doing all the talking. Brown tried to draw Aykroyd out. Aykroyd seemed to be supporting his partner, but he obviously didn't feel as strongly. Perhaps he didn't even agree. It was hard to tell.

John went on. Avildsen was not responding to their kind of humor. He didn't get it. Avildsen is a writer, a film editor and a cameraman, John said, and he thinks like that, in narrow, technical terms with no larger vision of what he wants. Fucking disaster, John said. Replace him.

Brown explained that Avildsen had that Academy Award, and he had the producers' confidence. And nervousness before starting was not unusual.

Basic problems, John argued. Avildsen has no sense of humor. He's no comedy director. It is a fundamental problem that cannot be papered over. All John's instincts told him no.

Brown felt he had now heard the worst of John's anxieties. He wasn't sure whether John was right or wrong, but he argued as forcefully as he could that different actor-director combinations had to be tried. The old cliché about Hollywood applied: No one could tell what made a great movie. The best actors and directors often made lousy movies, and the worst occasionally made great ones. But everyone on this one was a proven commodity. He and Zanuck could not promise a great movie, but it had a real chance. They had to back their director. Perhaps it would seem like the old period of cronyism during Hollywood's Golden Age, but there were no grounds for a change. And there were practical considerations. The Christmas release date had to be met. Avildsen had spent months working on this, and a new director could never get up to speed. It would cost hundreds of thousands of dollars to fire Avildsen; he would have to be paid. Let's wait and see, Brown said. I'll be there on the set every day. Let's all stay cool and wait.

John wanted action, but Brown could see that he had swayed Aykroyd. "Let's get this shit over with," Aykroyd said, impatient with his partner. "We're getting the money. Give the guy a break."

Reluctantly, John gave up.

Brown left to go home. He'd seen cases of opening night jitters, but this was severe. John was apparently so full of self-doubt that he was laying it off on Avildsen. John's intensity was both terrifying and reassuring: terrifying because he could slip off track and wreck the project; reassuring because if it were ever captured on film, they would have a real success. Thank God for Aykroyd. Surely John would listen to him.

Whatever the outcome, Brown did not want the inmates to take over the movie, but he was not sure yet who the inmates were. He called Zanuck, who was skiing in Sun Valley. "There's a catastrophe on this thing," Brown explained, "and we haven't even started. The boys want to dump Avildsen."

What! Zanuck replied. What happened to all the good fellow-feeling?

It was gone, Brown said. But they were both used to Hollywood egos and agreed to wait. The shooting was to start within a week.

The strike by the Writers Guild created a major dilemma for Tim Kazurinsky. Kazurinsky, thirty, a short, scholarly-looking former actor and head writer at Second City, had been in the same company as Jimmy Belushi and had met John during the filming of *The Blues Brothers* in

Chicago. Both John and Aykroyd had helped Kazurinsky get a job on "Saturday Night Live." Kazurinsky had done one show, April 11, before the writers' strike was called, and now he was left high and dry—no job, no apartment—and he was tossing in the towel and returning to Chicago.

Kazurinsky drove out to the *Neighbors* set on Staten Island to say goodbye to John, his chief benefactor. In John's trailer, Kazurinsky explained that New York hadn't worked out. His bags were packed and he was going home.

"Wait, wait," John said. "There may be a part for you in this script." He started thumbing through his copy of *Neighbors*. He said that no one had been cast yet for the part of Pa Greavy, a sixty-five-year-old who ran a gas station and towing service. John gave Kazurinsky the script and told him to look over the lines. "Now sound old," John said, and he called Avildsen over to hear Kazurinsky read the part.

"It sounds nice," Avildsen said when Kazurinsky had finished his lines. "But, John, this part is for an older man."

"I am thirty," Kazurinsky said.

Avildsen was apologetic, but Kazurinsky couldn't have the part.

When Avildsen left, John didn't hold back his anger. "I know what I'm doing. This movie needs Second City actors who understand comedy." They went to see the makeup man on the set, and John pointed to Kazurinsky. "Make him look sixty-five," he ordered.

A little while later John called for Avildsen to come for another reading, and this time Kazurinsky, with gray hair and a wrinkled, deeply creviced face, not only sounded sixty-five but looked the part as well. It was obvious that John was not going to be satisfied until he got his way. Kazurinsky was hired.

14

Sheldon Schrager, the Columbia executive production manager, was on Staten Island on Monday, April 20, for the first day of filming. Schrager, who had thirty years in the movie business, liked to be present for the first day on all Columbia films. As the studio's senior representative, he welcomed everyone, tried to sense the problems, to see if anything was needed. There was an air of anticipation, Schrager noticed, but that was always the case.

One of the first shooting scenes was scene 14, in Earl Keese's living room. Earl, sitting down watching television, was to go to the window and notice the arrival of his new neighbor.

John was waiting off to the side of the set. He sat, stood up, then sat again, moving his chair back and forth.

Avildsen was finally ready to start. John flew into the TV chair, prepared to be Earl Keese.

"That hair doesn't look convincing," Avildsen said. "It won't fool anybody." He wanted more gray. Earlier, Aykroyd had suggested that John's hair turn white over the eighteen hours of Keese's life in the film. John had rejected the idea. He didn't want to look middle-aged.

"Don't I look in my forties?" John asked.

"No," Avildsen said curtly. It was now time to direct this movie, and he was tired of being second-guessed.

"What a thing to say," John said. "I'm trying my best." He stood up and walked quickly off the set.

Avildsen turned to the crew and made a half-joke about temperamental actors, then went to find John, who was watching TV and listening to music in his trailer.

"I've got to say what I think," Avildsen said. "You've got to look older." Part of the theme is a kind of generation clash; you are the older generation, Aykroyd the younger.

John said he looked old enough.

"I want you to be as good as you can," Avildsen said. That means the right suits, right props, right lights. And it means the right hair color to conform with the whole character.

"What difference does it make?" John said. "People don't come to a movie to see me look older." Besides, hair didn't determine age. Being old was walk and voice and manner. He had played old people many, many times.

Avildsen realized he could end up fighting John's vanity for hours, and he was worried about the delay; it was costing hundreds of dollars a minute to keep the cast and crew waiting. But John was going to make him work for any concession. After about twenty minutes, John agreed to have the makeup man brush in a little more gray. It did not come near what Avildsen had in mind, but he saw no alternative to accepting the situation. John was a spoiled and outrageous brat. Yet these were the same traits that made him potentially a wonderful actor—fierce convictions, self-certainty. If only Avildsen could get John to shift his devotion to character and plot instead of concentrating on the performance John Belushi was more or less living.

By contrast, Aykroyd was flexible and experimental. He was willing to bleach his hair blond, put in contact lenses to change the color of his eyes, even wear a silver tooth, all to give him a wilder, more youthful appearance.

It took an hour to get John back on the set, and the shooting and the movie at last were underway.

After the first day, John took Brown aside and repeated his complaints about Avildsen. He was vehement.

Brown held his ground. It's too late, he said.

John called Brillstein: Avildsen was arbitrary. Ovitz was brought in. By the second day of shooting, Frank Price was bombarded by Brillstein, Ovitz, Brown and Columbia's production people on the set. The stories continued throughout the week. Price smiled. He would watch without saying or doing anything. A hot atmosphere on the set often resulted in the best movie. It meant that nothing would go unchallenged. Columbia was spending about $200,000 each day. The only possible thing was to move ahead.

Price screened the first dailies, and they looked good. They were trying to create something different; the project was risky, but no more so than it had been from the start. He adopted a policy of aggressive listening and active nonintervention.

Brown was familiar with the old saying that the sure sign of trouble was applause at the dailies, but he remained optimistic. The tension on the set intensified, and Brown came to regard himself as a baby-sitter.

One day John ran to him. "That son of a bitch is trying to be a cinematographer!"

Brown sprang from his chair and ushered John out of earshot. He had been in the middle of an interview with a reporter and didn't want to read about conflict on the set in the next day's newspaper. Finally, he convinced John not to discuss matters with Avildsen on the set. It was delaying production, and the inevitable flare-ups were poisoning the atmosphere. Brown told Avildsen, too, that if there was a dispute about how to shoot a scene, it would be easier to do an extra take the way John and Aykroyd suggested.

Brillstein was getting a daily earful, and he told John to watch out: it was going to get out of hand and he'd end up slugging Avildsen. John said not to worry. Brillstein bet him $1,000 that there would eventually be a fistfight. John said it was a deal.

Judy Belushi had been looking forward to the shooting of *Neighbors*. John would be commuting nearby, to Staten Island, five days a week, and they could have some pretense of a normal life. They could go to parties, movies, have weekends. But John's disputes with Avildsen spilled over to everything else, and he was very tense and distracted.

After three and a half weeks, Avildsen scheduled a couple of weeks for the nighttime scenes. The first was to begin on Wednesday, May 13 at about 7:30 P.M. and last until daybreak. That Wednesday, Mark Lipsky called Judy to say that John had been by to get $1,000 in cash. There was nothing more to say. Judy confronted John. "Do you have coke?"

"No."

"I think you're lying," she said, "and I don't want to stand here and call you a liar. Can I look in your coat?"

John admitted he had cocaine but said he needed it that night for the shooting. It was the only way he could stay up until dawn. Judy got Bill Wallace to take it away from him. She didn't think she could stand more drug battles. She decided to consult Dr. Ron Siegel, a Los Angeles cocaine therapist who had a number of Hollywood stars as clients. Siegel said it was possible that John's difficulty was caused by some sort of chemical imbalance. He suggested she read Dr. Ronald R. Fieve's *Moodswing*, a book published in 1975 that noted the beneficial effects of antidepressant drugs such as lithium. Judy wasn't convinced that John's current distress was depression, or anger, or whether it was simply John.

One night Judy went out with Carol Caldwell, and they complained to each other about the problems of living with comedians. John and O'Donoghue saved their best for their audiences. That was the direction the wit and the charm flowed; it left little for them.

"What the fuck are we the ones going to psychiatrists for?" Judy said. "They're the ones who are crazy."

Bill Wallace was upset that John was using drugs again. He was not sure how far his mandate extended. Was he to enforce a no-drug rule as Smokey had? He called Brillstein. "John's getting back into the shit," Wallace said.

"Oh, no," Brillstein moaned.

"Do I have permission to keep it from him?" he asked.

Do whatever is necessary, Brillstein replied.

"Will you keep me from getting fired?"

Yes, Brillstein said. Wallace would be fireproof.

Some time later Wallace saw John take two women into his trailer on the set. They were there a short while, and then John came out to shoot a scene. Wallace went into the trailer, took a look at the women and began searching.

"I'm tired of this," he said. "You're supplying John."

"Who the fuck are you?" one shouted.

Wallace found some packets of drugs in a fold-out drawer, which he confiscated. "I'm the guy who just threw you off the set."

They started to walk away.

"I hate to do this to you girls," Wallace said.

"We'll see about that," one of the women said.

"There's nothing to see," Wallace said sharply. "You're gone."

They found John and complained. John raced over and grabbed Wallace. "What the fuck are you doing?" he screamed.

"If I didn't care about you, I wouldn't care what you did," Wallace said. "I love you like a brother."

Tears came to John's eyes. He calmed down. He gave Wallace a big hug.

At every opportunity, John continued to make disparaging remarks about Avildsen. Brown was getting tired of it. "You forget he's the director," he said. "We're not going to replace him." But John persisted in talking as if it were his movie, as if the decisions were his.

He called John Landis late one night. "Come do this movie," John said. "I hate him . . . he's fucking up my movie."

"Wait," Landis said. "Aren't you shooting now?"

"Yes," John confessed.

"I can't do that," Landis said. "Are you fucking crazy?" He laughed at the notion of a palace coup with John marching in and installing his new director.

"Fuck you," John replied, and hung up.

In Los Angeles, Zanuck was receiving daily reports from Brown. It was obvious that the tension never subsided and that the movie was emotionally draining for his partner. Zanuck was worried more about what this might do to Brown's health than about what it might do to the movie. Brown was going to be sixty-five that summer.

Brown had to go to Europe on other business, and a rest would be good, but they could not let matters on Staten Island go unwatched for a single day. This movie was important for their reputations. Zanuck headed East to take his turn on the set.

Avildsen was still shooting night scenes when Zanuck arrived. John ran up to him as if they were old buddies.

"For Christ sakes," he said. "Thank God you're here. Come, let's go to my dressing room. We've got to get rid of this fucking director."

As they walked to John's trailer, Zanuck, a physical-fitness nut, was almost offended by John's heaviness and general slovenliness. When they sat to talk, however, it was obvious that John could muster his energy on one point. He battered away at Avildsen. They had to act, he argued. No disaster would be greater than to let this go on.

"We've gone this far—" Zanuck started to say.

"I don't goddamn care," John said. Zanuck and Brown had a responsibility to do something, but they were treating Avildsen with kid gloves. "You're destroying me," John said. He pointed to an imaginary movie screen: "It's *me* that's up there." Avildsen was a complete bum.

"A complete bum didn't make *Rocky*," Zanuck said.

"*Rocky*'s not funny," John said. "No one can tell me about two things—comedy and music. And he's fucking this up."

"Okay," said Zanuck. "He's a bum. But nobody can destroy you, John. You're a fantastic comedian. My ten-year-old son could direct you. You're great. Look at the dailies."

John would have none of it.

Zanuck was to endure four nights of duty on the set before Brown returned. The next night, the scheduled scene called for Aykroyd, on the roof of the house in a frogman outfit, to fire seven shotgun blasts at John as John tried to rendezvous with Aykroyd's wife.

When John emerged from his trailer, he could hardly talk. Zanuck was shocked. John tried to speak, but his words were a mumble. Zanuck looked around at Avildsen, at the cameramen, the rest of the crew. It wasn't simply that John didn't know his lines, or that he had had a few drinks; he was blitzed. Everyone stood around looking at one another. John, aware that he was not making sense, finally stumbled back to his trailer. There was silence on the set, and Avildsen announced that they would wait.

Zanuck went to John's trailer. There was music playing. John was drugged up and worn out. Do you want some coffee? Zanuck asked. They're waiting for you. It's your scene.

"Not if that fucker is out there," he said in a hostile whisper.

Zanuck tried to plead with him.

"You direct the picture," John said.

"I don't want to direct the fucking picture," Zanuck replied. It was like arguing with a child. There was no telling what, if anything, might work. Should he be reasonable? Get angry?

"Well," John said, as if offering the perfect solution, "let me direct it."

Jesus, no.

"Let Danny direct it."

"Look," Zanuck said, "just go out there."

John got up and staggered outside. He was able to work for about half an hour before he was back in his trailer.

Lili Zanuck was on the set and went with John. She had never seen anyone on a movie set so unfit to work. John was blaring "Hey 19," a song by the rock group Steely Dan, on his tape deck. He told Lili he wanted to do a movie based on the song. It would be about a child of the sixties who tried to explain the importance of the decade to a punk rocker. When the song was over, John rewound the tape and played it again and again, pounding the table in front of him like a set of drums, stoned and mellow at the same time. Lili deduced that he was on some kind of drug combo platter—probably cocaine for high and Quaaludes for down.

About 1 A.M. a doctor came in and examined John, and gave him a shot of B_{12} in his hip. "While he's here, do you want one, too?" John asked Lili.

"No thanks," she said. She thought she knew now what it must have been like for people to work with Marilyn Monroe.* Just to watch was nerve-wracking.

Zanuck wasn't sure what to do, and he didn't know the people or the situation well enough to act alone. If someone said or did the wrong thing at the wrong moment, there would be an emotional conflagration. And he could see that neither Avildsen nor Aykroyd were facing the real issue. No one wanted to discuss the problem, and Zanuck didn't want to light the match.

Avildsen walked around tight-lipped and solemn, pretending to be busy with other things.

Finally Zanuck asked Aykroyd, "Let's see if you can get him out here."

"Yeah, I'll go in," Aykroyd said, walking over to John's trailer. After half an hour Aykroyd came out alone, shaking his head. But he went back, and finally he got John to come out. After another take, John returned to his trailer.

There was another scene scheduled for that night, but at 3 A.M., Avildsen closed down.

Zanuck called Brown in London. "The whole night is down the drain," he said. "The guy was mumbling. He couldn't talk." Unless there was a miracle or some sleight-of-hand editing, the night was wasted.

Zanuck approached the next night's shooting with apprehension, but John reported on location in pretty good shape and was able to work. Avildsen decided not to reshoot the previous night's scene, hoping that he could patch something together by cutting and dubbing.

By Thursday, May 21, Brown was back from London. The script called for John to fall in a swamp and be dragged down in quicksand. He was in his trailer rehearsing his lines with Avildsen. Both Judy and Brillstein were with them. Brillstein thought that Avildsen was merely watching, not giving any directions or even suggesting what he wanted. John was simply going through his lines on his own, working out what to say and how to say it.

The crew had installed a deep watertight tank in the ground to act as the swamp. A special forklift arrangement would allow John to be raised and lowered in the mushy liquid. He was supposed to sink in over his head, but when he tried it, he got to chest level and floated.

---

* Monroe was found dead at her home on August 5, 1962, from an overdose of barbiturates.

Avildsen proposed that they construct a set of foot straps on the forklift that John could slip in and out of; the power of the forklift would carry him down, and when the scene was over, John would just slip out and rise to the surface.

John said no, he wanted sandbags taped to his ankles.

Avildsen said it was dangerous. If John slipped off the forklift, he would sink in the dark, mushy liquid and they would have trouble getting him out. He might drown.

John went into his belligerent, take-charge mode. Heavy three-inch tape could be used to strap a sandbag to each leg, he insisted.

This is a bad joke, Avildsen said. It's not the professional way to do it.

"I hate professionals!" John shouted, and walked off. The bags were taped on, and John was testing out the ankle weights, walking clumsily around the edge of the tank, when suddenly he misstepped and toppled over. Before he could sink, his double, who was testing out the forklift at the time, reached over and grabbed him.

Shaking the water off, John said, "When I fuck up, I really fuck up." He left sheepishly with someone from the costume department, a hair stylist and someone from makeup. He was back in about fifteen minutes to do the scene with Avildsen's foot straps. It worked without a hitch.

On Friday, May 29, they were finished with night shooting. There was just a month more, but the relationship between Avildsen and John stayed sour. John left the set on one occasion, delaying the shooting for an hour so that he could talk with his mother. Later, John and Judy had a fight, and John pleaded with Avildsen for a break in the shooting. "I need a favor."

It was raining anyway, and Avildsen cancelled the filming so that John could go. There had already been enough fights.

Louis Malle, the famous French film director, enjoyed testing the boundaries, pushing into new territory, not only for artistic value but for shock value. Malle always tried to work out of curiosity, and that meant exploring. How much daring was possible? America continually tested itself in this way. The search for national identity was as strong today as in de Tocqueville's time, but American movies did not have this pioneer spirit. They were now too often resorting to the cliché formulas derived from the lowest common denominator of the culture—television.

Malle had been making movies for 24 years, and he had explored controversial and provocative themes. *The Lovers* (1958) contained shocking hints of oral sex during a moonlit garden love scene; *Murmur of the Heart* (1971) showed a young boy's seduction by his mother. In Malle's first American movie, *Pretty Baby* (1978), twelve-year-old actress Brooke Shields played a child who was raised in a New Orleans brothel. After that film, Malle wanted to live and work in America.

In the summer of 1981 his most recent movie, *Atlantic City,* was receiving critical acclaim. It had been a Canadian tax shelter that had allowed him to operate outside the American studio system, which he loathed. And he had worked closely with playwright John Guare (*The House of Blue Leaves,* the musical adaptation of *The Two Gentlemen of Verona*), a scholarly forty-three-year-old who looked somewhat like the young James Joyce. Malle, forty-eight, and Guare had become close friends and were looking to team up on another "city" movie set in some uniquely American setting. While filming in Atlantic City, they had become fascinated with the Abscam congressional scandal, in which an FBI agent, posing as an Arab sheik, had been introduced to congressmen through a longtime con man named Mel Weinberg. Half a dozen congressmen had been secretly filmed taking money. It would make a wonderful political farce.

Malle also decided he wanted Belushi and Aykroyd to star, with Belushi as the con man and Aykroyd as an uptight FBI agent. Political films were anathema in Hollywood, but these stars were big enough so that the studio would leave them alone.

In September 1980, Malle had married Candice Bergen, and he had heard many of her stories about the three times she had hosted "Saturday Night Live." He tried the idea on her. What did she think of Belushi and Aykroyd in an Abscam movie?

The drugs, Bergen said, were out of control.

Malle agreed that might be a problem, but it was really the only one. The craziness and inventiveness of "Saturday Night Live" had never really been duplicated in the movies. He wanted to give it a try.

Malle went to Mike Ovitz, who had represented Bergen and was Belushi's agent. By presenting a package deal, Malle hoped to retain the most control. The studio would get a director, screenwriter, script and stars all together, which would keep interference to a minimum.

Ovitz liked the idea. He wanted to get as much money as possible for everyone and was out to kill because Columbia had high hopes for *Neighbors.* A development deal was struck.

Malle and Guare arranged a five o'clock dinner at the Odeon with John and Aykroyd about a week before shooting on *Neighbors* was scheduled to end. Guare had arranged to meet his wife, Adele, there, but he and Malle were about 25 minutes late, and they entered the restaurant apprehensively.

Guare had no idea what to expect of Belushi, and he was worried that his wife might have been cornered in some awkward situation, with John standing over her ranting and raving like the "Saturday Night Live" weatherman. For all Guare knew, John really was a thug, a drugged-out crazy man.

But there was Adele talking with this dashing figure, his hair combed, leaning comfortably and knowledgeably against the thirties-style bar like a character lost from a Noel Coward play.

Belushi and Adele were talking about a double solitaire card game Adele knew called Racing Demons. John loved the name and was asking about the rules. Guare was surprised by John's boyishness, his sunniness and openness.

Soon Aykroyd and a girlfriend arrived. They all sat at a large table, and Guare felt there was a sort of shipboard atmosphere—people thrown together, trying not just to make the best of it but really working to have a good time. The conversation wandered, and neither Malle nor Guare tried to direct it. There was no urgency, and they both wanted to watch and listen to Belushi and Aykroyd.

After a while, Malle presented the story they had in mind. The FBI was in trouble—bad public opinion, hostile Congress, corruption from within—and so they hire criminals like Mel Weinberg to lure congressmen into taking money, all to salvage their reputation. It would be a "buddy" movie, like *Butch Cassidy and the Sundance Kid;* male bonding, except that the two characters, each completely different, would never let up on each other. It would be a love-hate relationship with no reconciliation.

Belushi and Aykroyd said that they would love to make a political statement.

The subject of Malle's movies came up. Aykroyd clearly knew several of them; John just as clearly didn't. Aykroyd and Guare explained that one of Malle's movies, *Lacombe, Lucien* (1973), perhaps his most popular, dealt with a seventeen-year-old French farm boy who became a Nazi collaborator during World War II.

"Oh, wow!" John said. Exploring the unpopular side of things appealed to him. The new punk music, John said, did that. All this bullshit about it being New Wave. That's just the media finding a polite name for it. Punk music came out of nowhere; it had no connection to other music.

Guare disagreed. Some opera, like Berg's *Lulu,* used words to intimidate and scare, which was precisely what punk rock was about.

No, punk is pure and original, John said.

Aykroyd turned the conversation back to the movie and said that playing an FBI agent was a lifelong ambition. Some of his family in Canada had been Royal Canadian Mounted Police; some others had been priests. He himself had been in the seminary until about age seventeen. It really had been a life in uniform.

Malle and Guare said they too had gone to Jesuit schools. Adele also had gone to a Catholic school. John said he had been an Albanian Orthodox. So they were, Aykroyd said, a bunch of fallen Catholics.

Guare was struck that neither Belushi nor Aykroyd was concerned about how the proposed movie was going to be funny. Obviously they felt that was the easy, natural part.

Malle did not discuss the characters. That had been the point of the dinner, but everyone seemed willing to skip it. He found something original and quick about Belushi and Aykroyd. *Playing characters* was what they were about, and it was, oddly, something that didn't require discussion—at least not for the moment.

Both Belushi and Aykroyd said they wanted to do the movie. As a rite of passage, they asked Malle and Guare to come to the Blues Bar. When they arrived, it was closed up with a chain on the door. Aykroyd unlocked it. Guare thought it was like a boys' secret clubhouse. Inside it was very dark. Blue neon lights came on. There was a jukebox and a pinball machine. Belushi started the music—the Dead Kennedys' "Too Drunk to Fuck." He turned it very loud and began dancing and jumping around the bar. Suddenly he stopped and took Guare aside.

"Listen to this, listen to this," John said. "They can't play this record on the radio. This is what's all wrong with America. This song can't be played."

Guare laughed. Summing up all the troubles of the country that way, of course, didn't make sense, but at the same time, it wasn't completely naïve.

John insisted that both Malle and Guare come out on the dance floor and learn slam dancing—a punk dance in which people violently crash into each other. He threw heavy body blocks as they stumbled around the small dance floor.

John smoked some marijuana. Malle and Guare said they had to leave.

"I have to get up early also," John said. He suggested they go back to his house on Morton Street before ending the night. Once there, he gave Malle and Guare a tour of the house. He did it without comment, seeming proud, particularly of the vault, where he gave them a few blasts of music and also played the drums briefly.

Malle and Guare left about 4 A.M., dead tired. Guare was particularly impressed with Aykroyd: He was smart, original and quirky. And neither of them seemed spoiled, although Aykroyd was surely the disciplinarian.

Malle agreed about Aykroyd, but he was especially taken with Belushi and his vast, raw appetite. Belushi had a kind of intelligence, a kind of knowledge, that derived not from culture or literature but from instinct. He seemed to want to know everything, live every moment. Belushi was so American. He was almost mysterious, naïve at times, often innocent, but brutally cynical and self-indulgent. The director in Malle—and that was how he looked at things and people—saw Belushi as a centerpiece for a strong movie. He represented much of the antiestablishment culture of the moment, as the Beatles once had. Though John and Dan were virtually unknown in Europe, Malle suspected that it would take only a few years before they were popular across the Atlantic. A couple of more movies and Belushi and Aykroyd would be giant stars everywhere. Malle had a feeling that he was in precisely the right place with them; they could be directed and guided; they were interested in portraying antiheroes and doing something unsettling.

The filming of *Neighbors* ended on Monday, June 29, and afterward John and Judy took a plane to the Vineyard for an extended summer vacation. There was little they had to do for two months, and the glories of the Vineyard were legendary: temperatures 10 to 20 degrees cooler than in New York City and a brisk breeze blowing regularly across its 100 square miles. Judy could almost see John pull the plug, wind down and relax. Aykroyd was at his own house on the island, and John often used the hot tub there or fell asleep on a couch. He loved the island life. Driving around in his black jeep on simple errands gave him pleasure. He'd stop at Sandy's for a fishburger, or at Alley's to see if there were any new Conan comic books, or at the market for fresh swordfish. He got oysters in nearby Tisbury Great Pond and barbecued steaks and hamburgers. He built a model airplane, watched afternoon soap operas or whatever was on TV. He spent many afternoons at a friend's clothing store, Take It Easy, Baby, buying things or just watching the women fold clothes. Or he went to the island bakery or played golf.

The beach in back of their houses was one of the finest on the East Coast of the United States—wide, clean and private. John and Aykroyd christened it Skull's Beach, and people needed a special skull-inscribed pin to use it. Even the Chilmark police wore the pins. John loved to swim or body surf in the large waves that came with a big wind. He once took a mud bath with Aykroyd's mother.

Other times, John liked going to the home of Pulitzer Prize–winning author William Styron (*The Confessions of Nat Turner, Sophie's Choice*), who had a house in Vineyard Haven on the north end of the island. On August 4 the Styrons were having a birthday party for one of their children. One of their guests was singer Carly Simon.

A serious, troubled woman, Simon was still attracted to John's daring and irreverence. She felt drawn to people with a Dostoevskian dark side. And in some way John seemed to be a window into the drug world that had demolished her marriage to James Taylor. She drove to the party about midnight. John was lurking among the cars, looking half like James Dean and half like the parking-lot attendant. He came up to Simon, who was wearing a dress so thin that she hadn't worn underwear because it would have shown through. John greeted her, and as if through some sixth, sexual sense, pulled up her dress. She pulled it down and grimaced. His eyes were alive and he was so high and crazy.

John took her to the lawn and put her on the ground. Ignoring the people standing by, he climbed on her and started doing a fake, exaggerated humping motion. Simon soon was laughing uncontrollably. Then he stood and picked her up, tipped her upside down over his shoulder and carried her into the house, parading her around among the guests. Simon was used to John's teasing, but this had gone too far. She had no control over the situation.

Simon tried to pull her dress down to cover herself. She was upset, humiliated, dazed with embarrassment and almost in shock. Having John around was a macabre thrill for Simon: he had so much courage and he was so dangerous. He took so much energy, patience, understanding; he almost stole them from you.

David Brown's wife, Helen Gurley Brown, had persuaded John to be interviewed for *Cosmopolitan*. She had promised it would be friendly. On August 19, writer Michael Segell flew to the Vineyard.

"You've got expense money, right?" John asked, greeting Segell at the small Vineyard airport. He wanted to go to lunch.

"I tend to do everything to excess," John told Segell as they toured the island in John's jeep. "You've caught me at a calm period of my life."

Segell said that some of John's friends had mentioned his self-destructive tendencies.

"It's taken me a long time to break out of that," John admitted. "I think I have, though. It's the kind of thing that tends to be cyclical, feeding off itself. You go through periods of deep depression."

Segell asked whether he was referring to drugs.

"I hate to reduce it to just that, but that's part of it. That brings it on," John said. "It's all false pressure; you put the heat on yourself, you get it from the networks and record companies and movie studios, and then you put more pressure on yourself to make everything that much harder because work is no longer challenging. You say, 'Well, I'll get all screwed up and then it'll be a real challenge again.' So stupid—I've often wondered why people do these things. You're so much happier if you don't, but I guess happiness is not a state you want to be in all the time."

They went to a house that John said was being rented by his friend Michael Klenfner. A sign on the door read: DAN IS NOT HERE.

Segell asked John whether the "Saturday Night" group would ever get together again.

"If the whole group got back together, I'd do it. But it had its time, you know? It's played out. The show took a lot out of us, out of our souls. . . . You know, in the bar Danny and I just bought in New York, there's some graffiti in the men's room—three lines, written by three different people: 'Film is king,' 'Television is furniture' and 'Rock and Roll is life.' I think that pretty much sums it up."

In the jeep again, John braked in the middle of the road.

"I lied about the house. It's not Klenfner's, it's Danny's." John shook his head. "Stupid. I was trying to protect his privacy. He doesn't care. . . ."

When they arrived at John's house, Segell noted that the 1967 Plymouth in the driveway, a former police car, looked like the Bluesmobile, and he asked John why the window on the driver's side was smashed.

"Uh, we got locked out once, I think."

But, Segell wondered, wasn't there an easier way? Some people would use a coat hanger to get in.

"Yeah," said John, "some people use coat hangers. Other people use cinder blocks."

•　•

One day John called his brother Jimmy, who was staying at the Morton Street house while John and Judy were on the Vineyard. Jimmy was rehearsing for a revival of *The Pirates of Penzance,* in which he was going to star.

Paramount, John said, had asked him and Aykroyd to do the movie version of *Sexual Perversity in Chicago.*

Shit, Jimmy thought. He had starred in the play, *Sexual Perversity,* a story of the singles scene in Chicago; it had been a hit, and now the studios had gone to his big brother instead of him.

What do you think? John asked.

"It would kill me," Jimmy said frankly. He had busted his ass to keep his acting career separate from John's. Jimmy had been asked to do the television spinoff of *Animal House* and had answered with a flat no.

John started to talk about the realities of the business.

Please, Jimmy said. Don't.

"What would you do if I did it?" John asked.

"It would tear me apart," Jimmy said.

John did not take the part.

On one of those carefree Vineyard afternoons, with Aykroyd behind the wheel, John and Dan went riding in the jeep. Aykroyd drove fast and hard, finally out to the beach and over the sand dunes. It was a bright and clear day, so beautiful it almost made him ache.

The topic of death was not, perhaps, out of context. The Hell's Angels, fast bikes—very, very fast bikes—were all part of Aykroyd's sense of doing everything possible in his youth. Death fascinated both of them. They talked about it as if it were a phase, the final movie. Aykroyd loved the short Schiller movie John had done, "Don't Look Back in Anger," in the third season of the show.

You know, John, Aykroyd said, I might go out on my bike like that.

Yeah, John said. He knew.

But Aykroyd thought it was just as possible that one day he might hear that John had died—his awkwardness killing him, his clumsiness, his driving. Aykroyd felt it was important to keep a superior, jaded attitude toward death and fate.

Who wants to live to be forty anyway? Aykroyd said. He had a tape and popped it into the cassette deck. Clear-sounding guitars strummed out hard, repetitive chords—the kind of instrumental music popular in the sixties, with a strain of punk.

"Wow!" John said. "What is that? What's that called?"

"It's called 'The 2,000-Pound Bee,' by the Ventures," Aykroyd replied, explaining that the Ventures were a four-man group that had been very popular nearly twenty years before.

John laughed, apparently reminded of the infamous "Bee" skits from "Saturday Night Live." They both howled and it became funnier. "The 2,000-Pound Bee" was a grand symbol of where they had come from, of where they were now.

"You got to promise me something," Aykroyd said. "If I die before you do, you have to play this tape at my funeral. . . . Because it's . . ." And he lost control with laughter, then continued: "Wouldn't it be great to lay this noisy, heavy tape on a church full of people!"

"Sure," John said. "And you do the same for me." He was serious: A perfect message—"The 2,000-Pound Bee."

"Absolutely," Aykroyd promised. "Absolutely."

By August, Avildsen had a rough cut of *Neighbors* ready for screening by the Columbia executives. It was the first selection of takes of the various scenes, essentially the first crude edit of the picture. The dialogue was not always clear, and the transitions were ragged. Since an original music score hadn't been written yet, Avildsen decided to use music from some old horror films on the temporary sound track—dark, spooky, mysterious music like *King Kong* and *Creature from the Black Lagoon*. On August 7, the top executives from Columbia, including Price and Sheldon Schrager, producers Zanuck and Brown and a couple dozen other people, filed into room 24 in the publicity and distribution building on the Columbia lot.

The executives were laughing so loud that at times no one could hear the dialogue. Schrager was elated. Zanuck and Brown were also pleased. It certainly was not the disaster that John had predicted. The atmosphere was eerie, chiefly because of the music, which killed some of the laughs. The original music score, to be done by John's friend, saxophonist Tom Scott, was to be ready in time for the first public preview.

Price thought the movie certainly was different, and it seemed funny. His only concern was that some scenes and bits he remembered from the dailies—funny scenes, including a line in which John gave a sarcastic "Ha, ha, ha, ha, hey"—were not in the rough cut. But he decided to wait. Movies could change a great deal during these final stages, and he wanted to stand on the sidelines, which was where he believed the studio belonged.

•   •

232

John and Aykroyd saw a rough cut later, and they responded formally in a letter to Zanuck and Brown on August 18:

Gentlemen:
We feel that the changes listed in the following communication are necessary for an immediate upgrade in the feel and quality of the picture. We want it to be the best looking release possible. Thank you.

Sincerely,
John and Dan

Included was the list of ten changes they wanted. The producers were a little nonplussed by the tone of the demands: One dialogue line, John and Dan said, "ABSOLUTELY MUST BE DELETED"; another "WILL REMAIN." The letter also said, "Send two (2) audio tapes of the film to us. We will determine which sequences require [changes]." At one point in the movie, Ramona—Aykroyd's wife—had gone to John's bedroom and asked him if he was afraid that her husband would "think you're up here chewing me?" In the letter, John and Dan said, "Replace 'chewing' with 'fucking.' THIS IS IMPERATIVE."
Zanuck and Brown agreed with most of the points, and two days later they passed the suggestions along to Avildsen in a letter.

Just before the release of *Continental Divide,* screenwriter Larry Kasdan accompanied John and a few other people to a screening. Having finished the script for Spielberg's *Raiders of the Lost Ark,* Kasdan had moved on to rewrite George Lucas's *Star Wars* sequel, *The Empire Strikes Back,* and he was preparing to make his directing debut on another of his scripts, *Body Heat.*
Kasdan was shocked at the difference between what he had written in *Continental Divide* and what showed up on the screen. The tone had been radically altered. He winced at some of the lines which now sounded like clichés; the movie, and Belushi in particular, seemed unsophisticated. John was sitting down front, and Kasdan could hear him laughing. Kasdan felt pain. The movie seemed to be a failure. Afterward, John came up to him, excited. "Didn't you like it?"
It was a finished product. Kasdan simply said, "Good work." *

* *Continental Divide* was now in the hands of the promotion department at Universal. On September 1, publicist Nancy Hurst drafted a memo to 24 key people outlining the radio promotion plans for 25 cities across the country. Two hundred seats were being given away for sneak previews in each city along with knapsacks

Louis Malle and John Guare had spent much of the summer in France working on their Abscam movie, now titled *Moon Over Miami,* and were ready to talk over details with Belushi and Aykroyd. The Belushi character was named Shelley Slutsky, a con man who had been raised in the Fontainbleau Hotel in Miami. He was a disgusting, overbearing, thoughtless person who threw money around and ran over people. Aykroyd was to be Otis Presby, a compulsively hygienic ten-year veteran FBI agent with a shrine to J. Edgar Hoover in his home, the centerpiece of which was the late FBI director's toupee.

Malle and Guare were curious about how John did in a romantic role and went to see *Continental Divide.* The audience waited for Belushi to be outrageous, and when he finally got off a lame line, "It's so quiet you can hear a mouse get a hard-on," they went wild. The rest of the time they waited in vain for John to unleash the energy in them, strike the familiar chord. Belushi seemed to be in a straitjacket. That, Malle and Guare felt, would disappoint his fans. But from their perspective it was a blessing. The outrageous Belushi they wanted for *Moon Over Miami* had not been used up. For that matter, from what they could tell, John's role in *Neighbors* also didn't touch that wild persona they wanted reserved for their movie.

Malle and Guare arranged a dinner at Malle's New York apartment on the day after Labor Day. Malle's wife, Candice Bergen, was there. When Bergen learned that Aykroyd was not coming, she was uneasy. She had kept her distance from Belushi since the last "Saturday Night Live" show they'd done together. The drugs were just too much of a barrier. Her husband enjoyed the outrageous, but she wondered if he could control John.

---

decorated with Universal and *Continental Divide* logos. Hurst wrote that the response from radio station managers was tremendously positive, adding, "Overall the feedback is: 'We're getting a great response' and 'Can't wait to see Belushi's new film!' "

She gave a city-by-city breakdown on the planned promotion, one of which was WCCO-FM in Minneapolis: "WCCO is giving us a 13-day promotion . . . [including] trivia questions over the air about great romantic film stars and romantic film comedies. They will mention couples like Tracy/Hepburn, Gable/Lombard, and Belushi/Brown!"

A week later, on September 8, Hurst followed up with a report on the promotions and sneak previews. She wrote: "Overall reaction to 'Continental Divide,' shown at sneak previews across the country Sunday night, September 6, was *GREAT!!* . . . The general consensus is John Belushi surprises and impresses all with his performance and everyone seems to like the chemistry of Brown and Belushi as well as all the great one liners used in the film."

The night of September 8, Malle and Bergen, John and Adele Guare waited for their guests to arrive. John and Judy showed up an hour and a half late with Mitch Glazer.

To Bergen, John seemed almost to have gone from child to old man. She tried to reach in, but he was too self-focused.

Judy was intensely quiet. She got out some grass and began smoking it. Guare, trying to engage John in conversation, mentioned that he had just seen a nice review of *Continental Divide* in *Time*.

What? John said. He hadn't seen it.

It's the issue just out, Guare said.

John left to find a newsstand.

Bergen went into the kitchen, and Mitch Glazer followed and made a pass at her. She was furious. Glazer seemed high, and she resented his presence in her home.

Out in the living room, there was not much talk. It seemed to Bergen that the room fairly dripped with tension. John finally returned with a copy of *Time* and read the review first to himself, and then aloud:

" '*Continental Divide* is superior. John Belushi has dispensed with his randy Neanderthal persona to play that most hallowed of Hollywood leading-man roles: the extraordinary ordinary guy.' " Concerning John and costar Blair Brown, John read: " 'If they are not quite Tracy and Hepburn, they will do until the real thing comes along—on the Late Show.' "

Guare could see that John was awed. He was clutching the magazine as if it were the only copy in existence, as if he didn't believe it. He half-whispered, "Fantastic. Spencer Tracy."

A buffet supper was served, and Bergen thought it was the longest dinner they would ever eat. The subject of the Abscam movie was touched on only briefly. Later, Jacqueline Bisset, who had recently filmed a movie with Bergen called *Rich and Famous,* and Alexander Godunov, the Soviet ballet dancer who had defected to the United States, stopped by. John tried some slam-dance moves on Godunov, but the tension remained. After everyone had gone, Bergen wrote in her diary: "Oh my God, we have been invaded by the enemy. There are evil forces without. Beware."

15

Marcia Resnick, a thirty-year-old photographer with a satirical photo column in the *SoHo News* called "Resnick's Believe-It-Or-Not," spotted John at the AM-PM after-hours club in New York about 6 A.M. a few days later. This was a prime time for the club. People were just back from summer vacations, and activities were picking up in the New York underground. The club was housed in an old rundown building with three floors and a basement at 59 Murray Street, three blocks from the World Trade Center. In the basement, the so-called VIP room, crates substituted for tables and chairs. It looked like a half-finished construction site.

Resnick, a short woman who dressed in punk clothes, had had her bouts with drugs, including heroin. She greeted John, and they shared quick updates on their lives. Resnick had photographed John twice and was anxious to do so again for her forthcoming book, *Bad Boys: A Compendium of Punks, Poets and Politicians.* She gave him a friendly elbow in the side and asked when she could take his picture again. They decided to go to her studio.

Resnick had a strong intuitive feeling about getting someone's picture at just the right time. There was something that people exuded almost subconsciously, and for her *Bad Boys* book, it was important to catch the *enfants terribles,* the unspanked children, as she thought of them, in their acts of defiance.

In her loft—a large room that overlooked the Hudson River with the photo studio smack in the center—she went right to work, loading her Nikon FTN camera with black-and-white Tri-x film, the only kind she could then afford, and setting up two self-standing portable strobe lights. She stood ready.

John was wearing old corduroy pants, old tennis shoes, a black leather jacket and a heavy, dark V-neck sweater revealing thick clusters of chest hair. He paced around. Resnick thought he was trying to avoid the camera.

"You know," he said, "Lynn Goldsmith's [she was another photographer] office has been calling me up, and she'd give her eyeteeth for this photo session."

Resnick nodded, looking for the moment. He seemed nervous, almost as if he were caged. "Do you have any props?" he asked.

She gave him two scarves—a white one, which he put around his neck, and a dark one, which he wrapped around his head like a thick bandanna. He grabbed a small, ten-inch globe of the world and strapped it to his left shoulder with gray duct tape. He put on a pair of dark sunglasses and sat on a stool and gave a quarter-smile. He looked like a pirate Atlas with the world on his shoulder.

Click.

Resnick felt that there was a healthy tension between them: They were both exhausted, and he was fighting the camera. He seemed almost afraid to sit still for a picture. His talent was in moving, being fluid. His face grew tough.

Click.

At the fourth picture Resnick got him to take off the globe and the sunglasses; at the fifth through eighth he put the sunglasses back on and peeked over them; then the glasses came off, then finally the bandanna. He was sweating and loosened the white scarf around his neck. He groaned, rubbed his face and touched his hair, revealing a bald spot in the front. By the thirty-second shot he was relaxed, but Resnick needed a new roll of film. John wanted a cigarette, then a beer; then the music changed.

One more roll, Resnick told him. He emptied his pockets, pulling out a video cassette of *On the Waterfront* and a bottle of nonnarcotic tranquilizers called Dalmane.

When they resumed, Resnick felt that John was again trying to outfox the camera. A mannequin off to the side had a dark wool ski mask over its head. John put it on so that only his mouth and eyes showed through. He sat in a chair and looked like the anonymous executioner, fat and sinister.

Click, click, click, click.

John took off the ski mask and finally his leather jacket. He dropped his cigarette. No props. He dodged the camera, turning his head. Resnick clicked away, still searching for the right shot. She inched forward, so close the lens caught only his head, then only his face: There was the Bad Boy, the exhaustion and frenzy captured. A bead of sweat traveled down his forehead; his face relaxed for just an instant; the soft light revealed his messy, greasy hair, the coarse stubble of his beard, and his penetrating, weary eyes.

She hovered a fraction of a second and snapped.

"That's it."

John went over to Resnick's bed and collapsed. His snoring soon filled the loft. Resnick cleaned up the room, and in about 45 minutes John got up from the bed and took some pills that she didn't recognize. It was about 11 A.M. when he left. After he had gone, Resnick found his tranquilizers and his tape of *On the Waterfront*.

John went home to Morton Street, picked up Judy and left for Amagansett, Long Island, to attend the wedding of Lorne Michaels, whose marriage to "Saturday Night Live" writer Rosie Shuster had ended in divorce. He was marrying Susan Forestal, a model from Texas. It was a large wedding, and most of the people from "Saturday Night Live" were there. Everyone except Aykroyd, who earlier had had a serious relationship with Forestal. He was in Whitehorse, Yukon, believing that it was bad luck to see old girlfriends get married.

Brillstein thought the wedding was like a party at Elaine's, the famous New York restaurant that caters to celebrities. Actors Jack Nicholson and Buck Henry, singers Paul Simon and Art Garfunkel, models Lauren Hutton and Cheryl Tiegs, *Rolling Stone* editor and publisher Jann Wenner, Lou Adler (owner of On the Rox), Bill Murray and Gilda Radner were all in attendance.

John arrived in such bad shape that Paul Simon took him in tow, cleaned him up and shaved him so he'd be presentable for the ceremony.

Judy told Brillstein that John had been on a binge for two days.

Oh Christ, Brillstein said, and went to find him. John was dazed and almost incoherent. Brillstein's heart went to his stomach. It had been some time since he'd seen this.

"You still represent rock and roll groups?" John asked. Brillstein, his manager for six years, had never managed a rock group. He sensed that John didn't know where he was, but Brillstein couldn't get through the drug barrier. He assumed that John was scared to see the old gang; he had never done well socially with people from the show.

Michael O'Donoghue noticed, as did everyone else, that John was virtually on fire. "John is really fucked up," he remarked to Brillstein. Brillstein insisted that John was all right. But John could barely stand.

As Michaels and Forestal prepared to come down the aisle, they noticed him standing there as a kind of family elder. Michaels walked toward him, worried about what might happen. Was John going to freak out at the wedding?

John leaned forward and threw his arms around them, giving them a big, long embrace. Michaels found this full of meaning and love—half-stupor, certainly, but also a small call for something. Michaels realized again that John wasn't so tough on the inside.

During the reception outdoors on the beautiful fall day, John passed out in a lounge chair. No one could wake him, and he looked terrible. Brillstein and Michael Klenfner lifted the chair and carried him behind some hedges. The fewer people who saw him this way, the better.

The next morning, Monday, September 14, John was back in New York to begin promoting *Continental Divide*. Universal was releasing two other movies and had arranged a massive press junket so that reporters could cover all three from the Saint Moritz Hotel on Central Park South.

The *Hollywood Reporter,* a movie industry trade journal, was already in with a review that began: "John Belushi plays it basically straight . . . [but] it also makes for a super-hard sell for Universal, like tub thumping a film in which Pavarotti doesn't sing, or Bo Derek stays covered."

John did seven television interviews between 9 A.M. and 11 A.M., broke for three hours of rest and lunch and then came back for three hours of print interviews, moving from table to table in a crowded room.

Blair Brown, who was pregnant, was also there. She noticed that John had gained weight again. That made them less likely candidates to fill the Tracy-Hepburn legacy in American movies, she felt, but the myth was being pushed by the Universal promotion department.

In a private moment, John acknowledged to her that he had tried to fuck her up in the beginning of shooting in Colorado. She said she knew that.

As they moved from interview to interview, Brown sensed that John felt uneasy answering questions about his work. He snapped off his replies, often lying, offering set routines. It was apparent that he wanted to deck the reporters, at least verbally, but he was sitting on his aggressions.

After the press junket, Brown, Michael Apted and John agreed that they would get a good box office and bad reviews.

The next night, Tuesday, September 15, John and Judy went for a 6 o'clock screening of the latest rough cut of *Neighbors* at the small Magno Penthouse screening room at 1540 Broadway. Avildsen had arranged to let the others see what progress he had made since August. Aykroyd, Brillstein, Zanuck and his wife and David and Helen Gurley Brown were also there.

Belushi was seated between Zanuck and Brown. Columbia executives, including production president John Veitch, filed into a row in front of them. Zanuck could tell that Belushi was not in good spirits. He was squirming and made an ugly crack about Avildsen in a loud voice.

A number of people turned around.

"John," Zanuck whispered, "shut up, for Christ sakes!"

The lights were lowered and the film began. Almost at once John began loudly criticizing the selection of takes and the way they were edited and spliced. "No!" "Fuck!" "Shit!" he yelled.

Both Zanuck and Brown tried to calm him. He lowered his voice but started hitting his armrest with his fist—bang, bang, bang—when he didn't like something. The whole row of seats shook. He reacted to every fragment of the movie as if he were hooked up to an electric charge. Zanuck wanted to crawl under his seat and out of the room, but he had to try to keep John under control.

As the movie progressed, Zanuck saw and heard some funny things. But Belushi was right: the tempo was wrong and the scenes were too long, the pace sluggish, failing to capture the Kafkaesque situation Earl Keese found himself in. And the best takes, some of the really funny stuff from the dailies, were not there. Zanuck could see the ingredients of a fine movie, but it had been chopped and mangled. He felt so tense he was sure he was losing weight just sitting there.

Toward the end of the film John took off one of his shoes and slammed it on his armrest. Bang! Bang! It was like Khrushchev at the United Nations, clobbering the podium. "That's not the right take!" he yelled.

John was doing it for the dramatic effect, but it reflected a deep inner rage, and his beef, Zanuck could now see, was legitimate. Avildsen had fucked it up. The question now was how would they handle it? They couldn't all take off their shoes and start banging.

When the lights came up, there was no applause—generally the polite custom at private screenings. Zanuck could see the Columbia executives, including Veitch, exchange steely looks. People were racing, almost fighting for the exits. Zanuck smelled disaster.

Zanuck, Brown and Brillstein wanted to get together with John and

Aykroyd and announced an urgent meeting at Elaine's. There was no point in inviting Avildsen. Zanuck feared a fistfight.

David Brown walked up Broadway with John. "If I talk to him," John said of the director, "I'm going to hit him!"

Aykroyd, concerned with his partner's reaction, realized he would have to be the rock. There wasn't much they could do about it now. "John," he said, "I kind of like it."

The dinner table atmosphere at Elaine's was glum. John was calmer and more rational but no less cutting. "It's everything I feared," he said, noting that the worst, the absolute worst movie possible, had been made from the footage they had. John said he wanted to edit it himself; he and Aykroyd could still fix it.

No, Brown said emphatically, the Directors Guild gives Avildsen the right to edit a completed version of the film and preview it to a public audience. But after that, Zanuck said, the producers and Columbia would have the right to make the final cut. We will repair it, he said.

Zanuck wavered between expressing his outrage with Avildsen and voicing some optimism.

But John wouldn't let it go, arguing that the prospects were only grim.

The next day Zanuck and Brown went to a 4 P.M. meeting with Frank Price at Columbia's New York headquarters on Fifth Avenue.

It was clear to Price that the movie had played a lot better a month earlier. Avildsen had obviously taken some steps back since then, had flattened it out. But from what he had seen so far, it was not that bad. Price weighed the complaints and laid out an action plan:

First, the music would be changed. What was on the sound track now was working against the comedy, killing laughs rather than supporting them.

Second, Price wanted to conduct some controlled tests with Belushi and Aykroyd fans to find out what they thought of the movie as edited. This, he said, had to be on-lot testing at Columbia—where the studio would control the audience—not out in a public theater where someone from a theater chain would certainly show up. Price didn't want bad word of mouth.

Third, they would delay the release of the picture for several weeks. The initial plan had been to open on December 11, but that had then been moved ahead to December 4 to make sure *Neighbors* got a jump on other Christmas movies. That decision had been made when they thought they had a hit. Now Price said they would delay the premiere until December 18.

Price didn't have to give his reasoning; Zanuck and Brown knew why.

It was the old "hit and run" theory. An early December release date for a good movie would build momentum toward the Christmas weekend, when more people attended movies than at any other time of the year. With a bad movie, an early release could mean the film would be virtually dead by that crucial Christmas weekend. With the December 18 release, they could hit the big market and run, at least making back their costs, he hoped.

Zanuck and Brown, badly shaken the day before, were impressed with Price's cool, businesslike handling of the problem. The tests, new music and new release date seemed the logical steps, and Price had ticked them off one, two, three. It was simple and perfect, the proper activist strategy.

That morning, John appeared on NBC's "Today" show with Gene Shalit. Then he and Judy took the American Airlines noon flight to Chicago for the premiere of *Continental Divide* the next night. As usual, John stopped by Second City. Bernie Sahlins loved having any of the old alumni back and let them drift onto the stage. That night, the troupe set up a skit in which a group was watching "Saturday Night Live" on television. Then John strolled out.

The audience jumped to its feet. There were screams, shouts, cries from a hundred throats. John, at least in Chicago, was like Elvis or Jagger or John Kennedy. It was a primitive ritual of welcome, atavistic and almost alarming.

After the show John told Sahlins he had high hopes for *Continental Divide*. It was a serious effort, John said, and he had put his heart into the acting.

Judy could see that John was upset with the publicity tour and premiere; he hated standing out in the open for everyone to judge him. One reporter had asked what he had been wearing during the love scene with Brown in the hotel bedroom. John had almost flipped out and had gone into a quiet rage: No one would ever ask that question of Robert Redford.

The anxiety and the Chicago environment became John's excuse for a binge. He went to the Blues Bar and hooked up with some old drug acquaintances. One woman had a bottle of about 100 Quaaludes. Judy thought she could buy them and throw them away.

For a moment that seemed like the logical solution. But this cop role was getting too old. There John was—agitated, driven, on the verge of a drug frenzy. She didn't want to be the enforcer; it was an impossible task and it made her weary—watching each handshake, each hello, each bump in a crowd, every visit to the washroom, each phone call, every private moment he sought. She couldn't live in terror that John might exercise his free will. And for a moment she had actually thought she could erect a barrier between John and the outside world: seal him up and buy the 100 Quaaludes, buy all the Quaaludes in Chicago, buy all of them in the United States—and all the cocaine and uppers and potentially abusive pills or whatever. Even buy all the heroin. He was asking about it, asking if someone had any, and that really scared her.

John eventually escaped her watch, and apparently he got something, because he seemed really down when they left Chicago on September 18, the day the major newspaper reviews came out. The Chicago reviews were the first John read. Gene Siskel said in the *Chicago Tribune,* "John Belushi is adorable. . . . The apparent success of this film should help expand his choice of characters."

The *Sun-Times,* Royko's own paper, gave it three stars, saying John came across in the movie with a "surprising tenderness and charm."

The *Los Angeles Times* was highly critical, however, saying, "In a film that must stand or fall on the engaging nature of its leading man, John Belushi just isn't very lovable. Or charismatic. Or sexy . . . the electricity between him and Blair Brown isn't enough to illuminate a night light."

There were eventually more good reviews than John, Brown or Apted had expected, but the box office did not turn out well. With a cost of about $11 million, the $18 million in receipts was not enough to take the movie into profits for the stars. Apted had tried to find a nebulous line through the material, half-comic and half-serious love. But he realized it was a failure. John's fans just couldn't or wouldn't accept him in this new role.

On Tuesday, September 22, John and Judy flew into Los Angeles and checked into a suite, Rooms 205 and 206, at the Beverly Hills Hotel. John had to be in town for the post-production work on *Neighbors.* He said he didn't like the hotel. The food was no good; the air-conditioning was inadequate; he hated walking through the lobby and being recognized. He said they should have rented a house.

Judy concluded he was unhappy about *Neighbors* and was taking it all out on the hotel. But she needed a place to work. She was designing the cover of the fourth Blues Brothers album, and the extra room gave her space to spread out; she could order food, and she needed a place that would take messages. John had a good deal of cocaine and was heading into a coke jag. She now decided to try a new technique. Rather than force a confrontation, she withdrew and ignored him. That, she hoped, would distress him enough so that he would force the confrontation. Then they could get it all out. So, for the moment, she left him alone.

Brillstein saw that the cocaine was damaging John's voice. And that would be a disaster because he had to correct or change dialogue—the so-called looping, when words and entire sentences on the vocal soundtrack were altered. John's voice had to sound the same as in the rest of the movie or it could be a catastrophe.

John and Aykroyd, working through Zanuck and Brown, had convinced Avildsen to let them make some dialogue changes on their own. It was highly unusual, but Avildsen said he would consider what they wanted changed.

The looping was scheduled for 2 P.M. Thursday, September 24, John's third day in L.A. and his third day on the binge. Before the session, Brillstein took him to see Dr. Robert J. Feder, a Los Angeles ear, nose and throat doctor who specialized in voice disorders. Feder, forty-seven, had treated John for three years for periodic colds, infections and overuse of drugs, especially cocaine. His office was lined with more than 50 autographed pictures of his show business patients—the top actors and actresses, singers and personalities, including Natalie Wood.

Feder had seen many ups and downs in John's personal and professional life—the up of *Continental Divide,* when John loved himself; the down of the first Blues Brothers concert, when John had come in crying, depressed, feeling guilty because he had not succeeded. John would call Feder's home sometimes for medical or other advice.

Feder saw John as someone who wouldn't take care of himself no matter what. He had a little boy's embarrassment about his drug use, and that made it hard to get angry. Several times Feder had tried to explain that so much cocaine would hurt his career, wipe out his nose, guarantee chronic voice difficulties, and eventually cause his voice to have a permanent unpleasant nasal sound. John's typical response was a theatrical performance. Once he had giggled and laughed and told Feder how he'd been out with a couple of women from the Playboy mansion and couldn't get it up because he'd had too much to drink. Soon Feder found himself laughing. What was to be done? Efforts at enforcement were futile, and Feder chose not to try.

The morning of September 24, when John came in with Brillstein, cocaine had so inflamed John's nasal passages that Feder had his nurses give him a shot each of Decadron and Celestone—two anti-inflammatory drugs that would take down the swelling and allow his voice to sound more natural. It was a treatment that Feder had given John more than a dozen times.

John said that he also wanted a shot of B_{12} to give him a boost.

Feder had given John several B_{12} shots before and had made no effort to explode the myth. B_{12} did nothing. But it had a mystique, and Feder thought a placebo might help John psychologically.

John also wanted some speed, saying that he had to be able to stay awake for the looping work on *Neighbors*. He'd been up for several days and needed something to keep from crashing.

Feder gave amphetamines, or uppers, to some of his patients if they needed to be "on" for a particular performance or day. But he was not at all sure that John could be trusted with such a prescription. When John had drugs, anything was possible; he might even try to take a whole bottle at once, and that could kill him. "You can't have them," Feder said. "Bernie is going to have to dole them out to you." Feder then told Brillstein: "I don't want to give him a prescription. I'll do it in your name," and he wrote out a prescription to Brillstein for 10 Dexamyls— 15 mg each. Brillstein had the prescription filled at the pharmacy downstairs from his office and gave them to John.

John had a limousine, and as he and Brillstein were riding up Sunset, he complained about his privacy; he had none, especially at the hotel, and it was getting to him.

There were lots of people gathered outside the Roxy Nightclub and On the Rox as they passed on Sunset. John lowered the window as they drove by and waved. There was a mild cheer, faint recognition, "Who's that?"

Jesus, Brillstein thought to himself, he *hates* the loss of privacy but would be miserable without the fans.

John gave him a slight smile; it was, Brillstein realized, full of self-awareness and just as completely lacking in it.

At the 2 P.M. audio looping session, Aykroyd and John had many ideas and changes; it seemed they could have redone the entire movie in several days. John particularly seemed obsessed and worked into the night looking for a way to salvage the film.

Judy was not seeing much of him. At times he stopped by the Beverly Hills but left quickly. She knew how he would—intentionally or not —leave behind little clues about what was happening. Her practice was to search or just follow the trail of litter he left behind. She found the bottle of Dexamyl with Brillstein's name on it. That was too much, and she decided to go to Brillstein's office to get an explanation. For some time she'd been wondering about the extent to which the movie industry people—agents, managers, studio executives—had a hand in John's drug use. Were they orchestrating it? Assisting? She wasn't sure. Judy was steaming when she entered the fourth-floor office suite of Brillstein and Company. Brillstein was out, but she found John's assistant manager, Joel Briskin.

What the fuck gives? Judy demanded.

Briskin explained it was a $40,000 looping session, and John had to be there. It was the only way to make sure he'd stay awake. There were only a few pills.

Let him fall asleep, Judy said. We've got to quit postponing the moment when the drugs cause a big fuck up. *Let him fuck up*. Don't you see? That's the only way he will learn. We've got to stop being his custodians. She walked out abruptly.

Briskin disagreed. Too much was at stake: not just one looping session but the whole movie. And if the movie got derailed, then John—whose reputation in the business was awful to begin with—could place his entire career in jeopardy. Then there would be no more million-dollar-plus contracts; no vacation houses, first-class travel, expensive dinners, accountants, lawyers, agents and *managers*. John—all of them—needed success.

Soon Judy found another Dexamyl prescription in Brillstein's name. She went to see him even more upset than last time. John abused every other drug and clearly was abusing this one. Alone, it was dangerous. Mixed with the cocaine and God knows what else, it could be deadly.

Again, only Briskin was in the office. He explained that Dr. Feder had written the prescription in Brillstein's name because it would be bad for John if he were ever caught with one in his own name.

Judy didn't care about the reason. She wanted them to stop feeding John speed under any name. She argued and begged: *Let John fuck up*.

Briskin said they couldn't. Not this time.

Judy left, and on the way out she pondered why putting the prescription in Brillstein's name protected John. It didn't make sense. In fact, it could be worse if John were caught with a prescription in someone else's name. The arrangement protected Dr. Feder, Judy concluded. If John was arrested while drugged up from the prescription, Dr. Feder apparently didn't want to be the one who had directly supplied him. Brillstein would then have to take the heat if that happened and explain how John had gotten his prescription.

Judy was sufficiently upset to talk with Dr. Wilbur Gould, their New York doctor and the person who had referred John to Dr. Feder. She wanted Gould to warn Feder to stop.

The next night, Friday, September 25, John was in the Guitar Center, a slick, professional music store on Sunset in Hollywood, looking for some new kind of computer drum machine. He was with Tino Insana, his old friend from the Universal Life Coffee House days, and Aykroyd. Also in the store that night was a tall, thin twenty-nine-year-old. He was rather conservative looking, except for the fishing lure dangling from one of his ears. John was introduced to him.

He was Derf Scratch, a guitar player for a punk band, Fear. His real name was Frederick C. Millner III; "Derf" was "Fred" spelled backward. He went with John and the others to On the Rox for drinks. John had a hundred questions about punk music and Fear, Derf's four-member group, which had been together for three years.

John called Dav-El, which provided limousine service to the Beverly Hills Hotel, and asked that a limo be sent to him at On the Rox.

Frank Corte, a driver for Dav-El, pulled the large Cadillac limousine out of the hotel at 9:45 P.M. He was happy to get a late-night assignment, particularly for a celebrity such as Belushi.

At On the Rox, Corte picked up John, Aykroyd, Insana and Derf.

John said he wanted to go to the Playboy Mansion.

Corte took the group down Sunset and over to 10236 Charing Cross Road in Bel Air. They arrived at the celebrated symbol of Hugh Hefner's magazine and sex empire—a well-kept 5¾-acre estate with luxurious mansion—at 12:25 A.M. Hefner allowed friends and show business people regular access, particularly at the Friday- and Sunday-night parties.

Derf and Aykroyd could see that John loved the opulence—food, bars, a game room, and the exotic pool and saunas, so often the backdrop for the magazine's famous pictorial spreads. John and Derf went swimming and horsed around in the water for a while. John told Derf he was living life exactly as he wished. Success, John said, had given him this entrée and freedom. "Success means you can get up and leave whenever you want," he added.

By 1:45 A.M. they returned to the limousine, and Corte drove back toward Hollywood. Aykroyd, Insana and Derf were tired and wanted to go home, and Corte dropped them off.

To the Record Plant, John said, an all-night recording studio at Third and LaCienega. Neil Diamond was supposed to be recording that night, but apparently nothing was happening, because John was soon back, doing a little Blues Brothers dance as he approached the car.

John told Corte to stop on Sunset. They picked up a girl and drove her to the parking lot between the Roxy and the Rainbow, a popular bar next door. They arrived about 2:30 A.M., shortly after the Rainbow had closed. The parking lot, one of the most popular pickup and drug-shopping centers in the city, was jammed with all kinds of people: young teenage-looking girls in hot pants, hookers, businessmen, East Coast preppies, even some people literally dressed in space suits and other costumes.

John moved into the crowd, apparently one last effort to buy some drugs before the evening was over, and looked for the telltale signs that someone was "carrying." Nods, fingers, a glance, a whisper, were the subtle stream of communication for the street buy. Quickly John found someone to take $100 and go get something. John told Corte that the guy would be right back; he knew the street people, he was one with them, and they wouldn't let him down.

Nearly a half-hour went by.

"Who knows that guy?" John started asking around the parking lot. A number of people stared at him, wondering, mouthing, "Belushi?"

"Is he going to come back?" John asked.

No one had an answer. He got back in the limousine, clearly upset that someone would burn him.

John directed Corte east on Sunset and up Kings Road to a large A-frame house just behind the Comedy Store.

Wait here, John told Corte. Without saying how long he might be, John went into the house.

After about an hour of watching people come and go from the house, Corte finally got out of the car and walked inside. It was about 4 A.M. A group of people he didn't recognize were sitting in a semicircle, crouched around all the apparatus, including a blow torch, for freebasing cocaine. Corte went to another room, and there, too, was another group engrossed in the same ritual. He figured that thousands of dollars' worth of cocaine were being consumed. Corte finally found John and explained that he was just checking up. John told him to wait in the limousine.

At the party that night John ran into Seymour Cassel, the character actor who had been nominated for an Academy Award for his part in the 1968 movie *Faces*. Cassel and John had freebased together before, sometimes at Cassel's house, which was next door to the A-frame on Kings

Road. John normally did about a quarter ounce ($600 worth) at a time, but once Cassel had seen him do half an ounce in one sitting.

That night, John talked about the problems he was having with the *Neighbors* postproduction. John said he was going to fire Avildsen. "I'll just convince the producers he can't do the job."

"Good luck," Cassel said.

"Fuck 'em. Let them throw me out of the editing room."

About 4:30 A.M., John went out to the limousine. "It's getting pretty heavy in there," he said. "Get the motor ready. I may have to get out of here."

Corte thought that John was displaying the freebaser's paranoia. It is one of the most intense uses of cocaine, and it often pushes someone into a highly agitated state. He was concerned, but he nodded and started the engine, ready for the getaway. John returned to the house, to come out three or four times during the next several hours to make sure the car was still waiting. Corte also went inside several more times to check on him. As the sun was coming up, John and Cassel left the house and walked to Cassel's house next door. Corte followed them inside.

John picked up the phone and started to dial Judy at the Beverly Hills Hotel. He stopped abruptly and hung up. "Remind me to call her in fifteen minutes," he told Corte. John started to phone a few more times but stopped as he was dialing, nervously replacing the receiver and again asking Corte to remind him to try later. He finally had Corte make the call. The driver left a message for Judy that John would be late.

John took out some more cocaine and signaled Corte to head back to the limousine with him. He got in the back and slouched down. "They're all assholes!" he said abruptly, almost violently. "They're all assholes!" He was referring, it seemed, to everyone, the world, to all those he had outlasted that night and every night, to the cowards who went home, those who went to bed, those who didn't know how to squeeze the last lingering moment of pleasure or wakefulness from the night.

The sun was now up. Corte was exhausted. The first stirrings of morning traffic were beginning down on Sunset.

John said he wanted to find a record and tape store.

Corte said nothing would be open, but John insisted they go look.

Corte drove down Sunset. John couldn't turn off the night, didn't know how to flick the switch and shut himself down and go to sleep. The tapes or records couldn't be important. But the idea had settled into his head, and there was no getting around it.

Corte drove to several places, and they were closed. John insisted on trying another and another. After an hour Corte pulled into Tower Records on Sunset, and they agreed to wait in the parking lot until the store opened. When it did an hour later, John went in and bought some tapes, then directed Corte down Sunset again. John noticed that the driver did not have any sunglasses, and he told him to pull into the Optique Boutique at 8653 Sunset. John got out and bought two pairs of $50 sunglasses on his American Express card—a pair for each of them. Corte was surprised at the nice gesture.

Next John directed him to Penny Marshall's house.

"I haven't eaten for fourteen hours," Corte said when they pulled in the driveway. "I've got to get something. I feel like I'm almost going to vomit."

"Wait here just a minute," John said, and he went inside.

Corte felt sick and was tempted to drive off to get food. He had never been on such a short leash. John was generous about the sunglasses, but he wouldn't give an inch on food or rest.

When John came back, Corte repeated his request, explaining he was absolutely ragged, hungry and getting more fatigued with each minute, each mile.

John promised a big tip. He steered Corte to the home of Nelson Lyon, an occasional "Saturday Night Live" writer and close friend of Michael O'Donoghue. Lyon was out of town, but a Frenchwoman was staying at his place.

Next, they stopped at Tino Insana's, several blocks away. Corte, exhausted and feeling sour all over, dazed and unclean, slumped over the steering wheel. He was physically shaking when John came back.

"Take this," John said, laying out a couple of lines of cocaine. "It will wake you up."

It helped. Corte wondered what fit of graciousness had overtaken Belushi, who was snorting coke every half-hour or so. Corte felt disoriented. John had projected himself into the Hollywood night and now he was doing it to the day. Corte asked again and again for permission to eat, but John repeatedly said no, the next stop was really important.

Late that afternoon, Judy was working on the design for the Blues Brothers album at the Beverly Hills. She was surrounded by a clutter of pictures, rough sketches, some notes and graphic art material, when John called.

Everything's solved, he said happily. He had arranged for them to move into Nelson Lyon's place, and the woman who was staying there —a French friend of Viviane, Nelson's girlfriend—was going to come to stay in their suite at the hotel.

Judy thought that was ridiculous. But it was a decision made in a cocaine fit and there would be no stopping him. Inconvenient as it would be to move, she agreed. John said the limousine would be by to pick her up later.

That evening, Corte dropped John at Lyon's, took the Frenchwoman to the hotel and brought back Judy. When Judy and Corte got to Lyon's, they couldn't get inside.

"But I left him here," Corte explained, and they stood in the dark and pounded on the door. Finally a neighbor got in for them and opened the door. John was on the living room floor, passed out cold in front of the television. Corte wanted to wake him up. "He said he was going to give me a big tip," Corte said, explaining that he had been driving John for almost 24 hours all over town.

"He's an asshole," said Judy, staring down at him. She authorized an additional $50 tip for Corte; along with the standard 15 percent gratuity he came out with a total of $140 over his salary.

Corte drove back to Dav-El. The total bill for 24¼ hours was $740.85, and Dav-El started a new policy for anyone assigned to Belushi: Drivers would no longer do more than an eight-hour shift.

When John finally woke up the next day, Sunday, he avoided a confrontation by telling Judy where he'd been. She just listened.

He'd gone to the Playboy mansion, and that neither surprised nor upset her. In many ways, she figured, that was the perfect environment for John: he would not be alone, he would have food and games, and he would be watched.

Then there was a party elsewhere and I was freebasing, he said.

Freebasing was heavy-duty drug usage, and that meant he'd been around the hardcore. Judy was terrified. Apparently John could see that she was trembling.

"What are you worried about—*heroin*?" He spoke offhandedly, mentioning it as if out of the blue.

"I never thought about it," she lied.

John said he'd never do that stuff "again."

Judy didn't reply.

Several years ago, John said, when he got out of the hospital after his knee injury in January 1977, he'd snorted some heroin. Once he even got shot up with it. But, he added, definitively, it had made him sick and he didn't like it.

Actually, Judy knew about that time. John had called someone and had paid $250 for a shot when he woke up in pain. She felt it was a big step for him to have told her now, even though it was years later.

Judy wanted to leave it alone. If she responded, it might be seen as a challenge. She couldn't, however, endorse even a casual, onetime use of heroin. But, she wondered, why had he brought it up? It was on his mind for some reason.

"Look me in the eyes," John said. "You can trust me."

16

Tom Scott, the thirty-three-year-old jazz-rock saxophonist from the Blues Brothers, rolled over in his bed in Los Angeles early Sunday morning, September 27. He popped open his eyes in bewilderment.

"Get up! Get up!" John was shouting, pounding on the front door.

Scott struggled out of bed, walked down to the first floor and opened the door.

John was standing there, clearly under the influence of drugs. He had come to talk about the musical score for *Neighbors*.

Scott had previously done the background theme music for a number of television shows ("Starsky and Hutch," "Baretta," "Streets of San Francisco") and a few movies, including Columbia's 1980 hit *Stir Crazy*. On John's recommendation, he had been given the job several weeks earlier of scoring about 50 minutes of original music for *Neighbors*. He was consumed by the task. It took a full day of detailed work to score about three minutes' worth of music.

For the final song, which would be the title song "Neighbors," Scott had made a rough demonstration tape so people at Columbia could get an idea of the melody he had in mind. He had done it sitting at home, playing the guitar and humming into a tape recorder. He'd sent the tape to the music people at Columbia, and they seemed quite pleased.

John sat down in Scott's living room and continued his attack on Avildsen. He wanted to make sure that Avildsen was not influencing the music.

"Never mind what he says," John said authoritatively. "Do your own thing." Scott would do fine following his own musical instincts. Avildsen was poison and could wreck anything.

Scott knew that adding music was one of the final stages in postproduction, and a score could be shuffled around, cut, or dropped based on the whims of producers, directors and stars; those who wrote the music had no leverage whatsoever. When a movie was in trouble (as this one was, considering what Scott had heard and seen of Avildsen), the music could become a convenient scapegoat.

On the second day of scoring with the orchestra, Wednesday, September 30, Scott got a call from John, who was to do the vocals on the title song and was over at a recording studio in town.

"There's a problem," John said. "Come down."

When Scott walked into the studio, John, Derf, and the three other band members from Fear were blasting forth with an angry, savage sound, composing their own punk title song, "Neighbors," for the movie. The music was an upheaval of noises and overinstrumentation.

"This is a punk picture," John said to Scott. "I want people to tear the seats out." There was a pause in the music. "This space here is for your sax solo," John said, inviting Scott to join the band.

Scott listened in silence, wondering whether John had finally flipped out. This was deranged. John couldn't unilaterally decide on new music, and no studio would put a punk song on a major movie release.

John told Scott that he could be the producer of the new song.

After hours of work composing an original score, that was the cruelest part. John assumed that Scott's acquiescence could be bought with a sax solo and a technical credit.

"This is where I want the music to begin," John said, pointing to a spot near the end of the script.

"The director and producers want it here," Scott replied, locating the point from which he had been working. He spoke distractedly, confused by his own anger, trying to figure out what had gone wrong. How was this happening?

"I want this, and what I say goes," John said.

Scott's wife, Lynn, was sitting off to the side with Joel Briskin. "This is fucked," she said.

"Tom's big," Briskin replied. "He'll handle it."

Tom walked over and asked, "Why am I here?"

"Because we must support John," Briskin answered.

Scott went home, took a pencil and a sheet of music paper in hand, and scrawled out a letter to John: "Certain admissions and apologies are in order before I can begin to resume our friendship, which is over as far as I'm concerned." Scott listed his complaints, ending with a demand that John admit, "You're sorry you have been a self-righteous, egotistical, pompous, inconsiderate asshole."

Scott put the letter aside and went back to finishing his score.

He was on the sound stage with the orchestra the next day, Thursday, October 1, when John arrived wearing shades and a bandanna wrapped around his head, very underground, a sign of trouble. He had obviously been up all night.

John wanted to take Fear into the studio again that night to work on their song. Scott made the arrangements and said coolly that he would meet them there. Later, Scott phoned a friend at the recording studio, said that he was expected, and explained that under no circumstances was he going to show up. The humiliation was too deep, and he wanted John to get some of his own medicine. Once at home, Scott told his answering service that if Belushi called, they should take messages. But put no calls through.

John stopped to see Judy before going to the recording studio. She was withdrawing more and more from the frenzy of his movie, his music and his drugs. John said that he was going to stay in Los Angeles until the Fear song was finished and perfect. After that, he had to get it accepted for the movie. "I'm not going to stop doing drugs until I finish," John said. He would, he added, fall asleep for days if he stopped now.

Judy could see that the Fear song meant a lot to him. He was looking for some way of putting his energy into the movie. If the music was frightening, he said, that was exactly what he wanted.

Judy and Lynn Scott went out together that night, and Lynn confided that Tom felt betrayed and was not going to show up at the recording studio.

Judy sympathized fully with Tom. John was being awful. But she was torn, knowing that John was being set up. She called him at the studio and put Lynn on the line.

"Where's Tom?" John asked.

"He's not with you?" Lynn said, feigning surprise.

"We're all waiting for him."

"Well, you know musicians."

The phone rang at the Scotts' home again. Tom Scott waited a few minutes and called his answering service. It had been Belushi.

"The next time he calls," Scott said, "tell him you can't find me, put him on hold for five minutes, then get back on and tell him you still can't find me."

John stayed up all night working on the music.

Judy decided the only thing she could do was return to New York.

When John breezed into the house, he said he would see her back in New York when he was finished with the music. Then he left. While packing, Judy stopped to read the new October issue of *Esquire* magazine. The cover story was headlined: THE LIFE AND DEATH OF A COMIC GENIUS —"With the National Lampoon and Animal House, he shaped the humor of an entire generation, Doug Kenney, 1946–1980."

The article strongly implied that Kenney had committed suicide by jumping off the cliff in Hawaii. Judy didn't believe it. Kenney would not have killed himself in such an ambiguous or potentially inconclusive way. It was a small cliff, and Kenney would have chosen the Empire State Building or the highest cliff in the world. Judy also felt that if he had wanted to commit suicide, he would more likely have done it with drugs.

The article was unsettling to her in a larger way, painting Hollywood success—big money, high expectations and drugs—as ruinous and the early passing of the bright comic lights as somehow destined. She read: "Kenney's brilliance was his humor, and everything it touched turned to gold. . . . His humor influenced an entire generation, yet his is not a funny story." Unfortunately, Judy thought, that part was true.

When she had finished packing, Judy told Viviane's friend, who was staying in the Belushis' suite at the Beverly Hills Hotel, to check out. Judy was appalled at the charges that had been run up—$10,360.35. The Frenchwoman had taken their offer to "charge what you like" literally, using the drugstore, flower shop, tennis courts, beauty salon, laundry and room service with an extravagance that Judy thought could be matched only by John. One dinner alone had been $1,019. Perhaps it was an absurdly fitting cap to the Los Angeles visit. She was determined to find a psychiatrist in New York to help her through this storm in her life.

The next morning, Friday, October 2, Zanuck and Brown were in their Columbia office when John, unannounced, burst in so fast that Zanuck thought he might go through the wall into the next office. John had his father in tow.

John explained that he had found the solution to all their music problems—a new punk group called Fear that would brilliantly serve the deep, radical, lawless drive of the movie.

Zanuck and Brown said they had never heard of Fear. Brown wondered whether it might not be a good idea to end the movie with something like Bing Crosby singing "Love Thy Neighbor." The irony would not be lost.

John threw himself into a tirade about the misconceptions that were guiding their movie. Punk was kids' music, and it would draw them to the movie.

Brown concluded that John would probably kill for his work if it did not go his way. His commitment to what he believed was right was frightening. Now, he was storming about like the Creature from the Black Lagoon. As usual, Brown tried to calm him, explaining that the movie, John's career, the existence of Western Civilization, did not turn on this one point.

John wouldn't listen.

Zanuck was very nervous. John was way out of control, hanging around like some kind of deadly affliction.

"Take me over to the head of the music department," John finally said. He would get support from someone in the know about new music.

Adam Belushi was standing quietly, looking embarrassed. He shook his head and in an aside asked Zanuck, "Who does he think he is?" But Zanuck and Brown set up a 3 P.M. meeting in the office of Dick Berres, the vice president and director of music for Columbia Pictures. In the meantime Sheldon Schrager, the Columbia vice president and executive production manager, was in his office when Bernie Brillstein called him to inform him that John wanted a hearing on the music. Schrager was well aware of John's feelings about the music. He had been squiring John around, trying to keep him calm.

Also, Brillstein said, John needs expense money—now.

John was getting $2,500 a week for expenses. Schrager said he would get the check out right away if it was that important.

"A check won't do him any good," Brillstein said. "He needs cash."

So Schrager got the cash for John. *Anything* to keep things moving forward.

Richard Berres, sixty, a former Los Angeles Symphony cellist (1946–52), was in his office waiting for John. They had never met, but Berres, who had been in the music end of film work for nearly 30 years and was due for retirement, had learned how to deal with stars.

Zanuck and Brown arrived; then Belushi and Schrager walked in. Berres noticed John's headband and his stomach hanging over his belt. Trouble, Berres thought, but there was some reason for this meeting. Maybe one of the big studio bosses wanted this new music. Executives, stars, producers and directors often had strong feelings, and you never could tell where the final answer might come from. John went over to the stereo and slapped the tape cassette inside. "You got to put this music in," he said, looking at Berres as if it were Berres who made the decisions.

Berres nodded.

The music began, and John turned the volume up. Berres tried to suppress a wince. It seemed to be a rhythm beat with some screeching in the background, an absolute atrocity. Punk music, the antithesis of the classics Berres loved.

The others in the room indicated in one way or another that they couldn't understand the lyrics, so John turned up the volume. He started dancing around the room, singing the words.

Berres tried to turn down the volume, but John wouldn't have it, starting the song from the beginning again and turning it up even higher. Each time the song was finished, he rewound the tape and played it again.

Schrager finally got up and told Berres that he had to get on to other business. "You son of a bitch," Berres whispered.

Zanuck and Brown couldn't stand it either and finally left.

Berres was now alone with Belushi, who was on about his fifth time through the song.

"Isn't this the greatest fucking piece of music you've ever heard?" John asked, at last stopping the tape.

Berres nodded as noncommittally as possible, a barely perceptible up and down movement.

John went to Berres's desk, sat down, picked up the phone and dialed a number. Berres stood by watching.

Having gotten Avildsen on the phone apparently, John commenced to bellow every four-letter word in the book, speaking in wild hyperbole and disjointed sentences, running backward and forward over the same thesis. Avildsen was a "fucking cocksucker," and the Fear song would be the "greatest song ever to appear in a movie."

John stood up, swinging the phone around as he spoke, and accidentally pulled the connection from the wall. Unfortunately, Berres saw, the wire didn't break. So John continued shouting into the receiver, and for emphasis started banging the base of the phone on the cabinet behind Berres's desk, gouging hole after hole in it.

Berres said nothing but tried to signal, as delicately as possible, that John should calm down. John ignored him. Berres decided not to intervene. John was a name star, and if Berres had learned anything about name stars, it was to let them run.

John was lighting and discarding cigarettes with the same abandon. Several were on the side of Berres's desk and were slowly burning into the wood. No use even moving within range, Berres concluded, and just stood where he was. Clearly this was drugs.

John cradled the phone on his shoulder, the angry burble of obscenities continuing. He opened one of Berres's desk drawers, apparently to look inside. But he pulled it too far, and it came all the way out, dumping the contents on the floor.

Berres started forward but then held himself in check.

John attacked the desk, pulling out two more drawers and this time throwing the contents on the floor.

It was clear to Berres that this one song was a symbol to John of a multitude of sins he attributed to Avildsen. But it was like watching a stage play, and for a moment Berres thought it had been contrived.

John finally slammed down the phone and looked at Berres as if Berres now understood his justification. Berres nodded again, and John walked righteously out of the office.

Berres called Brown on his damaged phone and gave him a brief report. Berres's main concern was not his phone, his cabinet or his desk drawers, but the song. It shouldn't ever be used.

Brown laughed. "Dick," he said, "there is no way that will ever go in the picture."

Later Brown received a call from John. "Look, John," Brown said, "you wrecked the joint. That's not the way."

"I was out of control," John said, only a note of contrition in his voice.

Brown decided to explain about the music. "John, it's terrible," he said. "I confess there is a double or triple generation gap. It's crummy. It's so—" Brown paused to search for the right word—"so dirty." The Columbia music people felt the Fear song had no commercial value.

"You've got to trust me when it comes to music," John said. "This is the music of the future."

"You can't just dictate it," Brown said.

John hung up.

Brown, furious, called Brillstein. This was not the way he expected to be treated by anyone—star or not.

Brillstein said he had airplane tickets to get John out of town, but he wouldn't go. They'd thought of just carrying him on the plane when he was passed out. He's got to drop soon, Brillstein said, because by our calculations, he's been up twelve straight days and nights—since he arrived here. If we can get him out of L.A., he'll be okay, but this is the worst environment for him.

How can we control it? Brown asked. How does he get the drugs?

"You can't give him any cash," Brillstein said. "The only way to keep him off the stuff is to cut off the cash."

Brown said he wasn't giving John any cash, except for the usual $10 or $20 loan when John didn't have any money.

"He's got to get out of town or I do," Brillstein said despairingly. "I can't stand it!"

Brown said goodbye and hung up. He was worried that John had tied too much of his self-esteem and career to this one movie—and now the music. It seemed that John could not take professional failure, that he wasn't ready for a disaster; there was no cushion, and Brown knew you needed cushions in the business they were in. John was destroying every relationship he had—with Judy, with friends like Tom Scott. Even his father and Brillstein seemed disillusioned. And all the while it was feeding an ugly reputation in the business. The incident in Berres's office would get around.

John called Brown again to apologize. Like everything John did, it was strong and effective, a sincere, self-deprecating, groveling apology. Brown accepted. He liked John, but he felt he had to issue a stern warning. As nicely and authentically as possible, he said, "If you keep this up, you're going to be dead."

John was silent for a moment. Then he explained that he had to go, said a friendly goodbye and hung up.

The next evening, Saturday, October 3, Columbia held their first on-lot screening of *Neighbors* for several hundred Belushi and Aykroyd fans. Two separate screening rooms were set up, and preview cards alerted the audience that the film was "unfinished and in the process of being worked on in many areas."

Five ratings were indicated:

—Excellent ("One of the best movies I've ever seen.")
—Very Good ("Better than most movies.")
—Average ("About as good as most movies.")
—Fair ("Not as good as most movies.")
—Poor ("One of the worst movies I've ever seen.")

Price, much of the Columbia brass, Zanuck, Brown, Avildsen, Brillstein, Tom Scott (whose new score was in place) and even executive producer Irving "Swifty" Lazar were there. The producers and Columbia executives had agreed to ban John from the screening. They did not want a repeat of the earlier shoe-thumping screening in New York, or a wild man trashing the screening room. The doors were locked to make sure Belushi didn't barge in.

Price wasn't sure what they would see. Everything he had been hearing was bad. But that had been the case since the start of the shooting. The dailies and the August screening had shown promise, but this would be a better test, with Belushi and Aykroyd fans passing judgment. Price listened to the audience and watched their reactions. They seemed disoriented. It was a different experience seeing Belushi as a punching bag, a victim. There wasn't much laughter, the music was way off, and the ending didn't work. When the lights came up, there was dead silence.

"We've got a fucking disaster," Price said, throwing an arm around Brillstein. Price needed a comrade. The reaction was like a club bashing him about the head. He felt panic. If word ever got out about this audience reaction, they'd be dead—millions of dollars down the drain. They'd never even get the movie into the theaters.

Lazar went up to Zanuck and Brown. "Jesus Christ. Where did we go wrong?"

Zanuck and Brown felt violated and mildly resented Lazar's sudden show of interest after months of noninvolvement—not that they had needed more input. Lazar said the music sounded "like a sound track for a documentary on Auschwitz."

"Look, fellows," Lazar said, "why don't we go have a stiff drink somewhere?"

Zanuck and Brown declined, deciding that they didn't need an executive producer around to depress them further.

By Monday, October 5, Frank Price had received the preview statistics. It was worse than expected—the worst screening results that he or any other Columbia executive had ever seen. In one room, one percent had found the movie excellent, and in the other, 2 percent. For even a moderate success, they needed a minimum of 25 percent rating the movie excellent. In one screening room, 56 percent rated it poor—defined as "One of the worst movies I've ever seen." By contrast *Stripes,* the Bill Murray Army comedy that had grossed $72 million that summer, had received excellent ratings from 33 to 54 percent of the test audience. A one- or 2-percent excellent rating was death.

Price was in agony. These people had come in for free, and usually they gave better ratings than a paying audience.

There were some tough decisions to make. Columbia, like most studios, made some movies that they did not release—preferring to cut their losses and eat the production costs. With advertising and other expenses, releasing a turkey could be more expensive than holding it, to say nothing of the embarrassment of presenting a movie that would be savaged by both critics and patrons.

But *Neighbors*, with all the big-name people involved, was different. It would be more difficult to leave this one in the can, and maybe it wouldn't be necessary after all, Price reasoned. There were two things he could do. First, Columbia had ultimate control on the final editing, so he could get involved in the remaining creative decisions. Second, he could revise the marketing plans.

On the creative front, the basic problem was that the audience was expecting something like *Animal House* or "Saturday Night Live"— John's trademarks. They needed to be forewarned that John was stepping out of his familiar role; and the darker, modern comedy had to be made more accessible to them. Price ordered up book reviews that extolled the dark and sinister comedy in Berger's book to be rewritten as if they were reviews of the movie. They would be run on the screen as a kind of introduction to the movie. Columbia would test this approach and compare it to audience previews without the new introduction.

Next, something had to be done with John's character. He was too much a victim. Some way had to be found, a new scene or a new ending, so that Belushi came out on top.

Price also agreed that a more positive, "up" music score was needed. The real problem was the movie, but the music made it worse; the score gave the movie a quirky, remote feeling. With fresh music, the film could be made to appear more in the mainstream of Belushi-Aykroyd comedy. Price authorized several hundred thousand dollars for a new score.

For practical purposes, Price and Columbia were taking over creative control of the movie. But Price wanted to avoid a power play, and he wanted to do it authoritatively and persuasively. The Directors Guild prevented a studio from arbitrarily editing and cutting a movie by generally giving a director the right to a public sneak preview with a regular paying audience; in effect, the studio couldn't edit the film without first finding out whether the public sided with the director. To Price's mind, the on-lot testing already proved they didn't, and a public preview would tip off the theater chains that *Neighbors* was a bust. So Price went to work on Avildsen to get him to adopt some new notions. But he also had to convince the director not to enforce his contractual right to public sneak previews.

Columbia might do a repair job, but the film would remain basically the same, and that meant it was not going to be well received. Word of mouth was going to be poor or even terrible. So Price next devised a marketing plan that he hoped would avoid financial disaster.

Normally, Columbia would open a movie like *Neighbors* in 800 to 1,000 theaters. Price instructed the distribution department to sign up 1,500. Along with the December 18 release date, they would get every dollar possible as fast as possible, before the bad word got around. Hit and run. Belushi, Aykroyd, Zanuck, Brown and Avildsen were all big, and *Neighbors* was perceived to be a big movie. People would be clamoring to see it, and Columbia couldn't afford to turn anyone away while there were positive expectations. The truth had to be kept from the theaters, especially the chains. If they learned how bad it was, they would book other movies in their theaters after a two-week run. A third and fourth week would be crucial to bringing in more revenue—several million dollars more. Without those additional weeks, Columbia could wind up several million in the hole.

Zanuck and Brown were not party to the marketing strategy though they could see what was happening and why. But both agreed with Price's creative suggestions. His instincts were good, and they joined in the efforts to persuade Avildsen.

Brown found that Avildsen was a brick wall, so he drove home one theme: Columbia and Price held all the cards. "They can cut this movie any way they want," Brown warned. Better to collaborate than to have them simply take the movie away.

Zanuck was dismayed. Avildsen was stubborn and arrogant. Many of the things that Belushi had been warning them about, Zanuck now saw firsthand. Price's suggestions made sense, but Avildsen wouldn't listen. It wasn't just bad judgment, though there was plenty of that, and it wasn't just stupidity and ignorance, though they were also there in abundance.

With Zanuck and Brown supplying the heat, and Price providing cool inducement and coaxing, they finally got the director to give up his three public previews. The next steps would be won with difficulty, they could see.

Meanwhile, John was devoting the week to working with Fear on perfecting their *Neighbors* song. On Monday they had a 6-hour session; on Tuesday, 13½ hours; Joel Briskin was overseeing the work and sending out for beer, pizzas or whatever John and the musicians wanted.

One night John gave Briskin $600 in cash and asked him to get a quarter of an ounce of cocaine. "I've got to have stuff for the kids," he said.

Briskin went to a supplier he knew and brought back the drug.

John told the band that he was going to get their music into the movie at any cost. If their song was not used, he promised to shave his head bald like a punk skinhead as a sign of protest. Then he would go on television talk shows, and when asked why he was a skinhead, he would explain about the music, the fucked director, producers and studio.

On Wednesday, John went to see Dr. Feder again. Feder was increasingly worried about the inflamed membranes in John's nasal passages. The insides were tender and raw. Using Pontocaine, an oily local anesthetic mixture, for the first time on John, he cleaned and swabbed John's nose, clearing out the passages and giving the damaged membranes a chance to heal themselves. When it looked as though John might be having an allergic reaction to the Pontocaine, Feder discontinued the treatment. And he gave John a round of anti-inflammatory injections to reduce the swelling.

At 4 P.M. that afternoon John went to another recording session with Fear. They didn't finish until 7 A.M. the next morning.

When the tape of the Fear song was finally completed, John took it to Avildsen, who had promised Price that he would at least listen.

Avildsen cringed. The music had no melody and it was ugly. But Avildsen tempered his remarks. Though the music was important, it was secondary to the movie itself, and there was no time for a prolonged argument with John.

"I don't think it's appropriate," Avildsen said. It seemed too jarring, he said, and it did not relate to what John's character was supposed to feel at the end.

John said they had to get a better stereo system. Avildsen obviously had not had a chance to get the full feel. John tried to find a better sound system but failed. He finally told Avildsen emphatically, "This music is going to be in the movie."

"Stranger things have happened," Avildsen replied.

"What do you mean?" John asked belligerently.

"Stranger things have happened than for inappropriate music to be in a movie," Avildsen said. He felt angry, not only at John but at the producers and Columbia for second-guessing him at every turn. "It doesn't have my vote. Go talk to the people who are paying for the movie. I just work here."

John called Brown and said that he was taking the music decision to the top, directly to Price.

Brown couldn't be reticent any longer. This was crazy. It was impossible not to be aware that John was on something. "John, you can't," Brown said, hesitating. "You're around the studio in a condition that's obvious to everyone. No one will listen to you that way."

John repeated that he was going to go talk to Price, that there was no use trying to talk him out of it.

"Nothing will change our minds on the music," Brown said. But he agreed to set up a meeting. "If you expect to influence Frank Price," he warned, "don't go like *that*."

The producers called Price and filled him in on everything. Price said he understood.

That night John and Fear spent six hours polishing another version of the song, and afterward John went over to Ron Wood's house.

The next morning, Friday, October 9, John was scheduled to be in Price's office at ten o'clock. Briskin was supposed to get a limousine and pick him up at Tino Insana's. When Briskin arrived with the car about nine-thirty, John wasn't there. At eleven, already an hour late for the meeting, he arrived by cab. He was absolutely livid and looked a mess.

"I couldn't get a fucking limo," John shouted, obviously having forgotten the plans.

Briskin had never seen John so ravaged with drugs and full of bile.

Getting into the limousine, John shouted, "You're not coming! I'm selling this!"

Briskin was depressed. He was sick of his degrading role in John's life.

In his office at Columbia, Price wasn't surprised that John was late, and wouldn't have been surprised if he didn't come at all. John was a one-of-a-kind actor, but, like most of them, he was an adolescent.

John arrived at about noon. He was very distracted and began by giving Price the full background on Fear. Price listened encouragingly.

Since this is a punk movie, John said, the music would be just right.

Price had heard some wild claims over the years, but this was one of the wildest. There was no point in disagreeing, no point in getting into an argument. John, who was grossly overweight, was sweating profusely.

They went to Price's outer office, where there was a stereo system. John looked it over and said the speakers were too small. The bigger system wasn't working, however, and they had to make do.

John turned up the volume, danced a little and sang the lyrics into Price's ear.

Price recoiled. It was an awful, mean song. He could see that John thought he had found the Holy Grail.

What do you think? John asked.

Good, Price said, but it might not be appropriate. And there are questions about how popular that kind of music is. Price promised to speak with the producers and get back in touch. John wanted more.

They would all have to wait and see, Price said. He wanted to plant some reservations, but no more. More would inflame John.

John said that the Fear group would work really hard to plug the movie, and he was going to get them on television shows.

Price said he preferred to wait and see what was best.

John tried to move Price. If there wasn't going to be a go-ahead, then it seemed he almost wanted to hear the truth, a rejection.

Price held to the neutral ground. He would confer and be back in touch.

Unable to rouse his one-man audience, John left.

Price felt very bad for John. Either he was sick or on drugs. Everyone was saying it was drugs, and Price could see that it probably was. He himself had learned his lesson years ago. When he was twenty-eight and writing for television, Price briefly had become hooked on amphetamines and couldn't write without them. He was able to pull back and eventually stop, but only after a tremendous act of the will. John obviously had graduated to more serious drug use, but Price could sympathize with him, feel pity. John just didn't have the will power and probably couldn't see himself very clearly.

Still, what could Price do about John? About drugs? Guys like Belushi had managers, agents, lawyers, accountants, public relations people, assorted hangers-on. He was their job, not the studio's. Like many actors, John had some private demon. Price was pretty sure that any attempt on his part to interfere would be futile. He couldn't prove drug use. His information was rumor and supposition. If Price suspected that drug abuse was holding up production, then he might act—call Belushi's manager, agent or lawyer. But he'd hate to accuse someone and wind up with egg on his face. That would really look stupid and unsophisticated. And his reward for any effort to reform John or others would likely be a big "Fuck you."

The business of making movies rested on the talents of so few. Price suspected that John felt he had to top himself, to do it again, better, funnier. The pressure must be terrible. Some talents were in a category between blessing and curse, and the more talent, the more driven the person, the more inexorable the curse. Price was glad he didn't have that monkey on his back.

The next day Price called John and said the Fear song didn't seem as though it would work. To end the movie on such a note, he said, would be too much of a downer. What they needed was something to give John's character a boost.

John was polite. He thanked Price and said goodbye.

That night John got a limousine and drove around until 6 A.M., stopping at more than half a dozen friends' in his search for drugs, banging on doors until finally he stopped at Ron Wood's house.

The next day, Sunday, October 11, he flew back to New York.

Larry Gelbart had not seen the film yet and finally decided to go to a screening and see how they had handled the script. Afterward he was heartbroken. Tom Berger was a friend, and Gelbart had wanted the movie to be just right. Instead, it was a mockery of his intentions: The tone was desperate and grim; John seemed lifeless and stone-faced, obviously uncomfortable with his part; and most distressing, the movie was simply not funny. They had turned Berger's dark piece of chamber music into a semi-rock concert. Gelbart thought of taking his name off the script, but he had just done that with a Burt Reynolds movie, *Rough Cut,* and didn't want to add to his reputation.

All the judgments, both large and small, were wrong. The money people at Columbia obviously had heard the cash register ring with the "star" directing, producing and acting combination, and common sense had flown out the window. It appeared also that someone had rewritten parts of the script during the WGA strike that summer, possibly in violation of the strike rules.

On Monday, October 12, Gelbart addressed a letter to the sunshine boys, Zanuck and Brown: "Enclosed are my suggestions regarding the cut of 'Neighbors' that I viewed. . . . I wish I could share your optimism about the film. In view of my far more negative feelings, I consider what follows, unfortunately, mere band-aids."

The music, he wrote, "is so counter-comedy, it sinks us almost before we start." In the opening, John and his wife, Enid, "seem like a pair of recluses living in a house full of menacing shadows rather than simply just a bored couple."

A scene with John singing in the shower after he has fallen into the quicksand: "Why . . . after all he's just been through? Muttering in disbelief and anger, perhaps, but singing? It makes him seem a moron."

On another scene, "Please cut 'jagoff' and 'asshole.' . . . We just had an 'asshole.' (This is another case of people 'improving' the script and the film right into the ground)."

Toward the movie's end, Ramona (Cathy Moriarty) goes down on John twice in a prolonged suggestion of oral sex. Gelbart wrote that this was "in the worst possible taste. . . . 'Come quick' is another cheap joke that was added. Cut it."

Gelbart folded his correspondence and dropped it in the mail. He had recommended 43 changes in 30 separate scenes, or one Band-Aid every two minutes. But he felt it still wasn't enough, not even close.

The next week, on Wednesday, October 14, Tom Scott got a call from Avildsen informing him he was fired. They were getting a new composer and a new score.

Scott wasn't surprised, but he was bitter about the contradictory, incomplete and misleading instructions he had been given.

Avildsen hired Bill Conti, who had composed the Oscar-nominated score for his movie *Rocky*—the ultimate in "up" music.

Scott received a telegram from John that said:

SORRY ABOUT WHAT HAPPENED. DO YOU KNOW HOW SLEAZY THIS BUSINESS IS? I HOPE WE GET TO WORK TOGETHER REAL SOON, REALLY. YOUR FRIEND IN TELEVISION, RECORDS AND FILMS. JOHN.

The next Sunday, October 18, Columbia held more controlled previews of the latest version. One included the prologue of rewritten book reviews, ordered by Price, explaining that the movie was brilliant black comedy; the other did not. This prologue bumped the excellent rating up to 3 percent, and the poor was only 11 percent. It was better but still not out of the disaster category.

Gelbart attended the screening to see if they had listened to him. Not much. All he wanted to do, spotting Avildsen across the lobby, was to tear out his little heart. He decided just to continue building his case for a grievance with the Writers Guild.

Back in New York, John started working on selecting the songs for a "Best of the Blues Brothers" album. That fall, Judy was spending as much time on the Vineyard as possible. She loved it in the autumn, when the island was cooler and less crowded. When things were right, she would stay for a long weekend and fly back to New York for her regular Tuesday appointment with her new psychiatrist, Dr. Jak Cohane. She'd stay for a Thursday appointment, then return to the island for another long weekend.

The week of Sunday, October 18, Judy wanted to fly back to New York a few days early, but the Vineyard was fogged in. Carly Simon had rented a limousine, and she invited Judy to come along. They took the 45-minute ferry ride to Woods Hole on the Massachusetts mainland, where the car met them. The days were getting shorter, and a heavy scent of autumn was in the air as they settled in the back for the five-hour drive through New England.

Simon felt a close alliance with Judy, a kind of camaraderie and solidarity between psychologically battered wives. Both were trying to cope with the same marital problems—drugs and infidelity. James Taylor was still having bouts with heroin and had gone off with Kathryn Walker, who played Enid, John's wife, in *Neighbors*.

At least John's infidelities were passing fancies, temporary attractions and probably not very sexual, Judy said. Still, she wasn't sure if she could stick it through and wondered how much one woman could take. When John was in California, Judy said, he went nuts, and that cast her back in the old role of the bodyguard, the cop.

Simon said she knew the feeling, playing the gargoyle, trying to keep the bad influences out of the house. There were too many people around who wanted to please their famous husbands, and those people were too quick with their drugs.

Simon liked John but felt that he snapped his fingers too often at Judy: fix dinner, make cole slaw, get a limousine, call so-and-so. Judy was good at being stepped on. At least Simon had her own career and identity. Judy was little more than John's wife. When you were at the end of your rope, when you needed something to fall back on, a career helped a lot. Judy's own interests and talents were being stifled by the magnitude of John's success, Simon felt.

How was Bill Wallace doing keeping the drugs away? Simon asked.

Wallace, Judy said, wasn't like Smokey Wendell, a keen drug enforcer. He wasn't as smart as Smokey, and John could trick him. You had to be on John's heels all the time to succeed. She'd been on duty a lot recently—particularly in California.

Judy asked Simon about children. She wanted to have a family very much but just couldn't, not with John so crazed, not until things settled down and their lives permitted it, if they ever would.

They arrived back in New York about midnight. Simon left Judy feeling rather certain that she was not going to stay with John much longer.

John convinced "Saturday Night Live" to have Fear as the music group for the Halloween show, Saturday, October 31, and he agreed to do a cameo appearance. Several dozen skinheads, avid and sometimes violent punk fans, were invited to slam dance on stage during the songs. Things got way out of hand, and a small camera was knocked over. Though the microphones on the dance floor had been shut off, one skinhead yelled, "Fuck you, New York!" It didn't go out over the air, but the incident hurt Fear's chance for other TV appearances. Some of the skinheads were bleeding as they walked off stage.

One morning John went to the office of his accountant, Mark Lipsky, and threw himself on the table in a conference room. "I have a lot of friends who are doing heroin," he told Lipsky's assistant, Shirley Sergent, for no apparent reason. It seemed to bother him. "It really must be good stuff," he added, "because so many people get hooked on it. I don't think I could ever do heroin. If I did, I'd have a very hard time stopping —if ever."

In Los Angeles, Frank Price was still trying to salvage *Neighbors*. The new music was to be ready soon, and the introductory prologue was also ready. The marketing strategy of hit and run was in place—1,400 theaters opening December 18, a week before Christmas.

Avildsen did not believe the research findings, so he went to a couple of screenings to gauge the audience reaction and look at the preview cards. It was grim.

Price and Avildsen met to discuss a new ending—a last-ditch effort. Price argued that the audience was seeing John done in. They needed a catharsis, something to show he was no patsy, like a big, dramatic "Fuck you" to his wife, so he'd go out on top. Price had an idea. They could add a new scene at the end and have John go back into the house before leaving, pick up the television set—the symbol of his suburban stupefaction—and throw it across the living room, setting the house on fire. There had to be something for the audience to stand up and cheer about. In the current version the house caught fire, but the audience didn't get to see how it happened. The act of defiance would symbolically cast off his old character and signify the beginning of a new life. The final impression was very important because, more than anything, it would help determine what people told their friends about the movie.

Avildsen was not buying it. Such a scene would be overdone, much too dramatic, he said.

Price stood, picked up an imaginary television and threw it across the room with great energy and release. John's character and the audience need that, he replied.

Avildsen suggested that maybe John could draw a mustache on his wife's picture.

Price said no. They needed to get Belushi back in control at the end. It would cost several hundred thousand dollars to reconstruct the living room and other props, but it had to be done.

They went back and forth. Price, normally flexible, wouldn't give an inch. Both men knew he held the cards, and it was his decision unless Avildsen wanted to bust ranks completely. Finally, Avildsen buckled and agreed at least to try it. After all, it was Columbia's money.

Now Price's problem was to convince Belushi to shoot the new ending with Avildsen.

John balked at the idea of flying to California to reshoot one scene, particularly with that asshole directing. He wanted Aykroyd to direct it, but Aykroyd refused. John proposed that he direct it himself. After much go-around, Aykroyd agreed to fly to the West Coast with John to be present for the shooting, even though he wasn't in the scene. They took the United noon flight to California on Monday, November 2, and by Wednesday they were ready to shoot.

The fire department was on the set to control the fire if it got out of hand. John and Avildsen almost immediately locked horns over what should be on the TV screen before John threw the set. Avildsen wanted a talk show scene with people discussing how awful society is. John wanted the screen to show a giant skyscraper exploding and tumbling down. They agreed to shoot it both ways.

In the first part of the scene, John was to come back into the house, take the family portrait from the wall and put his head through it, giving a Samurai grunt. There was no disagreement over that, since Price had vetoed Avildsen's mustache suggestion as too soft.

In the next part of the scene, John threw the television. Avildsen envisioned a small flame in the corner with the curtains catching fire.

No, John said. He wanted a roaring, frightening fire; he wanted to go out in flames, a conflagration, something to substitute for the energy the Fear music would have supplied. But Avildsen and the others had made up their minds. In one take, the fire did get big, but it was quickly brought under control.

They worked late that day to finish, and John left despondent. He soon flew back to New York.

Price, Zanuck and Brown had all agreed on further changes, and they were still wrestling with Avildsen. On Monday, November 9, they had two meetings with him.

Avildsen was uncompromising, drawing lines in the sand all over the place. Both Zanuck and Brown marveled at Price's firmness and tact. He was understated; yet he quietly overpowered Avildsen. Only a few pieces of dialogue and the editing of the new ending remained. Price stayed right on the edge of issuing a threat. Zanuck could read an unmistakable message; Price was intimating, Look, if you don't go along, you'll never work at Columbia again, and everyone will know why. It was less direct than that, but the message could not be denied. By the end of the afternoon, Price had Avildsen in control.

The next day, Tuesday, November 10, the *New York Times* had a story about the Christmas movie season. Predicting generally dismal prospects, the article said, "According to every studio and exhibitor poll, the one movie with a chance to 'break out'—to reach toward dizzying box office heights . . . is Columbia's 'Neighbors.' . . . The 'Saturday Night Live' team of Belushi and Aykroyd together again will definitely have lines circling the block."

17

Jay Sandrich, who had directed television's successful "Mary Tyler Moore Show" from 1970 to 1977, had spent some time reading a 116-page feature movie script called *Sweet Deception*. It was a romantic comedy adventure about a young, honest unsophisticate who takes a new California wine to a New York wine-tasting contest, falls in love, becomes involved with a diamond-smuggling ring, but triumphs in the end—winning wine, diamonds and woman.

Sandrich, forty-nine, felt that *Sweet Deception* could be a little like Alfred Hitchcock's *North by Northwest,* or like *Charade.* The male lead might be a variation of Cary Grant or James Stewart, the female a Grace Kelly. He asked Chevy Chase if he was interested. Sandrich's one feature film, *Seems Like Old Times* (1980), had starred Chase. It had not done well, and Chase said no to *Sweet Deception*.

Then Sandrich got a call from his agent, Michael Ovitz. "What would you think of John Belushi?" Ovitz asked.

"Goodbye," Sandrich replied.

"No, no, wait," Ovitz said. He was serious. "Look at *Continental Divide*."

Sandrich went to a screening and sat up close so he could look at John's eyes carefully. He had heard about the drugs and wanted to see for himself. John's eyes were clear, and, more important, he was sweeter than Sandrich had expected. The movie was pretty bad, but John had raw appeal, and if the power he displayed would ever be harnessed, there was great potential. John did have that quality of Brando's: the eye fell on him naturally and was inclined to stay.

Ovitz sent the *Sweet Deception* script to Brillstein and John. Later he set up a meeting between Belushi and Sandrich in his conference room. Ovitz introduced them, stayed for about ten minutes and left.

Sandrich decided to lay it out directly. I don't want to go to work and fight, he said; comedy does not come out of anguish. I don't like destructive comedy—violence and car chase scenes—like *The Blues Brothers*.

John talked about "Saturday Night Live" and said it had been a struggle with all the egos. All I want is to be heard, he said. He was having a very bad experience with John Avildsen on his current project.

Sandrich detected an extreme anger at authority, but John seemed attracted to the *Sweet Deception* character's lack of worldliness. At least they were talking the same language: a straight romantic comedy with an adventurous diamond caper thrown in.

Now, about drugs, Sandrich continued. John had a reputation, a bad one.

"I was on coke," John said. It had come close to destroying his life and his marriage. He said he had essentially given up cocaine, and he used it only when the pressure got bad.

Drugs are out, Sandrich said. I will not work with someone on coke: it wrecks their timing and alters perceptions.

John agreed. They shook hands and left.

Ovitz, Brillstein and John had a number of discussions about the kind of movie to do next. Perhaps it was time for John to return to what he did best, another *Animal House,* something suited to his unique brand of physical comedy. For Ovitz, that meant part Bluto, part slapstick—a harder-edged comedy. For Brillstein, it meant pie throwing. Too much energy and money were being wasted experimenting with John's talent. It was time for him to drop his pants again.

John asked to meet with Sandrich again, and Sandrich flew to New York and went to the Phantom office at 2 P.M. on Thursday, November 19. It looked like a clubhouse and had the feel of a college dormitory—chaotic but comfortable—with Blues Brothers and other memorabilia scattered around. Sandrich was on time, and John arrived twenty minutes late. They talked for a few minutes, and John announced that they were going to walk over to the *schvitz* and take a steam bath. On the street some kids stopped John to talk. A police car hit its siren and pulled over, and an officer asked John to sign his ticket citation book. John's naturalness impressed Sandrich.

After a steam bath and massage Sandrich asked, "Why do you want to do this movie? It is not a John Belushi movie."

"You've got to change and grow," John explained. They left the *schvitz,* and John said that he had to go home to have dinner with Judy and said goodbye.

Sandrich was a little surprised. He thought they would spend more time together and talk about *Sweet Deception*. But John had turned and was heading down Morton Street toward home.

Sandrich took a plane back to Los Angeles. On the professional level, he felt he had not fully connected with John, but they seemed to have the same goals. On the personal level, he felt better. John was magnetic and carried a stage presence wherever he went. Sandrich called Brillstein to sound him out, not only about the script, but about John. "I've heard all these stories about drugs," Sandrich said.

"They're exaggerated," Brillstein said. John, like a lot of people, used some drugs, but it was not a problem.

Sandrich told Ovitz that he felt positive about the matchup with Belushi. Now it was Ovitz's job to sell them and the script as a package to a studio. Columbia was not the place to go because of *Neighbors,* so Ovitz sent it to Universal, where it was read by Sean Daniels, vice president and keeper of the Belushi portfolio. Daniels thought it was the wrong part for John. Spencer Tracy hadn't worked, and it was not likely that Cary Grant or Jimmy Stewart would either. Still, he didn't want simply to say no, so Daniels called John and said, indirectly, that the project didn't seem quite right.

"You don't like it?" John asked.

Why not wait for a better script? he suggested. But Daniels knew that John wasn't good at waiting.

After the lukewarm reception at Universal, Ovitz sent the *Sweet Deception* package to Warner Brothers. Lucy Fisher, John's friend for six years and former best friend to the late Doug Kenney, was now a vice president at Warners and the senior production executive. She read the script carefully. It was clearly a vehicle for a sexy leading man.

Fisher's heart sank. John could be warm, sweet and playful, but he simply was not the traditional Hollywood leading man. He could be a star and leading man like Woody Allen, but not Cary Grant, and John had to learn to accept that. The whole deal smelled: somebody wanted John to work and was pushing him into this, Fisher concluded. Instead of providing a good, positive feeling, the likely failure of such a movie would make John feel rejected, not only as an actor, but as that sexy leading man he no doubt wanted to be.

Warners didn't want the movie, but Fisher decided to get involved anyway. She called John in New York, and he seemed glad to hear from her.

"Are you really serious about it?" she asked.

He was.

Fisher told John it probably wasn't right for him, and he shouldn't do it.

John argued back.

Fisher realized that he didn't want to hear what she was telling him. In his own mind, the boat had already sailed. She didn't back off but expanded on her reasons. The conversation ended with rather terse good-byes.

For November 25, the day before Thanksgiving, Lorne Michaels had put together some of the old "Saturday Night Live" cast for a live Steve Martin prime-time special. Aykroyd had a major part, and John had been brought in at the last minute for a 70-second cameo appearance. There was no money left in the budget to pay him, so instead John drew up a list of "presents" that Michaels would have to give him, making John an artist in residence at Broadway Video, the independent production company Michaels had started in New York after leaving "Saturday Night Live."

John requested:

(1) Access to tapes in library, use of editing, duping (such as all Saturday Night Live shows with me, etc.) and cost of tape;
(2) General use of everything I can have fun with and people to give assistance when I need it;
(3) Use of location crews or sound stages once a month;
(4) Unlimited access to refrigerator;
(5) Every time I come by the office, I would like people to be nice to me and make me feel at home;
(6) All the above for free for one year. If you agree to this, sign Lorne Michaels' name.

_____

Agreed to and accepted by
Lorne Michaels

Michaels was sure. All John wanted was love and acceptance.

On the show Aykroyd and Martin were to play two Czechoslovakian brothers, immigrants who try hard to adapt to America.

Dressed in flowered shirts unbuttoned to the chest and tight polyester pants, they are talking nonsensically when suddenly John walks on stage to screams of hysteria. He is dressed in a drab brown skirt and a black wig, and his light-colored blouse swishes about with giant water-balloon breasts that sway around his belly. He grabs Aykroyd and Martin in affectionate half nelsons, the epitome of a big, burly sister who has spent her life milking cows on a Czech farm.

"I had to leave Czechoslovakie," he says, almost yelling above the laughter of the audience. "The government wouldn't let me swiiiiiing!"

Barbara Howar, journalist and author of the best-selling *Laughing All the Way,* a personal memoir of her life as a Washington hostess, celebrity and onetime intimate of Lyndon Johnson, arrived fashionably late to the Sunday night, November 29, party being given by Michael O'Donoghue and Carol Caldwell. The party theme was an Hawaiian Luau, complete with roast pig. Howar was just putting in an appearance and quickly realized she wouldn't be staying long. At forty-eight she felt old and out of place. Evidence of the generation gap was all about: marijuana cigarettes were being passed around; the people lined up at the bathroom, she surmised, were waiting to get inside to snort cocaine; the place was full of what she called "meat hook girls," young, pretty women in their twenties who would take all the interesting men. Howar had recently ended a long, stormy affair with a married man and was glad simply to be out socializing.

She walked into the art deco bedroom. John was on the oversize bed, watching television and eating a chunk of roast pig. They were introduced, and Howar continued her rounds, concluded there was nothing there for her and headed toward the door.

"Do you have to go?" a voice said.

She turned and there was John. She looked at him and smiled, getting off one of her favorite lines: "I'm too old, too tired and too rich for this." Howar knew how to flirt with a man, keeping it just ambiguous enough so that no one's feelings would be hurt if one or the other said no.

She went to get her coat and scarf. When she walked outside, John was waiting on the steps. He said he was freezing, and Howar wrapped her scarf around him. "I'll get you a cab," he said, stepping out into the street.

John hailed a taxi, opened the door for Howar and followed her inside, leaving Judy at the party. He told the driver to take them to the Odeon.

Howar knew how to sound as though she were on the Johnny Carson show—lots of gossip, inside stories. John had several drinks, and they made light talk.

Howar found John sort of a mess—young and difficult. He lived up to his reckless image. She looked at him and shook her head. "You need a keeper. You ought to get married."

"I am married," John said.

Time to go, Howar thought. She had just been portrayed as a home breaker and had vowed never again—and certainly not with someone as prominent and unlikely as John. It would be in the gossip columns in one day. Howar got up to leave and they walked outside. John hailed a cab, said goodbye and hopped in beside her again. No, Howar said. John resisted. No, no, she said, shooing him out. He acquiesced, and Howar went home alone.

The next day John called Carol Caldwell. "You had a hard night," he said, and probably need to get out. He'd be right by. He arrived in a limousine and took Caldwell to "103," a new-wave-style restaurant on Second Avenue.

John got right to the point. What was Howar like? What was she doing now? Tell me about her book. Tell me about southern women. Caldwell gave Howar's background. John continued the interrogation. What else has she written? Who are her friends? Are southern women manipulative? John was smitten and consumed by a new interest in the southern mystique. It would have been charming, Caldwell thought, if John weren't married.

Later, Caldwell got a call from Howar, who asked more indirectly but no less pointedly about John.

That afternoon, Howar heard a knock at her door. She wasn't expecting anyone, and the doorman, usually scrupulous about announcing guests, had not called up. It was John, who apparently had dazzled or bullied his way through. He had come to return her scarf.

She invited him in briefly. He was going to leave some of his Merit cigarettes, he said, so that on his next visit—which he promised would be soon—he would have them.

Howar had the feeling she was being courted—not precisely as a lover or a friend or a mother, perhaps a little of each. Quite strange. They made an unspoken pact not to meet in public. Neither of them needed that, and her Fifty-fifth Street apartment seemed to be the chosen rendez-vous.

Tom and Lynn Scott were in New York that week. Lynn called the Phantom offices to say hello, and John came on the phone and brought up *Neighbors* and the confusion over the music. Lynn wanted to avoid the subject.

"It's Tom's fault," John said. "I told him to ignore Avildsen and do the right score."

"You don't do that as a composer," Lynn said, siding with her husband, who was still hurt and humiliated by the whole incident. "You must listen to the director."

"Well, he should have listened to what I said to do—ignore Avildsen," John argued. "Tom has to learn about dealing with people and scoring a film. He must learn that you don't have to listen to the director." He made a knowing sound of disgust and added, "Well, that's right. You shouldn't have anything to do with this anyway."

Lynn was furious and told her husband about the conversation. Tom had never mailed the scathing letter he had written John, but he'd read it over many times. It was time to let John have it between the eyes.

"John," Scott said when he reached John on the phone, "your behavior really screwed me up. You don't think—that's the problem. You just do stuff and let the chips fall as they may. You're careless, and you don't examine the consequences of your actions."

John started to protest, but Scott interrupted him. "A blanket apology won't do, because I want you to understand what you did. I hate to say it—I don't like to flaunt my credits—but I know more about the music industry than you do. There's been too much disrespect."

"Well," John said, "the reason I got you this gig—"

"You are not the sole reason I was picked," Scott interrupted again. "I have credits. . . ."

"You should have written the score we talked about," John argued.

"John, I did," Scott said. "One final thing. You use people in a professional capacity and then revert to your friendship." If a professional disagreement arose, Scott said, John played the friendship card to get his way. In a personal disagreement, he played the professional card.

"That's not true," John said. He was upset.

"It is."

John banged the phone down.

Aykroyd had a name for John's behavior though he probably was the most tolerant of it—"a state of trance and venom," he called it. Scott felt relieved that he'd called John on it.

Back in California, Avildsen was finally finishing the editing. There were still some disputes, but Avildsen had given way. On the ending, they adopted John's idea to have a large collapsing building on the television before he throws the set and starts the fire in the house.

In the last line of the movie, John joked that his wife, Enid, "never did like to come home to a dark house." And he and Aykroyd shared a big laugh as they went off with Cathy Moriarty, the house burning in the background. It was one of the few times John had laughed during the entire film.

Price was satisfied, or at least as satisfied as he could be, given the raw product they had been given by Avildsen. It was such a damn shame. If Avildsen had only been able to capture some of the spontaneity in John and Aykroyd. It was obviously there, but virtually none of it came through in the movie.

In early December, John and Dan started giving press interviews for *Neighbors* and learned that the book quotes were being used as a prologue to prepare the audience. Aykroyd was furious and went to his office and typed a letter to Price, Zanuck, Brown and Avildsen.

> Gentlemen:
> It is difficult for me to express the true degree of disappointment and anger which surged through me. . . . I was disheartened . . . because I feel the use of these Quotes to be an example of Hollywood-executive paranoia in the worst order . . . a transparent marketing ploy which will be sure to damage this product. . . .
>
> D. Aykroyd

Louis Malle and John Guare went to a private screening of *Neighbors* on Tuesday, December 8. Aykroyd had previously mentioned how proud he was of the rewriting he had done; they might get a sense of how good he was at fixing a script. They also wanted to see if any of the comic characteristics and tensions they planned for *Moon Over Miami* had been used up by Avildsen. What happened to *Neighbors* would set the initial tone and the spirit in which they would undertake their project with Belushi and Aykroyd. For movie stars the last movie was like the last war for the generals: To some extent John and Aykroyd would be trying either to answer the criticisms or recapture the success of *Neighbors*.

After the screening, Malle and Guare were a little stupefied. They had not been prepared for the crumminess of the movie. Guare found it garish, a comedy that just was not funny. The two neighbors were locked in mortal combat—the reason was not always clear—and then they go off together. John's wife was made the villain, again for obscure reasons. John looked discomfited throughout. Guare felt a little frightened at first, because the movie showed dismal judgment about comedy. That could have been the director, but Belushi and Aykroyd had to shoulder some of the blame.

Malle and Guare had scheduled dinner with John and Dan at Mary Lou's restaurant the next night and waited nearly an hour for them. Was there a mistake about the date or the restaurant? Were Belushi and Aykroyd out stoned someplace? Should they leave?

John and Dan finally arrived, apologizing for being late. They had gone to see Malle's film, *My Dinner with André*.

Guare was amused. Everyone was looking at everyone else's work, sizing each other up.

Both John and Aykroyd said they were worried about the reception *Neighbors* was going to get from the critics. They had just done lots of interviews that had been very hostile. The press didn't understand the movie, but John and Dan still had high hopes for the box office.

When they turned to the script of *Moon Over Miami,* Aykroyd was relaxed and plausible. He had questions, ideas, and showed a keen interest.

Guare explained that the movie had to show how the model FBI agent, a man who wouldn't cheat a nickel on his income taxes or park illegally, would use any means to trap congressmen. The con man and the FBI agent don't get along—not because they are so different, but because they are so much the same.

"We'll commit now, right now," John said. He had not been talking much. "Right, Danny? We've asked around about you"—indicating Malle—"and you're wonderful. Everyone says that."

John was putting on a little ironic performance, playing the Hollywood mafioso, the man wired into the show-biz grapevine.

"And you," John added, motioning at Guare, "we haven't heard too many bad things about you."

They had brandy after dinner and shared stories until everyone wanted to leave but John.

"Come on, have another brandy," he said, trying to keep the conversation and the evening alive. The others had had enough already and, over John's vehement protests, got up to go. Malle and Guare promised to have another drink with him sometime soon.

Two days later, Friday, about 2 P.M., John showed up at Malle and Guare's office on Fifty-seventh Street. "Come on, you guys," he said, "let's have that after-dinner drink now." He was wearing the same clothes he'd worn on Wednesday. They were dirty and wrinkled and molded to his body. He seemed to have little control over his words and actions, and he smelled. He said he'd been to the Turkish baths and felt great.

Without warning, he took hold of a woman in the outer office and began to teach her slam dancing. Guare could see that John was very high on drugs. John went into their office, picked up the phone, dialed a number and turned on the speaker phone so they could all hear the conversation. Neither Malle nor Guare had any idea whom he was calling. When the person came on, John said, "Hey, have you seen *Atlantic City,* Louis Malle's latest film? What did you think of it? Wasn't very good, was it?"

This was over the line. Guare couldn't tolerate such a thoughtlessly cruel thing and reached over and switched off the speaker before the person could answer.

Malle and Guare sat in silence. On one narrow level, Guare could see that this was John's character for *Moon Over Miami.* But John wasn't just playing it. How are we going to work with this guy? Guare wondered. He and Malle exchanged worried looks. Should they call someone for help? Or to take him away? Who was taking care of him? Who was responsible? It wasn't as if John had fallen down and hit his head; in such a case they could call an ambulance to get him out of there. That would have been easier.

John kept thrashing about, returning to the theme of the too-long-postponed after-dinner drink. He was sweating as if there were a flame under him.

Word was being spread around the fifth floor that John was there, and people from some other offices popped by to see him or hang around outside.

"Where's the fucking script?" John asked. "I want to read it." He stood and pounded the table. "Where is it? Let me see it. Let's get going on this thing. Where is it? Where's the fucking thing?" He seemed convinced that they were intentionally keeping it from him. They tried to redirect his attention.

The force of John's presence and the force of the performance were extraordinary, Guare felt. It was like Mardi Gras and all of a sudden a John Belushi float had entered the room. All by himself he created a feeling that everything was askew. The progression over the six months that Guare had known John was a study in contrasts—from the debonair, Noel Coward character at the Odeon, to this total wreck, a Lenny Bruce extravaganza.

After about an hour and a half, when it was clear John was going to get neither the after-dinner drink nor the script, he finally left. He just sort of blew out the way he had blown in.

Both Malle and Guare felt immense alarm, and they asked the obvious questions out loud.

"We'll rely on Danny," Malle said.

That night John attended a party given by Boaty Boatwright, the head of East Coast production for MGM. He spotted Carrie Fisher and grabbed her. Fisher felt how small she actually was as John carried her effortlessly into the bathroom and locked the door.

"Where are the drugs?" John asked. He was serious.

"There is eggnog," Fisher said, smirking and laughing. She needed someone like John to liven things up. They were soulmates, she still felt.

Both agreed that the party was boring, boring—a party for adults. But they were stuck. "The eggnog was lovely," Fisher joked. She could see that John wanted to escape. "What is this fuck party?" he asked. Watching him was like watching spinning plates on the ends of long sticks: you see them, but it's hard to believe. They stayed locked in the bathroom for close to half an hour. John wanted to do a revival of *Guys and Dolls* with her. He finally opened the door and left to search for drugs.

John found Judy and said it was time to leave. They walked out to the hall and waited for the elevator. Suddenly, for no apparent reason, John bolted for the steps and raced downstairs, leaving Judy to find her own way home.

John began making periodic visits to Barbara Howar's. Her apartment was a hideout whenever and for as long as he wanted. He generally brought a prop of some kind. Once it was a bunch of little battle ribbons which he pinned on her and said, "You're a good soldier." Or a funny costume. Or fresh turkey sandwiches—not turkey roll, which he detested. John's eye frequently traveled down the many books in Howar's large library, reading off titles and authors. Do you know him? Ever met her? What's that about? They talked about the happiest times in their lives. His, he said, were the road trips with Aykroyd—just the two of them. He was proud that Louis Malle wanted to do a movie with him and was looking forward to it.

John made it clear he liked Howar, and she, in turn, liked the fact that he liked her. He kissed her on the mouth and neck but never went any further.

They talked about Hollywood, the studios, the agents. "Do you trust those guys?" she asked.

"Do I have a choice?"

Several times they talked very seriously. What does it all mean? Where does it all go? John was almost boyish, as if he half-expected Howar to have real answers.

"Have you ever tied off?" John once asked, inquiring if Howar had ever shot up drugs.

"No," she said.

"It's like kissing God."

After filming *Neighbors,* Tim Kazurinsky returned to work at "Saturday Night Live." Even though they were about the same age, Kazurinsky considered John a big brother.

"You've got to stop looking like a hayseed," John said one day. He grabbed Kazurinsky, took him to a clothes store and selected a brown leather jacket and a handful of thin neckties, saying this was the way to dress in New York.

Kazurinsky was not happy with the way things were going at "Saturday Night Live"; the calibre of the show wasn't high enough. He was doing a lot of writing, and he was getting material on the air every week, but his favorite pieces were continually being rejected. "Fight, scream, refuse to do things," John advised Kazurinsky. "Demand things, be an asshole." Kazurinsky was fighting, but it wasn't working for him. By December he'd decided to quit the show. He called John to tell him of the decision.

"Look," John said, "the show's not everything you want it to be, so you're going to piss it off. You've had other shit jobs, but this one happens to pay more."

Money wasn't the point, Kazurinsky argued.

"You can still occasionally communicate an idea to 25 million people," John said, "and that's an opportunity you shouldn't pass up. You have something to say. Where else are you going to get access to network TV?"

Kazurinsky equivocated, but John drove home his point. "So what if the show is a bowl of shit. Stop feeling responsible for the whole thing. If you hold yourself responsible for the failure of the show, then some part of you must want to be responsible for the success of the show. If it's bad, it's not your fault, and if it's good, it's not all your credit. If it's bad, then make it better. But if you leave, what does that accomplish?"

Kazurinsky decided to stick it out.

At just thirty-nine years of age, Michael D. Eisner was president and creative head of Paramount, responsible for the studio's feature films and TV productions. Eisner was a tall, thick-faced man, and he could be brutally candid and persuasive. And he didn't like package deals. He wanted Paramount to develop its own ideas and translate them to scripts or series, as Eisner himself had done when he was a vice president at ABC, overseeing the development of "Happy Days," "Charlie's Angels" and the TV spectacular of *Roots*. Whoever owned the material had the leverage.

Though Ovitz was a close friend, and Ovitz's brother Mark worked for Eisner at Paramount, Eisner sneered at Ovitz's package deals. They were too expensive and permitted the agent to do the studio's job of selecting. Eisner had turned down so many that he was surprised when Ovitz approached him with *Sweet Deception*.

It doesn't sound right, Eisner said. The script, Belushi and Sandrich are an odd mixture.

You've got to hear Belushi discuss it, Ovitz said. He wants to go back to the character from *Animal House*.

Eisner didn't have many promising movies scheduled for the next crucial Christmas season, and he was a big Belushi fan. The least he could do was listen.

Ovitz said he would send the script over and bring John by for a meeting when he was in L.A. later in the month.

Ovitz told Brillstein that they could get big money from Paramount. Eisner was an unabashed fan of John's, and he was seeing big dollars for the next Christmas. John went through the script and told Brillstein he'd do it if either Don Novello (Father Guido Sarducci) or former "Saturday Night Live" writer Alan Zweibel—both clients of Brillstein's—could be assigned to rewrite the script. Zweibel was busy, but Novello was interested and was sent the script.

John and Judy had dinner with Novello and his wife, Kathy, at Raoul's restaurant, a French bistro in SoHo. Novello said the script was a can of worms, and he couldn't believe anyone would want to make a movie out of it. It wasn't funny, and much of it didn't make sense; for example, a person is found dead in one scene, then reappears later in the script. It seemed more like a puzzle. It needed to be completely rewritten.

John didn't care. It would be *their* movie; they would take control, rewrite the script and oversee production, cast and every detail themselves.

John called Bill Wallace and said, "I need you." He was starting another movie, and Bill should come right away. Wallace quit his job teaching physical education at Memphis State and flew to New York.

The December 12 preview tests showed that *Neighbors* still did better with the prologue of book reviews than without them. Though an excellent rating was given by only 4 percent of the audience, it was the highest so far. Price decided to keep the prologue in no matter how angry Aykroyd was.

The first article on the movie was good, a Sunday, December 13, *New York Times* feature article about Cathy Moriarty. It featured a picture of her stretched out suggestively and was headlined: THE BLONDE FROM THE BRONX RETURNS.

Newsweek had the first real review the next day. David Ansen said:

Thomas Berger's paranoid comic novel could have been made a fascinating movie in the hands, say, of Roman Polanski, who knows how to make a comedy of menace. John G. Avildsen (*Rocky*) doesn't have a clue: you can't twist reality if you can't establish a reality to twist. Belushi and Aykroyd obviously got cast because they're "bankable," but no one seems to have asked if they were appropriate. The parts demand subtle comic acting—they do TV turns. Just how much blame falls on Larry Gelbart's disjointed script is hard to say (Avildsen could make any writer look bad), but without question composer Bill Conti has come up with the year's most offensive score—a cattle prod of cartoonish cuteness that only underlines the movie's desperate uncertainty of tone. The ads for *Neighbors* call it "a comic nightmare"; it's more like a sour case of creative indigestion.

Larry Gelbart filed a complaint with the Writers Guild charging that Belushi, Aykroyd and Avildsen had engaged in "scab" writing on the script while the guild had been out on strike, but he got nowhere with it.

John told Judy that he wanted to see Dr. Rosenbluth. An appointment was made for Thursday, December 17, and John was given a complete physical, blood test and electrocardiograph. Rosenbluth's thirteen-year-old daughter was in the office, and John read to her and gave her some autographs.

John told Rosenbluth that he had been off drugs for about a year, though there had been some exceptions: one period of three weeks, another of two weeks, one of three days in a row, and several others. He didn't like going home when he was high, he said, so he would wait until he was down. That often kept him out all night. At least, John said, I'm not shooting it up.

Ever since Rosenbluth had first seen John five years earlier, a doctor-patient relationship had been impossible. He wanted to *order* John to quit but thought that if he pushed too hard, too fast, John would walk. The doctor didn't want to frighten him away. It was best that John had a doctor he knew and trusted, who knew the details of his dangerous habits and could counsel reform patiently.

Neighbors opened at 1,384 theaters around the country the next day. Research tests in public theaters showed the movie getting ratings of 9 percent excellent and 43 percent poor. It was sure to die fast, Columbia executives realized, but during the first three days it took in $6,481,368, more than any other movie that weekend. It did well the next week, too, but then ticket sales fell off sharply.* The reviews were mixed, but the hit-and-run strategy had worked, and the projections guaranteed that Columbia would make a profit of several million dollars.

Price told Brillstein that, given the problems, everything had turned out sensationally. "We did the best we could," Price said.

* By the third week, January 1–7, the box office had slipped to $4.9 million; the fourth week, $2.3 million; the fifth week, $1.6 million; and by the sixth week, to only $900,000.

18

The day after *Neighbors* was re-
leased, John and Wallace took the 11:45 A.M. TWA flight to Los Angeles.
The meeting with Eisner on *Sweet Deception* was set for 2:30 P.M.,
December 21. But first, Brillstein, John and Sandrich went up to Ovitz's
office to discuss strategy. Ovitz made it clear that they had one purpose:
They had to sell it to Eisner, and Eisner wanted slapstick comedy.

With that settled, they drove over to Paramount. Also present at the
meeting were Stanley Chase, owner of the *Sweet Deception* script and
the designated producer, and Jeff Katzenberg, the thirty-year-old senior
production vice president at Paramount and Eisner's right-hand man.

The seven men greeted each other. Brillstein told a joke and shared
some gossip. He wanted John to have a moment to get a sense of the
room.

John likes the script, Brillstein said, but it needs work. Yet we've
made a big decision. *Continental Divide* proved John's an actor, and
Neighbors proved it again.

Eisner broke in to say that he had just seen *Neighbors* and he loved
it, a great movie. He could understand if it didn't turn out to be a big
commercial success, but it was interestingly dark.

Then John began talking. "I don't want to be anything other than
John Belushi," he said. "That made me all my money."

Everyone laughed.

The script isn't funny enough, John said, and we have ideas to make
it funny. The film will open with me being brought back to my father's
winery in a police car after being found passed out in a Shell station
men's room. The character can't touch wine without getting crazy drunk.
Remaining in his chair, John did the moves of the drunken son.

Everyone was laughing. Ovitz saw that once John got going, it
seemed to come with no effort.

John explained that he wanted to expand the scene of the wine-testing competition at the World Trade Center. Everyone would be there —Orson Welles with his wine, and the Blue Nun. It would degenerate into a kind of wine fight, and he would swing down like Tarzan after the judging.

Eisner's eyes widened. If John could keep them laughing from his chair, imagine what he could do with an improved script and the World Trade Center.

John then said he knew just the person to rewrite—Don Novello. Sandrich had never heard of Novello, but everyone else said that his work was brilliant.

John acted out a few more moves. The character would be a grown-up version of Bluto, he said, but not as gross.

Sandrich was getting worried. He was seeing and hearing more and more Bluto. What had happened to the idea of a romantic comedy?

Eisner was overjoyed. John saw the script's flaws and was going to make it funny. The movie must appeal directly to kids, Eisner said, and it must contain slapstick humor.

John was saying that he wanted to go back to the character he understood, a character that was even a little shy. But his movements were bold, Bluto moves.

Sandrich said that the style would be important. They could make a picture that would please on lots of levels, that both kids and adults would want to see. The humor would be slapstick, but it would grow from the character.

Eisner thought they had a good match: Belushi wanted to make the audience roar, and Sandrich could keep it on a high level. He liked just watching John. It was one of the best meetings he'd ever had on a new project.

When it was over, Katzenberg thought they had a winner. John was articulate about his role; he realized he was best at playing himself—and that was pure Bluto. He wanted to go back to his roots. It was unusual for someone in the film business to recognize his strength, Katzenberg thought.

Both Ovitz and Brillstein assured John that the meeting had gone exceptionally well. That night Brillstein took John and Novello to dinner at Morton's, a show-business restaurant on Melrose Avenue in Hollywood. Everything about the project looks perfect, Brillstein said. Tackle the script and make the movie.

"We've got to stay on top of this," John said, "and do it *our* way."

He kept returning to that theme. As few outsiders as possible should be involved in the movie—only "our people," he said, which meant young, "Saturday Night Live" people.

At about 11 P.M., John and Novello went on to a Christmas party being given by one of John's old Wheaton friends, Dick Blasucci, who had been in the Ravins, John's high school band, and was now a TV writer. Tony Pavilonis, the guitar player for the Ravins, also came along. He, Blasucci and John hadn't played together since 1967 at the Turnabout Dance in the Wheaton Central High School cafeteria, and Pavilonis hadn't seen John in fourteen years. The three played some of the old music—the Hollies' "Bus Stop" and the Kingsmen's "Louie, Louie." John was excited and happy, strumming hard on a Fender Telecaster guitar; his voice filled the room, as if he were trying to make up for its poor quality by singing louder.

John said he was coming back to L.A. in January to rewrite *Sweet Deception*. The draft they had was just plain shit. The last thing the studios worried about was content. The movie business, John said, was all about making deals; the rest was easy.

He suggested they get together the next night to play some more music at "Open Mike" night at the Central club on Sunset. On Tuesdays, the club let anyone come in and play for ten or fifteen minutes.

"I don't have any equipment," Blasucci said.

"Don't worry. I'll take care of everything," John told him.

The next day, Tuesday, December 22, Novello and Sandrich went to John's Beverly Hills Hotel bungalow to outline the rewrite plan. Sandrich gave his notes to Novello. Sandrich liked their proposed beginning —John being hauled in by the police. The movie, Sandrich said, had to be revised more to focus on the relationship between John and the woman; and the end needed work.

John hadn't said much until the mention of the woman. "I can't end up with this beautiful woman," he said emphatically. "I would have nothing in common with her. I don't want to do a sappy love story."

Okay, Sandrich replied, but you have to have touched each other, changed each other in a big way. It's true you don't have to end up together, but it *is* a story about an evolving relationship. He didn't get much of a response and soon left.

Novello was concerned. This guy is in love with the script, he said. He's talking about polishing the existing pages when it needs a complete rewrite. Is this the right director? There's some kind of generation or culture gap here.

"Don't worry," John said. "Man, those guys are nothing. It's my movie, and we'll do what we want." He started calling Sandrich "Malibu" because he lived out by the beach.

John was up at Brillstein's office later when Jimmy called. He was in Seattle starring in the New York Shakespeare Festival's *The Pirates of Penzance*. Jimmy said he had received a bad review in San Francisco from the second-string opera critic for one of the papers. The critic really blasted him, saying his "vocal credentials lie somewhere between a bray and a gurgle."

"He's a faggot," John said. "Faggots don't like Belushis."

Jimmy said he was thinking of buying a house in Chicago.

"Real estate is a good thing, I guess," John said. Lipsky says so. In fact, he and Judy were thinking of buying a house on West Tenth Street in the Village.

Jimmy sensed a quick close coming.

"Stay off the white stuff," John said. "I got to go, bye."

John went over to Blasucci's to tell him to be at the Studio Instrument Rentals (SIR) studio on Sunset at 8:30 P.M. John had made the arrangements.

When Blasucci and Tony Pavilonis arrived, some punk musicians were rehearsing, belching into the microphones, screaming and throwing bottles around. About 10:30 P.M. John came in with Derf, and the four of them practiced until midnight, when they went to the Central. As they discussed movies and money, John said with conviction, "What I really like doing is playing the drums."

The Central was a madhouse, with a new group getting up to play every ten minutes. The place was packed, loud and very dark. They took to the stage, the Wheaton Ravins on Sunset Strip.

They played mostly the old music—"Gimme Some Lovin'," "Johnny B. Goode," "Route 66," "Louie, Louie," "I Feel Good." John seemed to find stability in the old gang, something basic, more than mere nostalgia.

John was sweating and happy. He promised they would do it again, for sure, and soon. Blasucci went home and took his dog for a walk about 2 A.M.

John came by and wanted to have a drink. Blasucci asked about Judy.

She's fine, John said. She's the most important person in my life. The old times, the mention of Judy, seemed to rekindle something. You know, he said, you were so lucky. Your father was always home. You had a happy family.

Blasucci didn't know what to say. He'd been to John's house many times in their high school years, but he'd only seen John's father once or twice. Still, he'd never known things had been that bad. Something obviously hurt a great deal. Blasucci had never before talked with John about these things and felt uncomfortable. There was nothing he could say.

The next morning, John was supposed to have breakfast at eight-thirty with Novello, Brillstein and Katzenberg. He didn't show up.

Katzenberg didn't like to give maybes or nonanswers. Eisner's instructions were to be quick and specific. John was to be guaranteed $1,850,000 for *Sweet Deception*—$185,000 a week for ten weeks, the estimated period for shooting. In addition, it was a "pay or play" deal. If Paramount decided not to make the movie, they would be obligated to pay John the $1,850,000 anyway. If the movie was a hit and made a profit (earning 2½ times the actual cost, the industry's basic definition of break-even), John would get a percentage of the gross profit ranging from 7.5 to 12.5 percent. His per diem payment for living expenses would total $2,500 a week while working on the rewrite and filming and during postproduction work.

The start date for shooting was set for April 19, 1982, about the last day they could begin and still get the movie out for Christmas.

That morning, December 23, John was scheduled to fly to Miami to meet Judy for a Christmas vacation. They were going to spend five days with Mike and Carol Klenfner in a rented house. Bill Wallace received a call to meet him at the airport. John arrived just in time to make the flight, chauffeured by a beautiful woman with long blond hair. He introduced Wallace to Debra Jo Fondren, *Playboy* magazine's 1978 Playmate of the Year, said goodbye to her and ran for the plane.

John and Judy, who was coming from New York, arrived in Miami at about the same time. The Klenfners met them, and they all drove to the rented house off Collins Avenue. Later, Joe's Stone Crab, one of Miami's largest and most famous restaurants, was abuzz with his presence, and the other diners circled by to get autographs.

By the next day, John still had not been able to push the relax button. Klenfner decided he had to schedule a lot of activities to keep John out of the Miami cocaine scene, which was big and dangerous.

Klenfner knew that John would try almost anything. One time years earlier in California, Klenfner, John and some others including Aykroyd had stayed up most of the night "hot knifing" opium. They had heated a knife on the stove, placed a piece of opium on it and snorted up the fumes through a straw.

To help keep John's mind occupied in Miami, Klenfner took him shopping at Saks Fifth Avenue, and John charged about $1,000 in gifts, including a necklace for Judy. Before they left, sales girls from every floor had abandoned their posts to come and gawk.

Next, they stopped at a video parlor and got a handful of quarters. We have only twenty minutes, John said, and in less than twenty minutes people had flocked around him, asking questions, seeking autographs or just watching.

John had brought a bunch of Quaaludes. Judy and Klenfner had each confiscated several the first day and had hidden them, leaving him only a few. That night, Christmas Eve, John popped them. Later he wanted more, and somehow he got the mistaken impression that Carol Klenfner had taken them. He said he was going to confront her.

Don't! Judy shouted, throwing a handful at him. "Fuck you!" she added, and stormed off.

John picked up the Quaaludes and bit into one, apparently to be funny or speed up the effect. Klenfner stayed up with him until he fell asleep.

The next day, Christmas, they rented a fishing boat and caught a five-foot shark, but back at the house John was bored, running through the newspapers and magazines, watching television. He called Brillstein and learned that Brillstein's eighty-four-year-old father was in Miami.

"Where, for Christ sake?" John said. "I'm going to see him."

John went over to the Diplomat Hotel, stayed several hours and cleaned out the elder Brillstein's refrigerator.

On December 28, John and Judy took a plane back to New York. They spent New Year's Eve, their fifth wedding anniversary, party hopping. Sean Daniels was in town and joined John, Judy, Mitch Glazer and his fiancée, Wendy, to see Bow, Wow, Wow, a new-wave group. John ordered champagne and toasted Mitch and Wendy's imminent wedding. He promised to be back for it in two weeks. The crowd gathering in Times Square spotted John as he left the club. Soon he was surrounded by a thick and almost threatening crowd. Daniels was amazed. This was not the John of "Saturday Night Live" or even Bluto fame, but someone else. He was paralyzed in the midst of these people, and the police had to rescue him.

Judy felt the whole evening strange. John ran off at one point—and she was sure he would be gone for the rest of the night—but he came back in five minutes. The night ended at 8 A.M. on New Year's Day.

Later that week John told Judy that he wanted to rent a house about an hour outside of New York City where he and Novello could rewrite the screenplay. She could live there too, and they could have a real winter with Snowmobiles and outdoor fun. But Novello wanted to stay near his home in San Francisco, and he talked John into that. When a violent rainstorm hit San Francisco in early January, killing 24 people and causing enormous mudslides, they compromised on Los Angeles. Don is the writer, John said to Judy; he had to go where Don would be comfortable.

He was scheduled to go to California January 5, 1982. It would take only a week or two to get *Sweet Deception* in shape, he told Judy. Her birthday was January 7, and she asked, "Can't you wait two days?" He said yes, but he seemed anxious.

On Friday morning, January 8, John and Bill Wallace took two first-class seats on United flight Number 5 to Los Angeles. They were picked up about 2:30 P.M. by limousine and taken to the Chateau Marmont, a hotel which looks like a French Norman castle, perched high above Sunset Boulevard in the center of Hollywood. John checked into room 69, rented a maroon Mercedes-Benz 380 SL sports car for $85 a day and drove to On the Rox, where he bought drinks for people who stopped by —six Alabama Slammers, eight shots of Johnnie Walker black. He ran up a $152 bill and added a $200 tip.

Novello arrived from San Francisco and also took a room at the Chateau. The next day he and John spent some time talking about the script. John was full of ideas that he tossed off staccato. Novello's job was to sort through them, select the best, add his own and put it all on paper. He enjoyed their conversations, but he was never sure what he had at the end. Times with John contained more pleasure than productivity; John was such a strange creature, so full of love and rage.

Monday morning, January 11, Sandrich stopped by John's room. John and Novello explained what they wanted to do with the woman. She was sophisticated, sensual and hard, but they wanted even more of the stonelike, unreachable side: she was the elusive, truly unfuckable woman. John would make love with her, but he would not really get through. They outlined a scene in which she explains her philosophy: She had fucked John because, like a mountain, he was there.

"This is a love story," Sandrich said, gasping. "The audience has got to like both characters."

Sure, John said, she'd be likable but tough. But he wasn't going to remake *Continental Divide*.

Sandrich said they seemed to be taking too much of the adventure and intrigue out.

They said they understood, but as Sandrich listened to their ideas, he saw that they were changing the script drastically. He wondered whether Novello knew how to rewrite a screenplay. Don had written short sketches built around one point and some funny lines for "Saturday Night Live," but this movie couldn't be a series of wild skits stitched together. That wouldn't carry any sense of narrative. John and Novello had promised him a finished script in about three weeks, February 1, and Sandrich knew one thing: It was what was on paper that counted, not theories or ideas tossed off in conversations. He should see some pages soon.

Barbara Howar was in Los Angeles that week, and John called her to say he had a great car and he wanted to take her out on the town to all the punk clubs.

"Yeah," Howar replied, "and I'll dye my hair purple." She explained that her trip was serious business: she was trying to arrange some TV appearances and finish the novel she was writing. Also, there was a new man, and that meant her nights were booked. She told John the best he'd get out of her was lunch.

John took her to a pizza dive on Melrose. He was full of talk about the script, one moment very up on the possibilities and the next down. Howar had a feeling that he thought that this time he had to deliver. He knew the chips were down. His remedy was direct involvement, his hand in the script and every other part of the movie. If it bombed, he said, he probably would be back in television, and he dreaded that.

Howar thought that John was looking for a new way through the thicket, unsure that the old John was going to get him through. She offered encouragement. He was, after all, the best.

19

Later that week on the Paramount lot, John visited the set of "Mork and Mindy," ABC's runaway hit sitcom that starred Robin Williams as Mork, the visitor from another planet. Williams, twenty-nine, known for his razzle-dazzle improvisations, imitations and quick, often-unintelligible verbal stunts, was delighted to see John.

Williams had met John in New York three years earlier, and John had taken him on a nighttime tour of music clubs. "Watch this, look at this, check that out!" John had exhorted. Williams was awed by his drive. On another occasion, Williams had sung backup to John's Joe Cocker at Catch a Rising Star, a New York night club.

That day on the "Mork and Mindy" set, Jonathan Winters, the moon-faced master of impersonation and characterization, was performing a routine about a Marine who had fought on Okinawa during World War II and now realizes that the people who are tending his garden had shot at him there. Both John and Williams were transfixed as they watched Winters for an hour. People came by, and made noise, and interrupted. "Shhhhh!" John said. "Shut up!"

Williams felt close to John. They both saw Winters as their mentor in kamikaze humor. They were young comics who'd had meteoric rises, and they always verged on burnout. Several months before, Williams had bought a ranch in Napa Valley near San Francisco, which he called a human game preserve. He was trying to slow down, though he still loved the Hollywood nightlife and the fast lane.

In Hollywood, Williams was anxious. The "Mork and Mindy" show had recently taken a dive in the ratings, and he wasn't sure what to do next. The movie *Popeye,* in which Williams had starred as the sailor man, had been a critical and box-office disaster. He had just finished filming

The World According to Garp, based on John Irving's best-selling novel, and was uncertain about its reception when it would open in five months.

As the "Mork and Mindy" ratings plunged, Williams was seized by self-doubt. Am I still funny? Will the show survive? Will I ever come back? Was I a one-timer? The common sentiment was: If you're not seen, if you're not doing something, you're slipping off track. Old Mr. Nielsen was lowering the boom. The situation made him try to pump it up, pump himself up. And the atmosphere around town invited more anxiety. Giant 50-foot record and movie promotions lined Sunset as if to say, "Hello! Behold!" That'd be real nice if I were there, wouldn't it? Williams thought. I'd like to do that. I'd like a picture of me like that . . . they're 50 feet tall and I'm only five foot eight. I'm nothing.

Then he was up there in the *Popeye* promotion with a 40-foot can of spinach alongside him. You're hot, wow! Once there, the pressure was greater for a repeat. You could start living on those billboards, living off the Mr. Nielsens, the parties, openings, lunches, dinners, even the break-fasts. To assert his identity, when he was not on the posters or tops in the Nielsens, Williams went out—everywhere. Finally, a local magazine, listing what was "In" and "Out," said it was Out to go to a party also attended by Robin Williams.

Williams could sense the same impulses and phantoms in John. They were enthralled with Winters and didn't talk much, but they agreed to keep in touch and get together again soon.

About 7 P.M. Thursday, January 14, John and Bill Wallace went to the gym on the Paramount lot. John was working out several times a week, trying to get in shape.

Wallace knew the only way to deal with John in the gym was to push and pester. They began with warmup exercises, stretching and light running in place.

"Come on, you pussy!" Wallace shouted, trying to fire John's competitive instincts. They went to the large punching bag for a three-minute round. John began sweating. "Come on! Come on!" Wallace yelled, angry when John took a halfhearted jab at the bag. After a short rest, John sparred another three-minute round, the bag always coming back, with Wallace giving it a little nudge. Then a third three-minute round. Next some jumping rope, then to the weights.

Wallace could curl 90 to 100 pounds; John could manage about 60. There were weights for all the parts of the body—stomach, chest, then the stomach again, to the biceps, back to the stomach as punishment because John's hung over the drawstring of his sweatpants. Then on to the legs.

"Come on, you pussy, you fat slob," Wallace shouted.

"Fuck you," John said.

"Now listen, pussy," Wallace said. "I know you're a pussy. You know you're a pussy. Let's not let everyone else know you're a pussy."

The building was empty except for Orlando Perry, the physical therapist who'd run the gym since 1935. "Don't you think you're working him too hard?" he asked.

"We've done this before," Wallace replied. He took John out for a mile-and-a-half run down Santa Monica Boulevard.

"You're worse than any coach I had in high school," John said. "We didn't have to be with them afterwards."

But Wallace was with John only when John wanted. Outside the gym, Wallace didn't have much influence. John and Novello were working mostly at night, and that meant lots of cocaine.

One time around this period Wallace went up to John's room at the Chateau Marmont and found Playmate Debra Jo Fondren in front of the mirror applying makeup. "John is upset because he didn't get what he wanted," she said.

Wallace didn't know what that meant and didn't want to ask. Fondren pulled out a vial of what she indicated was cocaine, stuck a small coke spoon into it and snorted some. "You want some?" she asked Wallace.

"No," Wallace replied. "I'd appreciate it if you wouldn't give any of that to John."

"I'm not supplying him," Fondren said.

Wallace left, feeling increasingly frozen out.

Paramount was filming on its lot a prospective television series called "Police Squad!," and the producers had devised a sort of guest death routine. Each episode was to open with a guest star dying, and Robert Weiss, producer of *The Blues Brothers* movie, asked John to appear.

"Wouldn't it be funny if I was an overdose victim?" John said.

Weiss had a better suggestion. John would be submerged in a river, chained to cement blocks, the victim of a mafia hit. John liked the idea and went to Paramount to film the scene on January 15. Using underwater cameras in a swimming pool, he did the scene and came up gasping for breath at the end. Executive producer Jerry Zucker, the cowriter of *Airplane!,* read a mock obituary: "John Belushi, who was just about to step into the big time with a guest appearance on 'Police Squad!,' died yesterday during a freak swimming accident on the set.''

The scene was the final bit of shooting for the episode, and in the tradition of television and the movies, the cast and crew had a party on the last day. John and the Wheaton Ravins were the musical entertainment.

The next day, Saturday, Mitch Glazer was getting married in New York, and he was furious that John had been out with his high school band instead of flying in for the wedding. Aykroyd came instead, announcing, "I'm here to represent my partner."

That day John called one of Judy's closest friends, Rhonda Coullet, an actress and singer in her midthirties who had been in *Lemmings*. Coullet had not seen John for several months, but she knew that he and Judy were having hard times, and she knew that John thought of her as a line to Judy.

At the sound of his voice—slow, depressed—Coullet pictured John: He had been on cocaine, was now down or heading down and was probably in some messy hotel room trying to take account of his relationships.

How's Judy, he asked? What have you heard? Is she happy?

Coullet explained that there was no immediate news and asked why John was not at Mitch Glazer's wedding.

John said he was sorry he hadn't made it but offered no excuse. More important was what he should do about Judy. He was looking for a quick remedy, ignoring the fact that his behavior might have something to do with the tension.

Rather than lecturing John, Coullet talked about herself. "I'm not doing coke anymore," she said.

John didn't acknowledge her remark. He felt he was not making Judy happy, he rambled, on and on; he wondered what might keep them together; he reminisced a little about all they had been through. Rhonda was really the only one who might understand, he said, the only one he could talk to about it.

"John," Coullet said, "you know she loves you very much and would do anything to make you happy and make things work." Coullet knew how fragile the Belushis' relationship was and was glad that John had called, even though he didn't make much sense. They had been on the phone for nearly an hour, and John was doing most of the talking, plowing the same damaged ground. At the end, he had one request: Don't, under any circumstances, tell Judy that he had called.

Coullet promised, adding, "John, anytime you need to talk I'm here. Feel you can call."

She hung up. Knowing John and being Judy's close friend put her in a precarious position. Coullet was going through a divorce and was turning away from drugs and alcohol. She wanted to help John, but he was so pained, so isolated, so stubborn. Once, years before, John had claimed to her husband that he was strong and indestructible. Her husband had actually taken John and shaken him to say, "No, you're not! No, you're not!" Coullet wasn't sure what to do, but she decided she would honor John's request.

On Sunday, January 17, Novello went over to the garden in back of the Sunset Marquis to do an interview for ABC television's "Entertainment Tonight." As Father Sarducci, he interviewed "SCTV's" popular McKenzie Brothers, Rick Moranis and Dave Thomas, who play beer-drinking Canadian backwoodsmen.

A number of reporters and photographers were around when John showed up. All eyes and cameras—both the still photographers and television crew—swung to him almost automatically.

"Fuck you, fuck you!" John screamed, raising a finger, then a fist. "Get your fucking cameras off me!" He was there to watch, he said, just a fan, and he hid behind a tree.

After the taping, John invited about a dozen people, including Moranis and Thomas, Novello, Tino Insana and his wife Dana, Joe Flaherty (also at "SCTV" now) and his wife Judith, to meet later at the Imperial Gardens Restaurant just below the Chateau. But first John and Tino went down to a store that sold punk music paraphernalia. They met Blasucci on Melrose, and he came with them.

Look at this, John said, handing a Fear T-shirt to Blasucci. He picked out a dozen pins and buttons inscribed with skull and crossbones or other symbols of death. John didn't have enough money to pay the bill and borrowed $40 from Blasucci.

At the dinner that night he passed out a death pin to everyone, extolling the virtues of the new-wave music. He paid the $399.36 check, and then invited everyone to On the Rox, where he drank hot chocolate and struck up a long conversation with Moranis, who with Thomas had a feature film planned (*Strange Brew*) and a TV special coming up. Moranis talked about getting John and Aykroyd to do cameo appearances. John wanted the McKenzie Brothers in *Spies Like Us* or *Never Say Mountie*, two movie scripts Aykroyd was writing.

John went on at length about his battle to get off drugs and how Martha's Vineyard was a good place to convalesce. When it was time to leave, they shook hands.

"Goodbye," John said.

Moranis paused. John's eye could cut through glass. Moranis had never felt such an incredible presence.

On the way to their hotel, he told his partner, Thomas, "He talked so much about straightening up that it was as if he was saying it more to himself than to me."

Back in his room, Moranis found the death insignia in his pocket. He had not put it on. What an odd thing to hand out, he thought. John had been perfect, except for that. It spoiled the meeting. Moranis almost never threw anything out, but he dropped it in the trash.

Anne Beatts was in her room at the Chateau Marmont the next day, Monday, January 18, talking to Howard Hesseman of the TV show "WKRP." Beatts was trying to develop for CBS a loosely autobiographical sitcom about her high school days called "Square Pegs." There was a thud at the door. John was paying an unannounced social call. He saw Hesseman and talked for twenty minutes, ignoring Beatts.

As John was leaving, she asked if he could help get her a membership at On the Rox.

"No," he said bluntly, and left. Obviously he didn't want one of Judy's friends to infiltrate the privacy of his L.A. hideout, Beatts concluded.

Beatts wished she could package his hostility and sell it by the pound. Earlier John had told Deanne Stillman, who with Beatts had coauthored *Titters,* "I'll give you and Anne $60,000 if you don't work with my wife again." Judy's job, John seemed to indicate, was to take care of him.

Beatts used to feel a little protective of John, but now that had evaporated. Too much of the male pig in John wanted Judy home, like a mother, with something always cooking on the stove.

The couple in the room next to John's at the Chateau had a baby, and they complained to the management about the noise coming from John's room—stereo, TV, loud talk. John complained about their baby, and on January 19 he moved to room 54, a $200-a-day penthouse.

John and Tino Insana decided to give a party. John had promised Tino's mother on her deathbed that he would help her son professionally, and Tino had been given a small part in *Neighbors.* John also had arranged for Universal to pay Tino $5,000 to work on writing a sequel to *The Blues Brothers.*

Tino cooked pizza for the party, and John invited Brillstein, Landis and Sean Daniels, and Fear. It was a quiet evening as John held court on the terrace overlooking Los Angeles.

"This is the way it should always be," he told Brillstein. "What I love is having the guys together." There was much talk about future movie projects—*Spies Like Us* with Universal and a *Blues Brothers* sequel, for which Insana had already done the treatment. It was also obvious to nearly everyone that this was part of John's effort to introduce Fear to movie people.

Landis had brought his wife, who was pregnant, and John made weak jokes about the forthcoming "Son of Landis." He described *Sweet Deception,* and Landis thought it sounded terrible, but he held his tongue. At least John seemed in good spirits.

John was also blowing his nose a lot and as usual tossing the used tissue on the floor. One time he hit Brillstein's wife, Deborah, on the shoe. She was sick of John's mess and snapped, "Is that how your mother brought you up?"

John leaned down, picked up the tissue and said, "I'm sorry."

The next day John hired a mature Englishwoman named Penny Selwyn to be his secretary at Paramount.

"Do you use drugs?" he asked.

"Yes," Selwyn said, "but very little." She took a line or two of cocaine occasionally.

"I'm the same way," he said. "We should get along fine."

Mickey Rooney, the famous pint-sized star and character actor, had been trying to reach John for several days and had left three or four messages for him at Paramount. Rooney, sixty-one, had been told that John was unavailable.

"Bullshit," Rooney said to an assistant in his office. "Can you imagine? The guy has so much success that he can't even call me back."

John finally did call back. "Mr. Rooney," John began, and then muttered something incoherent.

"John, I'm calling because I want to do a picture with you. I have an idea for a movie, *The Picture Nobody Could See*." He described John's role.

John tried to talk, but he didn't make any sense. Rooney figured that he was fried on drugs.

"Okay, John," Rooney replied. "I'll talk to you later." He hung up, turned to a friend and asked, "Why is it that the youth of today can't accept God's gift of success?"

• •

Jay Sandrich couldn't get John on the phone, and after two weeks of what was supposed to have been a light polish and a partial rewrite, he had not seen a single page of the script. He talked to Ovitz, Brillstein and producer Stanley Chase. His message was, "I may not do this picture."

Brillstein explained that he had extracted a promise from John and Novello to involve Sandrich.

"If I don't like the script," Sandrich said emphatically, "I'm not going to do it."

"I understand," Brillstein said. "I don't blame you."

Brillstein asked John about progress.

"I'm writing," John said.

On Thursday, January 21, Sandrich and producer Chase met John and Novello in John's office at Paramount. Three or four meetings had already been cancelled, and Sandrich was not sure what he was going to find.

Punk music could be heard in the hall. In the office it was unbearable. Was this where John and Novello were working? "Can you turn down the music?" Sandrich asked.

Novello could see John almost bust a seam. "Turn down the music" was a call to arms for his generation—the demand of parents, establishment, teachers and cops to play by their rules. John got up without a word, went over to the record player, lifted the needle, turned the volume up and started it again.

After it was over, John said that the script rewrite was going great.

But can we see some pages? Sandrich asked.

Soon as we're done, John said. He had some great ideas for the movie, what punk music they would use, and he also had some casting ideas.

Sandrich said he was interviewing for a casting director.

John said he wanted the following people in the movie:

—Aykroyd, of course, in a cameo appearance;

—Danny DeVito, one of the stars of TV's "Taxi," as John's brother;

—The Green Grocer, a local Los Angeles news personality who gave a fruit and vegetable report;

—Richard Belzer, a stand-up, improvisational comedian and close friend;

—Gary Watkins, an actor and friend.

John did not mention that Watkins was one of his drug suppliers.

Sandrich and Chase left, feeling more and more cut out. "I've got to see it on paper," Sandrich said.

Novello went back to San Francisco later that day.

The next evening John went to the At Sunset club, a private after-hours club in a building where Lenny Bruce used to perform. He met a blond, sexy, rather hard-faced woman named Jeremy Rain. She was from West Virginia and had been in L.A. about three years, first working in the promotion department at NBC, and now at CBS. John asked if he could drive her home. Rain said yes, and they went for something to eat at another after-hours club.

John had tapes of the punk group the Dead Kennedys in his red Mercedes, and they listened for several hours, driving around and talking.

"Do you get high?" John asked.

No, Rain insisted.

By 6 A.M. they wound up at Fat Burger, an all-night hamburger stand where they bought some burgers and threw them to stray dogs.

Rain couldn't believe that John wanted to stay up so late. Why? Where did he get his stamina? What was he looking for?

"I've left bodies dead in the street who couldn't keep up with me," John said. He dropped her at home on Cynthia Street, just about a block from At Sunset. "You'll hear from me every day," he promised before leaving.

That evening, Saturday, January 23, John went to the airport to meet Judy, who was coming from New York on a 7 P.M. flight to be with him for his thirty-third birthday the next day. She was surprised that he came to the airport to pick her up. He had never done that before. As they greeted each other, she had the certain feeling that he had been doing a lot of cocaine, but she decided not to say much, sticking with her strategy of ignoring him.

She found a Quaalude on the floor of their room at the Chateau and was put off by the seedy hotel; it was old and musty and reminded her of staying at a great-aunt's house. "Are you sure you want to stay here?" she asked.

John said he was.

The next day, Brillstein had a small birthday party for John. It was Super Bowl Sunday, and Aykroyd, Derf, Alan Zweibel and Judy went to Brillstein's to watch the San Francisco 49ers beat the Cincinnati Bengals 26–21.

Brillstein felt down afterward. He loved his house and kept it neat. Even a five-minute visit from John could inflict remarkable chaos, and the birthday party and a three-hour football game had been a disaster.

There was no telling what was gone or broken or misused. It seemed that John had dipped his fingers into everything in the refrigerator.

Christ, what a pain, what a big kid, Brillstein thought. He loved John, understood his impulses, his resistance to some things, including much of Hollywood. When it worked—when a deal was made, a movie put together—well, then the millions could roll in, and Brillstein shared the wonder of that. But that night it all felt grubby and cheap.

Up in the Hollywood Hills, writer Carol Caldwell and Michael O'Donoghue were working on separate screenplays. They shared some deep apprehensions about John's attempt at writing. O'Donoghue knew that John could be verbally witty, but he had no discipline. Writing was like doing term papers, and John would have no more to do with that than neat rooms or a daily routine. And behind his back, many of the other "Saturday Night Live" writers were saying ugly things about John's writing.

Caldwell was glad that Judy had arrived. John had been strange during the preceding weeks, calling at all hours of the night. That part was not unusual, but there was confusion in his voice. He'd try to get a little writers' conference going, but there were two constants to his conversation. "Do you have any drugs?" She was trying to stay off and said no. Second, "I'm just so lonely." Caldwell would invite him up, even suggest they could sleep in the same bed, but he just wanted to talk.

For John's birthday, Caldwell bought the biggest plaster cast of Jesus Christ nailed and bleeding on the cross that she could find; it was nearly three feet high. She had it boxed and took it over to the Chateau. It was a perfect punk gift. Christ had died at age thirty-three. Her own thirty-third year had been wretched—a divorce and a bout with cancer. So she wrote on the card:

"Beware of 33. Tread fucking lightly, just get through this one. Love Carol."

Eisner tried to keep his family and private life separate from the movie business. That meant very little socializing, and certainly not a lot of personal visiting with the stars. Katzenberg handled most of that; he had the breakfast, lunch and dinner meetings. Eisner sometimes checked Katzenberg's schedule and if it sounded interesting or important, he'd invite himself.

That week he noticed a dinner at Morton's scheduled for Tuesday,

January 26, with Belushi and his wife. Eisner and his wife, Jane, tagged along.

John began the evening by quizzing the waiter about the wine list, showing off what he had so far learned while doing research for *Sweet Deception*. He ordered several kinds but said that he was just going to taste them. Judy knew that wine would go right to his head. As the wine was delivered, John first sipped it, but soon he had drunk several glasses. He loosened up and began performing the script.

Everyone seemed to love it, Judy could see, but she withheld judgment. John was a fabulous storyteller—he could improvise anything— but things often came out differently on paper and film. The dinner guests certainly were learning, often word for word, what was in the script. And the Paramount executives at the dinner—even to Judy's skeptical eye— were spellbound.

Jane Eisner mentioned that she was from Jamestown, New York, near Chautauqua Lake.

"My cousin is from there!" John said, beaming with recognition. He and the cousin, Gary, used to hunt and fish there in the summer. He described the times they had spent by the lake. Once he had hitchhiked there from Illinois. Gary, he said, is an idol, a very important person in my life. He's the straightest person in the world, shoots one deer a year, and he fishes all the time. John and Jane were able to pinpoint a stream and a single large tree they both knew.

Eisner was impressed. It was nice to see that John had people he valued outside the movie and television business, a down-to-earth cousin who lived on a lake. It made John seem more real.

When they all left, John was a little tipsy, and he asked Judy to drive. The two of them went to On the Rox and then to Open Mike night at the Central, where John took to the stage for two hours. Afterward two people, one carrying a large bass instrument, asked them for a ride to the valley. John said yes. Judy knew they couldn't all fit in the Mercedes and got angry. John ran off, and she had to drive back to the Chateau alone. He called later and finally came home to sleep.

The next day John and Judy left in the Mercedes for the 380-mile drive to San Francisco. Judy was surprised to find that John had made some arrangements: the car had tapes, oranges, a pillow and a blanket. They spent the night at the San Ysidro Ranch in Santa Barbara, 90 minutes north of L.A., and the next morning went on to San Francisco, where they were renting a house for a week near Don and Kathy Novello.

Novello had some more pages, but John wanted to make sure they got to the chief purpose of the trip, which was to comb through the wine country and learn everything about grapes, vineyards and the selecting, bottling, aging, tasting and drinking of wine. It's all got to be real, John said.

One night a friend of Novello's brought about a gram of cocaine for all of them to share. John can handle coke now, Novello told Judy. She felt ill.

On Tuesday, February 2, John, Judy and the Novellos drove to the Sonoma wine country to visit the 40-acre Remick Ridge Ranch, a vineyard owned by Tommy Smothers, the blond, "dim-witted" half of the Smothers Brothers. Smothers gave them a tour and pushed on them as many technical details about wine as they could stand. The conversation turned to the finest, the best wines. What was the secret?

Oddly, Smothers explained, the best wine comes from grapes infected perhaps once in a lifetime with a fungus or rot called "botrytis." It adds a distinct sweetness that is impossible to capture any other way. The rot—the little bit of bad—makes the good, the best, Smothers said, and it is called the "noble rot."

"Yes, that's it," John said. They'd rename their movie *Noble Rot*.

It was a beautiful day, and Smothers took them out to Chateau Saint Jean in Sonoma, and then to a small organic winery and to dinner afterward.

John said they planned to do some filming in the region.

Smothers asked why they didn't have a location manager or producer scouting for places to film.

"I don't trust them," John said. This was his movie, and Hollywood was not going to wreck it. "Someone's going to get involved and fuck it up," he said, and his plan was to control each detail carefully. "I'm going to do it myself."

Oh, come on, Smothers said, it's not all bad; you're exaggerating. Hollywood is miserable, but not everyone is screwed up.

"No," John said defiantly. "Everyone will fuck you."

In New York City at 2 P.M. the next afternoon, February 3, Mark Hertzan, John's friend and a top-level drug dealer, was followed into his apartment building in the Village at 41 Great Jones Street by a young man who pulled out an automatic gun and shot and killed him, execution style.

John and Judy were shaken by the news. John told her there were three possible explanations—the government, a bad drug deal or the "Kingpin" script. He had no idea which.

John called Brillstein from San Francisco. "I know all about the wine business," he said.

"You don't drink," Brillstein said.

John explained about what he had learned about the rot on the vine and said that the new title of the movie was going to be *Noble Rot.*

"That's a terrible title," Brillstein said.

John changed the subject. Was "Malibu" Sandrich holding on and staying calm?

John, Brillstein said, you've got to keep him clued in.

On Friday, February 5, John and Judy turned in the Mercedes at the San Francisco airport and took the 5 P.M. United flight back to Los Angeles.

John went alone to On the Rox, where he bought drinks for everyone and ran into actor Michael Brandon. Shortly before 4 A.M., Brandon took John and Marcy Hanson, *Playboy*'s Miss October of 1978, to the Playboy mansion. They left about 6 A.M.

The next evening, February 6, John and Judy went to "Taxi" producer Ed Weinberger's house for a Hollywood celebration of Danny DeVito's recent wedding. Penny Marshall, John and Judy, Weinberger and several other guests went upstairs, where there was lots of coke. Weinberger was amazed at the amount John was doing. It seemed that he could not get enough of it. Judy took a hit.

John asked all of them about "Malibu" Sandrich. Was he good enough? Too soft? Too square?

Weinberger argued that perhaps John needed a little squareness for balance. Marshall said that Sandrich was good: he followed the script.

Marshall also announced that Paramount had offered her a chance to direct her first feature film, *The Joy of Sex,* a comedy to be based on Alex Comfort's 1972 best-selling sex manual.

"Yeah," John said, giving her a deeply suspicious look as if to say: Who are you to be a big Hollywood director? He then softened up. Try something new, he said. Anything to get away from the prime-time shit like "Laverne and Shirley."

"How long can you stay in Second City?" she responded, striking close to the bone.

Marshall knew John well and loved him as a friend. She thought he could probably get away with anything. He acted from his gut, and his need for attention and approval was boundless. He had said to her many times, "Maybe I'm no good."

When John had gone to the Academy Awards with Lauren Hutton in 1978 he was really proud.

"Why do they go out with you?" Marshall had asked John. "Why? Why?"

John just looked at her.

"Because you're so good-looking?"

John said he went into acting because of the access to women.

When John was on *Newsweek*'s cover in 1978, he asked Marshall if she had read the article.

"No," she said truthfully.

"You don't care," he told her.

"You never watch my show."

He wrestled her to the ground in a friendly way.

At times he would bring his cocaine to Marshall's place and spill it all over himself and her house. Once, Marshall suggested to him that he take a shower to clean it off.

It was about this time that John had said to her, "Hey, I got smack."

"Don't you ever fucking use this!" Marshall shouted, grabbing the heroin and running to flush it down the toilet. Marshall had used heroin once. It was dangerous and had made her feel carsick.

The Police, an English new-wave music group that had scored big in America with their hit song "Roxanne" (1979), had a three-night concert stand in Los Angeles beginning February 8. John, Judy and Aykroyd, who was in Los Angeles, hired two limousines and took a group of friends to the first performance.

The next night Judy and Aykroyd took the American Airline red-eye flight to New York. Aykroyd wanted to get back to work on *Spies Like Us* and another movie script, *Ghostbusters*. Judy left L.A. feeling bad. John wasn't working though he was still insisting that Novello and he needed only another week to finish the script. Novello wasn't even due back in Los Angeles for several days.

After Judy and Aykroyd left, John called Jeremy Rain. He had kept his word, calling her nearly every day, often shouting, "Party! Party! Party! Party!" Rain was beginning to like him. He took her to the second Police concert that night. And then the next night John planned to take Rain again, along with her roommate, Alyce Kuhn. He had also asked Judith Flaherty to the concert. Judith called to remind him that afternoon.

"Judith, oh Jesus, I forgot," John said. Okay, meet us at the Imperial Gardens. We'll eat and go to the concert. Judith was surprised and angry that John had another woman with him and said little during dinner, but on the way out of the restaurant, she pulled him aside. "What am I supposed to be, a chaperone?" She felt that John was taking advantage of her and her friendship with Judy. He knew she wouldn't squeal to Judy.

"She's just a friend," John said.

"I don't believe you," she replied.

"I know," he said. "I'm such a lousy liar."

After the concert, at On the Rox, John called Judy and woke her up. Judith Flaherty also took the phone to say hello, but that was all, and she felt guilty and used. The owner of the club, Lou Adler, and Jack Nicholson came by, and they all went off to a party.

Lorne Michaels was in Los Angeles that week and he was supposed to meet actor Buck Henry, a frequent "Saturday Night Live" host, at the Playboy mansion on February 12 for the Friday dinner and movie Hefner gave for his friends. He arrived about nine-thirty, a little after the movie had started. It was a preview of *I, the Jury,* a film based on Mickey Spillane's private-eye classic.

Michaels noticed John and Peter Aykroyd, Danny's younger brother, in the front room of the mansion. Earlier John had gotten $400 cash from Brillstein's office, and he was pretty wrecked. Michaels wanted to keep his distance. John would certainly offer him some drugs, and that was always a hard choice.

"Let's go to the game room," John said.

"I should go say hello to Hefner," Michaels replied, "and look at some of the movie."

"The movie is no good. Boring shit," John said.

Michaels went into the large living room, where about 50 people were watching the film. As usual, Hefner was in front on the couch in silk pajamas with his current girlfriend. Michaels sat down in the back. About 45 minutes later John came in and began lurking about. He sat down next to Michaels and passed him a large chunk of opium.

No, Michaels said.

John insisted. Michaels, pretending to eat it, palmed it.

Soon John was on his hands and knees quietly crawling up the side of the room toward Hefner, who had his Pepsi and bowl of popcorn. This was definitely supposed to be Hefner's own supply, a symbol of his authority. Bowls of popcorn and drinks had been handed out to the other guests earlier. John stopped behind Hefner's table, reached for the Pepsi, drank it and put the empty bottle back. Then John took the popcorn, ate it all, and replaced the bowl. A short while later Hefner reached for his drink and popcorn, but he didn't register any surprise when he found them empty. No big surprise, Michaels thought. Not as John likes it.

After the movie John and Michaels walked over to the game room, a separate cabin that had several dozen of the latest electronic games. Hefner stopped by, still in his silk pajamas, and put on a leather driving glove that he wore while playing the games.

John took Michaels into one of the two small, private back rooms, where he laid out some cocaine. John snorted a lot of it himself and offered some to Michaels, who hesitated. To refuse would be to appear to judge John, to stand above him. What good would that do? There had always been, always would be, a cultural gap between the two. Not just because Michaels had once been the boss; not just because John was now infinitely more famous and powerful; not just because Michaels was private about his drug usage and John almost hysterically public about it. But John was reaching out, and the two had shared a lot.

Michaels took a little cocaine.

John mentioned how funny *Noble Rot* was. Novello was perfect. They were working together wonderfully, John said. He had never been able to get that close to Aykroyd, especially while writing. He felt closer to Dan's brother Peter. John had helped Peter, twenty-six, get a job on the fifth season of "Saturday Night Live" and had become his biggest fan and promoter.

There's a scene in *Noble Rot* for you to act in, John said to Michaels. A guy drives a car down a dock and jumps it twenty feet over water onto a ferry. You're included.

Michaels thought that John took drugs to get his emotions to the surface. He was talking fast, and he mentioned "Saturday Night Live." You and I, John said, should go back and do it for a year. We were the only two who believed in the show. Every night here in L.A. I close On the Rox and watch the reruns. There was a skit from the fourth year just last night—one of those scenes I didn't want to do, but you had pushed me. How funny it was, John said. How well it holds up. Peter Aykroyd had seen it and agreed completely.

What a great time the show had been, John said. It was what we were meant to do, what we were best at. The movie business is shit. The show was important. It was not rock and roll only, it was not Second City only, it was not "Your Show of Shows," but it was a special time. We didn't know it then. Now we are all playing it safe—all agent stuff, no hazards, too pat.

John wanted Michaels to go with him to On the Rox.

No, Michaels said, he just couldn't tonight. John was too jumpy. He was trying to be close, to go back. But Michaels figured they both knew the truth about that. There was no way there. They'd never go back.

Just before noon on Saturday, February 13, John drove over to Audio Video Craft on Melrose. Even inside the store, The Who could be heard blasting on the stereo in John's Mercedes, though the car windows were rolled up. He wore a hat and sunglasses, and a glob of white stuff, apparently cocaine, was hanging from one of his nostrils. He seemed frightened. He spoke softly and backed into a corner. It wasn't hot, but he was sweating heavily.

John told the sales manager, James Morgan, that he wanted a complete portable video camera, recorder and playback system for shooting in the wine country, perhaps even from a small airplane. After looking at a few systems, he selected Japan Victor and RCA equipment, paying $3,290.77 with his American Express card. He packed it all in his car and took it to Jeremy Rain's place, carried it inside and announced it was a present for her so she could watch *The Blues Brothers,* which she'd never seen. He had taken some Quaaludes, he said, and he was worried that he was going to pass out unless he got some cocaine. He left, apparently to buy more drugs, and Rain set up her new video system.

That night John went to Le Hot Tub Club on Santa Monica Boulevard in Westwood, where he met Leslie Marks, a pretty, brown-haired, fresh-looking woman of twenty-five who had worked as an assistant to a film art director. John and she went back to her apartment in Westwood and smoked some marijuana and did some cocaine. Later, he took her to Jeremy Rain's.

Rain thought it was a silly infatuation and told John that Leslie was too young. About five o'clock that morning, John called Rain and said, "I'm okay. You were right."

On Valentine's Day, Sunday, February 14, John stopped by director Steven Spielberg's house, but Spielberg wasn't there. John convinced the housekeeper to let him in, helped himself to a drink out of the refrigerator and left a note: "Hey Steven. I came by. See you soon, John."

The housekeeper later explained to Spielberg, "I couldn't keep him out."

Later from the hotel John called Judy and said that he had been to a party with some members of the Pretenders, a popular new-wave band that had played a Valentine's Day concert at U.C.L.A. in Westwood. "I have a problem," he said. "Chrissie Hynde [their lead singer] has passed out. What should I do?"

Call her road manager, Judy said dryly.

John also called Cathy Shields, another old Wheaton friend in L.A., to say that Hynde had passed out in his room and to ask her what he should do. It was 6:30 A.M.

Call her road manager, Shields also said, wondering what kind of prowling John was doing now.

Part Three

TUESDAY, FEBRUARY 16

About sunrise on Tuesday, February 16, John turned off Mulholland Drive and drove his Mercedes through the private gate to Jack Nicholson's house, deep in the Hollywood Hills. He wanted advice about his *Noble Rot* deal. Nicholson said that $1.85 million plus a percentage of the gross was okay, but John could have done better. Without you, Johnny boy, there wouldn't be a movie, Nicholson said, so you're entitled to a bigger piece of the pie. John should talk to him next time before he made a deal.

Since *Goin' South,* John's first movie, Nicholson had recognized an enormous potential in him. He wanted to be a father-brother-advisor-mentor to Belushi, and he was trying to inspire him to riskier work, and to get him to stop flying from coast to coast, a week here, a month there. Only by focusing, Nicholson argued, could John dispel the commonly held notion that he was only Bluto.

John insisted that finally he was in charge of a movie project—just like Nicholson. He was going to be involved in every step. He had questions about the preproduction mechanics and budgets.

Nicholson rarely permitted visitors to interrupt his routine or life. After a string of critical flops, including *Goin' South,* a remake of *The Postman Always Rings Twice* and a horror film, *The Shining,* he was taking time off. His house was always open for friends to swim, take a Jacuzzi, watch basketball games. If they wanted to do drugs while they were there, they could. John insisted that he was cutting back on drugs, but as the day wore on, Nicholson could see it wasn't true. Nicholson smoked pot regularly and had, at one time, kept two kinds of cocaine—the "downstairs cocaine" for visitors and acquaintances and the "upstairs cocaine" for special friends and women.

By midafternoon a few friends had come by to pass the rainy day, including Ed Begley, Jr. Begley entered Nicholson's large TV room with its U-shaped couch and big viewing screen and saw John, who had his shirt off. He was shocked at the immensity of John's stomach and the deadness in his eyes.

"Hey, Begley," John said, grabbing him affectionately. But Begley couldn't get hold of John's eyes.

John said that he was overdue on the script rewrite for *Noble Rot,* and it would be a race to get it out for Christmas. "They're busting my balls," he said.

Nicholson and Begley wondered why John was hanging out if he was so far behind schedule.

"They can wait," John said with scorn. He picked up a guitar and strummed some chords aimlessly; he couldn't find a pick, so he took a knife and made one out of a plastic cassette case.

Actor Harry Dean Stanton, a close friend of Nicholson's, arrived. A joke contest began, and soon John was on the floor acting one out. He stood up suddenly, said he needed another beer, and walked out.

"I can't believe it," Nicholson said to Begley. "Johnny came by at 5 A.M. and he's on a terror, trashing the place."

Belushi took a Jacuzzi and returned wrapped in a towel and wearing a bandanna on his head, looking like a Buddha. He said he planned to do a musical with director Ken Russell, and play the role of God.

Begley asked after Judy.

"The last time I saw her, she told me to do my own thing," John replied. He paused. "I can't keep this up, Begs."

Maybe they should talk, Begley said.

John asked for his phone number, and Begley handed him a business card with his home phone. John placed it in his portable address book, a quagmire of paper scraps and cocktail napkins with phone numbers written on them.

He finally left to do some errands. He stopped by Brillstein's office to collect $700 in cash and then arranged for the delivery of $848 of new Yamaha stereo equipment to Susan Morton, Bill Wallace's girlfriend. When he got back to the Chateau Marmont, he collected his belongings, his script and wine maps, and moved from room 54 to bungalow number 3, a two-bedroom hideaway in the back of the Chateau with a private entrance.

That evening at 7:50 P.M., John drove through the gate of the Playboy mansion with actor Gary Watkins, still one of his regular cocaine suppliers. It was Watkins's first visit, and John introduced him to Hugh Hefner.

Hefner always welcomed John and his friends. He didn't know that Watkins dealt drugs, however. Playboy Enterprises, the mansion in Chicago, and Hefner himself had been targets of a 1974 federal grand jury investigation after Hefner's executive assistant, Bobbie Arnstein, was sentenced to fifteen years for conspiracy in a large cocaine sale. Arnstein had committed suicide before she could go to prison. Shortly afterward, the Justice Department closed its investigation of Hefner for lack of evidence. Arnstein had always claimed Hefner was innocent, and Hefner was deeply disturbed by her death. After that, Hefner insisted that no one would dare bring cocaine into the mansion or anywhere around him.

John and Watkins headed for the Jacuzzi located behind the mansion in a lavish area of Polynesian design with private rooms.

In guest house number one on the Playboy grounds, Kym Malin, a nineteen-year-old aspiring actress from Texas, was watching television. She had just posed for a nude pictorial spread as the May Playmate of the Month. Malin (36-20-34) hoped it was a break that might lead to films or TV. When she was told that Belushi was outside and wanted to meet her, she slipped on a robe and found him sitting with Watkins on a cushion by the jacuzzi.

Malin had lived in a suburb of Chicago, and she chatted with John about the city. They talked about music. After a while Watkins took out a small spoon and a little vial of cocaine and gave them both four hits— two in each nostril.

John invited her to go on a tour of Hollywood night life, and at eleven forty-five the two left the mansion and headed for Sunset. Once in the Mercedes, John grew distant and formal. There were no more smiles.

"You know, I'm married," he finally said.

"We all are—in one way or another," Malin replied.

At On the Rox John had Malin try an Alabama Slammer, a mixture of sloe gin, Southern Comfort, orange juice and crème de banana. She hated it. He ordered two $90 bottles of champagne and ran up a $285 bill. Next, they went downstairs to the Roxy, where John left her alone for nearly half an hour.

There, that evening, was a young, attractive couple—April Milstead, twenty-five, a slim, striking woman with large, pretty eyes, and Charles

W. Pearson, thirty-two, a well-dressed rock-and-roll singer who had released two minor albums. Pearson looked a little like Mick Jagger, and he had cultivated the same droopy, hip look.

Milstead, an Air Force brat, was happy in Los Angeles. Her ambition was not to have to work. When she and Pearson had arrived eighteen months earlier, in the summer of 1980, she had not looked for a job, but when Pearson's music career didn't flourish, she had started working as a waitress in the Moustache Cafe, a bistro on Melrose Avenue in West Hollywood. She had been there a month when a well-to-do Englishman came in and fell in love with her. "I think I can help you out," he said. When the Englishman opened a bank account for her, she quit her job and told Pearson, "I've hit the jackpot."

They moved into a $375-a-month apartment on Martel, just south of Sunset, and the Englishman gave her money for rent, food, expensive clothes, a car and her growing drug habit. She used a lot of cocaine and some heroin, at times shooting it up.

Pearson, who had grown up near Washington, D.C., had been around drugs since age thirteen. He felt that Milstead, who was down to 105 pounds, was doing too much and that it made her unattractive, but he was very much in love with her.

John was infatuated with April. He hovered over her, following her around and teasing her, suggesting they run off together. Milstead teased him back. She invited John to join Pearson and her at a private party five minutes away at Dodson's, an art deco furniture store.

John retrieved Malin, who wondered why he wanted to go to a party at a furniture store. She was left alone again as John ran off to find Milstead, whom he backed into a corner to say that he liked her a lot. Milstead shared some cocaine with him. It was some of the best in Los Angeles, Milstead thought, almost pure. John was impressed and grateful.

Pearson was annoyed with John's attentions, but if somebody like Bo Derek ever fell for him, he thought, April would probably go along. Belushi was hardly the male equivalent of Bo Derek. He wasn't threatening. And with his contacts in the music world he probably could help Pearson.

John played cat-and-mouse with Milstead, dividing his attention between her and Malin. Finally, tired and bored, Malin convinced John to leave, and at 5:05 A.M. they arrived back at the Playboy mansion, where they took another Jacuzzi and John taught her how to slam dance. At 8:30 A.M. he drove back to his bungalow.

WEDNESDAY, FEBRUARY 17

About 9 A.M. he called April. "Why don't you come over?" he asked. "If you can find some coke, bring it."

Next, John called and awakened Briskin, who was in charge of John that week while Brillstein was out of town. "What are you doing today?" John asked. "Are you terribly busy? I've got a lot of stuff you could help me with."

Briskin said he'd be right over. He had never told John where he lived; he did not want Belushi showing up at any hour on his doorstep, which was on Sunset Plaza near the Chateau.

When Briskin arrived at the Chateau, John escalated his demands. "I'm going nuts. I can't find my phone numbers, can't find my messages." Briskin looked around. There were scripts, pieces of paper, food, bottles all over the living room and back bedroom. John was unshaven and complaining that he didn't have a fresh razor, but more important, he had talked to Nicholson the day before and Nicholson had better movie deals.

"How come Nicholson gets this?" John asked. "I should be getting this." Apparently Nicholson got a percentage of each ticket sold—10 percent or more—and John didn't get his percentage until after the studio started breaking even.

Briskin tried to tell John that he had a great deal.

"Well, I don't understand it . . . I'm not going to do the picture." He demanded to talk to Ovitz.

Briskin got out a pen and yellow legal pad and went through the scraps of phone messages, asking each time whether John wanted to return the call. Within an hour John was somewhat more organized. They had coffee and juice.

John said he'd had a good night's rest, but Briskin noticed that the bed hadn't been slept in. John wanted some cash; Briskin gave him $400.

Milstead and Pearson arrived some time after 10 A.M. and walked to the back bedroom with John. Milstead sold John two grams of cocaine for $300. Briskin went back and found them looking at some white lumps.

"This is really fabulous stuff," April said. She thought she was helping John to avoid being ripped off on drug buys.

Briskin asked to look.

"Do you want to buy some?" she asked.

Briskin asked to see it closer.

"Why?" John snapped.

"I want to see what you're doing to yourself. You can't do that."

John told Briskin to go buy a Deering grinder to break down the lumps of cocaine.

John and April stayed in the back bedroom. John suggested they write a song together and started singing, "I once met a girl named April." He told her Briskin would get them whatever they wanted; they drew up a list.

John took out a black bathrobe with leopard skin sash that Tino Insana had given him. Holding it up, he told her that it was a birthday present from a good friend—Keith Richards of the Rolling Stones.

Briskin and Pearson drove to a head shop and purchased the grinder. Briskin also stopped around the corner at Schwab's drugstore—a tacky but chic breakfast hangout on Sunset—to get John a new toothbrush, toothpaste and a razor. He was trying to arrange an emergency meeting for John with Ovitz, and he did not want John to be unshaven and messy. He had played manservant before, and no doubt would again.

When they returned to the bungalow, John ran the coke through the grinder, took a picture off the wall in the living room, laid out the fine white powder in long narrow lines on the glass and snorted several. "You know, Joel," he said, "I just love cocaine."

Briskin knew. It might be okay this time, he reasoned, because John and Novello were planning to do some night work. The script was overdue by nearly a week, and Novello was flying in from San Francisco with a new draft. The script would be finished within a week, and then there would be less reason for the cocaine.

Briskin was struck by April Milstead's arms. He could see little dark bruises on the inside of her forearm. Needle marks. Briskin had lived in the Hollywood fast lane, where drugs were a part of everyday life, but needles were not fashionable. He was a little stunned.

John settled in to make some phone calls. About 1 P.M. he reached director William Friedkin (*The Exorcist, The French Connection*). He launched into manic jive talk, claiming that he was working around the clock on his wine script.

Friedkin felt he could never have a straight conversation with John. He mentioned that actor Nick Nolte was in the office having lunch.

"He's a real candy ass. He takes it up the ass," John said, though he had never met Nolte.

"He's right here, why don't you tell him yourself?" Friedkin said.

When Nolte picked up, Friedkin introduced them, and they joked in star-to-star camaraderie, all to no point.

Briskin left the bungalow and went home to call Ovitz back-channel. John's been up all night and has been tooting coke, he warned Ovitz. He's on a real rampage about his deal, and there's some girl over there. Ovitz agreed to stop by John's bungalow after lunch.

Briskin returned to the bungalow with some soft drinks. Milstead had to get to the bank before it closed at 3 P.M. and left. John took a shower and shaved, and Ovitz arrived. Citing unnamed friends, not mentioning Nicholson, John said it looked as though he'd been screwed.

Ovitz responded that he didn't know anyone who had a better deal. He explained the way it was constructed. With the $1.85 million guarantee, Belushi was effectively getting 7.5 percent of the receipts from every ticket up to the studio's break-even. After break-even he would get 10–12.5 percent of ticket sales. If they had a runaway hit like *Animal House,* John could make millions.

It took half an hour to explain, but John was considerably calmed down. Though he appeared dishevelled to Ovitz, that was part of his charm: the clothes never matched, the shirt was never tucked in. Belushi was a study in contrasts, and Ovitz liked being his agent.

Just before four-thirty that afternoon, Judy reached John, and they talked for five minutes. She could tell from his voice and his hurried manner that he was doing coke, but he said he was almost finished with the script and would be home soon.

Novello arrived in L.A. late that evening, worried about the deadline. They needed some typing done on a crash basis. John said they could get his Paramount secretary Penny Selwyn, but he didn't have her home phone number. He finally got a message to her to call him. When Selwyn got through to him about eleven-thirty, she thought from the sound of his voice she'd awakened him.

Can you come over? John pleaded. We're in chaos and the pressure is on and Don is here and the pages are all mixed up. We'll send a limousine for you.

She got dressed and waited for the driver. After waiting a half-hour, she called the Chateau again. Novello answered. There was really no need to come tonight, he said. "John thinks you do, but I don't. Let me talk to John again."

Selwyn waited. About 1 A.M. she called John and asked, "Do you want me to come over? What's the story?"

"I've ordered a limo, and the driver will be on his way," he said.

After another 45 minutes she called again. John reassured her that the car was coming.

It was 3 A.M. when she walked into the bungalow. John was asleep on the couch, and Novello was in an armchair writing on a yellow legal pad. Papers, food, bottles, ashtrays, clothes were thrown all around. "Be careful not to make a mess in here," Novello said. He added that he felt bad that she had been hauled out in the middle of the night.

"Well, I'm here. What needs to be done?"

"As you can see, John is asleep," Novello said, going over to shake him. "Penny's here. Penny's here."

John woke up long enough to say "Hi, Penny," and went back to sleep. His snoring was incredibly loud. A few minutes later he got up, went to the refrigerator and took out something to eat. He got out some cocaine, chopped a few lines with a razor on a picture and snorted some. "Help yourself whenever you want," he said to Selwyn. The cocaine woke him up, and he asked Novello, "So where are we? How far did you get?"

Penny reviewed a section with Novello. It was confused, with photocopied pages from the old and new drafts mixed with yellow legal pad inserts. The planned rewrite had turned into much more. They were changing the whole thing—plot, jokes, characters, even some of the names.

With several trips to the pile of coke, John managed to stay up, and by about 6 A.M. they had 31 pages, which Selwyn took down to the waiting limo and then to Barbara's Place, a 24-hour Hollywood typing and reproduction service.

During the day Novello and John sifted through another section of the script, with John contributing occasional ideas and Novello executing them. By 7 P.M. another 29 pages were ready for Barbara's Place.

That night, Thursday, February 18, John invited Peter Aykroyd over to help write one of the opening shots for the movie—an aerial view of the rocky coastline and lush hills of the Sonoma County wine region and Highway 101. Peter was pushing and tried for several hours to insert some laugh lines. Novello was wondering why they were spending so long on a technical matter of how to pan in with a camera from a helicopter. It was only a paragraph or two. But Peter was spaced out, insistent and anxious to help. After a while John, despite his fondness for Peter, was dropping hints that perhaps he should leave. There was writing to be done. Novello went to his own room in the Chateau for a while.

Early in the morning John asked Peter how he thought each of them would die. Peter guessed he would die of a head injury at about thirty-five.

"I'll die in a flaming jet crash," John said, "and it will be spectacular."

Peter said he thought John would probably go out in his sleep.

When Novello returned, they got back to the opening aerial shot. Peter was out of hand. He was being unreasonable, loud and aggressive.

"Let's finish this," John said, and turned to Peter. "And we'll see you tomorrow."

Peter was not getting the message.

"Peter, *leave!*" John shouted, slamming his fist down on a table, shattering a glass. It cut John's hand and snapped Peter's daze. At last he left.

Later, Anne Beatts saw Novello. "How's John?" she asked.

"Fine," Novello said. "We're working nights."

"Is John doing coke?" Nights and John meant cocaine.

"Yes, on occasion."

"Aren't you worried?" John knew no such thing as doing coke "on occasion."

"No," Novello said, "he's learned."

Beatts was incredulous.

Novello told Bill Wallace that coke was necessary for the night cramming. They were on the home stretch and had to squeeze as much work as possible out of a 24-hour day.

FRIDAY, FEBRUARY 19

The next day, Joel Briskin took $600 in cash to John. He knew it was for cocaine. He said to Penny, "Do you realize he's going through a ton of this stuff?" She did, but after weeks of relative inaction on the script,

Novello and Belushi seemed to have achieved a certain momentum. Perhaps the cocaine was the price to pay.

Later John called Gary Watkins for more—using the code word "watermelon." He told Selwyn to make the pickup and gave her $500 for five grams. Take the Mercedes, he said.

Selwyn, certain John could talk anyone into anything, drove to Watkins's home at 1202 Harper, a few blocks south of Sunset. After she handed over the money for the drugs, she broke into a cold sweat and vowed, Never again.

After she returned to the bungalow, the phone rang. It was actor Robert De Niro. John loved De Niro, called him "Bobby D." Several years before, the two had taken some cocaine together and De Niro had hurt himself and had had to get stitches.

"Yeah," John answered into the phone, "I got some." Pause. "No one," John said. He hung up and turned anxiously to Selwyn. "He's coming over to get blow. He's totally paranoid, and you'll have to hide. I promised no one would be here."

John called Novello. Come on up, he said, there's someone I want you to meet. Selwyn went down to Novello's, and Novello walked up the steps from his room down by the pool.

In bungalow 3, John introduced his two friends. Novello had written a comedy script about a Mafia trainee, *A Man Called Sporacaione,* and John promoted it to De Niro. They discussed Italy and the *Godfather* movies. Just before midnight, John and De Niro went to the Playboy mansion and stayed for about 2½ hours.

DeNiro, thirty-eight, adapted his five foot ten frame to his characterization, gaining 60 pounds to play boxer Jake LaMotta in *Raging Bull* (for which he won the best actor Academy Award), dropping 35 to play the psychopathic cabby-assassin in *Taxi Driver*. He had also won an Academy Award for best supporting actor for the young Vito Corleone in *The Godfather, Part II*. Once dubbed "The Phantom of the Cinema" by *Time* magazine, the reclusive De Niro played his roles with clinical concentration. "My joy as an actor," he once remarked, "is to live different lives without risking the real-life consequences."

His immersion in character roles, "method acting," was famous. "There is a certain combination of anarchy and discipline in the way I work," he said in 1977. "The physical feeling of the character, the props, costumes, the way he stands, gestures. I am aware of the physical. It is important. Sometimes it is easier to distinguish a character physically. . . . People don't try to show you their feelings, they try to hide them.

"You know what I wonder about? Indecision. I think about it. There are so many alternatives one can take in life. I think about guilt. I wonder why people feel guilty about things they have nothing to do with. If I do something out of weakness, I feel guilty. If it turns out bad, I feel guilty. If it turns out good, I feel guilty."

Tim Kazurinsky answered the telephone in his dressing room at "Saturday Night Live" and heard Belushi in hysterics. Someone had written a letter to *Rolling Stone* magazine about their recent long feature story on him. Listen to this, John said: " 'Your article on John Belushi was cute. That's all—cute. That kind of reporting can be characterized in one sentence: "The operation was a success, but the patient died." Come on, give us more meat. The cover photo was great. However, my curiosity concerning our greatest American folk hero has not been satiated.' "

John roared some more, obviously pleased, and went back over the letter to hit the high points: "Give us more meat!" he shouted into the phone, barely able to contain his laughter. "Our greatest American folk hero!"

"That's a pretty tough bill to fill," Kazurinsky said to John. "America's greatest folk hero."

SATURDAY, FEBRUARY 20

By midday the next day, Novello and Selwyn decided to bring in someone for an all-night marathon typing session. They found a woman named Leslie Werner through a temporary help agency. Werner, thirty-eight, arrived about 5 P.M. John was asleep in the back bedroom. Penny told her, "I've got to warn you. John and Don have been up a lot. Tempers could be short. This is really crazy."

Werner, a slightly heavyset woman with a sweet face, took a section to type and quickly realized that there were a lot of repetitions and many things that did not make sense.

A little after 8 P.M. John came out, showered and smiling. Werner thought he looked like a cross between Zero Mostel and a shaggy beast. At 1 A.M., they needed to know where Mogen David wine was made for the New York wine-tasting contest scene. When they had no luck getting the information over the phone, John announced that he would find a liquor store and get it from the label. He drove down Sunset to Gil Turner's liquor store, a Hollywood fixture. Run by Turner himself from a paneled office with eight closed-circuit TV monitors and a public address system, which he used freely, the store boasted the largest wine collection in Southern California.

It was around closing time when John arrived, and there were dozens of people in line. He went behind the counter and became pushy, wanting answers, demanding service. Turner came out of his office and told him to cool down. John, who seemed stoned, flicked a cigarette at him. Several clerks moved on him, but Turner grabbed him by the arm and escorted him to the door, which was promptly locked. John had lost his car keys, and he started pounding on the glass door. The clerks couldn't find them in the store. John continued to bang on the glass, but he finally left, abandoning his car. It was after sunrise by the time he made his way back to the bungalow. He stormed in, issuing wild threats, and then made some frantic telephone calls and finally went back to bed.

SUNDAY, FEBRUARY 21

Several hours later the next day John got up and was off to a party in Benedict Canyon at a house that Michael O'Donoghue and Carol Caldwell were renting.

De Niro came with his two young children, and actor Christopher Walken was also there. Caldwell tried to make Walken comfortable. Three months before he had been present on Robert Wagner's yacht when Natalie Wood had drowned during the night. When Caldwell touched Walken, he seemed almost to jump out of his skin.

The members of the Fear band were there. Lee Ving, the guitarist, was glad to have John on their side; Belushi still seemed dedicated to their success, in spite of the negative response there had been to their Halloween appearance on "Saturday Night Live."

"Don't worry," John said. "It will happen soon. It's happening."

John went back to a bedroom and threw up. Caldwell, who by this time was drunk, came back and asked John if he was okay.

Of course, he assured her. "I can't stay. Got to go finish the script."

Caldwell brought some Fear members to the bedroom to comfort him, but he soon took her aside. "Come back here, you need some coke . . . you're hostessing and you need some."

She protested, but when John put some on her hand, she snorted it. Within minutes she felt slightly sick and had to lie down on the bed; then she was overcome by nausea. Soon she couldn't move her fingers and her eyes wouldn't focus. She lay immobile. My God, that's heroin, she thought. Heroin could make you immobile. Maybe someone had convinced John that it would slow the speeding from the cocaine.

Lucy Fisher, the Warner Brothers vice president, had not seen or heard from John since she advised him not to take on the *Sweet Deception* movie. She went over and sat on his lap, kissed him and gave him a hug.

John didn't respond. For the first time she couldn't break through. He looked horrible and fat.

Harold Ramis noticed that John was flushed and that his eyes were drooping. John came over to Ramis and silently put his arms around him, dropped his head on his shoulder and moaned softly, "Oh, Harold."

By 8:15 P.M., Belushi was back at the Chateau. He didn't have his keys and climbed over the gate to get in.

"Is Don gone?" he asked Werner, who had been working for 27 hours, with only 4 hours of sleep on the couch.

Yes, she said. He had to go meet someone for dinner.

"Do you like him?"

"Sure."

"He's the best. Is it all done?"

"Yes," Werner said, "I've got to take it now." She had the last 48 pages ready for retyping and photocopying, and Novello was going to pick it up from Barbara's Place after dinner.

"Oh, you have to go now?" John asked.

Werner saw something plaintive. He was pleading. John hugged her. "I want to give you something," he said. "What do you want?"

She hesitated.

"What do you want? Want my guitar?"

Werner said she would love something she could frame and keep. It was obvious that Belushi was on drugs. He was so worked up that she felt a sense of danger. John went to the living room and started looking through the piles of paper. His body and hands were flying around. Werner wanted him to relax. She urged him not to look so hard.

"What are you looking for?" she finally asked. He was rooting around in the debris, and breathing heavily.

"There is the scene—my favorite scene," he said, sending stacks of paper floating into the air. At last he pulled two pages out, got a stapler and, his hands working awkwardly, stapled the pages together. He grabbed a ballpoint pen and scribbled at the bottom: "Thanks. Could not be done without you. Love, John Belushi. XXX. Feb. 21, 82."

Werner read the two pages. Johnny Glorioso, John's character, and the female lead, Christine, had just slept together:

JOHNNY: Why can't you be straight with me? I could tell you enjoyed it as much as I did. Maybe more.

CHRISTINE: Do you know why I went to bed with you? It was because you were there. Did you ever hear them say the reason they climbed the mountain was because it was there? Well, it was the same with you. It was because you were here, that's all!

JOHNNY: You're not so tough. Beneath the cold exterior is a warm and vulnerable woman.

CHRISTINE: Beneath this cold exterior is a cold interior. You're a sweet guy, Johnny. And I'm a spoiled and pampered woman. When I was 18, I met a rich man and ran off to New York with him. Then I met another rich man and then another and the rest is history.

JOHNNY: So you fucked 'em all, huh?

Werner wasn't sure what it meant or why he had selected it. John looked at her and said, "You sure you have to leave?"

She said she did. John went to On the Rox.

MONDAY, FEBRUARY 22

About 6 A.M. the next day, John arrived back at the bungalow. Novello, who had to fly that morning to San Francisco and then on to Toronto, was disappointed in John. They had worked well on Wednesday and Thursday, but then John had simply dropped out. For the past three days he had been only a face coming or going, or a shape under the bed covers.

"Where have you been?" Novello asked tensely.

"Out celebrating," John said. Novello's thin face fell.

"I celebrated for the both of us," John added.

They decided to eat breakfast at Schwab's. The few finishing touches on the script could be made by Novello in the limousine on the way to the airport. And Novello would call later in the day with any additional changes. They were both convinced they had a terrific script.

That day John received four separate cash disbursements—$500, $500, $400 and $400—from Brillstein's office.

By late afternoon Selwyn had the last changes that Novello had phoned in from a gas station in San Francisco. She went to Barbara's Place, and soon John appeared, wearing a black tuxedo jacket and sneakers, to oversee the production of the finished script. He moved into the manager's office, phoned Briskin and demanded that he come down with the maps of the wine country. There were decisions to be made—the color of the binder, the typeface for the title.

When Briskin arrived, John had the place in turmoil. He was treating the script like a top-secret document, carefully limiting the distribution, not wanting the Paramount executives to see it yet. And producer Stanley Chase shouldn't see it either, John decided.

John chose burgundy for the color of the binder but was complaining loudly. "I wasn't meant to do this," he told Briskin, Selwyn and anyone else who would listen. "Why isn't Judy here? She should do this. This is her field."

John told Les Miller, who worked at Barbara's, that the typing had to be done so that the script was exactly 126 pages. Miller figured it was some good-luck number for John or Novello. John chose gold lettering and ordered his limo driver to go out and get some soda water and beer.

Then there was the question of the title page. Since the script was an adaptation of the earlier *Sweet Deception,* it had to say so: "By Don Novello, adapted from . . ."

No, John decided, his name should be on it too. "By Don Novello and John Belushi, adapted from . . ."

Penny talked to Novello in San Francisco on a few points. She mentioned the credit line—Novello and Belushi. Novello asked to speak with Belushi. John threw everyone out of the office and closed the door. "Okay, no authors!" he shouted. "No names on the credit line!" Novello was thunderstruck. All that work and no byline? The title page was in and out with various combinations. They finally agreed to share the credit, still listing Novello first.

John called Jeremy Rain. He needed some rest, he said, and he couldn't relax at the Chateau. Could she leave work and let him into her house on Cynthia?

She said okay.

Several copies of the script were made, and Belushi left the original to be retyped again and bound. Back in the limo, he directed the driver to Century City and to Mike Ovitz's plush offices. Unannounced, script copies and maps in tow, John blew into Ovitz's office and delivered a flurry of incoherent summaries about how hard he had been working, about the production, the sets, where they were going to shoot. Dragging out the maps, he pointed to certain vineyards and tried to show his mastery of the subject and script. He was making no sense.

Ovitz was stunned. He had heard about the Belushi Binge, but he had never seen it. John's self-parody was wrenching. When John left, he couldn't find his way out of the office down to his limo, and Ovitz summoned two people from the mailroom to show him.

Ovitz called Brillstein to sound a sharp warning. Later he reached Dan Aykroyd, and they talked for a long time. Aykroyd said that maybe he should get on a plane and come help straighten John out, take him out of that Hollywood environment.

John went to Rain's house and slept for an hour. When he woke up, he told her that he had to go to a dinner party. Bill Wallace's girlfriend, Susan Morton, was making a pasta and fruit salad dinner as a thank you for the new stereo system.

John arrived and tried to unwind, but both Wallace and Morton noticed that he couldn't let go of the script. Morton felt particularly sad; the legendary eater hardly touched his food. He played the sound track from the movie *Chariots of Fire* on the new equipment and made some suggestions about mounting the speakers.

John said he'd read them Johnny Glorioso and Christine's meeting on the flight to the wine contest in New York: Christine was debating what wine to drink; the punchline was that the wine tasted like Janitor in a Drum.

Wallace and Morton told him it was funny.

"I better get going," John said. "Got things to do."

He went to Gary Watkins's house, then to April Milstead's, and finally, at 11:38 P.M., he pulled into the Playboy mansion by himself. He stayed for about two hours and left at precisely the time 1978's Playmate of the Year Debra Jo Fondren left in her own car, 1:41 A.M. John and Fondren stopped back at Milstead and Pearson's place on Martel.

"I got to get some coke so I can get up on that airplane and go back to New York," John said. He was going home the next day. He seemed very unhappy about leaving. Milstead asked why he was going.

"I'm going to get some sleep," John said.

Milstead had lots of cocaine that night, and Fondren used several hundred dollars' worth. Milstead had rarely seen anything like it. At the end of the night, it turned out that Fondren didn't have the money to pay. Milstead realized that she would have to dispatch someone to get the money from Fondren.

TUESDAY, FEBRUARY 23

The next morning the bound copies of *Noble Rot* were ready and John was on the 9 o'clock Pan Am flight to New York.

At the Paramount lot, after weeks of waiting, Jay Sandrich took a copy of the script into his office. He closed the door to read.

"OPEN ON: COCKPIT OF CARGO PLANE—DARK—OVERCAST DAY" There were six quick scenes in which a young pilot intentionally ditches his plane in the ocean to deliver a small steel box to two Portuguese fishermen.

Sandrich recalled that the original *Sweet Deception* had begun at the TWA terminal at Kennedy Airport with the main character, David Reed, "a simple honest guy," meeting Christine Walsh.

The new script "SMASH CUTS TO NORTHERN CALIFORNIA—BRIGHT SUNNY DAY," as the police bring in, not David Reed, but Johnny Glorioso, "wearing crumpled clothes, a four days' growth of facial hair and handcuffs." The father compares the son to the fungus—the noble rot that creates the best wine.

The father's speech went on for a page, 250 words. Comedy, Sandrich knew, depends on fast pace and interaction. He read on in bewilderment. The wine label was a skull and lightning bolt! There were a number of references to drugs.

Sandrich was not laughing. He didn't like the principal character; there were no romantic possibilities in him. And the woman was hateful —hard and manipulative.

He got up and went to see Stanley Chase. "I'm at page 40 and have not laughed yet." He went back to his office and continued reading. There were fast cars, limos, Mercedes, talk of death, references to Belushi friends like Keith Richards, Hugh Hefner and Robert De Niro.

At the end Christine double-crosses Johnny, and he double-crosses her back and gets the diamonds. The comedy, the romance, the adventure, had been obliterated. In *Sweet Deception,* the antihero wins over the woman. He hides the diamonds in a wine bottle, and in the climactic celebration, he pours them into their champagne glasses.

Sandrich and Chase went to lunch. "I may not do this movie," Sandrich stated.

Chase said he could get another writer.

"I think this is what John wants," Sandrich replied.

Sandrich took the script home and read it again. He was hard pressed to find a funny line, but more important, there was not one character an audience could identify with or care about.

That afternoon Bernie Brillstein settled into his first-class seat on the British Airways flight to London, where he was going on Muppets business. He had saved *Noble Rot* for the 9½-hour flight.

Brillstein approached a script like a date with a woman: You could tell how it was going to work out in the first fifteen minutes. On the top of page 15, Johnny and Christine were on the plane. He says, "I'll tell you something I bet you don't know. There are only three beverages mentioned in the Bible and wine is one of them. . . . Wine. Water and milk. Those are the three." Brillstein felt like jumping out the window.

Halfway through, Brillstein could see more problems. Boy, are we in trouble, he thought. There were too many autobiographical droplets from John's life. It looked as if Novello, a good writer, had been intimidated by John. The absurd part was that nothing was funny.

At about 6 P.M., John arrived at Kennedy airport, and a limousine took him to Morton Street. Judy was not home. He called Ovitz in Los Angeles, and they talked for five minutes; Ovitz was having some of his people read the script, he said, and held off on his reaction.

Judy had been meeting with Anne Beatts about another book—a parody introduction to women's literature. When it was time for John to arrive, she raced out. Deeply suspicious about what had been going on in California, she returned to Morton Street to find John asleep. She looked through the clothes he had brought from Los Angeles and found a lot of cocaine. She tossed it into the fireplace.

WEDNESDAY, FEBRUARY 24

In Los Angeles the next day, Ovitz read the script with apprehension. It was awful, reflecting the drug-crazed atmosphere in which it had obviously been written. And Ovitz, the salesman, was alert to the fact that the script didn't deliver what John had promised Paramount and Eisner. It wasn't what they had sold. This was not Bluto in any form. Several people in Ovitz's office read it and had more savage things to say.

Ovitz called Sandrich.

"Hi, Mike," Sandrich said.

"It's terrible," Ovitz said. "No one will ever make this picture." Don't talk to John, Ovitz said. We've got to discuss this and work out a strategy.

When Brillstein arrived in London, he called his wife, Deborah. "We got trouble," he told her. She urged him to read it again, to give it another chance. He did, knowing that John's comedy was not on the page but in his performance. If this was the movie in which John was going to let his pants down again, Brillstein couldn't see any pants on the floor. Nor could he find a sustained laugh. He called Ovitz. "How much trouble are we in?"

Big, major, total, Ovitz said. The script not only failed, but it was bad for them, as a business team, to have sold such a product. It might be possible to fix, he said, but the chances were slim.

It was not a time for big speeches. Brillstein wondered if anyone from Paramount had weighed in with an opinion.

Not yet, Ovitz said grimly.

"I've got to talk to John," Brillstein said. As he hung up, the phone rang. It was John, who had just awakened, calling from New York, where it was 1 P.M. John had not put himself on the line as a creator in a long time, so Brillstein wanted to start tenderly. "It needs a lot of work, John."

John said the fixes would be easy.

Brillstein said he didn't agree, and Ovitz also had problems.

All we have to do is sit down with Paramount, John said.

It's more complicated than that, Brillstein said. He did not feel it was the moment to come down hard. After all, he didn't know what Paramount thought, and the executives there were the ones that counted; people always had radically different opinions about scripts, and everything else in the business.

"I know this character," John said. "It's me. I'll make it work. They're committed. I'll fix it."

Brillstein called Novello in Canada. He was franker with Novello. The script was not okay, and they would have to stay in touch.

At Morton Street, John began a round of phone calls. Just before 2 P.M. he called Ovitz and left a message. By four-thirty he had reached Novello. "They don't like the script," John said. "I'll have to go talk the script to them now."

Fuck 'em, Novello said. This is character humor. It may not be in the script, he said. Some of these things are not necessarily funny on paper. "Food Fight!" wasn't intrinsically funny, but it was hysterical when John announced it in *Animal House*. They had to take into account John's performance; that's when things would come alive.

Just before 5 P.M., John left another message for Ovitz. From 5:01 to 6:46 he tried Paramount five times. Just after 8 P.M. he got his sister Marian on the phone and talked about summer plans. He told his eleven-year-old nephew, Adam, how to deal with a bully: Beat the crap out of him.

At 10:15 P.M., John took a cab to the Odeon, his favorite restaurant. He went on to the Blues Bar, where he met Danny Aykroyd and Michael Budman, the owner of Roots footwear, a shoe store and clothing manufacturer in Toronto. Budman had known John for several years and often gave him clothes.

Bob Beauchamp, the fashion director of *Gentlemen's Quarterly,* and a date, Linda Hobler, arrived with Betty Buckley, John's old pal from *Lemmings* days. She had just finished filming *Tender Mercies* with Robert Duvall. Belushi was behind the bar wearing a plaid shirt with the sleeves rolled up, reminding Beauchamp and his date of Jackie Gleason.

A big brown bag of pot was brought out, and John and Dan got up and danced a routine from the Blues Brothers.

Buckley withdrew from the macho humor. John and Aykroyd were having an unarticulated pseudo-druggie communication.

Pretty soon a pile of cocaine was placed on the bar. Buckley was astonished at the amount—not the tiny bottles of earlier, less successful times, but a huge pile. Some of them scooped it up with a piece of paper, almost like a shovel, and snorted it. John, in particular, was taking large amounts.

Buckley was surprised that John was using so much in front of her. He knew she had stopped, and she thought he might have been concerned about her reaction, perhaps even refrained in her presence. But that would have taken extraordinary discipline. She knew the drug trap well —intense dramatic encounters, communications that seemed to have meaning. Slums like the Blues Bar suddenly looked attractive.

She sat at the bar drinking her beer. She was in a dive when John came over and sat down. It was one of his outreach programs. He told her how much he liked her, attempting to bring their closeness to life. She was truly happy to see him, and she wanted to connect. But the cocaine was a barrier.

John wanted to talk about the punk music on the jukebox. They used to talk about the past, the old street music, blues, rock and roll.

"Punk *demands* a response," John said. That was the new music. Listening could no longer be passive. The audience had to be made to respond—slam dance, scream, make a gesture of some kind.

Buckley thought that they weren't talking about music, they were talking about boredom. John could live now only on the outer edges, in a state of overstimulation.

"Why are you doing all these drugs?" she asked finally. "What are you doing all this for? This is not good for you."

John didn't reply. Buckley thought he wanted her to demand a response, to force an answer, as she had done nine years earlier when she had pushed him up against a wall after *Lemmings*. Distraught, she looked into his eyes; she wanted desperately to find him. But she would have had to reach inside and pull him out.

He told her about *Noble Rot* and the rejection.

Buckley realized John could talk about his feelings with her. The script was his attempt to tell about himself, how a noble young kid moves and grows. It seemed to be a dramatization of everything that was most rebellious in him—his bad-boy reputation, the Blues Brothers' mystique, drugs, the Blues Bar, music. It all lived in John, and it seemed that he had found a way to put his feelings on the screen. When the studio rejected the script, they rejected John, and the impact was sharp and personal.

As he talked on, Buckley realized that John was not addressing the practical side of the issue; the outpouring was all personal. It was big business, show business, she told him. He had so much money and success that he had lost perspective and now he wanted total artistic license. Instead of paying the small price of working and reasoning with the authorities—the agents and studio executives—he was acting like a petulant child—Mr. No Compromise. It seemed to Buckley that he was taking his anger out on himself, as if one more line of coke would dull the pain or change the rules of the game.

It was after 2 A.M. when Judy called John at the bar.

Hobler asked him, "Did your wife want to know when you're coming home?"

"My wife wants to know *if* I'm coming home," John said, arching an eyebrow.

A private communication between Aykroyd and Budman indicated that Budman was in charge of John for the rest of the night. Aykroyd went up to John, punched him in the arm affectionately and said, "Take it easy tonight and get home, okay?"

John clearly wanted the night to continue, and they all crowded into Budman's limousine and headed uptown. John sat in the front seat and began playing with the radio, switching stations, trying to take care of Buckley, who was depressed. "This?" he asked, turning around and looking at her in the back seat. "Do you like this music?" In quiet despair, she answered yes or no each time. He finally tuned into a jazz station, knowing that she'd like that.

Beauchamp and Hobler were dropped off, and John got in the back with Buckley.

"It's just a movie," she said. Take a vacation, a break, don't move so fast. Go to the islands, sit in the sun and don't do any drugs. It's just a script, and you can make it work. But you have to work with them.

John said they weren't letting him be who he was.

She reminded him that he was playing at the highest level for big bucks and big fame. They had just rejected a first draft.

Buckley wasn't buying his childish assumption that "they" were supposed to let him do anything he wanted; it was too easy to blame the business. John had accepted the high-echelon game plan—the money and fame—and he had to accept the boredom and discipline that were part of that. He had a choice: Be self-destructive or grow up. In her own mind she kept coming back to the cocaine—too fast, too insidious.

As she attacked around the edges of his bitterness, John finally asked for her advice.

"You've got to stop doing drugs," she said.

The limousine pulled up in front of the Carlyle Hotel, and John and Budman wanted Buckley to come upstairs with them.

"No," she said. "I'm going home." It was the first time that Buckley had ever checked out on Belushi before 4 A.M. John seemed disappointed, but she was determined. He walked around the back and opened the door, and for one moment his eyes were clear and he was all there.

"I know it all seems down, Buckley," he said, "but it's only temporary. The next time you see me, it's going to be great."

He shut the door and the limousine drove her home. When she arrived, she started to cry.

John went up to Budman's room, where they talked for a while and he made a few phone calls. Later, he hit some after-hours spots, and around sunrise went home and went to sleep.

THURSDAY, FEBRUARY 25

When John woke up late the next day, he had a series of phone calls, including a 24-minute talk with Novello and a four-minute conversation with Ovitz. Early the next morning, at one-forty, he talked for 15 minutes with Tino Insana, whose advice he frequently sought on business and personal matters. John had decided to return to Los Angeles. His strength was his presence, and he had to reproduce the dinner when Eisner and Katzenberg had been howling on the floor.

He called the Chateau Marmont. He was going to be back Sunday night and had to have his old bungalow, number 3.

Soon after 4 A.M., John arrived at AM–PM, the trendy after-hours club. It was the perfect place for him; it didn't open until about 4 A.M., and it had VIP and VVIP rooms, a giant sound system and a mammoth dance floor.

Vito Bruno, the twenty-six-year-old owner, usually had his Rolls-Royce and driver standing by in case a celebrity or friend needed a car. He worked as an architect, but during the night, Bruno was willing to send out for drugs for someone like Belushi. That night John wanted a half-dozen Quaaludes. Bruno didn't like Quaaludes; they were dangerous. But he sent for them. John was flying and needed something to bring him down. After the drugs were delivered, John left.

FRIDAY, FEBRUARY 26

About 10 A.M., John walked into his office at Phantom on lower Fifth Avenue. He was wrecked. Usually there was a hug and a kiss for Karen Krenitsky, his secretary, but this time he hurried by, calling out, "Get me Steve Jordan."

Jordan, the drummer from the Blues Brothers band, was also a night person, and Karen apologized for waking him so early. John, who was back in his private office, picked up the phone. Can you get me some coke? he asked.

I'll check and call you right back, Jordan promised. It was better to help John get coke than to have John parade all over town in search of it. Jordan made several calls from his bed but struck out.

At Phantom, John, not having heard back from Jordan, was impatient, and he told Karen that he was leaving. He was at the elevator when Jordan called back. Karen rushed out to grab John, and he took the call in the outer office.

Jordan explained that he'd had no luck yet but he could get some soon. He told John to wait where he was; he'd be over shortly.

Who you calling? John asked. Who says no? "They don't trust me for the money?" He was astounded.

No, Jordan said, that was not the problem.

Who is it? Tell me, John insisted. Jordan gave John a name and number but told him not to call the contact directly.

John said he was tired, and Jordan thought he sounded depressed. He urged John to come over to his place, just a block down Fifth Avenue.

"I'll be right over," John said. Jordan waited most of the day, but John never came. John did, however, call Jordan's drug contact but apparently didn't get anything.

A limo picked John up outside Phantom and drove him to accountant Mark Lipsky's office, where he got $500 in cash. Shortly after that, Judy called Lipsky. John was distraught, she said; they had to keep cash away from him. Lipsky put out the word in the office that under no circumstances was Belushi to get any more money. It was ridiculous for John to have cash, Lipsky knew. The studio's per diem payment of $2,500 a week was absurd. Brillstein's office in L.A. got it and doled out cash to John whenever he wanted it. But Lipsky's office paid all the hotel, rental car, restaurant, On the Rox, American Express, phone, limousine and taxi-service bills—and everything else under the sun. John could live on zero cash: the support system was total. The only thing John had to pay for with cash were drugs, and that was clearly how he used the studio per diem.

In Los Angeles, Michael Eisner plowed through *Noble Rot*. He felt contempt. He wasn't going to make a movie like that at his studio. He phoned Ovitz. He could be candid with Mike, and he was relieved when he found that Ovitz recognized the script for the piece of shit it was.

Ovitz decided to be cooperative. Though the deal was pay or play—

technically and legally giving Belushi the upper hand—he did not want to cram the script down Paramount's throat. With so much money on the line, Eisner might be willing to find another movie project, and the pay-or-play contract could be shifted. Ovitz didn't want his clients getting money for no work.

Ovitz and Brillstein wanted Eisner to do the dirty work and deal with John. They warned him that John was intransigent.

On an average working day Eisner probably had to deliver as much bad news as good. He wasn't a rookie. He reached John by phone that afternoon. There are some problems, he said. I don't like the script very much; it doesn't work.

"We disagree," John said.

"I want to talk to you about it," Eisner said.

Coming on lightly, John said he'd fly out and Eisner would see how wrong he was. I'll be on the next plane and we'll spend the weekend together. I'll even stay at your house, John said.

John, Eisner said, I don't have any extra beds at my place.

"I'll sleep with your kids."

That's no good, Eisner said, joking back. He cherished his weekends, his kids. It could wait until Monday.

Okay, John said, I'll be there first thing Monday morning and we'll go sit in the steam baths, a great place on Pico Boulevard.

Eisner loathed steam baths. But if that was the price, he'd do it.

John said one thing had to be clear: It would be an endurance contest. They would sit in the Turkish bath until one convinced the other. None of these agreements to disagree.

Sure, Eisner said, glad the conversation was ending on a humorous note.

John headed to Mitch Glazer's apartment on Tenth Street, just off Fifth Avenue. He entered and took over the room, driving Glazer's new wife, Wendy, to the back bedroom. Sitting down by the coffee table and grabbing the phone, elbows out, John began to dial, informing Glazer that everyone was circling the wagons, with him and his new script on the outside. Ovitz and Brillstein should be on the outside with him, against Paramount, but they had caved.

John got Ovitz on the phone and explained that Eisner was negative.

Ovitz knew that an equivocation, a soft answer, might turn aside the fury, but he had to give it to John straight. "It needs some more work," he said, "and it shouldn't be done as it is."

"Why?" John snapped, his voice coiled and tense.

It's not good enough for you, Ovitz said. If the script had come in from another writer, I wouldn't recommend it. It's not funny enough. The comic premises are not funny enough to play off; you'd be left having to improvise too much. And, Ovitz emphasized, you *could* do that, but who needs it? There'd be too much pressure on you; the script itself should carry more of the weight.

John wanted more reasons.

Too much of the relationship was taken away from the woman; she was no longer a leading lady but an obstacle.

"I totally disagree," John said sharply. "What do you know about comedy? You have no idea what's funny."

"You're probably right," Ovitz said, "certainly compared to you. I'm just one voice, one opinion. I don't know a lot about comedy. Talk to others."

Others have read it, John said, and they love it.

You ought to have more people read it then, Ovitz said. There's no doubt you could make it work. But why put yourself under that kind of strain? Why improvise through an entire movie? You're at the top of the profession, and we have the luxury of being able to get a good script. Bring someone else in to work on it; having someone more removed frequently helps.

"I don't need to hear the truth from you. Just sell it." John told Ovitz that he clearly didn't know shit about comedy and maybe they should not be working together.

"That's your prerogative," Ovitz replied.

John hung up and told Glazer that Brillstein was next on the chopping block. "I'm going to fire fucking Bernie if he gives me any shit," John said, dialing London.

"I fired Ovitz," John told Brillstein.

"He's your best friend," Brillstein said. "What do you want—us not to tell you the truth?"

John railed on about Ovitz.

"Hold it," Brillstein said. "You haven't asked me what I think of the script. . . . Nothing happens."

"Fuck 'em. It's pay or play. Let them pay."

"John, it's a first draft. They're like this. It takes time." There's hardly a script in Hollywood that doesn't go through one, two—sometimes as many as half a dozen—soul-wrenching rewrites.

"I know this character," John repeated. "It's me."

The call ended without a second firing. John apparently was not willing to cut the cord with Brillstein.

Glazer, who had not seen John recently, thought he should roll better with the rejection. John put it in terms of fighting the system, fighting Hollywood and the clique of self-interested agents. It was a battle he could wage righteously.

What are you doing tonight? John asked.

Glazer said he was going to see Mink DeVille, a new-wave band, at the Savoy.

"Right. We'll all go, all four of us," John said, inviting himself and Judy.

By 4 P.M., John was at Dr. Wilbur Gould's to be treated for an earache. He learned that Carly Simon had been in earlier with a severe headache. John called her apartment on Central Park West and soon after arrived with a brown paper bag containing a large bottle of baby oil and alcohol. He stormed in, breathing heavily, with his script under his arm, and announced that he would give her a massage and drive her headache away.

Simon still loved John. His crazy, impulsive boldness broke down her acute shyness. And they were both reaching for more in their art.

John couldn't hide his distress; Hollywood was fighting him on the script, he said. He asked her to read it and give him her evaluation. Simon said she had to hear him read it; that was the only way it would come to life.

Helping himself to the entire apartment, John went into Simon's bedroom, where there were two phone extensions, picked up the phone and started dialing. He was calling one of the people fighting him in California, he said. "I want you to hear what these motherfuckers say."

The secretary who answered the phone said the person was out. John put his hand over the phone and whispered to Simon, "Bullshit, I heard he was there." John then shouted "Bullshit!" into the phone and slammed down the receiver. He reached in his pocket and took out some cocaine, snorted it, and then swallowed half a Quaalude.

After excoriating the movie bureaucracy some more, he lay back on Simon's bed for a moment. "Goddamn," he said, "it's not her fault." He called back the secretary to apologize. She understood. In fact, her boss had just walked in and would talk to John. John signaled Simon to pick up an extension. She did, reluctantly. All she heard was: "John, it's just not funny." Simon almost died for John as he began protesting. Feeling self-conscious, she got off the line.

After the call, John complained, "They don't have the imagination to see what it would be when it's directed."

John made a few more calls and finally collapsed on the bed and slept for an hour. He got up and played with Simon's kids for a few minutes. "I've got some great music," John said, pulling out the Fear tape. He had obviously forgotten about Simon's headache.

Simon, one of the best melody singers of soft rock, humored him. She could see that the more bullish he became, the more fragile he was. He related the entire *Noble Rot* story.

I'm no script reader, Simon said, but when you want to be funny, you can be hilarious. She did not want to be negative about anything since he was laying himself open so completely.

"How's Judy?" Simon asked.

"Fine."

Simon knew that Judy was at her wits' end, but again, it was not a moment to press on anything—Judy, the script, punk music, the drugs.

At 8 P.M., John left.

Later on at the Savoy, Glazer was not surprised to find that he and Judy and Wendy were waiting for John. About a third of the way through the performance John arrived and sat for a while at their banquette. But he was restless, going back and forth from the table to the phone. After the show he invited the band to the Blues Bar and went on ahead by himself.

At the Blues Bar, Aykroyd and John sat down over a few beers. John said his frustration with the business team of Ovitz and Brillstein had peaked, and he had just fired Ovitz.

Too radical a move, way too radical, Aykroyd said. He was taken aback by John's tone—harsh and uncompromising. Aykroyd had never seen him so down on their business team.

"It's only one script," Aykroyd said. Take a rest, let the business people handle it, go to the Vineyard, cool out.

No, John said, he was going out to Hollywood to meet with Paramount alone, stare them down with no one else around, no manager, no fucking agents.

Do it on the phone, Dan urged.

"No, no. I got to meet with them. Got to go out there."

Aykroyd could tell that John was on drugs, probably downers. "Take two weeks off. That's what I do as a writer," he said. He reminded John that it was always three, four or five passes, occasionally ten times through the mill for a script.

No, John said, this was different. The arrangements were made. He could deal with Eisner.

I'll help, Dan said. I'll sit down with you and make the script well. We'll fix it together. John had never really written anything, Aykroyd knew, had not learned how to suffer writer's rejection. It was a standard process.

Come on, John, Danny said, you have to write it and leave it alone. That's a writer's life; you know that. No matter how good a script it is, there is despair in knowing that it's going to have to be changed, fixed, even overhauled. It's awful to go write it over again, but that's the job. Happens to me all the time.

John was inconsolable.

The two friends talked about Judy and her new psychiatrist, Dr. Cohane.

"Ah, shit," John said, "you know her shrink is telling her yarns about me, telling her stories, telling her that I'm no good for her, telling her that I have a repetitious bent on partying and getting high and stuff." Dr. Cohane had told Judy that he might have a life pattern of binging, John said. Cohane said Judy's problem was how she was going to deal with it, because each binge and disappearance triggered recollections of the former ones, compounding the impact on her.

Aykroyd had had psychiatric counseling when he was twelve because of a nervous disorder, and it had helped. But one of his old girl-friends had a psychiatrist father, and she had spoken about him with such venom that it had left a lasting, negative impression.

"Well," Aykroyd said, "I hate shrinks, John. You know, we should blow them away. They're the worst . . . he's sowing the seeds of dishar-mony."

John was angry that someone else had the power to intrude on his relationship with Judy. How can I get her away from this man? he asked.

Put him away, Aykroyd suggested facetiously. Violence. He could not have agreed with John more.

When the mob arrived from the Savoy, the music and company seemed to put John in his element and bring him out of the dumps. Aykroyd couldn't face the crowd and left. John soon went out roving himself and stopped at JP's, a small bar on the Upper East Side, where he saw Jimmy Pullis, the owner. Pullis knew that he would have to give John some drugs if he wanted him to stay. It was almost a first principle: Share the coke, or you never saw John at your bar.

Also at JP's that night was Richard T. Bear, a twenty-nine-year-old piano player and singer who had appeared on some big-name albums—

including the sound-track from *The Blues Brothers* movie—but had never made it as a solo artist. His real name was Richard Gerstein, and he had known John since *Lemmings*. Besides music, the two had another love in common, and Bear generally had at least a gram with him. He hated to go to the regular gram dealers, who either cut and diluted the cocaine or charged an arm and a leg. Over time, Bear had developed a great connection and was willing to split an eighth of an ounce, 3.5 grams, with friends. Bear did not think of himself as a dealer. But a number of people, including John and actor Robin Williams, considered him someone who could provide cocaine regularly.

When John and Bear spotted each other, they exchanged warm greetings. Soon John, Bear, Pullis and several women left in John's limousine for Bear's apartment on York Avenue. At the apartment, John asked Bear about music for *Noble Rot*. He explained the opening scene. "But I got a problem," John added. "I went to Paramount and they don't think it's funny." He explained the movie some more. "I think it's funny."

"Yeah, John, when the band laughs for a comedian, that means you're bombing with the audience. We think it's funny, you know, and we got these little inside things. But the public ain't going to laugh at it. Maybe that's just what they're trying to tell you."

John got very upset. The script was funny; he was not the band laughing at his own inside jokes.

Bear had a lot of cocaine at his place that night—at least half an ounce (14 grams)—piled in one big mound in the kitchen. Pullis bought a gram for $120. He also noticed that John was scooping some into a small plastic bag while Bear was out of the room. Just then Bear walked in. John had taken about two grams. Though the pile was so big that it made no apparent difference in the size, Bear was surprised and asked John what was going on.

"I'll take care of it in L.A.," John said, explaining he didn't have any cash on him. Bear often played piano at the Improv in Los Angeles. John said he was returning to Los Angeles soon, and since Bear was going back also, he'd pay him there.

He left after a few minutes.

"That son of a bitch," Bear said to Pullis. "He didn't pay me. I'm going to get him in L.A." Bear was livid; it was one thing to come and use cocaine; it was another thing buying some; but it was outrageous to come and steal it.

Bear felt that John had changed. The theft showed a dark side. There was no longer anything recreational or social about John's cocaine use.

Pullis felt that Bear was overreacting and tried to calm him down. After all, it was only two grams, Pullis said. "You know John."

"Yeah, I know John," Bear replied. But this was over the line of decency, and he just didn't expect it from a guest and friend.

Later, John was back at the Blues Bar, and by 4 A.M., Glazer and his wife, Wendy, were going home. "Come on," John said, running out to them on the street. "You leaving so soon? Don't go yet." John leaned on Wendy very hard. Glazer knew that even when they were aware that John was doing a routine on them, they might still succumb. He felt he couldn't any longer be available to John for these late-night rounds. He took his wife home. Judy, too, had had enough. She went back to Morton Street.

About 5 A.M., John went back to the AM–PM club. Vito Bruno had been able to keep the after-hours club open for more than a year, making a handsome profit on the illegal sale of liquor. Drugs were readily available. In the crowded basement washroom, the loudest sound was often the sniffing. Drug transactions occurred regularly. Bruno had once stuck his head in the washroom and shouted, "This is the powder room, but not that kind of powder."

"I'm fucking still up," John groaned. He had not slept the night or day before. He wanted two grams of cocaine and two black beauties—a straight Methedrine (speed), which came in jet-black capsules and was one of the most potent uppers. Bruno saw that the drugs were provided, but he pulled John aside. In his best Italian-Brooklyn spirit of friendship, Bruno said, Hey, John, aren't you pushing this a little far, overdoing it some?

John gave no response but cocked his head back, as if he were looking at the point where the wall and ceiling intersected, and closed his eyes. The response seemed to say: "Oh, please, don't you say it too; not you on my case too?"

Bruno backed down, and John was on his way.

SATURDAY, FEBRUARY 27

About 8 A.M., John went back to Bear's place and finessed his way by the doorman. Bear was surprised to see him.

"I brought you the money for what I took," John said, handing him $240.

"Okay, John," Bear said.

John indicated, indirectly, that he was embarrassed.

"Look," Bear said, "I got to go because I have a meeting."

"Can you get me any blow or anything?" John asked.

"I don't have any," Bear said. "See?" The mound was used or sold.

"All right. Take my car and go to your meeting and come back." John wrote a note to the driver on the back of an airline ticket envelope saying, "Take my friend anywhere he wants to go. John."

"Can you make any calls?" John asked. "Can you get me anything?"

"It's nine o'clock in the morning!" Bear said.

John put on the pressure sweetly. Bear made a call, but he couldn't get through. He went to his meeting and came back, then got in touch with his connection, who brought over several grams.

John went back to Morton Street and climbed into bed.

That afternoon he woke up coughing and asked Judy what was wrong with him.

You're doing this to yourself, she said. He sounded like a drowning man, and he was spitting up blood.

"I'm out of control," he said. It was half a question, half a statement.

Yes, she said.

"I'm out of control!" he bellowed. He seemed to be both asserting it and asking for her evaluation. Then he went back to sleep, to wake up a few hours later.

"What did I take?" he asked. "Heroin?"

For an instant, this struck Judy as funny, and she had to laugh. Then John laughed. On top of everything else, it was too disturbing to think about. She knew he had almost a romantic notion about heroin—the great forbidden, the drug of last resort. But John seemed fine now, after his sleep.

John had given Glazer the copy of *Noble Rot* to read the day before, and he wanted it returned. He called Glazer and said, "I got to get the script back."

"But John, you just gave it to me and you wanted me to read it."

John was angry that Glazer hadn't done so. "You promised to read it!" John said, his voice rising to a scream. "Give it back now!"

"You're crazy," Glazer said. "We've been together since you gave it to me. When was I supposed to read it—in the bathroom at the Savoy?" He promised to read it right then and walk it over afterward.

Now! John insisted, and he handed the phone to Judy to referee.

Glazer called a taxi to deliver the script, and while he was waiting for the cab, he read nearly the first third. It was absurd to be too concerned about the script one way or the other. John rarely read the things until he got on the set, and anyway his performances were all face and body and action, seldom the words.

Director Jay Sandrich reached John from Los Angeles later in the afternoon. Sandrich, knowing the immense personal and emotional investment that could go into a script, felt sorry for John. He wanted to be gentle. He was angry that John had excluded him from the writing process, but now was not the time to bring up the machine guns.

The basic problem, Sandrich said, is that the romance is submerged, but you've done good things with your character—Johnny Glorioso.

"Best script I ever read, wonderful," John said.

Sandrich retreated. He didn't have to be the one to scuttle the movie. Clearly, Paramount would.

At 8:45 P.M., John called Brillstein, who had just returned home from London, and they talked for 25 minutes. Brillstein made his essential point: Ovitz is the best, and don't cut yourself off from him. John agreed to try to repair the damage.

Just after 9:30 P.M., John called Jeremy Rain in Los Angeles. Using the name "Jonathan Remmy" for her, apparently because Judy was around, John said he was coming to L.A. the next day and not to make any plans.

An hour later John and Judy went to the Sabor, a Cuban restaurant on Cornelia Street, to meet Michael and Carol Klenfner. They had a quick dinner because they wanted to catch the late showing of *Quest for Fire,* a much-praised film about prehistoric cave men and women searching for fire. John had seen the movie and loved it—"a fucking good movie"—and he wanted the others to see it, too. "Meet you there," John announced, getting up from the table. That was just a grubby excuse to get drugs, Judy knew. Klenfner promised John, "I'll get some blow." But John left and stopped back at Morton Street, where he called Ovitz at 11:56 P.M.

John assured Ovitz that everything would be resolved; no matter how strong their positions, they could find common ground. The firing was off. The call lasted two minutes.

The Ziegfeld Theater on West Fifty-fourth Street was crowded, and Klenfner and his wife sat right behind John and Judy. John fell asleep halfway through the film but woke up and walked out to the lobby.

After the movie Klenfner saw John with a bandanna wrapped around his head, looking like Mr. New Wave in his black engineer boots and fatigue pants, standing with a group of fans. "I was in that movie," he was joking. "Did you see me with the spear?"

They got into Klenfner's brown 1980 Buick Century and went to the Odeon. Klenfner drove and insisted that John sit next to him so the cigarette burns and the inevitable mess would be limited to the front seat. John slammed the Fear cassette into the car stereo system and started rocking intensely. Judy smoked some pot on the way.

At the Odeon, John slipped the Fear tape onto the music system. The lyrics, barely decipherable through the heavy instrumentation, reverberated through the chic restaurant like so many dinner plates sliding off a waiter's tray:

> . . . My house smells just like a zoo
> It's chock full of shit and puke
> Cockroaches on the walls
> Crabs are crawling on my balls
> I love living in the city
> Where junk's the king and the air smells shitty. . . .

Klenfner yanked the tape and put it in his pocket.

"Let's get him out of here," he said to Judy, guiding John to the door. At six feet two and nearly 300 pounds, with broad shoulders and a thick neck, Klenfner looked like a professional football player and was frequently taken for John's bodyguard. As they were getting into the car, John saw a group of Spanish men who looked like a small street gang.

How you guys doing? John said, walking over. You got any blow? In the drug skits on "Saturday Night Live," he told them, he was actually using real blow.

Klenfner moved in and tried to place himself between John and the group. John persisted, and while making his plea, he touched one of the men, perhaps too aggressively. Klenfner's heart was beating quickly by the time the gang drifted on. John, his bandanna askew now, was hyped up, dancing, almost punching the air. He opened his fly and began urinating against a wall.

"Hey, that's John Belushi peeing!" someone shouted from a passing car.

"Fuck you, faggot!" John yelled, and chased the car down the street.

Klenfner finally got him back into the front seat. "Let's not go home," John said. He turned to Judy and Carol. "I want you to see the places where I go at night. I want you to know where I go when I disappear."

Carol Klenfner was touched, sensing that John, the godfather to her four-year-old daughter Kate, was feeling vulnerable and needed companionship. He was going to share a secret with them.

The first stop was Stilwende, a bar decorated in the style of 1930s Berlin, four blocks north of the Odeon. Despite the crowd, the doorman saw John and let them in. John's heavy biker outfit contrasted sharply with the preppie look of the crowd. He hustled up to the sound booth, put the Fear tape on and took over the dance floor. Soon he had about 50 people slam dancing. After two songs the novelty wore off, and the tide turned quickly from John the charming to John the intimidating. Klenfner moved to get him outside.

It was now after 3 A.M., and they went to the Greene Street Restaurant in the SoHo district. The current "Saturday Night Live" cast was supposed to be having its postshow party there.

"He's really fucked up," Klenfner told the maitre d'. The party had already broken up, so they went back to the car, and John started giving directions, ordering Klenfner around. He knew no addresses and shouted "Turn left! Turn right! . . . Turn here!" He banged the window when Klenfner made a wrong turn.

"I'm not your fucking driver!" Klenfner shouted.

"Park here," John said, at an illegal spot near the AM–PM. The doorman knew John: it was his third night in a row.

Klenfner stuck to John like glue as they hit the VIP and VVIP rooms. John was wild, looking for drugs, announcing it, calling it out, and trying to lose Klenfner.

Carol was fed up and could hardly stay awake. The excitement of exploring John's mysterious nightlife had worn thin. She told her husband it was time to go home. Klenfner left with her, promising John and Judy he would return.

John found Vito Bruno and got a gram of coke. He marched up and put the Fear tape on the sound system. It was not well received. John began slam dancing on the packed floor. Judy was getting angrier and angrier, hanging in the background. John fell, tumbling down half a dozen steps, and Bruno was worried that he might have hurt himself. On the way out John got into a dispute with the bouncer and smacked him. Bruno was concerned. That was too dangerous. To get John moving on, he loaned him his Rolls-Royce and driver.

"I'm going back to L.A.," John said to Bruno. "See you. I don't know when."

John then said to Judy, "I'm going to take you to this club. It's really raunchy." They drove to a place around Third Avenue between Thirteenth and Fourteenth Streets. As she walked through the place behind John, hands grabbed at her, pinching and feeling. Facing John down, she explained she didn't like being mauled by a bunch of strangers.

"I didn't know they did that here," he answered.

After about 45 minutes, she wanted to go.

"I'm staying," he said.

It was no use arguing, and Judy walked out to find a cab. John followed. A limousine was parked on the street and John knocked on the window. "Would you take my wife home?" he asked. The people in the back wanted to take John instead. Just then a cab pulled up and Judy got in. It was the corner where they'd had their first apartment in New York in 1973.

As Judy's cab pulled away, she glanced back at John leaning against a car, almost wistfully watching her cab dart away in the predawn chill.

SUNDAY, FEBRUARY 28

By 7 A.M., Belushi was at the *schvitz* on Tenth Street, where he met Christopher Giercke, an underground moviemaker. Giercke was attempting to put together a movie project with Johnny Thunder, one of the original punk rockers. John got a $290 cash loan from the *schvitz,* which he put on his bill.

By early afternoon John was over at Giercke's fourth-floor apartment above an automobile repair shop at Hudson and Laight streets.

Jim Martin and Steve Aeister, two artists who had studios in the building, joined John and Giercke. Martin, a wood sculptor, was aghast at John's condition. He was first blasting the Fear tape, and then he seemed overcome with laughter at a pornographic comedy tape of a couple making love.

John had the bottom section of a cocaine grinding mill and was snorting coke out of it through a straw, not even bothering to make lines. Blood flaked around his nostrils, and Martin was sure John snorted several grams as he sat there.

About 1 P.M., Giercke called Marcia Resnick, the photographer who had taken pictures of John before Lorne Michaels's wedding. She said she had the contact sheets and would be right over. John asked her to bring the phone number for Laurel Rubin, a beautiful friend of Resnick's from Chicago whom John had met while filming *The Blues Brothers.*

Resnick knew that Giercke represented an extreme of counterculture. He was the rebellion and the underground that John flirted with, the hardcore. When she arrived at about four, Giercke was telling John how to join the alternative filmmaking world. John said he was fed up with Hollywood and that he wanted Giercke to do the movie about the Mafia trainee in Italy that he and Novello had discussed with De Niro. He needed to restructure his professional life, to get out of Hollywood, to ditch the establishment that was fucking over his projects.

Resnick gave John one of her postcard photographs of Laurel Rubin (a shot of Rubin from the back with her skirt hiked up to show her underwear). On the card, she wrote the phone number of Rubin's father in New York. She also returned John's *On the Waterfront* video tape, which he had left in her apartment.

John called the Chateau Marmont just before 5 P.M. to make sure he had bungalow number 3. And with his underground audience in attendance, he called Joel Briskin in L.A. "What the fuck plane am I on?" he bellowed. "Why do I have to set up the deal? . . . And you expect me to be there and do everything? You're fucking up."

"Do you have your tickets?" Briskin asked him.

"I don't know where anything is," John said, and hammered the phone into its cradle.

Briskin immediately called Judy at Morton Street. "He's making me nuts. Why's he yelling at me about what plane he's on? He knows damn well what plane he's on."

"He was out all night," Judy said. "I haven't seen him." For four years she and Briskin had talked about how they could help John. "We've got to do something," she said now. Maybe getting Smokey back, or perhaps she should talk to a doctor again; it might, she said, even be time to get him formally committed. She couldn't do it herself. And, she said, her concern was greatest when he was out *there,* in L.A.

Briskin said he had reached his limit; it wasn't just the behavior, but now the personal abuse as well.

"Things aren't getting any better," Judy admitted. "What can we do? I don't know how much longer I can take it. He's destroying me."

Briskin called Brillstein at home. "We're really going to have to put him away," Briskin said. "It's going to be up to you."

"I'll get into it," Brillstein said. "I'm here."

John soon called Judy. He seemed aware that she felt despondent. "What time am I supposed to be at the airport?" he asked.

The limousine is here, she said. So is Bill Wallace. "Shouldn't you come here?"

No, he said, I'm close to the airport.

What—how is that possible?

"I'm in New Jersey," John lied.

Judy agreed to pack his clothes but included only three shirts, hoping that would encourage an early return to New York.

John called a Communicar taxi from Giercke's, which picked him up outside at 5:25 P.M. Before he left the apartment, he opened the envelope containing Resnick's contact sheets. Small square-inch reproductions showed his sweaty face and greasy hair, the vacant eyes and fat body.

"These are terrible," he said, handing her back the sheets.

John met Bill Wallace at the airport, and he slept all the way to Los Angeles.

At Morton Street after 7 P.M., Judy tried to reach Tino Insana and Brillstein at their homes, but they weren't in.

After checking into bungalow 3 around 9:30 P.M., John called Leslie Marks, but she didn't answer. About 5 A.M., he rang the doorbell at Milstead and Pearson's Martel Street apartment. April got up to see who it was. "What are you doing here?" she asked, inviting him in.

"Couldn't stand New York. It was real boring. All I did was sleep."
Milstead laughed.

"I'm hungry. Can I have a couple of dollars to go get some food?"

Milstead was amused that a rich movie star had no money. She gave him $5. "You want some coke?" she asked. She had an eighth of an ounce, and they shared some. John left after about fifteen minutes, promising to call later.

Next he stopped by Jeremy Rain's on the edge of Beverly Hills. He had brought the *On the Waterfront* tape for her, but *Noble Rot* was the only thing on his mind. He had a copy of the script and read her the scene in which Johnny Glorioso shows up at a New York hotel, discovers that the only room available is a $250-a-night suite, and wonders aloud to the hotel desk clerk if they are charging so much because he looks like an Arab.

Rain sensed it was a genuine effort, though not very funny. She told him it worked when *he* did it.

John told her that he had no money and wanted to get some nasal spray. A few minutes later she caught him doing some coke. "You're not sick," she said. "You're doing it to yourself."

"It's not even good—lumps in it," John said. April's coke generally had lumps because it was so pure.

Rain and John then had a brief dispute over drugs, but he kept going back to the script. His friend Tino would fix it, he said. And the French movie director Louis Malle wanted to do it, he lied.

Rain asked about vineyards and wine. He gave a quick answer and said suddenly, "I wish you'd got a chance to see me play football."

"Maybe your mother has some old high school pictures," Rain said.

John's face seemed to light up. "No one could love a stomach like this."

Rain said she did, and gave him a hug. She really did care for him and worried that he didn't care enough for himself.

MONDAY, MARCH 1

Across town near the downtown section of Los Angeles, in a small apartment at 133½ Bimini Place, Catherine Evelyn Smith was getting up. Smith, thirty-five, had cut her heroin habit to about $25 a day, down from $500 a day in the good times when she'd been dealing. But she had close friends in the trade, and for $25 she could get what was referred to as half a tenth—one-half of 1/10 of a gram of heroin. At 70 percent purity, it kept her going.

That morning Smith and John Ponse, forty-seven, her roommate of three years, a Dutch Indonesian waiter at the Polo Lounge in the Beverly Hills Hotel, began the day at Jerry's Family Coffee Shop, 525 South Vermont Avenue. Ponse had breakfast. Smith had a double vodka with orange juice. Drinking made the heroin habit almost bearable, considering that the addiction kept her from sleeping. When it was time for her fix later in the day, she would already have the hot and cold sweats, would be shaking and feeling weak. Her muscles could ache to the bone. It was hard to think of food, and she was often swept with waves of physical nausea. Her sinus passages drained, her eyes were huge, she was depressed and crying a lot these days. It was a rotten life. Ponse thought Smith had a light addiction. On a scale of 1 to 10, she had a 6, and was getting by.

Smith's life had had its ups and downs. It had begun down. Born in a small town in Ontario, Canada, on April 25, 1947, she was put up for adoption by her natural parents. Her adoptive father was a salesman and his wife an ex–Ringling Brothers circus performer. Smith became pregnant at seventeen and had to give up her baby, a great trauma given her own adoption. She started dating Levon Helm, who went on to play the drums and sing for Bob Dylan's backup group, which later became The Band. The group recorded five gold albums in the late 1960s and early '70s. Smith went to Toronto and worked for a steel company. She was five feet six, with a very good figure, and was quite beautiful. She married a man named Paul Donnelly, but it lasted only thirteen months.

Smith met the folk-style singer-songwriter Gordon Lightfoot ("If You Could Read My Mind") and lived with him from 1972 to 1975. During that time she recorded the backup vocals for "High and Dry" on Lightfoot's "Sundown" album. From 1975 to 1977 she drove the tour bus for Hoyt Axton and also sang backup for him. Smith and Axton together wrote "Flash of Fire," which got on the charts briefly and continued to earn her modest royalties. In 1977 she was with Rick Danko, the bass player and a singer for The Band. Later Richard Manuel, also of The Band, flew Smith to California.

Once there Smith and Sandra Turkis, a stunning model called "Sam" who was a friend from Canada, rented a house in Bel Air and became deeply involved in the drug scene, hanging out with rock bands and going to parties.

Turkis was a friend of Ron Wood, the Rolling Stones guitarist, and used to spend some time at his home, where she saw just about every drug, though no needles. Turkis introduced Smith to the Rolling Stones, and Smith quickly latched onto them. They took her wherever they went. That began a period of jet-setting—Paradise Island, Paris, New York, skiing in Colorado. During this period, Smith was first introduced to heroin. By 1978 she had a very secret heroin habit that she kept from friends who were nonusers.

She had an even darker secret; she had become a dealer. Smith went to Thailand as a middleman under an assumed name to arrange for the purchase of a kilo (kilogram—1,000 grams, or about 2.2 pounds) of China White heroin for a dealer in the States. It took three weeks to recruit, coordinate and get passports for the carriers, and when the heroin was finally smuggled in, Smith never got the $10,000 she had been promised. She contacted a friend to see if she could have the dealer killed but never followed through.

The next year, 1979, Paul Azari, a thirty-three-year-old drug dealer who operated under thirteen aliases, was helping wealthy, prominent people leave Iran after the fall of the Shah. Some of these people had access to large amounts of pure heroin.

Azari arranged for the delivery of 19 kilos (about 42 pounds) of Persian Brown heroin to Smith's apartment, number 502 in the Sunset Towers on Sunset Boulevard at La Cienega. The street value was about $13 million ($700 a gram), and Azari had paid just under $4 million ($200 a gram). Smith sold the heroin, and Azari came by and picked up the money each day; Smith's share of the profit was taken out in heroin, which she kept in tin boxes in her closet. Instead of shooting, she smoked it, using a time-consuming method called "Chasing the Dragon." Putting a small amount of the brown, sandy-looking heroin on a piece of tinfoil, she heated the foil and tilted it so the heroin burned and ran down the sheet; she then inhaled ("chased") the fumes, using a tinfoil straw. While the heroin burned very slowly and sluggishly, she had to run it up and down the same piece of foil until it was all gone. The tinfoil straw collected pure residue, which was then put out on a new piece of foil and "chased."

Smith gave a lot of parties in her apartment, and she sold to hundreds of people—many she knew, many she didn't. Some were just faces, or people in cars, or chauffeurs in limousines. Several drivers delivered movie scripts with cash inside. Smith kept a small book with the names, phone numbers and addresses of her Hollywood customers.

One was Victor Marquez, a native of Colombia who had become an American citizen when he was a teenager. Marquez had lived in San Francisco, Detroit, Miami, Los Angeles and Bogota, Colombia. Using his Colombian connections, Marquez had started out importing marijuana and, after amassing enough money, became a marijuana financier, insulating himself through a web of underlings who made the transactions.

Smith's friend, Turkis, and Marquez lived together for several years. Both became addicted to heroin for about six months and kicked the habit only after a doctor rescued them by prescribing Valium and other drugs. Marquez continued financing large marijuana deals and used his smuggling profits to branch out into legitimate real estate transactions and shopping malls.

Smith was secretly sleeping with Marquez and had a temporary falling out with Turkis when Turkis discovered it. Smith set up a date for Turkis with Jack Nicholson and then told Marquez about it, causing a storm.

Another entry in Smith's address book was Gary Weis, who had made many of the short films for "Saturday Night Live" and had directed the movie *Wholly Moses,* which starred Dudley Moore. Weis used the Persian Brown while filming at night, and he was afraid that word about him and heroin might get around.

After eight months, the 19 kilos were gone, and Smith turned down other chances to deal large amounts. She was frightened of being caught.

By early 1982, Smith was relying on Ponse for money, and for a while he was willing to give her $50 a day for her habit. But in a period of deep anxiety, she had accidentally taken 50 Stelazine tranquilizer pills, thinking they were Valium. The paramedics had to be called and her stomach pumped. After that Ponse cut her back, but he often gave her $20. So her question each morning was where would she find the next fix, the next $25 or $5.

By 9 A.M. Monday, March 1, Smith was at Rudy's, a small, windowless bar with a pool table on Santa Monica Boulevard. There she could find a bookie to bet on the horses. If she won, there might be a little more money. While waiting, Smith exchanged jokes with the regulars. It was a life of jokes, waiting and heroin. By 4 P.M. she would hit happy hour at Theodore's Cafe on Santa Monica, where the juice and double vodkas were only $1.58.

John was not happy to hear that the Pico baths, where he was to meet Eisner, were closed that Monday. He had Seymour Frishman, a grandfather figure who was his regular masseur, come to the Chateau to give him a massage. Frishman kept a warmup table, oils and towels in his car. John could enjoy Frishman, who extolled the virtues of good health without pontificating about the side effects of fast living. Frishman worked on John's 220-pound body for about an hour.

Michael Eisner had not been looking forward to the 150-degree steam room and was delighted that the meeting was moved to the Chateau. When he arrived, he at first couldn't find number 3 because the bungalows were in back on Monteel Road and the entry to them did not connect through the lobby. After wandering in circles for a while, he finally found

John's bungalow. He was disgusted. There were pizza boxes thrown around; the place looked like a pigsty.

But Eisner had come armed with an idea. With the support of both Ovitz and Brillstein, he was going to talk Belushi out of *Noble Rot*. He wanted to shift the $1.85 million guarantee to another movie. In practice, pay or play was an agreement to do business; the contract gave each side leverage. It was time for Eisner to exercise that leverage by suggesting a new project, and he had the perfect candidate—*The Joy of Sex*.

Paramount had bought movie rights to the uninhibited sex manual years earlier. It had been offered to a dozen directors—currently it was being proposed for Penny Marshall—and the script had been through a number of rewrites. The current one, dated January 26, 1982, was a third revised final. Called *National Lampoon's The Joy of Sex, A Dirty Love Story*, all it needed was Belushi's name. Eisner called it a big idea, meaning big money.

John listened patiently and argued for *Noble Rot*. He dragged out maps of the wine country and started in on locations.

Eisner was stunned that someone would try to talk him into a script with a map. It made no sense. So he spent some time reviewing the problems with the script; essentially it was not funny and it was badly written, he said. He had to be frank.

Turning to *Joy,* Eisner tried to get the enthusiasm rolling. It's the subject, he said—Sex, Belushi, National Lampoon. That's a better comic premise than a wine and diamond caper. The *Joy* script is as bad as *Noble Rot,* he said, and we don't like it. But the broad theme—a child's, boy's and man's sexual initiation—has tremendous possibilities. Eisner said they were looking for John's point of view on that; it could be funny and even full of insight. And John could play all the stages of the main character's life, all the sexual rites and passages—the infant in diapers grabbing the aunt's breast, the six-year-old playing doctor with the girls, learning the facts of life, the college student, the old man.

John at once started improvising some sex material—his first date, picking up girls in a bar.

Eisner thought it very funny and original. Do John Belushi's version of a sex comedy, he said. Take the script and read it. See if it gives you any inspiration. It's a script that doesn't work. Make it work. What you're doing right here convinces me even more that it could be great— different and better than what Woody Allen did in *Everything You Always Wanted to Know About Sex.*

John agreed it would be funny if he played all the parts, but he wondered about Penny Marshall as director. It would be her first picture, and they had been close friends for years.

She's good and has a marvelous, natural sense of humor, Eisner said. She has immense potential as a director. But, he added, they did not have a deal yet, and Paramount was not absolutely committed to her.

Eisner and Belushi agreed to get together again soon; maybe with their wives some night at one of John's favorite clubs. Eisner left thinking that he was well on his way to changing John's mind.

At 3:40 P.M., John reached Leslie Marks and arranged to see her that night. He also found the postcard with the picture of Laurel Rubin. Through her father, John got her Chicago number and reached her there at 3:47 P.M. Rubin had a sweet, open voice, and she adored John. She hadn't heard from him in months, and now she bubbled.

John said he missed her and the times they had spent together during *Blues Brothers,* when they had ridden motor bikes and gone to the zoo. I miss Chicago, John said. "I wish I could just drop everything and come visit."

"John," she said, "I care for you. You're welcome in my house whenever you want. Call whenever you want."

Someone's at the door, John said, and he left for a few seconds. Rubin could hear a woman's voice; then John came back and said he would have to call back. She hung up feeling angry; her phone rang many times for several hours, and she assumed it was John. She didn't pick it up.

By about 6 P.M., John was at Rain's once again. "You've got to get me some money," he said.

Rain went to her bank and got $100 from the automatic teller's window. After she got back and gave John the money, a man came by to look at a room that was available to rent in Rain's house.

"I'm not safe anywhere!" John said, and he ran from the house.

Leslie Marks, the young woman John had met at a hot-tub club several weeks earlier, arrived at bungalow 3 and went with him fifteen blocks east down Sunset to Milstead's. April answered the door, and John insisted on coming in. He wanted some heroin, he said. Did she know where to get any? Just a little, perhaps a tenth of a gram. "Just get me what you can," he said.

The going rate for a tenth is about $60, Milstead said. Several weeks earlier, she had bought a tenth from Cathy Smith, whom she had met the previous fall at Dan Tana's, a bar on Santa Monica. Milstead could call

Cathy and get the heroin herself, and John would never even have to see Smith.

Smith was at her apartment watching TV when the phone rang that evening. She'd already had her own heroin for the day.

"John Belushi is in town and is looking for some stuff," Milstead said. "Can you get some?"

Smith had met John and talked with him briefly during the second season of "Saturday Night Live," when The Band were the musical guests, and also during the filming of *1941* three years before, when he'd been doing lots of cocaine. She had never associated him with heroin.

"I'll have to check and call you back," Smith replied.

Three years earlier Smith had formed a relationship with Janet Alli, a twenty-six-year-old Los Angeles native who was heavily involved in the local drug scene. Most serious heroin users lived in feast or famine. Good connections came and went; and at times, as in 1979 for Smith and in 1980 for Alli, there were opportunities to deal. Their salad days were over for now, but Alli had a good connection, a man named Lou Dolgoff, who supplied relatively pure China white. Smith called Alli. "Is there anything happening?" she asked.

"Yeah," Alli said.

"Can I come by and talk to you?" She didn't like to use Ponse's phone for drug transactions.

Alli said fine. Smith went out to her car, a light-blue 1964 Plymouth, the kind with the old push-button transmission. Ponse had bought it for her for $500.

It was raining hard, and the car wouldn't start; the battery had been acting up for some time. Smith flagged someone to jumper-start the car with cables. She went north several blocks and got on the Hollywood Freeway for less than three miles, then off and directly to 1958 Gramercy.

Alli was trying to organize several buys and to work out the logistics for delivery. She insisted on the cash first, and then she would deliver the heroin. Smith called Milstead to find out how much she and Belushi wanted.

A couple of hundred, Milstead said. That was enough for four-tenths of a gram—a good, long party, particularly for those who weren't regular users.

Smith said she'd come by Milstead's for the cash. "I have other places to go," Smith said, "and this has to be fast." She too had other customers to meet.

The three miles to Milstead's was a long drive in the rain. The apartment was set back, and Smith noticed a Mercedes in the driveway.

From inside, Pearson saw Smith arrive. "Ah, shit," he said. He had never liked her, going back to 1979 when they had been introduced by Keith Richards, lead guitarist for the Rolling Stones. Pearson had accompanied Richards when he went to Smith's apartment to buy some of her Persian brown, and Pearson had been struck by what a hard, chewed-up woman Smith seemed. He had seen her since from time to time, especially around Dan Tana's restaurant. He regretted having introduced her to Milstead. Obviously, they had become friends, and as far as Pearson was concerned, they were a little too simpatico.

Smith walked up to John's car. John was behind the wheel, and Leslie Marks was in the passenger's seat. Milstead was standing outside having an intense argument with John.

"Well, John," Milstead said, "are you going to do it or not?" John seemed worried that he was going to be ripped off and was asking questions. How long will it take to get the stuff? Where would they meet, here or at the Chateau? What was the quality? How many people were going to step on it (cut and dilute it) before it was delivered to him?

"Hi, John," Smith said, "long time no see . . . last time at my place when you were making *1941*."

"Hi," he said.

"How long you in town for?" she asked.

"About a week," he said.

"I've got to meet Janet," Smith said. "Make up your mind."

Just then Smith's car started idling down as if it were going to stall. She ran back to it, ripping her jeans and cutting her leg on the sharp bumper.

"I want my money back," John said to Milstead. "Forget it, I'm not getting it. That's it. I don't want it."

"Here's your money," Milstead said, handing $60 through the window. But, she said, if he wanted some stuff again, Smith wouldn't do it. Milstead was bored by his indecisiveness. "When I have it and you don't, don't ask me for any."

John reconsidered. "Okay," he said, handing back the money.

Smith returned to the Mercedes, and April gave her $200—three-tenths for herself and one-tenth for John—$50 a tenth. (John was paying Milstead an extra $10 for her role as a middleman.)

"Well," John said, "how long is it going to take?"

"It's just a matter of I have to pick up money and go get it," Smith said, estimating 30 to 45 minutes. "The quality is excellent."

Smith backed out and drove about two blocks when her car stalled. She heard honking behind her and turned around. John pulled over, got out and walked up to the window. "I want my money back."

"Here, take your money," she snapped, shoving $50 at him. "I don't have time for this." She asked if he could help start her car.

"No," he said, "it's a rented car, and they don't have jumper cables." He started walking toward his car and then turned back, saying, "Wait a minute," and handed her the $50. "How long is it going to take?" he asked for a third time.

"It's not getting any shorter talking to you."

John pulled his car around and headed off. Smith flagged a camper whose driver helped start her car. She drove to Theodore's Restaurant, where other customers gave her $100. Smith was in a hurry to join Belushi, so she told them that Alli would be back shortly with the heroin. She then drove down to the parking lot of Miller's Outpost, a clothing store at the corner of Pico and Robertson.

Alli and Dolgoff were there in an old green Volkswagen waiting for the cash. Of the $200 from Milstead and the other $100 from the customers at Theodore's, Smith kept $25 for herself, handing Alli $275 for a total of six-tenths. The implied agreement with John was that Smith would get some for herself. That's the way she'd done it with others when she had provided the connection for the drugs.

Alli was buying for three other customers, and all told, she passed about $700 to Dolgoff. Her profit was about $100. Dolgoff didn't like dealing with too many people and used Alli as intermediary whenever possible. He left and returned about fifteen minutes later. Alli met him by the phone booths, where he passed the packets to her. Alli then gave Smith her share.

"If it's good, I'll want more," Smith said.

When she got in her car, it stalled again.

John and Leslie Marks, meanwhile, had gone to the apartment of comedian Richard Belzer. John brought a bottle of wine from Tommy Smothers's vineyard. Belzer, a stand-up comedian, was preparing a routine for the Johnny Carson show the next week and got out a tape of his recent performance on the "David Letterman Show." He wanted John's help. But John was distracted and not very helpful. He couldn't sit still and pulled out some cocaine for Marks and himself. Later, he called Milstead's to see if Smith was back with the stuff. She was.

Back at the Chateau at 9:49 P.M., John again called Laurel Rubin in

Chicago. This time she answered the phone. "What are you high on?" she asked.

"A little of this, a little of that," he replied. He missed her and wished he could drop everything and come to Chicago.

John sounded sentimental and wanted to talk, but he kept repeating himself, and after ten minutes Rubin said he should call again when he was straight.

Shortly after that John and Marks arrived at Milstead's, where Smith was waiting. April took John aside and warned him that Smith was bad news; she lived off other people's money and drugs. At that moment, Smith was shooting about ¾ of one of the tenths into her own vein. She welcomed the extra shot.

Milstead did not like to shoot herself up and asked Smith to do it for her. Smith, thinking Milstead didn't know enough about shooting and might be careless injecting herself, agreed. It was safer. She gave April about half a tenth, not sure how big a load her body could handle.

John and Marks seemed fascinated with both the process and effect, watching intensely in Milstead's bedroom. "You think you could do that for me?" John asked.

Smith considered herself a superb nurse with a full working knowledge of drugs. She had read books and articles about how to revive overdose victims, and she had once saved the life of someone who had overdosed in her apartment. Better to have her shooting John than letting someone like April do it.

"Do you have a syringe?" John asked.

"Yes," she replied.

"Shoot me up."

"I don't know why you'd want to do that." Smith explained that she really didn't like shooting drugs into people, and she expressed mild surprise that he did heroin.

John said that he'd taken heroin before, back in New York, but he didn't like people to know. He said he wanted a speedball—a mixture of cocaine and heroin. The high of the coke and the dulling effect of the heroin, mixed properly, could create a wonderful sensation, he had heard.

The China white heroin did not have to be heated, and neither did the cocaine. Taking a small amount of coke and even less heroin—$10 to $20 worth of each—Smith placed them together in a teaspoon and added a small amount of bottled water. She mixed the substance and then wadded a cotton ball as small as possible and dropped it into the liquid.

Sticking the needle into the cotton, she then drew out the mixture into the syringe; any impurities would tend to adhere to the cotton.

Next she tied off John's arm with a web belt to make the vein come to the surface. Then she quickly, deftly, jabbed in the needle.

John seemed to love the impact, which normally hit in ten to twenty seconds. In Southern California, Smith knew, it was often described as the feeling of scoring a touchdown in the Rose Bowl.

John turned to Milstead. "Hey, I like it. It feels great," he said.

"You're thirty-three years old," Milstead replied, "so you know how you feel."

"Will you do Leslie?" John asked Smith.

"I don't want to shoot someone who's not—"

"Do it as a favor to me," John interrupted forcefully.

Smith agreed. She was not, however, going to give Leslie a speedball mixture with heroin. Instead, she shot her with a tiny bit, maybe $10 worth, of coke, the equivalent of a thin line that someone might snort. Leslie was so small, so innocent and tender in appearance. An extreme rush of a coke shot could be overpowering, an almost electric jolt to the system.

Marks liked it and was back soon at Smith's side, pestering her for another shot. The high from a cocaine shot dissipates rapidly.

About midnight, the party—John, Marks, Smith, Milstead and Pearson—moved to John's bungalow. As they stepped over the threshold, John grabbed Smith's arm. "Let's go in this bathroom," he said, turning hard right into the small bathroom nearest the living room. "I want to do another hit."

Smith wanted to keep it as private as possible, so she closed the door. John took out some cocaine, a fresh supply neatly wrapped in small paper bindles, and handed her one. Earlier he had given her the heroin to hold, but he kept charge of the cocaine. They agreed this shot would be only coke—not a speedball.

"As a precautionary measure," Smith said, she would do a shot first. She wanted to be careful not to give John too much and needed to test the purity. "I don't know what the quality of this coke is. If the quality is appreciably more, there could be problems." She prepared about a line and injected herself. She didn't particularly like coke; if she took a lot, she needed just that much more heroin to come down.

Next she prepared a shot for John—all coke, and only about half what she had given herself. How is it? she asked.

"Great," he said, and he left the bathroom with a big smile on his face.

Marks got another shot of cocaine later. John turned on some loud music and talked scripts and wine while the drugs continued. The hazy bull session lasted for hours. John snorted some heroin. Milstead was snorting coke and drinking wine. After John got another coke shot, Marks barged into the bathroom where Smith had set up shop. She wanted another.

"Stop following me around," Smith shouted. "Get out of here . . . listen, I can't. I'm sorry, sweetheart, but this is way out of your league."

"Can't I do some more of that?" Marks persisted.

"No. Leave me alone!" Smith shouted again, pushing Marks out and locking the door. Smith then gave herself a full tenth of a gram of heroin to compensate for all the coke she'd done. Cocaine made her jittery, and this damn baby was following her around. Smith hurried out of the bathroom and took John aside.

"John, I'm sorry; she is going to have to go," Smith said in her raspy voice. They had no idea who Leslie was—some girl from a hot-tub club. "This girl looks only seventeen. She's impressionable. Let's get rid of her . . . or I'm going."

John prepared to take Leslie home. At 2:34 A.M. he called the home of William Schumer, a thirty-five-year-old importer of leather, furniture and cars. He knew that Richard Bear was staying there. Schumer woke up, answered the phone and said Bear was not there.

He then called Jeremy Rain and woke her up. He wanted the phone number of Alyce Kuhn, Rain's old roommate who had accompanied John, Rain and Peter Aykroyd to the Police concert the month before. Rain gave him the number, but John held off calling.

He left with Marks to get some more cocaine. They went to a place south of the Chateau, but no one was home and John had a temper tantrum outside. From there he dropped Marks at her home in Westwood and returned to the Chateau, where the party continued.

Both Pearson and Milstead watched Smith shoot up John. Once, when the front bathroom was unoccupied, Milstead went in to check out her eyes in the mirror. John followed. Milstead continued to stare into the mirror. He undressed and took a shower with her standing there. She bit her cheek; he seemed incapable of embarrassment.

TUESDAY, MARCH 2

About 7 A.M., when all the drugs were gone, John said he would take Smith, Milstead and Pearson to breakfast. They drove over to Duke's

Diner in the Tropicana Motor Hotel on Santa Monica. John ordered a cheese blintz, and after finishing it, he started eating from Milstead's plate with his hands, putting on a Bluto show.

John and Smith drove over to Smith's place on Bimini so she could change clothes, and then they went back to the Chateau. John called Brillstein's assistant, Gigi Givertz, and said that he didn't have his credit card and he needed money to buy some cassettes. She sent over $600 with Bill Wallace.

Smith wondered how John always had so much cash. He seemed generally to have $1,000, and when his cash got low, he was resupplied at once by Brillstein's office, usually through Wallace. The money clearly went for drugs. He seemed to have four to five grams of coke most of the time. She asked him how it worked.

"There's several thousand dollars of cocaine built into the contract," he said. "Extra money for the length of the contract . . . not said, but that's what it's for." In the current movie contract, he got a $2,500 a week per diem, even when he was just working on the script and not acting. But everything—hotel, limo, credit cards, everything—was paid by his accountants in New York. So he had the money to use for drugs; that was its purpose, he said.

At 10:13 A.M., John called Judy in New York. She wasn't home, and he left a message: "Tell Judy I love her." Later, he tried again but dialed the wrong number. Just after 1 P.M. New York time, he tried the Phantom office. She wasn't there either, and he left the same message on the answering service: "Tell Judy I love her."

Nelson Lyon, a forty-three-year-old writer and close friend of Michael O'Donoghue, dialed John at the Chateau. Lyon, a tall, heavyset man who liked the perverse exuberance of the "tonight-anything-can-happen" quality in John, had heard that his old acquaintance was in town.

Lyon, a friend of Robert De Niro and Belushi, had never quite made it. His 1973 X-rated movie, *The Telephone Book*—about someone who falls in love with an obscene call—had received some favorable reviews but had not made money. He lived on the edges of show business, writing articles and scripts.

John suggested they get together. Lyon invited him to his house, the same one John and Judy had stayed in during the postproduction of *Neighbors.*

"I'll be right over," John said. He turned to Smith. "There's a friend of mine that's in town who has never shot up, and I'd like him to try it."

They drove to Lyon's house, where John and Lyon went back to the den and put on some music.

"I'm being fucked over by Paramount," John said, repeating the whole *Noble Rot* story. And now instead they wanted him to do a sex movie. Speaking of his agent and manager, John said, "They're not backing me up. I want someone who will, instead of pushing me into this shit like *Joy of Sex*."

Lyon asked about Cathy Smith.

"Oh, she's a good girl," John said. "She does lots of errands." They went to get her, and John said to Lyon, "Let's go in the back. . . . Have I got something for you."

They walked to the rear of the house, where Smith shot herself with coke, compensating afterward with a shot of heroin. She then gave John a shot of coke. He was needing more and more to get the same feeling— highly dangerous, she realized, but she tried to keep the increases down.

"Will you do this for Nelson?" John asked.

Smith looked up at Lyon, his large, animated face encouraging. It was no use resisting. He evidently knew his way around drugs, though apparently he had never shot up. She injected a modest amount of coke into his arm.

"Wow," he said. "It's great." He got shot up four times that afternoon. They used a necktie to tie off once and a black belt with punk cleats the other times.

Smith called Alli and asked if more heroin was available. Alli said yes; she was going over to where Dolgoff was staying just south of Beverly Hills. She told Smith to call her there.

Shortly after that Smith reached Alli and said she had a couple of hundred dollars. She arrived twenty minutes later in John's Mercedes and handed Dolgoff $200. He gave her about four tenths of heroin.

"Did you like what you had last night?" Dolgoff asked.

Smith said yes, and Dolgoff replied that this was brown.

Smith remarked that Belushi liked the China white.

White would be available later, he said.

About 5 P.M., John called Penny Selwyn at his Paramount office. She asked where he was. John lied and said he was at Jack Nicholson's house. Were there any messages? What else was happening?

Stanley Chase, the producer on *Noble Rot,* had summoned her to his office the day before, she said. He was twitching and sweating, putting her through the third degree on every phase of John's life, the script and the mounting negative reactions to the draft.

"Fuck him," John said.

Selwyn realized that John was blitzed on something. He was nearly incoherent. She told him that a copy of *The Joy of Sex* had been sent over.

"Fuck. Have you read it?" John asked.

"No."

"Well, read the fucking thing."

Selwyn also told him that she had a temporary secretary for the next day as he had requested. As she understood it, John and a friend were going to ride around in a limousine, and the secretary was to take notes on ideas for some other script.

Right, John said. He wouldn't give her any more details.

Selwyn said she had arranged with Leslie Werner, who had done the marathon *Noble Rot* typing the weekend before last, to do it. She happened to be in the office.

John asked to speak to her.

Selwyn handed the phone to Werner and whispered, "He's high."

"Do you still have the thing I signed?" John asked.

Werner said she did.

"I want to give you something else, something better. We're going to have a lot of fun tomorrow."

John, Smith and Lyon got in John's Mercedes and went to the Guitar Center. Smith noticed that Lyon was trying hard to control himself so he wouldn't look high. He seemed very paranoid. The Guitar Center was like a candy store for John, and he began wandering around, looking, grabbing, holding, plucking.

Lyon told Smith that he liked John but couldn't keep up with him.

"Yeah, I know," Smith said. "He never sleeps."

John bought two pairs of Ludwig drum sticks for $10.60; he also purchased a small amplifier for $106 so he could play his guitar at the bungalow. Hooking the amplifier to a guitar, John set it up on a counter in the back and strummed away. He bummed cigarettes from the manager, Jim Fox, and took a sip of his coffee.

John picked up a phone and asked Fox to dial a number, explaining that they were calling one of the bigwigs, whom he didn't name, involved in his latest script.

When the phone was answered, John gave the receiver to Fox and told him to hold it up in front of the amp. He then strummed loud, powerful rock chords for about 30 seconds. His plump hands weren't very adept, and he compensated by playing louder. Taking the phone back, he said, "So what do you think of that? Pretty good, huh?"

John listened to the other end for a moment.

"Fuck you!" John yelled, and slammed the phone into its cradle.

When John and Smith got back to the Chateau, he said he had to go to a meeting with some Paramount executives and asked her to leave. Smith took a cab to Milstead's. "I'm exhausted," Smith told Milstead. "I don't want to go all the way home. My car's broken. Do you mind if I stay here?"

Milstead said okay, but she'd have to sleep on the couch. After the last 24 hours, Smith was grateful to have anything. She lay down and fell asleep.

By 9:45 P.M., John and Tino Insana were at On the Rox. The club was not crowded. John ordered a limousine to come and wait for him in the parking lot. Soon Eisner, his wife, Jane, and assistant, Jeff Katzenberg, joined them at a table, as had been previously arranged. Insana was shocked that John would meet such important executives in such bad shape. He was burned out and sloppy. And Eisner and Katzenberg could make or break a career, turn thumbs up or down on $10-million or $20-million movies.

Eisner wanted to keep up the momentum of the day before, slowly edging John away from *Noble Rot* to *The Joy of Sex*. Eisner selected several of the scenes and acted them out at the table. There was something inherently funny about sexual awakening, and in John's hands it would be hilarious.

In rebuttal, with a copy of *Noble Rot* in hand, John did a few scenes from that script. Everyone laughed or chuckled. "How can you not think this is funny?" John asked.

Someone asked how John would remember the long speech on the history of the great wine that comes from rotten grapes—the noble rot.

Insana realized that the speech was not from John's character, Johnny Glorioso, but the father. John seemed to stiffen, and seemed insulted, as if they thought he could not remember lines and was just a guy who spit potatoes.

"Well, I want my money," John said. "Contact my lawyers—Jacoby and Meyers," a local law firm that advertised on TV.

Eisner laughed, glad John had a sense of humor about it but aware of the potential threat.

"No, no, I'm kidding," John added.

There was a note of ambiguity. John had invited Tino as a possible rewrite person on the script. He ran through some more scenes.

Eisner and Katzenberg said that the current *Noble Rot* was a step backward from the earlier version.

Then we'll do some work, John said, and he tried a few more lines. Katzenberg noticed a dismal refrain in John. John said he couldn't understand how they could commit and after one rewrite, want to walk away. It didn't make sense.

Eisner tried to keep the conversation focused on *The Joy of Sex*. That was the perfect answer to their problems.

John was eating a lot—hamburgers, Chinese food—and he was leaving the table often. Eisner thought it a little strange, but maybe that was John's way. On the Rox was like his own living room, and he was probably very comfortable moving about. In any event, Eisner was trying to be optimistic. Perhaps something good would come out of this.

But after an hour, they seemed to have reached an impasse, and Eisner and Katzenberg liked to get home early. No more headway was going to be made tonight. It was 11 P.M., and a rerun of "Saturday Night Live" had just begun on the oversized Advent at the other end of the club. Eisner and his wife headed down the steps to the parking lot. He was glad to be leaving; the club reflected the seedy, nightlife side of Hollywood which he tried to avoid. And he was quite tired.

Suddenly Belushi appeared in the parking lot. "You got to see this," he pleaded. "One of my best . . . please, please." He almost had to drag them back to the television.

It was a show that had aired three years earlier, November 4, 1978, three days before the national midterm elections, and two weeks after John had made the cover of *Newsweek*.

On the big screen, Jane Curtin introduces " 'Weekend Update's' political analyst, John Belushi."

The audience goes wild—clapping, cheering, a welcome for the star.

Sitting at the commentator's table, John begins: "You know on Tuesday, we all have an opportunity that doesn't come around very often. I'm talking, of course, about our right to vote. . . . I mean, you can vote when you're 18 now." He turns angry and belligerent. "I couldn't when I was 18! I couldn't even drive when I was 18! I got my license when I was 16, but they took it away when I was 18 because I had too many tickets! That's when I was in Chicago. I just went back to Chicago in 1976 and I saw my friend Steve Beshekas. I said, 'Steve, who'd you vote for—Ford or Carter?' He said, 'I didn't vote. All politicians is the same.' I said, 'Who do you think makes the laws, Steeeeeve? Politicians!' He said, 'It doesn't make any difference.' I said, *'Doesn't make any difference? Possession of an ounce is a misdemeanor now! You know how far we've come?'* "

The television audience roars with laughter at the Belushi they love —loud, mad, the righteous tyrant pounding sense into America about drugs. Eisner was chuckling as he saw John building.

"There's still some people in prison in Texas eating rats because they were caught with a seed in 1965!"

Thunderous laughter and applause.

"In Europe, in Amsterdam, everyone votes there, and they smoke hash in the streets." (Laughter) "Don't tell me it doesn't make a difference. I've got this to say and I'm going to say it. Why am I up here wasting my valuable time telling you this? To tell you the truth, I'd rather be out smoking hash on the streets!" (Laughter)

"I could be out smoking hash on the streets, but *noooooooooooooo*" (intense laughter), "I got to be here to show you lame-o's, because an informed public is the only hope, hope we have if we want to smoke hash in the streets." (Laughter)

"In the Communist countries—I've been there; I've been to Mexico and Canada—suppose nobody voted on Tuesday, then where would we be? The Russians would be all over us the next day! You think they'd pass up a chance like that? *Not on your life.* There'd be some Commie goon kicking down your door. . . . How'd you like to drive to work someday and all the street signs are in Mongolian, huh?"

John is raging at the audience now, berating, arguing, condemning. Eisner and his wife watched John watching himself in a trance.

"Can you read Mongolian? I can't . . . not even Mongolians can read Mongolian. Have you ever smoked Mongolian hash? Huh? You don't even get high . . . your heart starts beating, and you think you're going to die. I want hard drugs. . . ." John pounds the table, physically out of control, and in a frenzy, falls over clutching his heart, dead.

The television audience cheered. Eisner smiled. John was proud. A few minutes later Eisner and his wife returned to their car.

Jane Eisner found John incredibly sad. "I feel as though I've just seen *Sunset Boulevard,*" she said, referring to the 1950 Paramount classic in which Gloria Swanson played an aging, washed-up silent screen star who lived to watch reruns of her old films.

That was about someone whose career was over, Eisner said; John's career is still active. John did seem a little tied to the past, and there might have been a little too much urgency in the way he had pulled them upstairs to sit them down in front of his old work, but Eisner didn't see any connection.

"*Sunset Boulevard*," Jane Eisner said. "I'm telling you. We just saw it."

WEDNESDAY, MARCH 3

From On the Rox John called Barbara Howar in New York. She complained that it was past 2 A.M.

John said he had a real problem and explained about the script rejection. He didn't think he was getting the straight story from the executives and agents. No one was telling him the truth. They had been so enthusiastic before, and now everyone was jumping on the rewrite, which was better. "Come out here and read it and tell me if it's funny," he said. He'd put her on the payroll.

Howar really cared for John, but L.A. was out of the question right now, she said. They'd talk later.

Finally John drove back to the Marmont—forgetting he had a limousine waiting or deliberately leaving it behind—and at five minutes past midnight tried to call Leslie Marks in Westwood. He then drove over to Milstead's. "I'm lonely," he said when Milstead answered the door in her nightgown. Cathy Smith was there asleep. John was really loaded, sweating and breathing heavily. "Will you come back to the bungalow with me?"

"John, I'm dressed for bed, you know." John came in. "Why don't you cool it?" she said.

"I'm fine," he replied. He turned his attention to Pearson.

Pearson, still trying to get another record deal, had a tape of a song he'd written with Nils Lofgren, an accomplished guitarist with a large cult following. It was a heavy blues tune called "The Raw Edge," about the seediness of heroin. John wanted to hear it, so Pearson put it on:

> It's the raw edge, back to haunt me;
> Makes me desperate, too confused to see;
> Well, it's the raw edge, destroying me.
> Sitting on the corner, got mud inside my shoes,

(Pearson explained that "mud" was a street name for heroin—specifically, Persian brown.)

Well, here I done forgot the point,
And I got the blues.

John apparently understood that "the point" was the needle.

"Look," John said, "let's get together and write some songs. Maybe there can be something for the movie." He urged Pearson to come back to the Chateau. "Bring your guitar." Milstead finally agreed to come along.

Before they left, Celeste, one of Milstead's drug connections, stopped by with an eighth of an ounce of cocaine for $300. Out in the driveway, Celeste asked John if she could drive his Mercedes, and he said okay. When they pulled up at the bungalow, John complained that some cocaine was missing from his car's glove compartment, and he accused Celeste of taking it.

Milstead found that a little strange. It was hard to believe that John would leave coke in the car; he usually kept it in a clear plastic bag with a zip lock top, generally in his breast pocket.

They left the problem unresolved and went to the bungalow. Pearson brought in his old electric Yamaha guitar, and John played some songs from his high school days.

John wanted Pearson to read *Noble Rot,* so Pearson went to the bedroom and read through it quickly. "I don't see it hitting Indianapolis," Pearson said when he came back, "but it could be a real subtle comedy." He threw out a few lines from the script, and John picked it up and recited the rest of the scene.

Later, Gary Watkins arrived bringing some more cocaine. When Milstead saw that John was going to buy some, she handed him $50.

"I don't want to take this," John said.

"No, we want to do it." It was only fair since she and Pearson were using it too.

"Okay," he said, putting the $50 in his pocket.

About 3 A.M., Celeste left. John was very tightly wound, nervous and jittery. He darted around, running in and out of the rooms, talking trash; it was neurotic babble as far as Pearson could tell. He was on a coke jag, acting like all three Marx Brothers wrapped up in one. "Taste this, taste this wine," he said. Then he was talking about the script, then one kind of music or another, then playing punk or blues or old rock and roll on his stereo or strumming it on his guitar. John could only play a handful of chords, but he made the best of it. "I got to get some sleep," he said. "I got to get some sleep."

Watkins had some pot.

"John," Milstead said, "I just can't smoke pot."

"I can't either," John said.

Milstead went to the kitchen, opened some champagne and poured herself a glass. John came in, and the two of them played hangman, the spelling word game. The forward thrust of the evening was gone, and Milstead wondered why they were all still there. Nothing interesting was happening; she'd played hangman in grammar school.

John called Bill Wallace at home and awakened him. "Bill, this is John. I need some favors." Wallace was to get a typewriter, some typing paper and a cassette recorder for the next morning. John didn't say why.

At 5:58 A.M., John called Leslie Marks and asked if he could come over to her place, away from all the commotion, for some peace and rest.

"I got to get some sleep; I'm going to Westwood," he told Milstead and Pearson. "You can stay."

Milstead and Pearson caught a cab. At 6:45 A.M., after nine hours and a $312.45 bill, John's limousine driver finally called it quits. He had never found Belushi.

At Marks's apartment, number 3 at 1661 Selby Avenue in Westwood, John came in seeking some antidote to his insomnia and his anger. He reached for the cocaine packets in his pocket and snorted some. Eventually he took a shower, and Marks noticed the several small, red needle marks on his arms from the day before. She got out a container of makeup, stretched out his arm and gently applied the flesh-colored substance to the little welts, painting them over and over until they disappeared, until it was almost as if they didn't exist.

Sickish and exhausted, John heaved over on his side and went into a senseless trance. He was almost blacked out but never quite asleep. Occasionally, he was consumed with coughing fits that wracked his body.

Wallace called the bungalow that Wednesday morning, letting the phone ring about fifteen times, but got no answer. He decided to go over to the Chateau and wait. He had a key to number 3, and he let himself in. The mess was worse than usual. Food, clothes, paper, glasses, bottles, cups, were not just dropped around; they were thrown about as if the room had been trashed.

He called Brillstein's office. Neither Bernie, Joel nor Gigi had heard from John. They would try to find him. At Paramount, Selwyn said she had not heard from John either. Wallace tried a few other places and then made some personal calls. He was planning to take the red-eye to Memphis that night to sign the final papers for his divorce, and he needed to make some last-minute arrangements.

By dinnertime, John had still not returned. Wallace ordered wine from room service, and at 7:25 P.M., he began an hour-long phone conversation with his estranged wife.

Brillstein was in a fury. "That son of a bitch, I'll kill him!" he shouted. John's career was hanging in the balance; it wasn't just one $1.85 million deal; that deal determined the next, and that determined the next. And John had pulled one of his disappearing acts. Brillstein kept saying, "I don't want to end up like Freddie Prinze's manager." *

Gigi was trying her best, the telephone equivalent of rounding up the usual suspects. It was the same old routine; soon the phone would ring and there John would be—mellow and sweet—and the idea of strangling him would dissolve by his third sentence. But this time the call didn't come, and Gigi ran out of ideas.

Penny Selwyn was alarmed. Briskin called her at home after work and said, "If John carries on like this with the coke, he'll kill himself."

Shouldn't they call the police?

"He's done this before," Briskin replied, remembering hours and days of waiting and wondering. You had to learn to live with the uncertainty; it was part of the job.

Smith woke up at Milstead's Wednesday morning and drove home to Bimini Place, where she called the bungalow and got a busy signal. Milstead was also trying to get through. By about 8 P.M., the two women were together at Milstead's, still attempting to contact John at the Chateau. The line remained busy; maybe it was off the hook. Smith, in particular, was worried. John was running too hard. Let's drive up there, she suggested. When they arrived, the front door was unlocked and they walked in. Wallace was sitting in the living room with a note pad and a pencil in his hand, apparently taking messages.

Something might have happened to John, he said. No one could find him, and they had tried everywhere. "You know where he is now?" Wallace asked. "I have no idea."

"Probably at Leslie's," Milstead said.

"Where is that?" Wallace asked.

"Westwood is all I know," she answered.

* Prinze, star of "Chico and the Man," a mid-seventies hit TV show, died of a self-inflicted gunshot wound in 1977 at age twenty-three.

He seemed angry that they didn't have an address or a phone number.

"He'll probably call my house," Milstead said.

Wallace thought he recognized Smith or Milstead—maybe both. They were the kind of women who were obviously involved in Belushi's drug life.

"Are you giving or selling dope to John?" Wallace asked.

"No," Milstead said.

"You don't know where he's getting it?" Wallace asked.

"Not off hand," Milstead stated. "I don't consider that my business."

Wallace said that he suspected them, and he urged them to stop.

Smith and Milstead decided to leave. April wrote a note and left it for John: "I helped myself to your 'roach'! Thanks again, 'Yet, I don't know what for!' Call me later when you're pulled together. Take 'Somanez' [sic] tonight and sleep—safe and restful sleep, sleep, sleep! Love, April."

Jeremy Rain was also looking for John, and she called the Chateau until finally she got through. Wallace wanted to know why she was looking for John, and Rain said that he owed her money.

"Don't give John any money," Wallace said. "Why did you do that?" His anger flared. "You're not going to see John anymore. He's not going to be walking or talking to anyone." This was the "Superfoot" karate expert talking; he would put John out of commission and stop this nonsense once and for all. Tough business—the way kickers talk around the gym.

"What are you talking about?" Rain asked, her sense of dread growing. What did no talking, no walking mean?

"John got into something over his head," Wallace said sharply.

Rain said she didn't have anything to do with John's drugs; she abhorred them.

Wallace seemed to relax. The two of them, he said, should get together over the coming weekend and work out a plan to control John.

Rain hung up, scared. She called On the Rox and demanded to speak to John, breaking through the normal barriers at the private club. She was able to find out only that John had somehow hooked up with Robert De Niro and that there was talk about their going to Las Vegas together. But it was unclear.

Wallace's words—"He's not going to be walking or talking to anyone''—were tucked in Rain's mind. Placing person-to-person calls to John Belushi, she began calling the hotels in Las Vegas—the Sands, MGM, the Hilton, all the big casinos. There were no clues, no Belushi, no De Niro. Rain tried Wallace again. He seemed to suggest another hotel in Las Vegas—if indeed that was where John was—and promised to try.

Please have him call me when you locate him, Rain said. The more she thought about it, the more John seemed in trouble. What had he said when he had run from her apartment Monday night? *"I'm not safe anywhere."* John needed sheltering, but she couldn't think of what else to do; she had to find him first, and he didn't seem to be in Las Vegas after all.

Bill Wallace caught a flight to Memphis after midnight. He didn't like leaving with John out on the town, but there was no way to postpone a divorce without giving everyone the wrong impression.

About 3 A.M., John woke up at Marks's apartment. He and Leslie watched a movie. He placed calls to Cathy Smith and Brillstein, and when he failed to get through, he returned to the bungalow.

THURSDAY, MARCH 4

At 5:50 A.M., John called Judy at Morton Street. It was 8:50 A.M. in New York, still too early for her. She had the flu and was angry that they hadn't talked for days. He said he would call back at a reasonable hour.

Later that morning, John called Phantom and left a message on the answering machine: "I'm coming home on the red-eye tonight."

At about that time, 11 A.M. in New York, Dan Aykroyd was just coming into the Phantom office, and he picked up the phone on the answering machine. He heard John's voice—not sure if John was actually on the line or whether it was an old message playing back. But there it was, his partner's voice: "I'm coming home on the red-eye tonight." Boy, Aykroyd thought, he really sounds down and tired. Aykroyd considered getting on the line, and he thought about what to say: Hey, what's wrong with you? You better come home. But that might set John off, so Dan hesitated.

Everything with John had to be very deliberate. Aykroyd had frequently had to sit Belushi down, eye to eye, and say, You have to see that this is not good, that you or your behavior, or this business decision we made, is not good. Or, I have a disagreement with you. He couldn't be short with John. Two or three lines on an important subject could be disastrous. And the tone in John's voice was bleak. A scolding could throw him off the path home.

It probably was John right there on the line, but the red-eye would put him back the next morning. That would be fine, Aykroyd decided, and hung up.

He turned to a script he was writing, *Ghostbusters,* about three exterminators who expel evil spirits from homes. Using the latest in high technology, they exorcise paranormal forces, not through witchcraft, but through quantum theory and proton packs, ion beams and neutron wands. Aykroyd loved that stuff. He sat down at this typewriter in the corner office for the day's work to start on one of the first scenes with John's character. Before he started, he told the secretary, Karen, "John's gone off the deep end."

John called Milstead. "I want to see Cathy," he said. Fifteen minutes later he called again. "Have you found Cathy?" he pleaded. Milstead promised to try harder.

Finally John called Brillstein.

"Where the fuck have you been?" Brillstein asked.

"I'm getting out of the shower. I spent the night at the Westwood Marquis," John lied. It was too noisy at the Chateau and he had needed some real sleep.

Brillstein issued a semi-ultimatum. They couldn't leave this deal hanging. What about *Noble Rot*? And now what about *The Joy of Sex*? There couldn't be this fucking disappearing act. They'd have to meet with Eisner soon, now, yesterday. John couldn't leave the head of Paramount dangling, couldn't treat him like his manager. Eisner held the key to their futures, the money.*

---

* John was spending a lot of money—anywhere from $40,000 to $75,000 a month. The previous month, February, his accountants wrote 81 checks on the Phantom Enterprises Ltd. business account. The total February outlay had been $49,988.32 from Phantom alone. That money went for taxes, travel, parking, legal fees, public relations ($1,500 a month to Solters, Roskin and Friedman, the firm that represented Frank Sinatra; their job for John, as with many of their clients, was to keep his name out of the news, not in it), limousine rentals, American Express, bottled water, miscellaneous cash, appliances, phone, doctors and delivery services.

Other regular monthly Phantom expenses included $1,625 for Karen's salary, office rent at 150 Fifth Avenue, $1,137, and $1,000 of the rent on Morton Street, which was now up to $3,000.

Over the last several years John had put many of his and Judy's family members on the Phantom payroll; the total monthly outlay, $4,380. Included were monthly checks of $625 to Adam Belushi, John's father; $550 to Agnes Belushi, his mother; $858 to Marian Belushi, his sister; $600 to Billy, his younger brother. Judy's father, Leslie Jacklin, got $667 monthly, and her mother, Jean, $1,080; Mrs. Jacklin had previously worked for a publisher for fifteen years, and John and Judy had agreed to let her quit, and they would pay her regular salary from John's income.

Another payment from Phantom was $4,171.47 monthly for medical insurance for John, Judy and the family members on the payroll.

From John's personal account in February the accountants wrote 35 checks for an additional $26,285.81 in nonbusiness expenses such as cleaning, food, plumbing, repairs and electricity.

In December, John and Judy had also bought a house at 56 West Tenth Street in New York; they had taken out a $500,000 mortgage on the property, and the monthly mortgage payments were $7,847. Other expenses were $3,059 for the Vineyard house mortgage; $2,000 of the Morton Street rent; a $1,024 mortgage payment for the California ranch John had bought for his father; another $866 monthly mortgage payment for a $60,000 condominium in Chicago which John had bought in June 1981 and which was being used by his mother.

John was paying all or most of his mother's and father's living expenses. In February he paid his father's $606 Visa card bill and his $649 Mastercard bill. Over the last several years John had also paid out about $60,000 to clear up his father's accumulated debts from the Chicago restaurants.

John had loaned thousands of dollars to friends. Lipsky had tried to get John to pressure some of them to repay the money. John would not. One was a demand note dated May 16, 1979, for a $10,000 loan made to a drug dealer, but John just let it go.

In order to maintain his current life-style for himself and his family, John needed an annual income of somewhere between $500,000 and $1 million. The promised $1.85 million for *Noble Rot* offered the prospect of continued prosperity for all. Apart from his current per diem, his only income was about $1,000 a week from reruns of "Saturday Night Live." He could get no money from *Goin' South* or *Animal House* because he had no profit share. He had a small share in *Old Boyfriends,* but there was virtually no chance it would ever realize a profit. The latest accounting statement from the studios showed that the prospects of income were unlikely on his other four movies too.

The Blues Brothers: Total gross receipts $58.4 million; but it was $15.7 million in the hole owing to claimed costs of $35.1 million to make the movie (up from initial costs, like the other movies, because of interest and other charges), $19 million in distribution fees to the studio, and $20 million in other expenses (including nearly $13 million for advertising).

Continental Divide: Total gross receipts of $12.3 million. But it was $12.6 million in the hole, according to the studio calculations—$3.7 million in distribution fees to the studio, other expenses of $8 million and a cost of production of $13.2 million.

1941 had taken in $27.7 million in net receipts from which John might eventually get a share. But cost of production was $34.4 million, and the distribution fees paid were $19.9 million, putting the movie $26.6 million in the red.

On *Neighbors,* John had a better contract, and it had been agreed that he would get a share of gross receipts after $25 million was taken in at the box office. But only $21.3 million had come in.

John promised to come within the hour.

Brillstein reached Eisner and asked if they could meet before lunch. He explained that he had issued an ultimatum; they were going to get John's career back on track.

John drove over to Gary Watkins's house. Watkins could see that John was not in the best of health. "Are you feeling okay? Have you had a checkup?" he asked.

When preparing for a movie, the studios require their stars to have an insurance examination in case of an accident. He'd passed,* John said, and anyway his grandparents had lived to be 100.

At 9:24 A.M., John placed a call from Watkins's home to Judy. She was now awake and took the call on the upstairs phone at Morton Street.

"I'm sorry I didn't come home Sunday," John began. "I'm going to stay for a meeting." This was a courtesy to the studio, he said.

Judy thought he sounded better, more frustrated than depressed.

"You can't believe what they want me to do," he said. "Now they want me to do *The Joy of Sex*. . . . You won't believe the script. They want me to put on a diaper." Maybe Tino could rewrite it, he said; he was going to go to his house later to talk about it.

Judy was glad to hear from him, but she knew the cocaine was way, way out of hand. She called Smokey Wendell; it was time to reenlist the drug enforcer.

Smokey was living in a Virginia suburb of Washington, D.C., and he got the message on his answering service. He called the Phantom office at once. Aykroyd picked up and said, "Look, Judy and I talked . . . what are you doing now? Are you free?"

Wendell was.

"I think it's time to get together again. Call Judy. She'll talk to you."

Just after 5 P.M., Smokey called Judy at Morton Street. She sounded very worried, her voice tense. "Would you be free to spend some time with John?" she asked.

"Yes. When?"

"Right away, if possible," Judy said.

"Okay," Smokey answered. "I can take a flight tonight to L.A." Smokey had heard from friends on the West Coast that John was back into his old habits.

* John had been given a routine insurance examination in February, and he had passed.

"I'm not sure we want to gang up on him," Judy said.

Smokey said that he had recently left messages for John at the Chateau but hadn't heard back. He wanted more details from Judy, though they had previously agreed to make no direct references to drugs over the phone.

"The problems are back again," Judy said. "But worse, stronger. He's having rewrite problems on the script . . . a script was rejected. He hates L.A., you know. And we're having marital problems."

"We don't have to get into that over the phone," Smokey said. Wouldn't it be best for him to fly to California now?

Judy said no.

"Are you sure? I can pack in fifteen minutes and get the first flight and be there in the morning."

"No," Judy said again. "I'm going to talk to him tonight, and we can talk tomorrow."

"We've got to get him out of L.A.," Smokey said.

Judy agreed. The conversation lasted thirteen minutes.

Smokey told his wife, Deborah, about Judy's call. "I think John has big problems again."

"Do you think you should call John?" Deborah asked.

"I could," Smokey said, "but it would be too coincidental." That night he packed a suitcase, ready to go the next day.

Judy also spoke with her friend Laila Nabulsi, who was living in Colorado with Hunter Thompson, the author (*Fear and Loathing in Las Vegas*) and gonzo journalist for *Rolling Stone* magazine. Laila was planning a trip to New York that week.

"I don't know what to do," Judy said. John was really acting crazy. "Should I give him an ultimatum?" It was so bad that she might have to have John committed this time.

"Don't worry," Laila said. "As soon as John gets home, I'll be there to help."

In Los Angeles, John called Milstead again to ask if she'd found Cathy yet. April promised to renew her search.

John left Watkins's house and returned to the bungalow about 11 A.M. and ordered a continental breakfast. Then he went over to Brillstein's office.

"For someone on a binge, you look pretty good," Gigi said as he walked in.

"I feel fine, feel great," John said, claiming to have slept about 24 hours straight. He took his stack of phone messages and had a cup of coffee.

Gigi was glad to see things calmed down. John was looking well, rested and strong.

John went into Brillstein's corner office and took off his Wilson warmup jacket—a recent present from Ovitz. It was time for a serious talk.

Brillstein explained that they were at one of those crucial points in John's career. He was still big money for the studios—they would pay close to $2 million for a picture—but that enthusiasm was going to run down if there was a fuckup on the Paramount deal. *Animal House* was a 1978 movie. That was really the last hit. It was 1982. We need a big, raucous hit, Brillstein said. We need it now. Do *Joy of Sex,* he implored. Afterward you can do Louis Malle's *Moon Over Miami.* The script is finished and Danny loves it. Next you could do one of the scripts Danny is writing—*Spies Like Us, Ghostbusters* or *Never Say Mountie.* Then maybe *Noble Rot.* It would be, at least, the equivalent of a four-picture deal. Brillstein had always argued that no one in show business could sit back and wait. It was necessary to keep active. Do a string of movies, and the chemistry would work on one and hit.

Brillstein was driving hard, confessing his anxieties. A lot of money and many other things—careers, credibility, clout, leverage—were on the line.

John seemed to be warming to the idea of doing *Joy.* "Okay, okay," he said. But he was up and down, and Brillstein couldn't tell where he would land. John always made him earn a victory.

"I want to buy a new guitar," John said, "and I need cash."

"How much?" Brillstein asked.

"Fifteen hundred."

Brillstein thought that was outrageously expensive. John explained that the guitar he wanted had been made especially for Les Paul, who had pioneered the development of the electric guitar.

"I'm not going to give you money," Brillstein said. "You'll use it on drugs."

"Am I here?" John asked. "Am I okay?"

As Brillstein well knew, John knew how to apply pressure with a new angle, a new hobby, a new excuse—always the same game, always new rules.

· ·

Over in Century City, Ovitz was struggling with one of his classic problems—two clients being sought for the same movie. Penny Marshall was tired and bored with TV. Under her contract with Paramount, which did the "Laverne and Shirley" TV series, she was to be given a directing opportunity for a feature film. Eisner had chosen *The Joy of Sex*. But Marshall had been very much on the fence and had been asking friends for advice. Then suddenly she'd decided to do it with her typical "Let's go" gusto. And now Eisner wanted John to star in it.

Ovitz didn't like *The Joy of Sex* script. It was juvenile and stupid. In one scene describing the female sex organ, a health teacher says, "Tuesday we will discuss how women use this extremity to get home furnishings, credit cards and clothing." The script had to be changed no matter which of his clients picked it up—Belushi, Marshall or both.

And Ovitz didn't think it was right for John. The sex material was too cute. Paramount had its own imperative. Money was on the line, and Eisner was trying to shift the *Noble Rot* commitment; and the momentum was on his side. Ovitz had expressed some reservations to John but had held off a final recommendation. That would hinge on the script changes and the director.

After Marshall had made up her mind to do *Joy,* she had scheduled a meeting with Eisner and Katzenberg to make the deal final. Katzenberg —whom Marshall privately called "Spiderman" because of his looks, his intensity and efficiency (he was the best in the entertainment business at returning phone calls)—had pushed the meeting back. "You're stalling," Marshall had told him. They had been so anxious, and now everything was in slow motion. That didn't seem like Spiderman. Something, clearly, was up.

About noon Ovitz called Marshall. They had offered the lead in *Joy* to Belushi.

"That makes a lot that is bad work," she replied. She realized that Belushi would have the right, as the star, to approve her as director. Her television experience wouldn't mean much. Paramount's offer to her was clearly back on hold.

She considered calling John, but she wanted to avoid mixing friendship and work, so she called Katzenberg. He said that they would know by tomorrow whether John would accept the offer, and then they would talk. In fact, he said, Eisner is meeting with John right now.

In New York, Aykroyd called Brillstein's office and John took the phone. Danny needled him about his disappearance the day before.

"How is it you can disappear in Canada for two goddamn weeks and everyone doesn't go crazy?" John asked. "Why me? Where were you yesterday?"

"Well, John," Aykroyd said, "I was here in New York writing a project for us. That's where I was." He told John that they had an offer from a U.S. Navy captain to cruise out on a ship leaving from San Diego the next week. John showed little interest. "Do me the solid favor of your life," Aykroyd appealed, "the solid favor of my life. Come with me on this Navy cruise. We'll have time to clean out physically and mentally, and we'll be able to plan the strategy for the next series of projects that we're going to do together and discuss their order. Come on, man."

"No," John said sharply.

"Why?"

"I get seasick," John said.

"You can take pills."

John wouldn't budge, and Aykroyd carped some more. He was worried and he didn't want to show his concern, but it came through. "You got to get on the ship," Aykroyd said.

"Who the fuck are you?" John screamed. "You disappear! No one says anything to you. You can go anywhere you goddamn please! Why are you picking on me?" He hung up.

Brillstein had to call Aykroyd back and send word that John apologized.

Eisner arrived. He was impressed that John was up so early and was happy to find him in good spirits, chipper and fresh.

Penny Marshall, Eisner said, is the person to direct this movie. She is brilliant and funny, and after one of the longest-running, most successful TV series, she is ready to direct.

John resisted. Brillstein knew he had immense problems working with women, especially when they were in authority. Brillstein wanted to focus on one issue: They needed a hit. With all the script and other problems, *Noble Rot* clearly was not going to be the next picture. On *The Joy of Sex*—Brillstein paused—"the title alone with Belushi would make a fortune."

John agreed that a commercial success, a movie that would put him on top again, should be next.

As far as Eisner was concerned, they had reached an agreement in principle—no *Noble Rot*, but another movie. He argued that *Joy* was the obvious choice. And, he said, in the meantime he'd be willing to have *Noble Rot* rewritten.

John brought up the guitar he had told Brillstein about earlier. It was just what he wanted, he said. Really.

Large decisions could turn on small ones, Brillstein realized. "Gigi," he called, "get $1,500." He turned to John. Buy the guitar, he said. It's on me—"a belated birthday present."

John walked out of the meeting to find Gigi. "Where's the money?" he asked.

She had to go get it.

He went back into the meeting but came out again. Gigi suspected that the guitar was an excuse to get cash, but it was so good to see John looking and feeling well. She knew that Judy was having a tough time. Had he talked to Judy recently? she asked.

John said Judy had the flu.

"I just saw *On Golden Pond,*" Gigi replied, the Henry Fonda and Katharine Hepburn film about an elderly couple who share their last summer together. I can handle being alone now, Gigi said. But I wouldn't want to be alone when I'm old.

"Judy and I will always be together," John said. "We just will." He reminded Gigi that he and Judy had started out together as kids. Their 1980 trip to Europe had been good because it was just the two of them, no outside distractions. They had had to count on each other and, he added almost pensively, "We were there for each other."

Gigi handed John $1,500.

He went back to the meeting but acted impatient. Finally he said, "What am I sitting here for? I do what Bernie says." He got up to leave and said goodbye to Eisner.

Brillstein, his eagerness apparent, walked John out to the elevator. "Two and one half years of work and $10 million in the bag," he calculated. At least "*two* daring movies . . . *Joy* could be raucous, socko!" He could see the deals and studios falling into place.

In Brillstein's office, Briskin could tell big deals were being made. He too was surprised that John looked so good, but he wasn't fooled about the $1,500. That was drug money. There was no doubt.

Ovitz had another piece of Belushi's business to handle that day. He called Louis Malle in France to say how excited he was with the script for *Moon Over Miami.* Danny loves it, Ovitz said, but John has been so busy that he hasn't read it yet.

Malle said he had left half a dozen messages at the Chateau.

Ovitz said Aykroyd was worried about John's reaction to his character. Shelley Slutsky is an obnoxious slob, artfully drawn, but it's a little close, perhaps too close. Guare has captured John a little too perfectly, and Danny wonders about it; John might be unnerved. But overall, it's wonderful, Ovitz said.

Malle said he wanted to start filming in the spring.

Both Dan and John should be ready for you in May, Ovitz promised.

Malle also spoke to Aykroyd in New York. "If I have to scrape him off the walls myself," Aykroyd said, "we're going to make this picture."

About 1 P.M., Wallace reached John at the Chateau and said he had been trying to phone him all day Wednesday. John said everything was okay.

Then John called Milstead. Had she found Smith?

Milstead said Smith would be over in half an hour.

"Great, fine," John said. "I'll be right over."

While she waited, Milstead got a phone call from her mother, who was at her office in a top-secret message center in the Pentagon. They were chatting when Smith arrived and let herself in.

"Hi, Cathy," Milstead said while talking to her mother.

"Who's that?" her mother asked from the other end of the phone.

"Oh, a friend, Cathy," Milstead said.

Smith went into the kitchen and started rummaging around.

"Where's the coke!" she yelled.

Milstead slammed her hand over the phone.

"What's that?" her mother asked.

"Oh, nothing."

Smith screamed out again: "Where are the works?"—meaning the needles.

Milstead slammed her hand over the phone again.

John arrived. "Hi, John," Milstead said.

"Who's that?" her mother asked.

"John."

"John who?"

Milstead decided to tell: "John Belushi."

"I know people in the office who'd like to talk to him," her mother said, indicating she'd like to pass the phone around the Pentagon.

"Forget it," Milstead replied sharply; she had to go. She got off the phone and kissed John hello. He took a half a gram of cocaine, put it on the television and said, "Here, this is for you."

"John, you look good, really good," Milstead said. He had some color in his face.

John had brought a lot of cocaine, and he and Smith did several coke shots over the course of the next half-hour. Suddenly John and Smith headed for the door. "We'll see you later, April," Smith said as she and John walked out.

"Wait! I want to come."

John promised to be back in half an hour.

He was supposed to have been at Insana's about 1 P.M., but Smith didn't drop him off until almost three-thirty. Before getting out of the car, he gave her $300 in cash for more heroin. She promised to pick him up after the buy.

Smith took John's Mercedes over to Alli's on Gramercy Place. She said she wanted five tenths of China white and handed the money to Dolgoff, who left to get the drugs. While she waited, Smith told Alli that she'd been doing some really good cocaine with Milstead. Ten minutes later Dolgoff was back with the heroin.

John apologized to Insana for being late. A meeting with Brillstein had delayed him. Tino had to go to an audition, so John waited with his wife, Dana. Usually when John visited, he and Dana would chat, but he seemed very hyper, pacing quietly, glancing outside, obviously expecting someone. "I'm really sorry," he said, noticing that she considered his behavior strange. "I'm just thinking." He paced some more. Usually he had juice when he came over. This time he asked for coffee but took only a sip.

The March issue of *Chicago* magazine had just arrived. Jimmy Belushi was on the cover, dressed like a pirate, a sword clenched in his teeth, for his appearance in *The Pirates of Penzance*. Dana held the magazine up to John's face and commented that Jimmy had blue eyes while his were brown. She noticed nothing in John's eyes to account for his agitation. John also seemed to have a cold and was leaving a trail of tissues. Tino finally returned, but then John's car arrived, pulling beyond the house, and John bolted out. He said he was going to Nelson Lyon's.

By early evening Aykroyd was finished writing the day's scenes for *Ghostbusters*. He had promised to go over to Morton Street to have dinner with Judy and watch the premier episode of "Police Squad!," a series that Tino had been involved in writing and for which John had taped a guest death to run sometime later. He also wanted to tell Judy that it looked as though John was coming home that night on the red-eye.

Aykroyd locked the Phantom office, walked out and down Fifth

Avenue to Washington Square and over to Morton Street. He and Judy had had many such talks as they now had. The cycle of John out of control on drugs was again in full swing, the first in four or five months.

"I may have to put myself on the line," Judy said. That meant a threat of divorce, something to whip John into shape. "If he doesn't come home soon, I'm going to move out."

The message on the answering machine said John was getting the red-eye that very night, Aykroyd said.

No, Judy said; she'd heard from him and he had one more meeting.

Aykroyd said that tomorrow was the limit. John couldn't be allowed to spend another weekend in that environment.

Judy said she was looking for a new way to convince John that their relationship couldn't go on the way it was.

Aykroyd recounted the last weekend in New York when he'd seen John. He was obviously on coke and downers and needed some time away from the business.

Judy wasn't sure what the next step should be. What should they do?

If he doesn't come home before the weekend, Aykroyd said, he'd go out there and somehow get him home, perhaps take him to the Vineyard, or figure out some program for the three of them—or just him and John —so that they could take off and leave the temptations of urban nightlife behind.

Maybe treatment, Judy said, maybe institutionalization.

Aykroyd was thinking more in terms of an environment in which they could all clamp down, stop all the drug taking and cut off the availability.

Judy said she had to look out for herself—her doctor was emphasizing that.

John hates your shrink, Aykroyd said. That's one of the things he's upset about. He's afraid it will provide the excuse, the justification for you to leave him.

Judy said she had to protect and take care of herself. Marriage to John was tough.

Aykroyd knew about that; he had said many times that he too was married to John. And in that relationship Dan was the wife, the supervisor, the cleanup person, the attendant, the one who did the dirty work with hours at the typewriter, watching the business end, answering mail. As a partner, he said, he had the same problems as Judy. And there were choices to make. He was detaching himself from John slightly, going to do a movie by himself—*Dr. Detroit,* a comedy about a college professor who becomes a pimp.

They tuned into "Police Squad!" on Channel 7 at 8 P.M. and continued to talk. John feels he needs to be this way, Dan said, because he works so hard. In some ways, he puts more into his work than anybody else. The intensity and pressure he puts on himself are enormous. He's new at actually developing a property and a script by himself; he doesn't know that you don't have to sit with the writer when he works. John apparently feels he has to put all his time into it. Perhaps he thinks that gives him a license for his behavior—that he needs or deserves some illicit thrill beyond the ordinary dinner and other rewards. And the harder he works or thinks he is working, the more he rewards himself.

Judy said that she had reached Smokey and that was the best chance they had. His watching over John was the only thing in the past that had really worked. Repressive as it might be, it was an answer.

If he isn't back tomorrow, Aykroyd said, he would go out there and take Bill Wallace or Smokey to track him down and bring him back. "We'll handcuff him if necessary," Aykroyd said, and get him on that plane.

It was about midnight when Aykroyd left to go home. He was torn by the extent of his responsibility. John was in charge of his own life. How much intervention was needed? How much good would it do? To force him out of Los Angeles—if it were possible—would tear a hole in John's soul, break his spirit. He would scream and kick and howl. Would that kind of intrusion help or hurt? There was a greater distance between the two of them than had ever existed before, but there would be future projects together. Now John was on his own, and maybe he needed that. Or did he? Was there a call for help? Aykroyd wasn't sure. There was no depression, just anger at things that John was right about—shrinks and Hollywood.

In Los Angeles, Brillstein was at home napping about 5 P.M. when John called. Bernie, he said, you really knocked them dead. Eisner would have done anything you asked.

"Should we okay Penny now?" Brillstein asked. Eisner seemed to feel strongly about that.

"Tomorrow," John said. "Why should he sleep? I love you."

Next John called Jeff Katzenberg at Paramount.

"I'm in," John said. "I want to do it. I have ideas." Katzenberg was glad to hear that John had a renewed sense of reality.

The matter of Penny Marshall's directing is still open, John said. He wasn't at all sure about that and wanted to talk with Eisner and Katzenberg tomorrow—a meeting with no agents or managers, just the three of them, John said.

Katzenberg wrote it on his calendar.

Call me at noon to make sure I'm up, John said.

Next, John called Eisner and said he was definitely in for *Joy*. We'll meet tomorrow and work everything out. It will be a great movie when we're done.

John then met Smith at Nelson Lyon's. He had many packets of new cocaine. They did about four more shots at Lyon's house and then went to the Guitar Center again and spent about a half-hour looking at musical equipment. John bought a foot pedal for his drum set in New York. They all agreed to meet at On the Rox later for dinner.

When John arrived at On the Rox about 9 P.M. he called Penny Selwyn at her home. "Where the hell have you been?" she asked. "We've been worried sick about you and tried to find you. For all I know you could have been dead on an overdose and in a gutter."

"I've just been around. I can't remember." He sounded in great spirits, and he said he'd talked to Judy and everything was fine. "Let me tell you what's been happening, but don't mention it to anyone. . . . It's really been fucked. I checked into the Westwood Marquis yesterday afternoon."

"What happened with Katzenberg?"

"They're so fucked over there. None of them had the balls to fucking tell me they didn't like it [*Noble Rot*]. They don't understand me."

"So what's going on?" she asked. "Is there a movie?"

"Can you imagine what those fuckers want?" John began in a cold, angry tone. "They either said we could go back to the original—"

"Why don't they like it?"

"They don't understand it."

"Have you been in to sit down with them and explain? Has Don talked to them?"

"We did exactly what they wanted, and now they want the original, and said I can bring Don back and make a few changes to the original."

"You certainly aren't going to do that? Surely you can't do that."

"Of course not. Now they fucking asked me to do *The Joy of Sex*. Did you read it?"

"You must be kidding," Selwyn said. "Yes, it's absolutely hideous. You poor guy." She felt sorry for him. *The Joy of Sex* was the biggest joke of all time on the Paramount lot. The script was foul, and the Paramount executives were desperate to get it off the ground. But they'd never been able to get a director, or a star, to do it. Selwyn felt it was insulting. "Did they ever intend to do *Noble Rot*?"

"Katzenberg's an asshole."

"What are your options? Either rewrite *Sweet Deception* or do *The Joy of Sex*? Does Don know about any of this?"

"Don just knows they don't like it," John said.

"*Sweet Deception,* well, there's nothing there. And *The Joy of Sex* is impossible."

"I talked to Eisner this afternoon," John said. "I'm going to meet him tomorrow. I've got to make those assholes fucking understand. None of those guys have any imagination. I'm going to have to just go in and show them."

"Great," Selwyn said.

John didn't reply.

Selwyn reminded him that she had someone in producer Stanley Chase's office who was keeping her informed.

"Good for you. Great," John said. "Keep it up." He said he wanted Leslie Werner to come over to the Chateau tomorrow before the meeting at Paramount.

What's it for? Penny asked. To work on the *Noble Rot* script?

"No," John said. "Tino and I are doing something. I need you at the office. . . . Tomorrow's the day everything is going down."

"When will I see you?" Penny asked.

"Call me in the morning."

"God, no wonder you've been so upset."

"It's going to be okay."

In fact, John had a plan for the next day. Tino and he were going to ride around in a limousine and work on the twenty-nine-page movie treatment they had written the previous summer about a thirty-three-year-old (John's age) public relations executive named Steve. Steve, John's role, goes to a convention in New York City and gets involved with a woman named Cheri and a punk rock musician, Johnny Chrome. Eventually Steve goes punk himself, leaves his job and wife, and dyes his hair blue. Johnny Chrome at the end is found dead in Cheri's apartment, leaving her to explain his death to Steve.

> . . . *Cheri explained, "Johnny's dead."*
> *They shared a moment of silence.*

"How did he die?"

"He was on the 'H.' "

"Heroin?"

"He O.D.'d." They shared another silence. . . .

"Listen," Steve said trying to cheer her up, *"what can anyone say when a friend dies? . . . Uh . . . Johnny wouldn't have wanted us to sit around and . . . uh . . . mope over this. . . ."*

"Yeah, let's go out and toast the great Johnny Chrome, who never had a chance. . . . Hurry up and get dressed. . . ."

"What are we going to do with Johnny?" [Cheri asks]

"I don't understand."

"Johnny died here last night."

"Johnny died here last night?"

"We both did the same heroin. He did more, a lot more. He died."

What the . . . in her apartment . . . the dead body of Johnny Chrome . . . the junkie . . . who died of an overdose . . . right there! . . . The whole time there's been a dead body in here. . . .

"Are you sure he died of an overdose?"

"Well, he looked and felt dead," Cheri remembered. . . . *"He's dead in the bedroom."*

. . . There, lying on the bed, was the young, dead body of Johnny Chrome. Steve hesitated, then lifted the dead arm to feel for a pulse.

"He's dead all right. God, look at his arm. It's full of holes. He was a junkie," Steve said.

"He wasn't no junkie," Cheri jumped in. *"The stuff was too strong. Maybe it was a setup."*

[Steve thought] I mean it's not like he was a victim. A team of surgeons hadn't tried desperately to save his young life. He did it himself. It took him time to fix up the heroin and shoot it into his young veins to euphoria, to death. It was his own fault. Was it society's fault?

From On the Rox, John next called Insana, who'd written most of the treatment. John explained that he wanted to do some work on the punk movie treatment the next day. It seemed important to him. Since Tino had written it the summer before, John had been pushing for a crucial new scene. Steve was going to be talked into shooting up heroin by the punk rocker, Johnny Chrome.

To lend credibility to the scene, John wanted to *actually shoot up on camera*. Insana, Judy and the Universal vice president Sean Daniels, who had seen the script treatment, were strongly opposed. Insana was horrified; Judy had been angry.

But John had raised the issue with Robert De Niro and had concluded that he had found a strong ally who agreed that doing the heroin on camera would significantly enhance the scene. De Niro was still a leading advocate of method acting: An actor had to experience the character, both physically and emotionally.

Insana was not that anxious to work on the script. John sounded drunk or high. The script had too much to do with drugs, and Insana didn't like drugs. They were a time bomb. But he loved John, and he agreed to get together the next day.

"We'll talk in the morning," John said, "and I'll come over to your place."

John had been trying all week to get in touch with Richard Bear, piano player and cocaine supplier. Bear had finally agreed to meet that night at On the Rox.

He arrived and the two had a talk. John explained the punk movie and how his character, Steve, shoots up heroin. "Well, listen," John added, "when we do this, I'm going to use real heroin."

"That's not acting, John," Bear said, rather surprised. Bear himself had never shot heroin, though he had snorted it once, years ago, in Europe. He said that it seemed like a bad, dangerous idea.

"No, no," John said. "I'll have a real doctor there." He seemed to be seeking support.

"I don't know, John," Bear repeated. ". . . That's very real, and if you need it to be that real, then you're going to do it. But I don't know."

John said there was going to be a punk band in the movie, and he wanted Bear to be in it, along with some of the Fear guys, like Derf. "You and Derf get along together great. We'll all have a great time. I've got to get you involved in punk." John said punk music was sort of like the blues—for and by the down-and-out. Punk was anti-everything, he said, and that was the way he was feeling, particularly anti-Paramount. John began a fifteen-minute harangue against the studio and the executives—all "motherfuckers" who were ignorant. John said he would like to punch out the head of the studio. "That's why punk music is so cool, because they'll never understand it. But we can do it. They'll never, never understand it, but it's going to take over the world."

Bear had a remake he'd done of a song called "Free Love," and he played it for John.

"Don't do that," John said. "Do it faster." That was punk, he said, faster and faster. "Maybe we can even do that in the movie . . . really fast."

John then asked Bear if he had any cocaine.

"All I got is this," Bear said. "I have a gram for myself."

"Come on, give me half."

"Here, have a line," Bear said, handing a bindle to John.

John went to the washroom and came back. Half was gone.

Bear had asked actor Stacy Keach to come meet John that night.

John admired Keach, who was a friend of another of John's cocaine suppliers, Gary Watkins. But Keach didn't turn up.

Soon Lyon and then Smith arrived, and John headed back to owner Lou Adler's private office, a seedy, small room that looked like an add-on attic. With a nod, John signaled to Lyon and Smith to join him. John handed Smith the cocaine. She prepared the cocaine and water mixture, shot herself and then Lyon and John.

John left and walked across the parking lot to the Rainbow. Smith and Lyon sat down to have some wine. Smith also ordered some shrimp. There were almost no other customers, and the bartender, Julie Baker, and Smith and Lyon watched *Papillon,* the 1973 Steve McQueen and Dustin Hoffman movie about an escape from Devil's Island prison.

Singer Johnny Rivers and Todd Fisher, Carrie's brother, arrived. John returned, and Adler introduced him to Rivers. They shook hands.

Baker had a new guitar, which was sitting in its case on a couch. John took it out and started strumming. "You want to sell it?" he asked. She did not.

John, Baker and Rivers went back to the kitchen, and Rivers sang "Kansas City." Baker had to get back to her customers. She was having trouble with her necktie, and John helped her tie it properly.

Meanwhile, both De Niro and Watkins had been trying to reach John at the Chateau. At 9:09 P.M., De Niro left a message for John: "At Dan Tana's if you want to meet." At 10:13 P.M., De Niro called and left another message: "I'm on way to On the Rox. Return to hotel at 10:30 P.M." Watkins also called the Chateau; he left a message at 10:51 P.M.

At 11 P.M., the "Saturday Night Live" rerun started. It was from the second season, five years earlier, January 15, 1977—the week John had been in the hospital with a knee injury and hadn't done the show. He had called in by phone during the "Weekend Update" news segment to speak to Jane Curtin.

John and Smith sat down before the large Advent screen.

A large, still head shot of John came on with the caption: ". . . in happier times." The audience listened to his conversation with Curtin.

> *"Hi, Jane. This is John Belushi."*
> *"Hi John, how are you?"*
> *"Well, ah, not too good actually. You probably noticed I haven't been in the show yet. Well, it's because I'm in the hospital. I have a hurt leg, you know; I got a knee injury, kind of like Joe Namath kind of thing. I've been here a week, Jane, and ah, nobody's even called. There hasn't been any publicity about me not doing the show. I mean when Chase was in the hospital there was a lot of publicity. . . ."*
> *"We didn't want to depress everyone during the first part of the show," Curtin says. "We thought we'd wait until the good-nights to tell them about it."*
> *"Oh, okay," John says. "I just want to tell everyone. . . . It got operated on. But I will be back next week, with or without my leg. . . . Who's this new kid in the show?"*
> *"Billy Murray. Isn't he terrific! He can do anything."*
> *"Yeah, sure. I'm sure he can. How about a Samurai? Can he do a Samurai?"*
> *"Oh John, Billy does the best Samurai I have ever seen. It's like watching Toshiro Mifune."*
> *"Yeah, well imitations are easy to achieve. Can he act, Jane? Can he act!"*

Smith noticed that John, wearing a broad smile, seemed lighthearted and self-satisfied.

> *"John," Curtin continues. "I've been doing scenes with him all week, and he is a gem to work with. And you know, he doesn't mind being a bee." She breaks into a nervous laugh.*
> *John's laughter—"Ha, ha, ha"—comes over the phone.*
> *"Hey John, I got to go. . . . Come up and visit us at the office anytime," Curtin says.*
> *"Listen, do I get paid for this show this week? I might like to buy myself flowers. . . ."*
> *"Bye, John."*

John was still beaming, childlike and happy. Smith hadn't seen him unwind, ease up on himself and those around him, all week long. It was always the phone, meetings, scripts, another shot, which he was growing to love. He seemed to soften while watching the rerun, and he lingered by the seat a few more minutes.

Todd Fisher came up to John. "John, it's Todd, Carrie's brother."

"How's she doing?"

"She's in London," he said, doing the third part of the *Star Wars* trilogy, *Return of the Jedi.*

"Yeah," John said. "I wish she and Danny had got married."

Derf Scratch arrived and ordered a screwdriver.

"Oh, hi, Derf," John said nonchalantly. In his long effort to promote Fear, John had been trying to get the band on Toronto's "SCTV," but the executives had said no, and John told Derf the bad news. "Those fuckers don't know what is good. . . . They don't understand."

"Don't worry about it," Derf said. "Those things happen."

John signaled Smith and Lyon; it was time again. They went to one of the washrooms, shut the door, and each got a shot of John's cocaine.

Derf got up and headed for the washroom and pushed open the door. He saw Smith and John.

"Don't come in now," John said, sounding overstrung. "I'll be out in a minute."

Derf went back to sit down, and John returned a couple of minutes later. Beads of sweat had formed on his forehead just beneath the headband he was wearing. "Are you all right?" Derf asked.

"Yeah," John said quietly. "Yeah."

Derf suggested that John get his guitar and come to Derf's for a jam session later.

"Yeah."

Derf left On the Rox and went home to wait for John.

In the washroom, Nelson Lyon was standing over the toilet. Something was making his stomach turn. He felt queasy, and then there was an abrupt flash of nausea. He bent and threw up violently.

FRIDAY, MARCH 5

About midnight De Niro walked in with actor Harry Dean Stanton. Smith and Stanton sat and chatted about getting together for dinner some time. John saw De Niro and asked him to come back to the bungalow when On the Rox closed. De Niro said he'd stop by.

John and Adler talked. Adler asked about Alyce Kuhn, Jeremy

Rain's old roommate whom he'd met at On the Rox after the Police concert in February. Kuhn, a beautiful, slender woman who played a lot of sports, was staying at the fashionable Rodeo Drive home of her sister. She was getting ready for bed when the phone rang.

"Hi, it's John. Lou Adler and I are at On the Rox. Why don't you come over and join us?"

Kuhn thought John was wonderful, one of the bright spots in her life, but she said it was too late. Besides, she was going out with them and Jeremy the next night.

"Well," John said, "maybe Lou can convince you." He put on Adler, who just said hello and confirmed their plans for the next evening. Then John came back on. "Why don't I come over?" he asked.

"No," Kuhn said, "of course not. It's too late."

"Let me come over, and I'll bicycle through your living room and roller-skate down your halls."

Kuhn laughed and said no.

"We've really had good times together, haven't we?" John asked. The Police concert? he reminded her. The party afterwards, the dinner, the limo? It was a lot of fun?

She said it was. He wanted to keep talking. "John," she said, "go home and get some sleep, and we'll all meet tomorrow."

John introduced Bear to Nelson Lyon, whom John said was going to direct the punk movie. Bear suspected that Lyon was on heroin, because he seemed so spaced out.

Later, Bear went down to the parking lot with John and told him he was thinking of staying, maybe moving out to Los Angeles permanently. That unleashed a torrent from John. "I can't wait to get out of this fucking town. I hate this fucking place. I hate the people, I hate the bullshit. I hate the studios. You come into this town for 48 hours, and then you better get your ass out. Thank God I'm leaving here. Thank God this will be my last night in L.A."

Bear said he had to go.

"Listen, meet me later," John said, describing where his bungalow was at the Chateau. They were going to talk about the new scene and the screenplay. De Niro was coming too.

Bear left for another party but said he might stop by.

About 2 A.M., while John, Smith and Lyon were waiting for the car in the On the Rox parking lot, John saw someone selling drugs and bought a gram of coke for $100. "I got some coke," John told Smith. "Let's go back to the Marmont." He asked if she would drive.

Smith loved the Mercedes. She got behind the wheel and headed east down Sunset. John asked her to pull over quickly. She turned into a closed service station. "I'm going to get sick," he said, opening the door. He threw up, heaving and gasping.

At the Chateau, Lyon and Smith helped him in. John went to the back bathroom and threw up again.

"John, are you all right?" Smith asked. ". . . What are you sick from?"

"I don't know," John said. "I ate all this greasy food at the Rainbow." He then told Lyon that he and Smith were going out for a little bit. They left.

That night, comedian Robin Williams had stopped by the Comedy Store on Sunset Boulevard. As he often did, he had showed up on an impulse to give a 30-minute stand-up improvisation. He took the 1:30 A.M. time slot, which he liked best; there was the least pressure at that time of the morning. From the stage he played with a drunk in the audience. Williams was getting ready for a long, 60-city tour, and he wanted to practice.

No matter how late it was or how sympathetic the audience, no matter how welcome he was by the management (he did not charge the Comedy Store for his appearances), there was still some trepidation in performing for a live audience. The danger and the performance itself were a release. If Williams didn't get up on stage occasionally, something backed up inside. The performance was therapy, proof that he still had it. When things were tense or bad, he generally went to perform. It was the cure; the moment of inventing on stage was his own emotional hydrogen bomb.

When he'd finished that night, Williams went a few blocks down the strip to On the Rox, but it was closed. The post–2 A.M. crowd in the parking lot was large. One of the bouncers noticed Williams and said both Belushi and De Niro had been looking for him. Williams phoned De Niro's room at the Chateau, and De Niro said they were meeting at John's.

Williams got in his silver BMW and drove over to the Chateau. Lyon let him in and said that John should be back shortly.

Williams called De Niro's room. "Hey, where are you?" he asked, feeling weird and out of place. He could hear the voices of at least two women in the background of De Niro's room.

"I can't," De Niro said.

Shortly after that the phone in number 3 rang, and Williams picked it up. It was Derf Scratch, who was waiting at home for John to come by for a jam session. Williams said John was expected soon.

A few minutes later John and Smith returned. John greeted Williams warmly and sat down on the couch with Smith.

Smith was delighted to meet Williams. She had seen him once at the Comedy Store, and he had put on a brilliant show. And here he was, sweet and low-key.

From the instant Smith walked through the door, Williams's discomfort increased. Williams had never seen John with such a crusty woman; she had clearly been around. Williams did not consider himself a spring chicken, but Smith was frightening. She and Lyon seemed somewhat out of place in John's life, at least from what Williams had seen. Even the room, tacky and messy, seemed part of this different ambiance. Dozens of wine bottles were open and scattered around. Williams wondered what John, who was overweight and depressed, was doing and why. He emitted a certain melancholy. He seemed, not embarrassed, but a little out of sorts because Williams was seeing him in this condition.

Grabbing his guitar, John strummed a few chords. He didn't find the sound he was looking for and put it down.

John stood up and got out some cocaine, and Williams had a little. Then John sat down and his head just dropped, as if he had fallen asleep or passed out. In about five seconds he lifted his head.

"What's up?" Williams asked. He had never seen anyone go out like that and come back so quickly. "Are you okay?"

"Yeah," John said distractedly. "Took a couple of ludes." He sat there on the verge of sleep.

Williams decided it was time to go. He felt sorry for John and thought that if he knew him better, he'd probe and find out what was going on—perhaps even recommend that John get away from this strange company and the aura of decadence of the room. But that was just a thought that flashed by. Williams realized he was an outsider. He got up and said good night.

As he was leaving, he noticed a map of the wine country and pointed to the road that passed by his ranch. "I live here," he said. He knew of John's recent excursion to the vineyards. "If you ever get up again, call."

John acknowledged the invitation and turned away.

Williams drove home to Topanga Canyon, some twenty miles to the east near the beach. When he arrived, he told his wife, Valerie, that he'd seen Belushi. "God, man," Williams said, "he was with this lady—she was tough, scary."

Back at the bungalow, De Niro appeared from the back through the sliding glass doors. Smith didn't want to shake his hand. His quiet, penetrating stare seemed to say, Back off, look out.

Help yourself to the coke, John said.

De Niro snorted a few lines from the table. He found Smith trashy and was surprised that John was with such a woman. De Niro also felt that John seemed strung out. There wasn't much to say, and he headed back to his room shortly after 3 A.M.

John then said he felt cold and turned up the heat. "I want everyone out," he said to Smith.

Lyon was the only other person left. In two and a half days, Lyon had had at least twelve shots of cocaine or a speedball mixture of coke and heroin. It was late, and Viviane was home alone; he felt lousy and exhausted. In many ways the evening had been boring, not like the exciting, high-pitched evenings that he and John had had when they were not using drugs this way, when John was a lot more fun and could talk and laugh.

"I'm leaving," he said to John. "You're in no condition to drive anybody, and I don't want to go with her," he said, indicating Smith. "I'll ring the desk for a cab."

"You don't have to do that," John said. "You can walk out on Sunset."

"You're really crazy," Lyon said. "You can't just walk out on Sunset and hail a cab."

"They're all over the place on Sunset," John said.

Lyon started to go, figuring he'd take John's word.

"You got $10?" John asked, apparently out of cash.

"Yeah," Lyon replied.

"Can I borrow $10?" John asked.

Lyon gave him $10 and walked out. Within two minutes, to his astonishment, he found a cab.

"Do you want me to leave?" Smith asked John.

"No, stick around," he said. "Can you get some more coke?"

Smith said she really wouldn't know how, especially at this hour. "You haven't had any sleep for days," she said. "Why don't you go to sleep?"

John produced a little more coke from his pocket. Smith mixed it with some heroin for a speedball. She gave herself the first shot and then made one for John that had a half a tenth each of cocaine and heroin.

John got up and took a shower, and she washed his back. Smith then showered. Her clothes were dirty, and John told her to wear his new jogging suit, the latest gift from Ovitz.

Sitting up in the bed, he wanted to talk. They reviewed the scripts and the various movie deals that were pending—*Noble Rot, The Joy of Sex,* Louis Malle's *Moon Over Miami,* and Danny's scripts.

Smith made a gesture of sexual intimacy. It was experimental, and it was more out of companionship. John was not interested and turned away. She knew well that heavy drug use killed any desire.

John said he felt chilly.

"Well, get under the covers," Smith said. "I'll turn up the heat." She tucked the blankets around him and pushed up the thermostat.

About 5:30 A.M., Richard Bear left another party and was trying to decide whether to stop by John's. He thought that because of John's talk about the movie there was probably heroin at the bungalow. Bear had an appointment with a rock singer the coming afternoon, and though he had used a good deal of cocaine and was awake, he figured he needed some sleep. But the group at John's sounded interesting. He was at a point midway between Schumer's, where he was staying, and the Chateau. Which way does the car go? Bear thought. He decided finally to head back and get some rest so that he wouldn't be burnt out for his meeting.

Back at the bungalow, Smith went to the living room and started to write a letter on a yellow legal pad to Bernie Fielder, the owner of the Riverboat club in Toronto. Smith had met singer Gordon Lightfoot there —the start of a four-year relationship she considered the best of times and the worst of times, so much worry, ambition and yearning.

My Dearest Bernie,
I'm not too long in writing, huh? Sorry about that! How on earth are you? How I miss you! Don't you ever come down this way any more? There's not another man on this planet with a sense of humor like yours . . . and I'm dying on the vine because of it! . . . Paul Donnelly offered to fly me up there if I wanted to visit, but he wanted me to stay with him and somehow I got the impression that he was seeing the whole experience through his dick! I mean Excu-u-use me! . . . I was considering coming back to Toronto and see what's shaking there for a while. I sure wished I had the money to lease a store, and pay somebody a percentage to run it, secure an import-export license and go

around the world doing all the shopping for it. What do you think? I love to travel, not to mention shop!—and I'm sure I have the good taste and a sense of what people would buy; the *best* stuff, of course!

Whatever, I must get out of LA soon. It's driving me to an early death, what with all my self-abuse! I'm such a sucker for a good time! Ho- ho- ho.

Speaking of ho- ho- ho's I've heard some very funny, I think, jokes lately. . . .

She stopped at the top of the third page.

Smith wanted to get back to Ponse's apartment on Bimini and wondered if she could take John's car. She got up and went back to his room. "Are you hungry?" she asked.

John mumbled something and waved her off, unfriendly.

Smith went back to the living room and tried to call Canada.

Coughing and wheezing—very strange noises—were coming from the bedroom, so Smith went back again. John was making heavy, choked-up sounds. She pulled back the covers. "John, are you all right?"

"Yeah," he said, waking up. "What's wrong?"

"You don't sound right. . . . Do you want a glass of water?"

She went to fill a glass, came back and handed it to him. He took a couple of swallows and said his lungs were congested.

Smith said she was going to get something to eat.

"Don't leave," John said, a plaintiveness in his voice. He eased himself down under the covers, rolled over on his right side and closed his eyes.

Smith dialed room service but couldn't get through. She called Milstead, but there was no answer there either. She tried room service again, and they answered. She ordered two pieces of wheat toast with jam and honey and a pot of coffee. It came about fifteen minutes later, around 8 A.M. Smith added a $1 tip to the $4.50 bill and signed Belushi's name.

About 10 A.M., Brillstein's assistant Gigi tried to get through to bungalow 3, but the desk said there was a do-not-disturb message on John's phone line.

At about 10:15 A.M., Smith checked John. He seemed okay and was snoring loudly. She put the syringe and spoon they had been using in her purse; the maid might come to clean up, and she didn't want her to find it. She left the bungalow, took John's car and drove over to Rudy's bar on Santa Monica to have a brandy and place a $6 bet on a horse.

About 11 A.M., both Leslie Marks and Paramount's Jeff Katzenberg left phone messages for John. Jeremy Rain, who still hadn't heard from John since she'd called all the Las Vegas hotels on Wednesday, called at 11:47 A.M. and was told the phone was off the hook. That, at least, meant John was back and finally sleeping, Rain thought. As far as she was concerned, for three days John had been on the moon. Rain told the operator to leave the following message for him from Jeremy: "Welcome back to planet earth!"

Bill Wallace, back from Memphis and his divorce, had left two messages at the Marmont saying he had returned. He and his girlfriend, Susan Morton, were driving around doing several errands during an early lunch hour, about noon. Wallace had to stop at Brillstein's and pick up a typewriter and tape recorder for John. Then Morton and Wallace drove up to the Chateau.

"Shit," Wallace said, noticing that John's car wasn't there. Wallace said he would take the typewriter in, and Morton dropped him off while she went around the corner to get gas. When Wallace got to number 3, he knocked several times. There was no answer, so he let himself in with his key. He set the typewriter down and looked along the 25-foot hall to the back bedroom. It looked as though someone was in the bed. If John were sleeping, there would be snoring and wheezing. There was not even a hint of the familiar harsh, raspy breathing. The place was hot, a dry, breathless heat. The mess and squalor were John's—that particular resoluteness behind the disorder. Wallace felt a slight eeriness as he moved down the hall. Someone was clearly gathered in a tight fetal position under the covers with his head under a pillow. Wallace recognized John's form. He walked slowly up to the side of the bed, reached over, touched John's shoulder and shook it gently. "John," he said, "it's time to get up."

There was no response—no groan, no pulling back from the touch.

"John," Wallace said again, "time to get up."

Nothing. Wallace pulled the pillow away carefully. John's lips were purple, and his tongue was partially hanging out. He was not moving.

Something like a flame ignited in Wallace. He had taught CPR— cardiopulmonary resuscitation—at Memphis State and recognized the signs.

Wallace flipped John's nude, heavy body over on its back. The right side, where blood had apparently settled, was dark and ghastly. Wallace, his heart leaping and racing, reached in John's mouth with trembling fingers and drew out phlegm, which spilled and puddled on the bed sheet in a thick stain. There was a rancid odor. Wallace, with one near-involuntary motion, clamped his own mouth down on John's and began mouth-to-mouth resuscitation. He tried for several minutes—training and horror in each motion. The body was cold, and John's eyes contained nothing. There was no movement, not the stirring of a response, a breath, a nerve, a moan. John was dead, gone. But there was an irrational hope and a requirement—the requirement that John not be dead. Tears flooded Wallace's face. He was disoriented.

The room was quiet. A glass of wine stood on the dresser. A script, *The Joy of Sex,* lay on the upholstered bar stool near the bed. Other things cluttered the room—an early issue of the new April *Playboy* magazine with Mariel Hemingway on the cover; a belt speckled with silvery punk cleats; some powder on the table; John's red jogging shoes on the floor.

Wallace jabbed at the body, tried more mouth-to-mouth. Wallace wailed, *"You dumb son of a bitch! You dumb son of a bitch! You dumb son of a bitch!"*

In shock, panic and confusion, Wallace called Brillstein's office.

"Is Bernie there!" he shouted to Gigi.

"He's in a meeting."

"I need Bernie."

Brillstein came on.

Uncertain, Wallace said, "We got real trouble . . . a problem . . . I need help . . . John's having trouble breathing . . . I can't get him up!"

Brillstein knew that Wallace presented everything as the end of the world. John was just trying to avoid the Paramount meeting, playing games, Brillstein thought. But Brillstein promised to get help and went out to Gigi. She had listened in on Wallace's call.

"Get Joel over to John's," Brillstein said.

"I'm going to get Dr. Feder over there," she said.

First she called Briskin.

"You'd better get over to John's," Gigi said. "Bill's just called, hysterical. Something is wrong with John."

Gigi then called Feder's office and asked that the doctor go to the Chateau. The nurse who answered the phone said that if John was having breathing problems to call the paramedics.

Gigi asked if she would summon the ambulance for John's bungalow. The nurse called them.

Wallace called Brillstein again two minutes later. "I can't get him to breathe. . . . There's something really wrong with John."

Gigi said that the paramedics and Briskin were both on their way.

Briskin ran down to his Mercedes 450 SL convertible, got in and raced the two miles up Sunset to bungalow 3. He walked through the open door and to the back bedroom. Wallace was leaning over doing mouth-to-mouth.

"Get out of here!" Wallace screamed. The next words almost flaked off his mouth incomprehensibly: *"John's dead!"*

Briskin began crying.

"If you can't take this . . . you'd better get out," Wallace said.

Briskin ran back to the living room and outside. He spotted the ambulance and started screaming for it. Just then Susan Morton returned. She saw the ambulance and suspected, almost knew, why it was there. She broke into hysterical tears.

At twelve thirty-six two paramedics came in and went to the back bedroom with Wallace. Briskin was pounding the walls in the living room and crying.

"Let's get him on the floor," one said.

They lifted John's naked body and rested it on the floor to examine it. Wallace urged them to try defibrillation to see if they could start his heart.

It was useless, they said. At twelve forty-five John was formally pronounced dead. One of the paramedics took a sheet from the bed and covered his body.

"Is that all you're going to do?" Wallace said.

John had been dead perhaps two, three or four hours. There was nothing they could do, one said.

"Is that all the fuck you're going to do?" Wallace asked, a high-pitched, accusatory strain in his voice.

"Okay, everyone out," one of the paramedics said.

"You'll play hell trying," Wallace said. "You touch me, I'll kill you. . . . I'm staying with John."

The paramedics stepped back.

"John, you dumb son of a bitch! You dumb son of a bitch!" Wallace screamed. A few minutes later he addressed the corpse. "John, the fucking game's over. Get up and let's go to the meeting."

Wallace was sure he had seen at least two needle marks on John's arms.

Brillstein and Gigi drove over to Cedars-Sinai hospital, just south of the Chateau on Beverly Boulevard. Whatever the problem, the paramedics would bring John there. While they waited, there was a call for

Brillstein. He picked up, and in fifteen seconds just dropped the receiver. There was a huge, eternal wave of remorse. Gone forever, his doomed, beloved friend.

Brillstein called Aykroyd at the Phantom office in New York. It was about 4 P.M. there. "Danny, sit down. John's dead."

Aykroyd was quiet. In about six seconds it had sunk in—confirmed, no mistake.

Karen and Aykroyd's brother Peter were both in the office. They told Dan he had to go tell Judy, must rush out and find her before someone called, before she heard it on the news.

Stiff and quick, Aykroyd moved out, through the door, down the elevator and out to Fifth Avenue. It was a beautiful day. He took the same route across Washington Square he had used the evening before when he had gone to tell Judy that John was expected home on the red-eye flight. Now he had news that would break both their hearts. But he wouldn't let the grief spill over until he got there. He had been one day late with his handcuffs.

Suzanne Jierjian, a young Lebanese woman who was manager of the Chateau Marmont, was not at the hotel when the desk learned that John was dead. She was summoned at once. The staff told her that Robert De Niro, who had room 64, one of the two penthouses, had been calling looking for John and was not able to get through. De Niro had phoned John just about every day recently. Jierjian often called De Niro her "favorite guest." He was on the line now, asking for her, the person on the desk said. Jierjian said to stall, put De Niro off, don't tell him yet. But De Niro was back on the phone shortly and wanted her. She took the phone.

"Where's John?" he asked. He had called earlier, and they said he couldn't talk to him, as though it was impossible.

"There is a problem," she said.

"What?"

"It's bad."

"Is he sick?"

"It's really bad."

It hit De Niro, and he started sobbing.

Brillstein went from the hospital back to his office on Sunset. There was nothing for him to do at the Chateau. He called Jeff Katzenberg at Paramount.

"John's not coming in for the meeting."

"Why?" Katzenberg asked.

"I just can't discuss it." The news wasn't out, and he didn't want to spread it.

"Why?" Katzenberg persisted.

"I just can't explain it," Brillstein said coldly.

Katzenberg walked down to Eisner's office, where Eisner was waiting for John.

"The deal's falling apart," Katzenberg said.

"Why's the deal falling apart?" Eisner asked.

"Bernie Brillstein is being real strange," Katzenberg said, relating his call cancelling the meeting.

Within about three minutes Ovitz called Eisner. "Belushi's dead," Ovitz said.

Eisner had figured the Belushi deal was dead, given Brillstein's call. Somebody, another studio or producer, had moved in. It was only one deal out of hundreds, and they would worry about the next movie. "Well," Eisner responded, "let's go on to the next thing."

"No, no, no," Ovitz said. "*He* is really dead!" Not the deal, the man.

"You must be kidding?" Eisner said. "What are you talking about?"

"A drug overdose," Ovitz said, "No, no, no—I can't say that, that's not fair. I'm not sure that's what it is. I'm just telling you he is dead."

Eisner was flabbergasted. His wife had been right; she had seen what he had missed—*Sunset Boulevard*. He felt a dull, icy despair.

Bill Wallace finally got home after five minutes of questioning by the police. He called Judy in New York. She was crying. He was crying.

It's not your fault, Judy said, an unbearable rage and occasional thin scream coming out between words. If it didn't happen this time, she said, it might have happened the next, or the one after that, or then there might have been . . .

She was inconsolable.

Word of Belushi's death reached Universal Studios in Universal City. There, John Landis, Sean Daniels and president of the studio Thom Mount rushed over to the office John still kept in building 125 on their lot. They personally conducted a careful search for drugs or anything else incriminating. They found nothing.

● ●

Jeff Katzenberg called Penny Marshall. "I have bad news for you," he said.

She thought immediately that John had turned her down as director of *The Joy of Sex*.

No, he explained; John is dead.

Lou Adler, owner of On the Rox, called Alyce Kuhn to see if she knew. She did. He was subdued. "This whole thing is a mess," he said. "It's better not to talk to the press, better to keep your mouth shut entirely and not get involved."

After the long night with John and Smith, Nelson Lyon woke up late. He called the Chateau at 1:54 P.M., and the desk said John wasn't taking calls yet. He left a message.

A little later Carol Caldwell called Lyon with the news. She could barely speak but said, "John's dead."

"You're out of your fucking mind!" Lyon replied, explaining that he had just left John several hours ago. "That's absurd." He hung up and dialed the Chateau and explained to the person on the desk: "Look, I'm a very dear friend of John's, and I just heard he's dead. I have to know. Is he all right?"

There was a long pause, and the person said, "We are not allowed to release any information on that."

"Oh, my God," Lyon said, and hung up. He stayed home and re-played the evening and the entire week in his mind again and again. It had only been a party. There had been no statement on John's part of acute depression, no sense that the world was coming down around him, no terrible melancholia or anything. What had happened?

April Milstead got up late, as usual, furious that she had spent the entire day before waiting for John to come by or call. She phoned the bungalow.

"Are you a member of the family?" the person on the switchboard asked.

No, Milstead said. She would call later. She went back to bed, thinking it was an odd question.

Inside the bungalow, police found a cocainelike residue apparently spilled in a dresser drawer, two folded paper bindles with traces of a white powdery substance, a plastic Baggie containing a marijuanalike substance, and a half-smoked, hand-rolled cigarette on the floor. They also found a slip of paper with April Milstead's name and address written on it. Later in the afternoon, Milstead heard a knock on her door and got up. There were two uniformed police officers. They took her and Pearson to bungalow 3. There was a crowd.

"Who lives here?" one of the officers asked.

"John Belushi," Pearson answered.

"He's dead," the officer said.

"What did he do?" Pearson asked, thinking the officer was joking. "Die of obesity?"

"He *is* dead," the officer said.

Milstead burst into tears. John had portrayed himself as indestructible and on top of everything—always winning in his career, with women, getting the best drugs, having the best friends, having the best future.

Milstead and Pearson filled out some police forms and were released.

About 2 P.M., Cathy Smith turned onto Monteel Road and drove toward the bungalow the wrong way down the one-way street, exactly as John always did because the access off Sunset was more direct. She noticed a small crowd, some police and a camera crew.

A policeman stopped her and came up to the car. "Don't you realize this is a one-way street?"

"I had no idea," Smith said. "I'm just returning John's car."

"John who?" the officer said.

"John Belushi."

"Will you get out and stand over at the curb?"

Smith got out, and after being identified by the room-service maid who had delivered breakfast that morning, was handcuffed and taken at once by police to the Hollywood station.

Inside the bungalow, Belushi's body was examined by Coroner Thomas T. Noguchi about 4:30 P.M., and the body was removed to the morgue. Noguchi put the time of death between 10:15 A.M. and 12:45 P.M. The coroner's investigator, Deborah Peterson, noticed numerous needle marks on the inside of both elbows. Dr. Ronald Kornblum, Noguchi's deputy, thought it would be obvious, even to someone with no knowledge of drugs and even without seeing the drugs on the scene, that it was an overdose. Police Lieutenant Dan Cooke, pending a lab report on the substances found at the scene, told reporters: "It appears to be death by natural causes. . . . The detectives here found nothing to make it seem suspicious."

· ·

Robin Williams was on the set of "Mork and Mindy" that afternoon when someone came by and said, "Belushi's dead."

"Pardon me?" Williams asked.

At once everyone seemed to hear it; it was soon verified. Williams felt the floor fall out from underneath him. He walked out, numb, to a back-lot street near a big tank and a huge painted sky. Williams didn't know what to do, where to turn, what to say, whom to call, whether to run or cry.

His thoughts raged: Could I have done something? Maybe, he realized, maybe not. He felt commanded, warned, a secret sharer in the experience—not just the drugs, but the whole life-style.

Down at the Hollywood station, Homicide Detective Richard D. Iddings, forty-one, a sixteen-year veteran of the L.A.P.D., began questioning Smith, recording the session on tape.

"To begin with," Iddings said, "be very candid with me, don't hold back anything."

"No, I . . . ," Smith said. "I have nothing to hold back." She feared that John had been busted, arrested for drugs or something. Or that they thought she had stolen John's car. ". . . What happened?" she asked. "Did something happen to John?"

"Well, he's dead, to start with."

"He's dead?" Smith asked softly.

"Yeah."

"My God." Smith said that Belushi had been alive when she left that morning. "He certainly wasn't dead, you know."

"Are you into heroin or anything?" Iddings asked.

"No," she lied. "I was into heroin for a while. I detoxed a year ago last April."

"Do you mind if I look at your arms?"

"No, look," she said. "They're pretty bad."

"They don't look too good, though," Iddings said, scoping her arms through a magnifying glass to find the track marks.

"No," she said. "It hasn't been too good for a while."

"You still have a little discoloration around there."

"Yeah, yeah," Smith said, as if she had nothing to do with it. "I've been noticing that, too."

Iddings took her purse and asked to look inside. He took out a syringe, needle and a spoon. "Okay," he said, "now, getting back to this candid part, okay. If that is your spoon and needle . . ."

"Uh huh."

"Tell me: It's your spoon and needle?"

"Well," Smith said, "it's been in my purse for a while, it's not . . . I don't use a spoon and needle. He would call me up and ask me if I would bring him . . . And he got into shooting cocaine. As far as I know, Nelson Lyon had just recently gotten into it, too." She explained that she had taken the spoon and needle from the bungalow so the maid wouldn't find them if she came in to clean.

Iddings then asked how it was done. She explained the water mixture, the cotton ball.

"Sick world, isn't it?" Iddings asked.

"Isn't it, God," Smith replied.

"You didn't shoot any there?" Iddings asked. "Because it does look like you might have had something fresh."

"I haven't since Monday, Tuesday, maybe Tuesday morning . . . ," she lied again.

"What did you shoot Tuesday morning?"

"Cocaine," she said.

Iddings asked for the names of the people who had been around that week. She mentioned Robin Williams and Robert De Niro from the night before. She put her own departure from the bungalow at about ten-fifteen that morning.

Iddings indicated he was finished with his questions. "Any death investigation is heavy . . . and the ghoulish press is hanging around. . . . And it's up to you, you know, as to whether . . . They would like to talk to you."

Smith said, "He seemed like a nice guy . . . and he wasn't one of those. I quite liked him. I thought he was very nice. I liked the way he treated his wife. He practically called her every day . . . loved her and all that . . . you don't see too much of that either, you know. So, you know, I was impressed with him."

Iddings picked up the syringe and spoon and needle and said, "I'll take these from you so you don't have to worry about the maid taking them from you."

The two shared a laugh, and Smith was released. She couldn't believe they were letting her go. During the interview she had admitted to twice being arrested. Just two months earlier she had been arrested and held for possessing narcotics paraphernalia. Under the terms of her probation, she was ordered not to "use or possess any dangerous or restricted drugs, narcotics or narcotics paraphernalia except with valid prescription.'' Here they had taken a syringe, spoon and needle from her purse, and she had admitted shooting cocaine. There had not been any real questions about the source of drugs, the suppliers. Smith felt she had never before gotten a break like that in her life. Apparently the police didn't want to know, didn't want to become involved with drugs, didn't want to find out what had happened to John.

About sundown in Gary Watkins's place at 1202 Harper, a group of several friends gathered, including actor Stacy Keach. They knew Watkins had been close to John and would likely be upset. If anyone had reason for remorse, Keach thought, it was probably Watkins. They reminisced about John and his work. The gathering turned into a kind of informal memorial service. On the floor Watkins noticed a ring with a silver setting and a black stone. A wave of irony hit him. He said it had belonged to John; John had said he got it from the Hell's Angels. Apparently he had left it there the day before.

They set up a round of drinks and toasted their lost comrade.

That afternoon at his home in the Virginia suburbs, Smokey Wendell was with his seven-year-old son, Joshua, who was watching television. Joshua said, ''John's dead.''

Smokey changed channels until he found it. Joshua began crying. ''That's not true, daddy.''

Smokey tried to get Judy on the phone, but the lines were busy. He tried all night. Each time he tried, John's death seemed to become a little more believable. His packed suitcase sat in the bedroom.

The next day, Saturday, Brillstein, Joel Briskin and Suzanne Jierjian, the manager of the Chateau Marmont, received permission from Los Angeles authorities to remove Belushi's belongings from bungalow 3, which had been sealed all night. The room was a sad, depressing mess— littered with newspapers, magazines, scripts, at least four opened bottles of wine, a large stack of unanswered phone messages, Cathy Smith's unfinished letter to her Canadian friend and, on the terrace, her half-eaten toast and used coffee cup. A poster of Karl Marx was pasted up in the front bathroom. Brillstein took the messages and letter, surprised that the police had not conducted a more thorough search. There were few of

John's clothes and no real personal belongings, no remnants of a private life. Brillstein could get no sense that John had been running his life from Los Angeles for the last two months.

A ring and necklace belonging to Cathy Smith, plus a black belt lined with silver cleats, were in the bedroom. Brillstein didn't want them, so Jierjian locked the articles in the hotel safe; she wondered why the police had not taken them.

Briskin found two Quaaludes in a drawer, an empty plastic bag with cocaine residue in it and the remains of a marijuana cigarette. He flushed the Quaaludes down the toilet and threw out the rest.

At 10:10 A.M. that morning, Dr. Ronald Kornblum, the deputy medical examiner, began the Belushi autopsy. There were four to five needle marks, probably no more than three days old, on each inner arm at the elbow. The brain weighed 1.620 grams, swollen 300 to 400 grams more than normal; Kornblum expected that in a sudden death such as a drug overdose. The bladder was distended and contained 750 CCs of urine— an extraordinary amount, almost 250 CCs more than most people could stand, which suggested that Belushi's body had not been sending him the normal urge to urinate; again, this was not unexpected in an overdose. His heart weighed 460 grams—very large, even for someone Belushi's size (222 pounds), indicating probable hypertension or the early stages of high blood pressure.

Overall, Kornblum's preliminary conclusion was an overdose death. After talking to him, the police wrote in the death investigation report that, pending further tests, "The final death classification will undoubtedly be ACCIDENTAL."

Later that afternoon, Richard Bear finally got in touch with Robert De Niro. Bear had heard about Belushi's death over the radio while driving to a meeting the afternoon before, and he had had to pull over to the side of the road because he burst into tears. Bear wondered what they should do. There was a terrible secret about all this.

"Don't talk to anybody about that," De Niro said. "We'll put our heads together. . . . We'll get together in New York."

But, Bear said, John was planning this punk movie and wanted to shoot up heroin on camera; he had the screenplay and a director.

"Well, I know John wanted to do that," De Niro replied. "You know, I knew John wanted to do that."

"Bobby," Bear said, "they rehearsed the scene. That's what killed him. . . . They were doing it!"

"Don't say a word to me," De Niro said. "Not to me. Don't say a word to anybody. . . . You, me . . . we'll put our heads together. But don't talk to anybody."

Over the course of the next three days, Kornblum and his assistants turned to analyzing parts of the body where telltale signs of drug use might be found—the blood, where indications of recent drug use would be detected, and the urine and bile, where drugs and their metabolites, the substances they become through interaction with the body, would have collected over the course of hours and even days. Kornblum took a standard 100 milliliter (3.38 fluid ounces) sample from each. Using normal screening procedures, he could then determine what drugs were present and how much of each.

There were .407 milligrams of cocaine or cocaine derivatives and .02 milligrams of morphine (the drug heroin becomes immediately upon injection) in the 100 milliliter sample of blood. The amount of morphine was above what would be given in a hospital as a pain killer, but it was probably not lethal. Besides, the blood cleansed itself rapidly, and the buildup, if there was any, would be in other areas of the body. In the bile, Kornblum found .279 milligrams of cocaine, and the amount of morphine, 2.1 milligrams, was more than 100 times the blood level—a large amount that had passed through the body and had probably accumulated over the last 48 hours of Belushi's life. In a 100-milliliter sample of urine, Kornblum found 55.72 milligrams of cocaine, a huge accumulation that must have been building over several days. The mixing of heroin and cocaine probably had a cumulative effect on the brain, slowing down Belushi's breathing and finally triggering respiratory failure.

Kornblum found traces of both heroin and cocaine at the injection points on the left arm. He felt it would be almost impossible to determine how long before his death Belushi had had his last injection, though usually the maximum time lapse between injection and death was three to four hours, if not considerably less.

The evidence from the bungalow was also tested and found to be cocaine and marijuana. The paraphernalia recovered from Cathy Smith's purse bore traces of both cocaine and heroin.

On Tuesday, March 9, Belushi's body was buried in Abel's Hill Cemetery on Martha's Vineyard just about a mile from the old McNamara place that John and Judy had bought several years before. Aykroyd, dressed in a black leather jacket and black jeans, led the funeral procession to the cemetery on his motorcycle. James Taylor sang "That Lonesome Road" at the gravesite as snow began falling.

In Los Angeles, Dr. Kornblum finished the autopsy and ruled that in his opinion, "John Belushi, a 33-year-old white male died of acute toxicity from cocaine and heroin."

Two days later, about 1,000 family members and friends attended a memorial service in New York at the Cathedral of Saint John the Divine. Aykroyd took a small tape recorder from his blue knapsack, held it up to a microphone and, as he'd promised John six months earlier, played a tape of the Ventures' "The 2,000-Pound Bee." At first everyone seemed stunned, but soon they were laughing.

Cathy Smith fled to Canada and granted an interview to the *National Enquirer* (for $15,000) in which she was quoted as saying, "I killed John Belushi." The article and a call by Judy Belushi for a thorough investigation led to the convening of the Los Angeles grand jury in late September. Smith denied the *Enquirer* quotation later, but on March 15, 1983, she was indicted by the grand jury and charged with murder in the second degree—killing with malice—and thirteen counts of furnishing and administering heroin and cocaine.

She hired expert lawyers and began a long battle to avoid extradition to the United States. Authorities in Canada overheard her on wiretaps in which she allegedly agreed to assist some drug dealers test the quality of their heroin. Before her indictment, in a series of long interviews in Toronto, she insisted repeatedly that John's death was a terrible accident. "It should have been me," she said. "I was a long-time user of heroin and it should have got to me. . . . There was not a lot that could be done for John. But I don't take responsibility for his death. I feel bad. I should have been more in tune with what happened. . . . There was never the thought or statement that, 'Let's do a lot and die.' "

Dan Aykroyd went on to star in the movies *Dr. Detroit,* about a college professor who becomes a pimp, and *Trading Places,* which co-starred the new "Saturday Night Live" sensation Eddie Murphy. He also played in a segment of *Twilight Zone—The Movie.* In April 1983, he married Donna Dixon, who also appeared in *Dr. Detroit.* In the fall of 1983, filming of his *Ghostbusters* script began in New York.

In three long interviews six months after Belushi's death, Aykroyd said, "Heroin is such an enjoyable stone. . . . It was the romantic image of it. I can tell you firsthand, right now, from my three or four experiences with it, that's the best stone on earth. Oh, absolutely. It's the warmest

. . . the poppy opiates are really warm, very soothing, very comfortable drugs to get accustomed to. . . . It's a real warm, nice, placid feeling. . . . Here I am relatively straight and industrious, and I will admit to you and to anyone else that's interested that sure I tried it. And that it's, it's good, it's good stuff. In terms of the high, it's the best there is. . . .

"And when he would ask me for money . . . I'd usually give it to him, even though knowing what it might, he might go out and buy something with it. And it was like, I would warn him and say, 'You shouldn't do it,' whatever, 'but I'm not going to refuse you money. Here it is, you take it. You go.'

"And had I been with him that night with Cathy Smith and everything, and he said, 'I want you to come on and try this stuff,' I probably would have been right there alongside him. . . . I liked the guy so much, I would have done anything for or with him. . . .

"But my life hasn't changed at all since he died. . . . And I'm not going to preach and proselytize, and I don't even think I want to become involved in these anti-drug-abuse things because, I'm, I'm—every man has his own free will. . . .

"As far as I'm concerned, it's like being in battle, looking over and seeing your best friend get his head blown off . . . and just turning back and going right into the battle again. Cold and hard and right over the top.

"Half my attitude is, 'Well, pal, you fucked up. You're missing out on a great ride. This next decade is going to be a wonderful ride. And you, you messed up, and I can't do anything about that, and I'm sorry.'"

This is the tough side of Aykroyd, the cold and rational, the automated writer, but he says there is another side. "I miss him and there's grief. . . . I wept at the funeral, and I wept doing an interview in the office maybe a month later. . . . I wept recently. . . . What was it that set me off? . . . In the house the other night a song came up: 'It's been a hard day for Johnny, you don't have to cry no more. One more mile, one more mile to go. It's been a hard day for Johnny, you don't have to cry no more.' And I wept."

Michael O'Donoghue, the humor writer, stayed in Los Angeles and said in an August 1982 interview: ". . . That guy that [John] pretended to be was the guy he was. He lived on the edge, played there. He would sweep you up for a while. He was one of those susceptible to motorcycle accidents and overdoses, and all that stuff that killed America's heroes. . . .

"Lots of people get to the edge of the fantasy and feel embarrassed and unworthy. They won't do it. John did—the limos, the drugs, the keys to the Mercedes, the deals, the clothes, shopping sprees, the generosity, the women."

Chevy Chase went on to star in *National Lampoon's Vacation,* which was directed by Harold Ramis, Belushi's former Second City and *Lampoon* colleague and one of the writers of *Animal House.* The movie was a critical and box-office hit, taking in more than $49 million over the summer of 1983.

Chase was interviewed on the Warner Brothers lot in October 1982 as he was preparing to film *Deal of the Century.* He said: "His tragedy was that John was just coming to self-knowledge. Entertainers want to be famous and recognized, and there is a long period when that does not happen. . . . So when we are successful, we want to go back, want to go home, which is when we were rejected—become a clown, a druggie, a fuckup. . . . Actors search for rejection. If they do not get it, they reject themselves."

Chase said that this applied to himself and that he spent a long time doing too many drugs and drinking too much. Several months after Belushi's death—but not, he says, in any way related to it—Chase went home and said to his second wife, "I'm an alcoholic and don't realize it." Chase said he was drinking half a bottle of vodka a night. His wife helped him clean out the liquor cabinet. "I hate alcohol and drugs now."

John Landis went on to direct *Trading Places,* which made $87.5 million in the summer of 1983. Landis also wrote and coproduced (with Steven Spielberg) *Twilight Zone,* which had a summer 1983 gross of $32.6 million. He directed one segment of the film, and during the shooting, actor Vic Morrow and two children were killed when a helicopter crashed. In July 1983, Landis and four others were indicted by a grand jury for involuntary manslaughter.

In a letter ten months after Belushi's death, Landis said, "Our failure to save him is a constant hurt and not a fair one—but a real one just the same." Landis was concerned with myth making and exploitation, "our fascination with self-destruction." He said that Belushi was part of a group of young show-business personalities who will never be understood because "They're not simple. Not tragic, not joyous, not silly, but extraordinary in their individual complex and sad and funny ways."

Steven Spielberg directed *E.T. The Extra-Terrestrial,* which set the all-time Hollywood box-office record, taking in more than $400 million. He also wrote and coproduced the summer 1982 hit thriller *Poltergeist* and then directed the sequel to his *Raiders of the Lost Ark.*

In an interview six months after Belushi's death while preparing to direct his segment of *Twilight Zone,* Spielberg said, "Overall, I could have been more involved in his life. He reached out. But I felt he would consume me. . . . I am a control freak and want to deal on my terms, my hours. His life-style was so opposite of mine. I liked him, and there is a tear in my throat about John, always will be."

After *1941,* Treat Williams starred in *Prince of the City* and was on the cover of *Newsweek* as one of a "New Breed of Actor." He also starred in *The Pirates of Penzance* on Broadway. Williams was cast as Stanley Kowalski, in Marlon Brando's role, in *A Streetcar Named Desire,* a made-for-TV movie. He was in an off-Broadway play when he was interviewed in December 1982 and said that he had given up drugs. "It's selfish, but to talk about John's drug use is to implicate oneself. I used drugs during that period. I never had any realization that it would kill anyone, never."

Williams stopped by Belushi's grave the summer after his death and someone had left a sign: "He could have given us a lot more laughs, but nooooo."

Williams said: "It takes a real good friend to say, 'Stop.' If you do, perhaps you'll lose a friend. I wasn't strong enough, man enough, to say it. I think people are afraid of the commitment of getting involved in someone else's life, even if they're ending it before your eyes.

"If he'd had a capacity for controlling his demons. . . . That's the heartbreak . . . so incredibly famous and not that good yet . . . but he had that capacity for greatness."

Michael Apted in 1983 was directing the movie version of *Gorky Park,* the vastly successful mystery novel set in Russia.

John Avildsen's next directing assignment was *Heaven,* a low-budget sexploitation movie about male strippers due for release in 1984.

Richard Zanuck and David Brown produced Paul Newman's Christmas 1982 hit, *The Verdict.* Their company has moved to Warner Brothers, and they are currently working on the development of five movies, including *Cocoon,* a science-fiction fantasy, and *Shattered Silence,* a spy story.

Louis Malle said in a fall 1982 interview that the planned Abscam movie, *Moon Over Miami,* might have prevented Belushi's death. "If we had been faster with the script, we might have saved his life. This probably wouldn't have happened if he had been working." After Belushi's death, Malle lost all interest in the project. He went to work on a movie called *Crackers.*

Betty Buckley won a 1983 Tony award as the best featured actress in a musical for her role in the Broadway hit *Cats*. She also recently starred with Robert Duvall in the movie *Tender Mercies*.

Anne Beatts produced the critically acclaimed "Square Pegs" for CBS until it was cancelled in 1983 because of low ratings.

Don Novello produced nine shows for Second City Television in Canada and continued doing various Father Sarducci appearances but undertook no new screenplay after *Noble Rot*. Novello said, "John was a casualty along the way of our generation. . . . His death also has to do with being out of town, being alone in a hotel room. The loneliness. . . . He could have been on Sunset Boulevard and someone had a gun and he jumped in front of it and he would have been a hero. The death, the means or reason of death, is overemphasized. . . . Whose fault? I don't know. It's so complicated. How can you place the blame? I don't think I can place the blame. I don't think anyone can."

Carrie Fisher starred once again as Princess Leia in the third part of the *Star Wars* trilogy, *Return of the Jedi,* which was the summer 1983 box-office favorite, grossing $209.6 million over eleven weeks, making it the fifth highest-grossing film ever. In the summer of 1983 she married singer Paul Simon of Simon and Garfunkel. She said that, at Belushi's memorial service, she thought: "All these people who I'd seen do drugs with him, and you know what they were thinking? Hoping? That what he died of was not what they liked to do best."

Neighbors screenwriter Larry Gelbart's hit TV version of "M*A*S*H" finally went off the air, to much fanfare, in March 1983, after almost eleven seasons. The next month, his script for Dustin Hoffman's movie *Tootsie* lost its Oscar bid for best original screenplay, though the film is currently ranked the eighth largest moneymaker in history.

Frank Price planned to leave Columbia at the end of his five-year contract in February 1983 to produce movies independently. He was quickly talked out of it with a lucrative four-year contract worth $10 million but then resigned on October 7, 1983.

Michael Eisner continued to shine as head of Paramount. Told that Paramount's $2,500-a-week per diem was the money that financed part of Belushi's fatal drug purchases, Eisner said, "We certainly didn't give him the money to go buy drugs. We tend to give a flat fee so we don't get into whether or not an actor should have 24-hour guards, twelve-bedroom suites, houses and a myriad of other things. . . . We do a flat fee, because if you do 'accountable up to,' you get into conversations about what is proper. So we don't do that."

Kym Malin was *Playboy*'s May 1982 Playmate of the Month. She became addicted to cocaine and spent $6,000 of her Playmate money on drugs. In the fall of 1982, she said she had given up drugs.

Jeremy Rain married actor Richard Dreyfuss on March 20, 1983, five months after Dreyfuss was arrested and charged with possession of cocaine and 31 tablets of Percodan. (The charges against Dreyfuss were dropped after he went into a drug counseling program.)

Robin Williams starred in *The Survivors* with Walter Matthau. In May 1983, Williams was spending about eight hours a day learning Russian for a new film, *Moscow on the Hudson*. He voluntarily testified before the grand jury investigating Belushi's death under an agreement that he would not be asked about his own drug use. Though Williams wasn't very close to Belushi personally, he said he had never been so near death, and that it had scared him—not just the drugs but the fast-lane life-style. He spent more and more time at his ranch in Northern California and vowed to keep to a minimum his visits to Los Angeles. "... I seemed to be running, if not as intense a circle . . . the same type of drive in terms of 'be out there.' Something in me said, 'Oh, man . . . you run that speed. . . . Get your shit together.' " Of Hollywood, Williams said, "The danger of the place is that if you don't have people there that can ground you down, that you just start whirling. There are people there that will support any mood you want."

Robert De Niro starred with Jerry Lewis in the film *King of Comedy,* which enjoyed only a brief life at the box office. He was interviewed by telephone for the Los Angeles grand jury investigation into Belushi's death. De Niro declined to be interviewed for this book.

Nelson Lyon wrote a screenplay with Michael O'Donoghue about motorcyclists. Lyon was granted immunity from prosecution and testified before the grand jury. He said in a letter a year after John's death, "My 'partying' role in John's life that last week makes me feel dark, foolish, miserable. The pain of his loss hits me from all directions."

One of John's frequent drug suppliers, Richard Bear, nearly killed himself about six months after John's death because of his addiction to freebasing cocaine. In a 1983 interview Bear said, "It's the most destructive, insidious, deadly thing in the world, cocaine. . . . I realized that when I put a gun up to my head and I was going to kill myself. . . . I had to call my mother up and say, 'Mom, I'm an addict.' "

Bear said he had been freebasing by himself. "That's when I knew I was an addict, because I did it alone. . . . I lost my wife. I lost my family. I lost my record deal. I lost a lot of shit, and I almost lost my life because of cocaine. You understand this? I'm just trying to survive now. I'm trying to get back on my feet and not end up in a mental hospital and not end up ever using it again. And that's the bottom line. I go to Alcoholics Anonymous and Cocaine Anonymous meetings, and I go once or twice a day, every day. I pray to God every day that I don't pick it up or shoot cocaine, which I ended up doing to see what it was like. . . . It's a nightmare, and it's a nightmare [that] will never go away for me. I mean, I was not there that last night of John's life, but I know where John was at the end because that's where I was the last week before I went in the hospital."

Gary Watkins was interviewed by phone three times in 1982–83 at his place south of the Chateau Marmont. He was acting in a local play and insisted that he was not Belushi's major cocaine supplier, though he acknowledged that at times he did provide drugs to him. "I was not his main source by any means. . . ." Watkins said he believed that John was making his own decisions. "I was not the guy responsible for his intake."

Michael Dare became the movie reviewer for a Los Angeles weekly.

April Milstead and Charlie Pearson left Los Angeles in late 1982 to return to the Washington, D.C., area, where they lived separately with their parents. Pearson got a job as a waiter at a plush Pennsylvania Avenue restaurant several blocks from the White House, and Milstead worked as a waitress at the Hamburger Hamlet in Georgetown.

Bill Wallace stayed in Los Angeles and traveled around the world giving karate seminars and exhibitions. Wallace said, "His friends killed John. I tried to keep him away from the drugs. It would have been so easy for them to say no, but they didn't."

Smokey Wendell moved to California and continued to provide security and temptation enforcement to various music personalities. Smokey said, "At the funeral I had to make the arrangements. I went to the open casket, and Judy called me in and was distraught. His hair and hands were wrong. . . . She said, 'You know what it was like.' And I had to fix his hands so they were folded."

Michael Ovitz and his agency, Creative Artists Agency, continued to flourish (100 employees, 36 agents). He still represents Robert Redford, Dustin Hoffman, Paul Newman, director Sydney Pollack, Bill Murray and Penny Marshall. In late 1983 he said, "John's death was a tragic loss to the performing world. He had not even started yet . . . a brilliant performer. The other night on ["Saturday Night Live"] reruns he was playing a transsexual, and no one could do it better."

Bernie Brillstein bought a house in Connecticut in 1983 and said he was tired of Hollywood and planned to leave it soon. In the meantime he continued to manage Jimmy Belushi, Aykroyd and many others from the old "Saturday Night" crowd. In an interview six months after Belushi's death, Brillstein was driving his Mercedes 450 up Sunset and said, "Look, Hollywood is so peaceful. . . . What do the stars do? What they've always been doing for decades—drinking and fucking and drugs."

Michael Klenfner continued in the record business as president of Brighton Records, a label distributed by CBS, and manager of several rock singers. He said in the summer of 1983, "I miss talking to John, those half-hour, hour talks cruising around in a car in New York. He was a good board to bounce things off, particularly when you'd fucked up. He was a little fuckup himself, so he knew. There is never a time when I'm in the Vineyard when I don't go by the grave and sit for a little while. . . . I really miss him, really, really miss him, not just for the bopping around or the parties, because the parties go on without him.

"I remember the night his body was brought into the Vineyard to be buried. It was Monday night about 10 P.M., three days after his death. It was a beautiful, clear, cold, very, very cold Vineyard night with the moon out, and the casket wouldn't fit into the seven-seater Warner Brothers plane, and so Brillstein brought him back [from Los Angeles] in a body bag. And we all had to see him out there on the wing, and the wind blew the cover off, and there his forehead was in the moonlight, shining off that clear white Albanian skin. It was so sad, so sad, so very, very sad."

Lorne Michaels's independent production company in New York City, Broadway Video, which does TV specials and has some of the best technical video facilities on the East Coast, continued to thrive. In the fall of 1983, he was planning to produce a live, prime-time adult variety program, "The New Show," for NBC's 1984 season. Late one night in the fall of 1982, Michaels said, "I thought I'd work with John the rest of my life . . . none of us knew what the limits were or if there were limits. . . . At the end, no one could say no. I think I failed. Bernie [Brillstein] said, 'It was not in your hands anymore.' . . . He stole the show so often on 'Saturday Night Live,' and here he did it again by dying. At the funeral we tried to keep it light because that's the way he did things. But underneath it wasn't light at all. He took it all in, had seen too much. I thought for a moment as he was lying there that he was like Christ and had died for our sins."

Jimmy Belushi made a cameo appearance in *Trading Places* and in late 1983 had agreed to join the cast of the new "Saturday Night Live" show. In a series of interviews, he said it was important to understand what had happened to his brother. He said that John was caught among competing pressures that never let up—the pressure from Wheaton to be successful and WASP; the family pressure to go into the restaurant business; the pressure of immense, instant fame; the pressure from New York, which Jimmy said "is a snotty fucking town. You always have to compete again no matter what you've done."

Jimmy said, "I looked up to the guy, and when you look up that far it's hard to stop him, to do anything, and I regret that. My chin was always up, looking, and it was hard to bring it down level. . . . It was really the American tragedy. Making it big and getting fucked by success. There is a message in his death as much as his life."

On February 19, 1983, Judy Belushi produced a five-minute tribute to John for "Saturday Night Live" called "West Heaven," consisting of photos from their sixteen years together and a ballad sung by her close friend, Rhonda Coullet. Judy worked on various projects and planned to write her own book about John and her life after his death, to be called "Don't Look Back in Anger." "I do not feel this way," she said, "but I look forward to the day that I do. . . .

"I don't have to apologize for John's life. There was a personality change with drugs. Always. The pattern was denial that he was doing them, then deceit—hiding them, lying—and then he would tell me. That was an indication, I believed, that he wanted to quit. . . . There was pressure to do drugs, to be *that* for people. . . . People would offer it to him. He would refuse and they would say, 'Come on!' That's what they expected, like he was letting them down."

In a letter, she noted that many of John's friends and other show business and movie people have "talked openly about drugs, people have incriminated themselves, all in hopes of supporting [my] desire for something good to come from John's death."

During one interview she said, "I wish someone had ruined John's career by writing about his cocaine use."

In another she said, "I've been aware all along that a lot of John's heroes were self-destructive. . . . John was insecure, but he *seemed* so secure and sure of himself. So I never thought of him as having low self-esteem. . . . John was, I think, five foot seven inches. He seemed bigger than he was. When we sat next to each other he looked much bigger. . . . I always thought John was handsome. John had soft skin and classical features.

"Amazing he could look like people you'd never think he could. . . .

Bogart is definitely an actor that he watched over and over and respected. *Casablanca, Key Largo, To Have and Have Not, Maltese Falcon, Big Sleep.* He'd watch them over and over. . . . That's part of Second City training and discipline. . . . We'd get stoned and watch movies at home.

"John did work with mirrors a lot and had a real good sense of how he looked. And he would talk to himself at times. . . . He'd just be thinking about those things—like the Bogart impersonation—all the time. You could talk to him, and he'd look at you and have no idea what you were saying. . . . He would also just talk to himself, practice how to say it. I'd hear him and think he was talking to me and say, 'What do you mean by that?' And he'd say, 'I'm just practicing my lines.'

"Brando was his favorite. He saw *On the Waterfront* the most and knew lots of the scenes. He knew three people. He'd do Steiger and the scene in the cab, Steiger-Brando, and then he'd do some with Karl Malden. . . . He really could do almost the whole movie. I must have seen the movie at least fifteen times in its entirety. . . . He was almost always practicing Brando. . . . He talked about Brando a lot. . . . Maybe he related to the characters he did, that's what I assumed . . . the guy who is fucking up but doesn't mean to."

Chapter Notes

These chapter notes provide the source of each scene or section of the text. Some verbatim quotations from the persons interviewed or from the author's or research assistant's notes are included to convey, as precisely as possible, what those interviewed actually said. The use of dialogue in the text is based on the recollections of those cited below. The listing or mention of a name or names means that the person or persons provided the information in an on-the-record interview. Generally, the primary source for each designated page number or section is listed first, the secondary second, and so forth. These notes are followed by a listing of the principal 217 persons who assisted; the dates of each of the interviews are also listed. About 50 people were interviewed and provided background information or confirmation but would not allow their names to be used as sources. Yet virtually all portions of the book have an on-the-record source or a source that can be sufficiently identified to give a good idea of the basis for the information in the text (e.g., a person's statement to investigators or police records). In some cases material was taken from documents, statements or testimony which is not specifically identified in the text but is cited below.

PART ONE

CHAPTER 1

15–16
Judy Jacklin Belushi interviews and dated diary entries, including July 4, 1979, entry: "John acting anxious. I suspect coke. When I ask him, he tells me the truth. I feel sad and panicked. Bob Weiss gave it to him. Bad situation. . . . [I am] turning down coke, don't mind. Need to get it out of our lives." July 6, 1979: "I talk with Bob Weiss about coke. Actually, I pounce on him about it . . . When I spoke to Bob, I was angry and scared." Weiss confirmed that Judy Belushi warned him about John's health and drug problem.

16–17
Dr. Bennett Braun, Weiss.

17
Judy Belushi's diary, Sept. 27, 1979: "Carrie, Penny and I take a 60s weekend . . . drop acid. Bought polaroids, documented the evening . . . left the tape recorder running." Carrie Fisher interview notes: Judy, Penny and I once took acid in Chicago—first time for me. Penny Marshall interview notes: Judy, Carrie and I took acid and took polaroids and did a tape cassette of the evening.

17–18
Carrie Fisher interview notes: "I smoked opium with him once." Says

her father was a drug addict and shot speed for 13 years. Eddie Fisher's manager confirms. Fisher wrote about his addiction in his autobiography, *Eddie: My Life, My Loves*.

18–19

Morris Lyda interview notes: So many people had blow. I didn't go a day or two days the entire time without doing it. Joel Briskin confirmed that at times he gave money to John for drugs.

19–20

John Landis, *The Blues Brothers* movie production schedule, Aykroyd. "They had rushed the project . . ." is from Brillstein.

20–22

Judy Belushi interviews and diary; she said it is possible she was present when Landis hit John; her diary says she returned when John was asleep; Landis said that he was alone with John. Diary Nov. 9, 1979: "John at Ron Wood's. Do some freebase . . . first time both John and I did it." Ron Wood declined to be interviewed.

22–24

Landis, Judy Belushi, Brillstein confirmed an angry conversation with Landis.

24–25

Brillstein interview notes: "I did go through a period when I gambled too much . . ."

25–26

Dr. Michael Rosenbluth's records and file on John Belushi from Nov. 12, 1976, through Dec. 17, 1981. Judy Belushi, Brillstein.

26–28

Jimmy Belushi. Del Close confirmed drug use with John that night. Judy Belushi; accountant Mark Lipsky's records (Waldwick Travel Agency receipt dated April 14, 1980).

28–33

Richard "Smokey" Wendell interviews and travel records. Bob Tischler and Lyda generally confirmed the events of April 16, 1980. Joe Walsh declined to be interviewed.

CHAPTER 2

34–37

Dan Payne, Wheaton High School records, 1967 Wheaton High School yearbook, Judy Belushi, Jimmy Belushi. Adrian Renner is deceased.

37–38

Judy Belushi.

38

Dick Blasucci, Tony Pavilonis, Pavilonis's written notes.

38–39

Judy Belushi.

39–40

Dan Payne; Tom Long is deceased. Background on Second City from the book *Something Wonderful Right Away* (1978), by Jeffrey Sweet.

40–41

Judy Belushi, Dan Payne, Jimmy Belushi, Rob Jacklin.

41–42

Dan and Juanita Payne, Steve Beshekas.

42–43

Jimmy Belushi.

43–44

Judy Belushi; Judy's mother, Jean Jacklin.

44

Carol Morgan, Judy Belushi.

44–45

Beshekas.

45

Morgan; Beshekas interview notes: I got caught with a bag of Rantoul . . . two years probation [for] 12 pounds.

CHAPTER 3

46–49

Bernard Sahlins, Beshekas.

49–51

Joe Flaherty; *Chicago Daily News* (Apr. 15, 1972) and other *Chicago Daily News* and *Chicago Tribune* reviews in 1972.

51

Harold Ramis.

51–52

Joe Flaherty.

52

Judy Belushi, Mrs. Jacklin.

52–53
Joe Flaherty interview notes: Nothing wrong with taking drugs. I felt strange [and did] not do that much. Judith Flaherty interview notes: I did a little drugs with John . . . we did mescaline. Sahlins.
53–55
Sahlins, Judy Belushi, Joe Flaherty.
55–57
Del Close.
57
Joe and Judith Flaherty.
57
Chicago Daily News (Apr. 15, 1972).

CHAPTER 4
58–59
Tony Hendra, Sean Kelly.
59–60
Judy Belushi, Sahlins.
60
Matty Simmons.
60–61
Hendra.
61
Simmons.
61–62
"National Lampoon Lemmings" (1973), MCA Records, Inc.
62
Judy Belushi.
63
New York Times (May 27, 1973).
63
Jimmy Belushi.
64
Judy Belushi.
64–65
Kelly interview notes: The most important thing he [Chase] brought to the show was that he ended up being the cocaine [intermediary] on that front. . . . Hendra interview notes: I'll get coke after the show [he told John] if you don't do it before the show. . . . We were all doing it . . . every day of the week . . . levied a drug tax on [the management]. . . . To start with I was the one to get [the money], but I got tired of it. Judy Belushi interview notes: "Coke . . . Chevy had most in *Lemmings* . . . always had on him."
65–66
Betty Buckley.
66–67
Kelly, Hendra, Judy Belushi. Excerpt from the Dec. 29, 1973, "National Lampoon Radio Hour" is from "National Lampoon Missing White House Tapes" (1974), Blue Thumb Records, Inc.
67–68
Dan Aykroyd.
68
Simmons.
68
Joe Flaherty.

CHAPTER 5
69
Herbert Schlosser, Schlosser memo of Feb. 11, 1975.
69–73
Lorne Michaels, David Tebet, Marvin Antonowsky. Dick Ebersol was not interviewed. Schlosser, Chevy Chase, Michael O'Donoghue, Judy Belushi. Some details about Belushi's audition were provided by Richard Belzer. Background on how Chase was finally added to the acting cast is from the *Los Angeles Times* (Nov. 18, 1979).
73–74
Bernie Brillstein, Judy Belushi.
74
Michaels.
74–75
Broadway Video tape of the first "Saturday Night" show, Oct. 11, 1975. All other references to "Saturday Night" sketches are taken directly from tapes and the Broadway Video timed summary of each show.
75
Michaels, Schlosser.
76
Judy Belushi.
76
New York Times (Oct. 20, 1975).
76
Tebet memo of Oct. 24, 1975.

77–79
Michaels, O'Donoghue.
79–80
Candice Bergen, Michaels.
80
Tebet memo of Dec. 3, 1975; Michaels.
80–81
Ebersol memo of Nov. 12, 1975.
81
Gary Weis interview notes: "I spend $25,000 a year on coke . . . I like it and it's worth it." Weis also did several lines of cocaine in front of the author in a December 2, 1982, interview in New York City. Anne Beatts.
81–82
Steven Spielberg.

CHAPTER 6
83–84
Michaels, Judy Belushi.
84–85
Judy Belushi, O'Donoghue.
86
Michaels, Chase.
86
Jane Curtin.
87–88
Aykroyd. Producer Hudson Marquez, who saw Belushi and Aykroyd twice on the trip, provided some details.
88
Joe Flaherty.
89
Michaels.
89
O'Donoghue.
90
Michaels, *It Sure Looks Different from the Inside* (1979), by Ron Nessen.
90
Michaels.
91
Michaels.
93
Aykroyd.
93
Weis interview notes: "Watkins is a dealer" and "I turned John onto Gary Watkins . . . John was using 2 to 3

grams a day it seemed. . . ." Judy Belushi said that Watkins was one of John's cocaine suppliers. Gary Watkins confirmed that he helped Belushi get drugs.
93–94
O'Donoghue.
94–95
Michaels.
96
Michaels.
96–97
Rolling Stone (July 15, 1976).
97
O'Donoghue.
97
Judy Belushi.
98
O'Donoghue.
99
Brillstein.
99–100
Michaels.
100–101
Aykroyd.

CHAPTER 7
102–3
Michaels.
103–4
Judy Belushi, Pam Jacklin.
104
Penny Marshall.
104–5
Dr. Michael Rosenbluth's records, Nov. 29, 1976.
105–6
Tom Brokaw, Jane Pauley.
106–9
Bergen.
109
Judy Belushi, Rob Jacklin, marriage license.
109–10
O'Donoghue interview notes: In limo [we] would turn up music loud, R and R tapes, smoke dope. Judy Belushi.
110
Michaels, Judy Belushi.
110–11
Judy Belushi, Watkins.

111–12
Mitch Glazer, *Crawdaddy* (June, 1977).
113
Aykroyd.

PART TWO

CHAPTER 8
117–19
Landis.
119
Judy Belushi, Brillstein, Aykroyd.
119–20
Brillstein, Judy Belushi, Beshekas, Gittes.
120–22
Harold Schneider interview notes: "I certainly did drugs with Jack [Nicholson]," but not on the set. But we would sniff all night. Gittes, Nicholson generally confirmed.
122
Bob Westmoreland.
122–23
Nicholson.
123–24
Judy Belushi; Ed Begley, Jr., notes: "I was at the height of abuses of drugs and alcohol. . . . He [John] brought ludes, and we would take them."
124–25
Landis, Daniels.
125–27
Karen Allen, Daniels, Landis.
128
Judy Belushi.
128
Don Novello.
129–31
Jimmy Belushi, transcript and script of Second City show.
131–32
Tom Schiller.

CHAPTER 9
133–34
Talia Shire, Joan Tewkesbury.
134
Michaels.

135
Tewkesbury, Shire.
135–36
Schneider, Nicholson, Brillstein.
136–38
Tewkesbury, Shire.
138–39
Landis, Daniels.
139–40
Aykroyd.
140–41
Glazer, Laila Nabulsi, Judy Belushi.
141
Brillstein.
141–42
Paul Shaffer, musician Doc Pomus, Donald "Duck" Dunn, Steve Cropper.
142
Judy Belushi.
142–43
Carly Simon notes: When I got together with James [Taylor], I did not know what it was like living with a drug addict. Taylor was not interviewed. Judy Belushi generally confirmed.
143–44
Daniels, Ned Tanen, Landis, Brillstein.
145
Landis; La Costa receipt dated Sept. 7, 1978. William Holden is deceased.
146
Aykroyd, Brillstein.
146–48
Dunn, Cropper, Scott, Jordan, Brillstein.

CHAPTER 10
149–50
Spielberg, Brillstein.
151
Newsweek (Oct. 9, 1978), *Time* (Oct. 9, 1978), *The New Yorker* (Dec. 11, 1978), *New York* (Oct. 30, 1978), *Washington Post* (Oct. 6, 1978), *Los Angeles Times* (Oct. 1, 1978).
151–52
Lorne Michaels.
153
Brillstein; Thom Mount confirmed contracts.

153–54
Rob Jacklin.

154
Daniels; open letter to students from Rutgers dean Howard J. Crosby dated Nov. 1, 1978.

154
Allen.

154–55
Spielberg.

155–57
Michael Dare interview notes: Capt. Preemo's [was] like a deli—hundreds of customers. [John] instrumental in starting . . . I a big dealer . . . He put up money, I became middle man. . . . I [was] eventually busted.

158
Aykroyd, Glazer.

158–59
Kathleen Kennedy, *1941* daily production reports, Spielberg, Janet Healy. Lauren Hutton was not interviewed.

159–60
Betty Buckley notes: You don't realize when you are younger and have an ideal of yourself as a hip artist that the whole task is learning how to handle it: Am I getting enough to eat? Am I getting enough sleep? Am I dealing with the consumption of drugs? It's a lifestyle that starts and becomes a habit. The person starts living at a high rate of speed and the habit escalates as the bucks increase. . . . You get bigger and bigger projects with more money and indulgence, and the drugs become more expensive and insidious. . . . We were [both] going through the same experience of drugs and the encouragement to narcissism. . . . I had to make a choice, and it was both a personal and career choice for me. I said, I'm in pain, my body hurts too much. I looked in the mirror and said I'm hurting myself because of the exaggerated life-style. I got help professionally.

160
Treat Williams.

161
Washington Post (Feb. 5, 1979), Dare.

161–62
Dunn, Judy Belushi, Lynn Scott.

162–63
Judy Belushi interviews and diary.

163–64
Michaels, Jane Curtin.

164–65
Judy Belushi diary.

CHAPTER 11

166–67
Tewkesbury, producer Edward Pressman, Michele Rappaport, Judy Belushi.

167
Spielberg, Michaels.

167–68
Time (April 16, 1979).

168
Judy Belushi diary.

168–70
Glazer, Brillstein, Universal contracts dated May 10, 1979, and May 25, 1979, Judy Belushi, Landis.

170
Judy Belushi diary.

171
Aykroyd.

171
Judy Belushi.

172
Aykroyd, Michaels, Brillstein.

172
Morris Lyda, Judy Belushi.

172–73
Judy Belushi interviews and diary, Oct. 6, 1979, entry: "Beautiful day. Danny and Carrie take acid."

173–74
Spielberg. Judy Belushi notes: We got a joint and smoked it. Penny Marshall.

174
Newsweek (Dec. 17, 1979), *Washington Post* (Dec. 15, 1979), *Los Angeles* magazine (Nov. 1979).

174–75
Spielberg.

175
Spielberg, Larry Kasdan.

175–77
Spielberg, Matthew Robbins, Hal Barwood.

431

177–78
Tanen, Kasdan, Robbins, Barwood,
Spielberg, Brillstein.
178
Michael Apted.
178–79
Wendell.
179–80
Lyda.
180
Paul Shaffer, Lyda, Landis, "Guilty,"
by Randy Newman.
180–81
Landis, Tom Brokaw.
181
Los Angeles Times (June 6, 1980), *New
York Times* (June 20, 1980), *Washington Post* (June 21, 1980), *New York
Times* (Aug. 17, 1980 and Jan. 18,
1981), Landis.
182
Lipsky, Shirley Sergent.
183–87
Wendell; Curtis declined to be interviewed, but through a spokesman denied the incident took place. *Chicago
Tribune* (June 29, 1980). Dunn interview notes: "I never did coke until I
met John." Cropper.

CHAPTER 12
186–87
Tom Scott.
187–90
Wendell, Judy Belushi, Penny Marshall, Jimmy Belushi.
190–91
Judy Belushi, Lucy Fisher.
191–92
Wallace, Apted, Blair Brown.
192–93
Carrie Fisher interview notes: It was
the only time I saw him afraid. I realized he could die because he realized
it.
193–94
Apted, Daniels, Brillstein.
194–96
Wallace, Wendell, Blair Brown,
Apted, Briskin.

196–97
Wendell, Judy Belushi, Apted, Blair
Brown.
197–98
Wallace, Blair Brown, Apted, Chevy
Chase, Judy Belushi.
198–99
Begley interview notes: Later I bot-
tomed out and finally went off booze
and drugs.

CHAPTER 13
200–204
Richard D. Zanuck, David Brown;
Neighbors (1980) by Thomas Berger;
New York Times Book Review (Apr. 6,
1980). Irving P. "Swifty" Lazar confirmed his deal with Zanuck and
Brown. John Avildsen, Lili Zanuck.
Producer Robert Stigwood's office
confirmed that Avildsen was fired from
Saturday Night Fever. Burt Reynolds's agent confirmed the incident
on *W. W. and the Dixie Dancekings*.
Screenwriter Steve Shagan confirmed
that MGM took *The Formula* away
from Avildsen. Larry Gelbart, Frank
Price (some details of the Feb. 20 meeting supplied by Columbia executives
Sheldon Schrager and John Veitch,
who were also present).
204–5
Judy Belushi interviews and diary en-
tries.
205–8
Smokey Wendell, Wendell's letter of
March 10, 1981.
208–9
Ovitz, Avildsen, Brillstein, Aykroyd,
Price, David Brown.
209–11
Gelbart; a detailed *Neighbors* chronology kept by Gelbart; Richard Zanuck,
David Brown.
211–12
Aykroyd, Penny Marshall, Kathryn
Walker.
212–14
David Brown, Richard and Lili Zan-
uck, Bill Kaplan, Gelbart and his
Neighbors chronology.

214–15
Tim Kazurinsky.

CHAPTER 14
216–17
Avildsen, Schrager, *Neighbors* production reports.
217–18
Frank Price, David Brown, Brillstein.
218–19
Judy Belushi, Carol Caldwell.
219
Bill Wallace.
219–20
David Brown, John Landis.
220–22
Richard and Lili Zanuck, Avildsen.
222–23
Avildsen, Judy Belushi, Brillstein.
223–27
Louis Malle, John Guare, Candice Bergen.
227–28
Aykroyd, Judy Belushi.
228
Carly Simon.
228–29
Michael Segell, *Cosmopolitan* (Dec. 1981), David Brown.
230
Jimmy Belushi.
230–31
Aykroyd.
231–32
Richard Zanuck, David Brown, Avildsen, Schrager, Price. Aykroyd-Belushi letter dated Aug. 18, 1981; letter to Avildsen from Zanuck and Brown dated Aug. 20, 1981.
232
Larry Kasdan.
232–33n
Nancy Hurst; Hurst memo dated Sept. 1, 1981; Hurst memo dated Sept. 8, 1981.
233–34
Malle, John Guare, Bergen, Bergen's diary for that night, *Time* (Sept. 14, 1981).

CHAPTER 15
235–37
Marcia Resnick and Marcia Resnick interview notes: Marcia used to be a heroin junkie and had quit six months earlier. Copies of the photographs Resnick took that night.
237–38
Bernie Brillstein, Aykroyd, Judy Belushi, Michael O'Donoghue, Michael Klenfner.
238
Blair Brown, *Hollywood Reporter* (Sept. 9, 1981).
238–40
Richard and Lili Zanuck, David Brown.
240–41
Frank Price, Richard Zanuck, David Brown.
241–42
Judy Belushi, travel records in Lipsky's files, Bernard Sahlins, Michael Apted, articles from the *Chicago Tribune, Chicago Sun-Times* and *Los Angeles Times*.
242–44
Brillstein; Beverly Hills Hotel receipts dated Oct. 3, 1981; Judy Belushi; Avildsen; interview with Dr. Robert J. Feder, in which he confirmed his treatment of Belushi on Sept. 24. Details from Feder's medical records on John Belushi made on visits from Sept. 9, 1978, to Feb. 22, 1982: "Sept. 24, 1981. Injections 3. B-complex, Decadron, Celestone," plus the Dexamyl prescription. Feder interview notes: John asked for speed and I said, "You can't have them. Bernie is going to have to dole them out to you."
244–46
Judy Belushi. Dr. Wilbur Gould was not interviewed.
246
Derf Scratch.
246–49
Frank Corte: "He gave me only two lines of coke." Seymour Cassel interview notes: John was freebasing a lot. I did it with him. . . . We'd freebase with Ronnie Wood, too. . . . I saw [John] do a half-ounce once in one sitting, one evening. He'd do it over at Wood's and a couple of times at my house. American Express receipt

dated Sept. 26 for the Optique Boutique; Dav El receipts and records dated Sept. 25, 1982, and Sept. 26, 1982.
249–51
Judy Belushi, Corte.

CHAPTER 16
252–54
Tom and Lynn Scott, Tom Scott's letter.
254–55
Judy Belushi; *Esquire* magazine (Oct. 1981); itemized Beverly Hills Hotel receipt dated Sept. 22 to Oct. 3, total $10,360.35.
255–56
Richard Zanuck, David Brown, Schrager, Brillstein.
256–58
Richard Berres, Richard Zanuck, David Brown; Avildsen said that he does not remember this specific phone call; Brillstein.
258–59
David Brown, Brillstein.
259–62
Frank Price, Richard Zanuck, David Brown, Tom Scott, Lazar; preview statistics from Columbia.
262–63
Receipts from Cherokee Studio. Briskin notes: He had me go get an eighth of an ounce of coke for $600. . . . So I went to someone I know. Derf Scratch, Dr. Feder records and interview.
263
Avildsen.
263–64
David Brown.
264
Briskin.
264–66
Price interview notes: Price also said . . . he took Dexamyl once and actually got hooked on them and at some point realized he couldn't write without Dexamyl and accordingly pulled back and stopped using them. Price's appointment calendar.
266
Limousine driver Daniel Houle, limousine records, travel records.

266–67
Gelbart, Gelbart's *Neighbors* chronology, Gelbart's Oct. 12 letter of suggestions.
267
Tom Scott; Western Union telegram dated Oct. 21, 1981.
267
Price, Gelbart.
267–68
Carly Simon, Judy Belushi.
269
Musician Lee Ving, Derf Scratch, Michael O'Donoghue.
269
Shirley Sergent.
269–71
Price, Avildsen, Richard Zanuck, David Brown, *New York Times* (Nov. 10, 1981).

CHAPTER 17
272
Jay Sandrich, Michael Ovitz, Sean Daniels, Lucy Fisher.
275–76
Lorne Michaels, Alan Zweibel. The Belushi-Michaels contract comes from *Rolling Stone* (Apr. 29, 1982). Broadway Video tape of the Nov. 25, 1981, special.
276–77
Barbara Howar; Carol Caldwell.
277–78
Tom and Lynn Scott.
278–79
Price.
279
Aykroyd letter dated Dec. 4, 1981.
279–82
Malle, Guare, Guare's diary.
282
Carrie Fisher, Judy Belushi.
282–83
Howar.
283
Kazurinsky.
284
Michael Eisner, Ovitz.
284–85
Brillstein, Don Novello, Bill Wallace.

285
Price, *New York Times* (Dec. 13, 1981),
Newsweek (Dec. 14, 1981).
285
Gelbart.
285–86
Dr. Rosenbluth's files.
286
Columbia Pictures files, Brillstein.

CHAPTER 18
287–89
Brillstein, Ovitz, Sandrich, Eisner,
travel records, Eisner's appointment
book, Novello.
289
Tony Pavilonis, Dick Blasucci, Pavilonis' notes of that night.
289–90
Novello, Sandrich.
290
Jimmy Belushi.
290–91
Blasucci, Pavilonis.
291
Brillstein; 25-page "Memorandum of
Agreement" between Belushi and Paramount dated Dec. 24, 1981.
291
Wallace. Debra Jo Fondren declined to
be interviewed.
291–92
Carol Klenfner. Michael Klenfner
interview notes: In California we
would "hot knife" opium. Judy
Belushi, Brillstein.
292–93
Judy Belushi, Sean Daniels.
293
Receipts from accountant Lipsky's office (Waldwick Travel Agency receipt
dated Jan. 8, 1981; Playboy Limousine,
Inc., receipt dated Jan. 8, 1981; Chateau Marmont Hotel receipt dated Feb.
23, 1981; Budget Rent-a-Car receipt
dated Jan. 8, 1982; On the Rox receipt
dated Jan. 8, 1982).
293–94
Novello, Sandrich.
294
Barbara Howar.

CHAPTER 19
295–96
Robin Williams.
296–97
Bill Wallace notes: She [Debra Jo Fon-
dren] pulled out a vial of coke and put
a spoon in and snorted. Orlando Perry,
Paramount gym records.
297–98
Jerry Zucker, Bob Weiss.
298
Mitch Glazer.
298–99
Rhonda Coullet notes: I had been living an uncentered, crazy life . . .
drinking and doing drugs. . . . I told
him I was not doing coke anymore.
299–300
Rick Moranis, Dave Thomas, Dick
Blasucci, American Express receipt
dated Jan. 17, 1982, for tne Imperial
Gardens.
300
Anne Beatts, Beatts's appointment calendar. Howard Hesseman and Deanne
Stillman were not interviewed. Judy
Belushi.
300
Suzanne Jierjian, Chateau Marmont
records.
300–301
Brillstein, Landis.
301
Penny Selwyn.
301
Mickey Rooney.
302–3
Sandrich, Novello, Brillstein.
303
Jeremy Rain.
303
Judy Belushi, travel records.
303–4
Brillstein, Alan Zweibel.
304
Carol Caldwell, Michael O'Donoghue.
304–5
Eisner, Judy Belushi.
305
Judy Belushi, American Express re-
ceipt dated Jan. 27, 1982, for the San
Ysidro Ranch.

305–6
Novello, Judy Belushi.
306
Tommy Smothers.
306
Judy Belushi, N.Y.P.D. homicide Detective Mike Flannery, *New York Post* (Mar. 17, 1982).
307
Brillstein, American Express receipt dated Feb. 5, 1982, for United Airlines; On the Rox receipt dated Feb. 5, 1982; Budget Rent-a-Car receipt for Jan. 8, 1982, to Feb. 5, 1982, for $3,829.89; Playboy visitor log for Feb. 6, 1982. Michael Brandon and Marcy Hanson not interviewed.
307–8
Penny Marshall interview notes: Ron Wood was freebasing in the bathroom. Tried it and it freezes your chest like a vise. . . . I used smack once and it was like being carsick. Judy Belushi. Ed Weinberger interview notes: "John did a lot of coke there . . . seemed he could not get enough."
308
Judy Belushi.
308–9
Judith Flaherty, Rain, Alyce Kuhn.
309–11
Lorne Michaels notes: John had a lot of coke [and] I had a little. To deny it was to appear to judge him.
311
James Morgan, Audio Video Craft receipt dated Feb. 13, 1982; Rain, John Belushi American Express receipt for $30 for Le Hot Tub Club; Leslie Marks's statements to the Los Angeles District Attorney's investigators: Went back to Selby Ave. [with John] . . . did coke and marijuana.
311–12
Spielberg, Judy Belushi, Cathy Shields. Chrissie Hynde could not be reached for an interview.

PART THREE

FEBRUARY 16
315–16
Jack Nicholson. Catherine Smith interview notes: Jack Nicholson has upstairs and downstairs coke . . . on lots of occasions I was there and he'd say let's go upstairs for the upstairs coke, which is better, not for the people down here. Diary kept by Nicholson's assistant; Begley.
316–17
Cash disbursement records from Brillstein's office, Belushi expense records, Playboy mansion visitor logs, Watkins.
317
Kym Malin notes: Gary then pulled out his little vial, and we each took four hits—two in each nostril. On the Rox receipt.
317–18
April Milstead interview notes: April during this period was doing a lot of shooting. Charlie Pearson interview notes: Charlie says they went up and did a little coke. Malin, Playboy mansion visitor log.
319–20
Milstead, Pearson, Briskin, Brillstein cash disbursement records, Milstead interview notes: April had very high quality, almost pure coke. April felt she was helping John get his drugs so he would not get ripped off. Said she sold $300 of cocaine to John.
320–21
William Friedkin.
321
Briskin, Ovitz.
321–22
Phone records, Judy Belushi, Don Novello, Penny Selwyn, Barbara's Place work orders.
322–23
Peter Aykroyd, Novello.
323
Anne Beatts, Wallace.
323–24
Brillstein cash disbursement records, Briskin. Selwyn notes: I'm going to buy drugs on Friday, February 19. She was to take the car . . . to a fellow named Gary Watkins, who's an actor, to pick up cocaine. Of the alleged sale of 5 grams of cocaine, Watkins said, "I don't recall that." Of drug sales to John, he said, "You're putting me in a

very delicate situation . . . I don't think it's in my best interests to pursue this. . . ."
324
Selwyn interview notes: John said to Penny, "He's coming over to get blow. He's totally paranoid, and you'll have to hide." Robert De Niro declined to be interviewed. *Time* (July 25, 1977). Judy Belushi interview notes: ". . . once several years ago De Niro did coke with John . . . he [De Niro] had to get stitches."
325
Tim Kazurinsky. The letter was in the March 4, 1982, *Rolling Stone,* which was on sale Feb. 16. The article referred to was in the Jan. 21, 1982, *Rolling Stone.*
325–26
Leslie Werner, Selwyn, Gil Turner.
326–27
O'Donoghue, Carol Caldwell, Lucy Fisher, Lee Ving, Harold Ramis.
327–28
Werner; copy of *Noble Rot* script (pp. 167–68) provided by Werner with Belushi's signature dated Feb. 21, 1982.
328–29
Novello.
329–30
Cash disbursement records from Brillstein's office, Selwyn, Briskin, Les Miller, Jeremy Rain.
330
Ovitz, Aykroyd.
330
Rain, Wallace, Susan Morton, *Noble Rot* script.
330–31
Milstead interview notes: Probably that night Debra used $800 worth of cocaine. Pearson, Playboy mansion log. Debra Jo Fondren declined to be interviewed.
331–32
Sandrich.
332
Brillstein.
332
Limousine records, phone records, Judy Belushi.

332–33
Ovitz, Brillstein.
334
Phone records, Novello. Details on call to Marian from *Rolling Stone* (Apr. 29, 1982). Communicar taxi receipts.
334–37
Betty Buckley notes: They were shoveling it. I don't know how much. . . . There was a huge pile of powder on the table. Aykroyd, Michael Budman, Bob Beauchamp, Linda Hobler.
337
Phone records, Novello. Vito Bruno interview notes: Vito says that he would get drugs for Belushi. . . . "We got two grams of coke and two black beauties for him [that night]."
337–38
Karen Krenitsky. Steve Jordan notes: He [John] said he wanted to get some coke. . . . I figured instead of him going all over town looking, I would help.
338
Cash disbursement records from Lipsky's office; Lipsky, Judy Belushi.
338–39
Eisner, Ovitz.
339–41
Glazer, Ovitz, Brillstein.
341–42
Carly Simon and her diary. Simon provided her phone records for this day, but it was not possible to determine whom John called.
342–43
Glazer, Aykroyd.
343–45
Jimmy Pullis. Richard T. Bear interview notes: I used to get blow . . . from somebody at a great price. . . . I split an eighth with you or you take a gram and I'll take a gram. . . . That's the way I do it. But not as a dealer . . . I can't remember it being to Robin [Williams] more than he would split a gram with me or something. . . . I know that Bobby [De Niro] uses it. I remember once splitting a gram with Bobby, but that was it. I mean, I'm no big-time dealer. I'm no dealer period. . . . Let me tell you—fucking cocaine

is like paint; it's everywhere. And it's like there was many occasions that I asked them if they had any . . . as opposed to them asking me. Robin Williams.
345
Glazer, Bruno.
345–47
Bear, Judy Belushi, Glazer.
347–50
Sandrich, phone records, Rain, Michael and Carol Klenfner, Judy Belushi, Fear lyrics from *SoHo News* (Mar. 16, 1982), Bruno.
350–51
Bill from the Tenth Street Baths, Inc., to Belushi's account. Jim Martin, Steve Aeister, Marcia Resnick.
351–52
Briskin, Judy Belushi, Communicar taxi receipt, Wallace.
352–53
Chateau Marmont phone records. Milstead notes: She [Milstead] had about an eighth of an ounce of coke then and they did some. Rain.
353–54
Catherine Smith interview notes: I was a longtime user of heroin, and it should have got to me. . . . "I was doing $500 of heroin a day—about a gram a day." At age 17 got pregnant . . . had the baby and had to give it up for adoption. John Ponse, Gordon Lightfoot, Hoyt Axton.
354–55
Sandra Turkis interview notes: Turkis also became addicted to heroin. . . . [Ron] Wood . . . the only [Rolling] Stone who owned a house in L.A. Never saw needles around there but everything else. Smith notes: Paul Azari . . . he supplied the drugs. . . . In 1980 he delivered 19 kilos of Persian Brown heroin to me at my apartment. Other background on Azari is from local Los Angeles police records and sources. Ron Wood declined to be interviewed.
355–56
Sandra Turkis interview notes: She went with Victor Marquez for several

years. . . . He was never a dealer directly but was the financier of big pot deals. Victor personally got into heroin. . . . Turkis also became addicted to heroin. Other Marquez background from a federal official with access to FBI files who said that in 1982 Marquez was a fugitive from the Drug Enforcement Administration. Weis interview notes: "Yes, I knew Cathy Smith and went up to buy the Persian Brown." Smith interview notes: I had earlier accidentally taken an overdose of Stelazine—I took 50—and that scared Ponse. . . . I thought they were Valium. Nicholson acknowledged he knew Smith.
356–58
Eisner, Seymour Fishman, *The Joy of Sex* script dated Jan. 26, 1982.
358
Phone records, Laurel Rubin, Rain.
358–61
Milstead, Smith, Janet Alli, Pearson. Marks declined to be interviewed, but the information was obtained from law enforcement sources familiar with her statements and testimony in the investigation of Belushi's death. Lou Dolgoff could not be located for an interview; his background confirmed by a Los Angeles law enforcement official.
361–62
Belzer, Rubin.
362–64
Smith interview notes: Overall, I did shoot Leslie twice, but just with coke . . . April did not like to shoot herself "so I shot her." Milstead, Pearson, phone records, Bear (Schumer confirmed the call), Rain.
364–65
Smith, Milstead, Pearson, Gigi Givertz, cash disbursement records from Brillstein's office, phone records.
365–66
Nelson Lyon, Smith. Alli interview notes: Cathy calls. Said she wanted to know if she could get more. . . . I told her I was going to Lou's. . . . She drove up. . . . She handed

me the money for three-and-a-half tenths.
366–67
Selwyn, Werner.
367–68
Smith, Lyon, Jim Fox, Guitar Center records.
368
Smith, Milstead.
368–71
Insana, Eisner, Broadway Video tape of Nov. 4, 1978 "Saturday Night Live" show.
371
Howar.
371–73
Milstead notes: April's supplier is a woman named Celeste. . . . Celeste brought an eighth of an ounce of coke for them that night . . . for $300. . . . Gary Watkins came up that night and brought some pot. . . . Gary also brought some coke that night. . . . April actually gave John $50 for the coke, just wanted to contribute some money to it. Pearson, phone records. Celeste could not be located.
373
Wallace.
373
Phone records, limousine records, Marks's statements to law enforcement authorities.
373–74
Wallace, phone records, Chateau Marmont room service receipt.
374–75
Brillstein, Gigi Givertz, Selwyn, Briskin, Smith, Milstead, Wallace, copy of Milstead's note to John.
375–76
Rain, Rain's diary; Wallace said he recalled the talk but did not recall the suspicion that John might have gone to Las Vegas.
376–77
Phone records, Judy Belushi, Aykroyd, Karen Krenitsky.
377–79
Milstead, Brillstein, Lipsky's monthly cash disbursement and balance sheets, studio records.

379
Watkins, phone records, Judy Belushi.
379
Wendell, Judy Belushi, phone records.
380
Laila Nabulsi.
380–81
Milstead, Chateau Marmont records, Givertz, Brillstein.
382
Ovitz, Marshall.
382–83
Aykroyd, Brillstein.
383–84
Brillstein, Eisner, Givertz, cash disbursement records from Brillstein's office, Briskin.
384–85
Ovitz, Malle.
385
Wallace, Milstead. Smith notes: John gave me $300 to buy heroin and I went to get it. Alli notes: Cathy called me . . . Lou was there . . . Cathy came by. . . . She gave the money to Lou—$250 to 300. . . . Lou went to get it [the heroin].
386
Tino and Dana Insana's account to Pam Jacklin.
386–88
Aykroyd, Judy Belushi.
388–89
Brillstein, Eisner, Smith, Lyon.
389–90
Selwyn.
390–91
Twenty-nine-page untitled, undated draft treatment of the punk script. Information on John's plan comes from Tino Insana, Judy Belushi and Richard Bear.
391–92
Daniels, Insana, Judy Belushi.
392
Judy Belushi and Insana said that John told them Robert De Niro agreed shooting up heroin on camera would help the scene. De Niro declined to be interviewed.
392–93
Bear interview notes: The night he died he asked . . . if I had anything. . . .

He finally talked me into giving him a half [a gram of cocaine].
393
Stacy Keach confirmed that he had planned to meet John that night.
393
Lyon. Smith notes: John would signal with a nod and the three of us [Smith, John and Lyon] would go back to Lou Adler's office. . . . [John was] interested in me showing Nelson how [to shoot up]. Julie Baker, Johnny Rivers.
393–95
Chateau phone records and messages, Broadway Video tape of Jan. 15, 1977, "Saturday Night Live" show; Smith.
395
Todd Fisher was not interviewed. Details from his brief conversation with John were provided by his sister Carrie Fisher. Derf Scratch, Lyon.
395–97
Alyce Kuhn. Lou Adler declined to be interviewed. Bear. Lyon denies knowing anything about the punk script. Smith.
397–98
Robin Williams. Smith: "Robin was funny, stuck a straw in the bag of coke." . . . De Niro came in and . . . did the coke from the table. Judy Belushi said in an interview that she spoke with De Niro in late 1982, more than six months after John's death, and De Niro said he found Smith a trashy woman and he was surprised that John was with her. Judy Belushi also quoted De Niro about his own cocaine use as saying, "Sometimes I do and sometimes I don't."
399
Smith, Lyon.
399–400
Smith, Smith's taped statement to police on Mar. 5, 1982.
400
Bear notes: And I was still awake because I had tooted that night.

400–402
Smith, copy of Smith's letter, Smith's statement to police, Chateau room service receipt for the breakfast, hotel maid Isabel Chavez, Givertz, Chateau phone records, Rain.
402–4
Wallace, Susan Morton, police photographs of the room, police reports.
404–5
Givertz, Brillstein, Aykroyd.
405
Suzanne Jierjian.
405–6
Brillstein, Eisner, Ovitz.
406
Wallace.
406
Landis, Daniels, Thom Mount.
407
Penny Marshall, Alyce Kuhn.
407
Lyon.
407–8
Milstead, Pearson, police reports.
408
Smith, police and coroner's reports, Dr. Ronald Kornblum.
409
Williams.
409–11
Smith's taped interview with Iddings, L.A.P.D. tape no. 89696; Smith.
411
Watkins, Keach.
411
Wendell.
411–12
Brillstein, Briskin, Jierjian, Belushi autopsy report.
412
Kornblum, autopsy report, police reports.
412–13
Bear.
413
Autopsy report, Kornblum.
413–14
Aykroyd, Kornblum, *National Enquirer* (June 29, 1982).

Interviews

The following people were interviewed for this book. Many assisted by providing their diaries, appointment books, calendars and other written chronologies, correspondences, pictures, newspaper and magazine clips, receipts, scripts, tapes and other personal and business documents. Dates are for main interviews; dozens of follow-up interviews, generally over the telephone, are not listed. In addition to the people below, there were many others who provided data and recollections but whose contributions were not substantive enough to warrant inclusion in this list. Other sources who did not wish to be named included Los Angeles police officials, secretaries, managers, attorneys, doctors, writers, movie and TV executives, federal law enforcement officials, actors, actresses and friends of John Belushi.

STEVE AEISTER	artist	12/2/82
ANDREW ALEXANDER	executive producer, "Second City T.V."	9/13/82
		9/15/82
KAREN ALLEN	actress	11/27/82
JANET ALLI	drug supplier	12/10/82
MARVIN ANTONOWSKY	NBC and Columbia Pictures executive	12/82
		10/24/83
MICHAEL APTED	director	10/16/82
JOHN AVILDSEN	director	10/15/82
		11/3/82
HOYT AXTON	singer/songwriter	6/22/83
DAN AYKROYD	actor/writer	9/21/82
		9/22/82
		9/23/82
PETER AYKROYD	actor/writer	9/21/82
DR. MICHAEL BADEN	provided expert testimony on drug overdoses to the grand jury investigation into Belushi's death	9/20/82
JULIE BAKER	waitress, On the Rox	10/22/82
HOWARD BARNES	Wheaton High School football coach	3/28/83
HAL BARWOOD	producer	4/83
RICHARD T. BEAR	musician/drug supplier	3/6/83

ANNE BEATTS	writer	9/23/82
ROBERT BEAUCHAMP	Fashion Director, *Gentlemen's Quarterly*	12/13/82
ED BEGLEY, JR.	actor	12/1/82
JIMMY BELUSHI	brother of John Belushi/actor	9/10/82
		2/10/83
		2/20/83
		2/23/83
		6/28/83
		7/5/83
JUDY JACKLIN BELUSHI	wife of John Belushi/graphic artist	7/15/82
		8/4/82
		9/9/82
		10/4/82
		11/23/82
		12/1/82
		12/6/82
		1/6/83
		2/19/83
		2/20/83
		2/23/83
		5/2/83
		5/5/83
		5/24/83
		6/10/83
		6/14/83
		6/27/83
		6/28/83
		6/29/83
		6/30/83
		7/1/83
RICHARD BELZER	comedian	10/23/82
		10/25/82
CANDICE BERGEN	actress	2/10/83
DICK BERRES	Columbia music executive	1/12/83
STEVE BESHEKAS	John's friend, Chicago Blues Bar manager	12/14/82
		3/30/83
JACKIE BETTENCOURT	John's secretary	10/26/82
DICK BLASUCCI	Wheaton High School friend/writer	12/9/82
CURTIS BLOCK	NBC vice president of press relations	4/83
DR. BENNETT BRAUN	physician/psychiatrist	11/24/82
BERNIE BRILLSTEIN	manager	8/21/82
		9/23/82
		12/8/82
		4/24/83
JOEL BRISKIN	assistant manager	8/24/82
		10/26/82
TOM BROKAW	NBC's "Today" cohost	6/27/83
BLAIR BROWN	actress	10/27/82
DAVID BROWN	producer	12/23/82
		12/24/82

VITO BRUNO	owner, AM–PM club	12/24/82
BETTY BUCKLEY	actress	12/1/82
		12/6/82
		12/18/82
JIMMY BUDMAN	owner, At Sunset	12/1/82
MICHAEL BUDMAN	owner, Roots Footwear	11/29/82
CAROL CALDWELL	writer	8/22/82
		10/24/82
MARK CARLSON	Wheaton classmate	3/29/83
PATTY CARTEN	Chicago friend	7/83
SEYMOUR CASSEL	actor	6/20/83
CHEVY CHASE	actor	10/21/82
ISABEL CHAVEZ	hotel maid, Chateau Marmont	10/22/82
MARK CHERENSON	Los Angeles friend	10/13/82
DEL CLOSE	director, Second City	2/14/83
		2/15/83
PAUL COOPER	record executive	9/21/82
FRANK CORTE	limousine driver	12/9/82
		12/20/82
RHONDA COULETT	song writer/actress	5/11/83
STEVE CROPPER	musician	10/22/82
JANE CROWLEY	NBC censor	4/8/83
JANE CURTIN	actress	6/21/83
SEAN DANIELS	Universal executive	9/20/82
		10/11/82
		10/13/82
		10/22/82
		2/3/83
		3/1/83
		3/20/83
MICHAEL DARE	Belushi friend/drug supplier	2/22/83
		6/20/83
SALLY DENNISON	casting director, *1941*	12/3/82
DANNY DEVITO	actor	10/19/82
EDDIE DODSON	owner, Dodson's furniture store	4/28/83
DONALD "DUCK" DUNN	musician	12/6/82
		3/3/83
MURPHY DUNNE	musician	10/22/82
MICHAEL EISNER	Paramount president	10/19/82
		12/22/82
DR. ROBERT J. FEDER	ear, nose and throat specialist	12/9/82
BUZZ FEITSHANS	producer	6/27/83
JIM FIELD	bartender, The Raincheck	10/19/82
CARRIE FISHER	actress	12/9/82
LUCY FISHER	Warner Brothers executive	4/29/83
		6/21/83
JOE FLAHERTY	actor	4/14/83
		6/11/83
JUDITH FLAHERTY	Joe Flaherty's wife/Belushi's friend	10/19/82
		12/10/82
		6/11/83
DETECTIVE MIKE FLANNERY	N.Y.P.D., homicide	10/5/82

JAMES FOX	manager, Guitar Center	10/23/82
WILLIAM FRIEDKIN	director	10/13/82
SEYMOUR FRISHMAN	masseur	10/14/82
LARRY GELBART	writer	12/20/82
		12/27/82
HARRY GITTES	producer	12/14/82
GIGI GIVERTZ	secretary	8/24/82
MITCHELL GLAZER	writer	9/9/82
JOHN GUARE	writer	1/7/83
JANET HEALY	associate producer, *1941*	11/30/82
HUGH HEFNER	owner/publisher, *Playboy* magazine	9/22/82
TONY HENDRA	producer	4/6/83
LAURIE HERTZAN	wife of drug dealer Mark Hertzan	12/3/82
MIKE HIGHTOWER	musician/employee, Guitar Center	10/25/82
LINDA HOBLER	New York friend	11/29/82
DANIEL HOULE	limousine driver	12/29/82
BARBARA HOWAR	author	10/4/82
		10/12/82
TINO INSANA	college friend/writer	10/21/82
JEAN JACKLIN	mother of Judy Jacklin Belushi	2/20/83
PAM JACKLIN	sister of Judy Jacklin Belushi/attorney	8/2/82
		9/14/82
		9/17/82
		9/29/82
		10/8/82
ROB JACKLIN	brother of Judy Jacklin Belushi	2/20/83
PAUL JENKINS	actor	10/24/82
		10/25/82
SUZANNE JIERJIAN	manager, Chateau Marmont Hotel	8/23/82
		9/27/82
SUSAN JOHANNESSON	owner, Barbara's Place	12/9/82
JEFFERY JOLSON	writer/editor	10/23/82
GARY JONKER	manager, Barbara's Place	10/19/82
STEVE JORDAN	musician	10/5/82
DAVID JOVE	producer	6/20/83
		6/22/83
BILL KAPLAN	soundman	10/20/82
LARRY KASDAN	writer/director	1/26/83
TIM KAZURINSKY	actor	6/20/83
STACY KEACH	actor	12/9/82
SEAN KELLY	writer	2/18/83
KATHLEEN KENNEDY	assistant to Spielberg	10/25/82
CAROL KLENFNER	wife of Michael Klenfner/friend	8/19/82
MICHAEL KLENFNER	record executive	8/19/82
		10/5/82
BILL KOPECKY	cab driver	10/23/82
DR. RONALD KORNBLUM	medical examiner, Los Angeles	10/26/82
KAREN KRENITSKY	secretary	9/9/82
		10/5/82
ALYCE KUHN	Los Angeles friend	10/27/82
		11/17/82
JOHN LANDIS	director	11/17/82
		3/25/83

IRVING "SWIFTY" LAZAR	agent	10/19/82
TIMOTHY LEARY	author	5/5/82
MEL LEMMON	assistant principal, Wheaton High School	4/4/83
GORDON LIGHTFOOT	singer/songwriter	6/23/83
MARK LIPSKY	accountant	9/10/82
		6/16/83
MORRIS LYDA	road manager, The Blues Brothers	12/6/82
		12/13/82
		5/9/83
NELSON LYON	writer	11/22/82
		12/10/82
		2/25/83
KYM MALIN	*Playboy* Playmate	9/28/82
		10/19/82
LOUIS MALLE	director	10/20/82
ALAN MANDEL	writer	11/29/82
HUDSON MARQUEZ	producer	6/23/83
PENNY MARSHALL	actress	10/20/82
		10/21/82
JIM MARTIN	artist	12/2/82
DENNIS MARTINO	manager, The Lingerie	10/26/82
TIM MATHESON	actor	12/15/82
LORNE MICHAELS	television producer	8/18/82
		12/23/82
		2/16/83
		8/31/83
JOHN MILIUS	writer/producer, *1941*	6/23/83
LES MILLER	employee, Barbara's Place	11/30/82
APRIL MILSTEAD	Los Angeles friend/drug supplier	3/31/83
RICK MORANIS	actor	10/12/82
CAROL MORGAN	Judy Belushi's college roommate	3/28/83
		6/22/83
JAMES MORGAN	manager, Audio Video Craft	10/23/82
GARRET MORRIS	actor	7/13/83
SUSAN MORTON	Bill Wallace's girlfriend	10/23/82
THOM MOUNT	Universal executive	10/82
LAILA NABULSI	secretary/friend	3/3/83
NILS NICHOLS	production assistant, Broadway Video	2/16/83
		2/17/83
JACK NICHOLSON	actor/director	10/23/82
DON NOVELLO	writer/actor	10/26/82
		11/23/82
		1/5/83
MICHAEL O'DONOGHUE	writer	8/22/82
		12/3/82
		4/5/83
JOSHUA OTTLEY	NBC censor	4/8/83
MICHAEL OVITZ	agent	9/21/82
		12/17/82
GUS PAPAS	landlord	10/19/82
		10/20/82

446

JANE PAULEY	NBC's "Today" cohost	6/4/83
TONY PAVILONIS	Wheaton High School classmate	10/27/82
DAN PAYNE	Wheaton High School drama teacher	2/11/83
		4/12/83
		5/30/83
JUANITA PAYNE	wife of Dan Payne	4/12/83
CHARLES PEARSON	Los Angeles friend/musician	3/31/83
ORLANDO PERRY	manager, Paramount gym	10/26/82
DOC POMUS	record producer/songwriter	3/4/83
JOHN PONSE	waiter/Cathy Smith's roommate	10/21/82
EDWARD PRESSMAN	producer	12/13/82
		3/10/83
FRANK PRICE	Columbia Pictures president	12/3/82
JIMMY PULLIS	owner JP's and Traks clubs	12/2/82
MARY QUINLAN	secretary, Wheaton High School	4/4/83
JEREMY RAIN	Los Angeles friend	10/18/82
HAROLD RAMIS	writer/director	10/20/82
MICHELE RAPPAPORT	producer	3/8/83
MARCIA RESNICK	photographer	11/24/82
		12/2/82
JOHNNY RIVERS	singer	11/29/82
MATTHEW ROBBINS	director	4/83
MICKEY ROONEY	actor	12/2/82
MIKE ROYKO	newspaper columnist	11/29/82
LAUREL RUBIN	Chicago friend	10/11/82
LATA RYAN	production assistant, *1941*	11/29/82
BERNARD SAHLINS	producer	2/14/83
		6/10/83
JAY SANDRICH	director	10/27/82
HERB SARGENT	writer	6/23/83
MELVIN SATTLER	Universal executive	10/83
TOM SCHILLER	filmmaker	2/83
HERBERT SCHLOSSER	former NBC president	4/7/83
		6/16/83
HAROLD SCHNEIDER	producer	12/82
		12/9/82
PAUL SCHRADER	writer	12/15/82
SHELDON SCHRAGER	Columbia executive	12/28/82
WILLIAM SCHUMER	businessman	11/20/82
LYNN SCOTT	wife of Tom Scott	10/23/82
TOM SCOTT	musician	10/23/82
		12/2/82
DERF SCRATCH	musician	8/23/82
PENNY SELWYN	secretary	9/20/82
SHIRLEY SERGENT	accountant	10/4/82
PAUL SHAFFER	musician	12/17/82
STEVE SHAGAN	writer	5/5/83
REX SHERMAN	Wheaton High School coach	3/28/83
CATHY SHIELDS	Wheaton friend/film editor	10/21/82
TALIA SHIRE	actress	3/3/83
HOWARD SHORE	musical director, "Saturday Night Live"	3/8/83

Dr. Ronald Siegel	drug therapist	10/26/82
Jan Simmons	secretary	1/14/83
Matty Simmons	producer/publisher	10/21/82
		8/31/83
Carly Simon	singer	11/2/82
		11/17/82
Joyce Sloane	associate producer, Second City	2/13/83
Cathy Smith	drug supplier/musician	11/6/82
		11/7/82
		12/11/82
		12/12/82
Tommy Smothers	comedian	11/26/82
Steven Spielberg	director	10/22/82
Ned Tanen	former Universal president	5/83
David Tebet	NBC executive	4/5/83
		4/6/83
		4/13/83
Joan Tewkesbury	director	12/16/82
		3/6/83
		6/21/83
Dave Thomas	actor	12/4/82
Bob Tischler	record producer	4/27/83
Sandra Turkis	model/friend of Cathy Smith	6/1/83
Gil Turner	owner, Gil Turner's Liquor Store	10/22/82
Mike (Marco) Urbanek	limousine driver	12/31/82
John Veitch	Columbia executive	1/4/83
Lee Ving	musician	12/21/82
		1/13/83
Kathryn Walker	actress	6/20/83
Bill Wallace	bodyguard/trainer	8/21/82
		11/16/82
Gary Watkins	actor/drug supplier	11/15/82
		2/4/83
Ed Weinberger	producer	10/21/82
Gary Weis	director	12/2/82
Robert K. Weiss	producer	10/25/82
Richard "Smokey" Wendell	bodyguard	9/17/82
		9/19/82
		5/19/83
Leslie Werner	secretary	9/22/82
		12/31/82
Bob Westmoreland	makeup man	12/14/82
Robin Williams	actor/comedian	5/19/83
Treat Williams	actor	12/2/82
Lili Zanuck	wife of Richard Zanuck	5/83
Richard Zanuck	producer	1/4/83
David Zucker	producer	12/1/82
Jerry Zucker	producer	12/1/82
Alan Zweibel	writer	12/17/82

Index